GATE KEEPERS

CREATED BY: KEIJI GOTO

ORIGINAL STORY BY: HIROSHI YAMAGUCHI

VOLUME 2

D1025913

TOKYOPOP®

Los Angeles • Tokyo

ALSO AVAILABLE FROM 🐾 TOKYOPOP®

MANGA

ANGELIC LAYER*
BABY BIRTH* (September 2003)
BATTLE ROYALE*
BRAIN POWERED* (June 2003)
BRIGADOON* (August 2003)
CARDCAPTOR SAKURA
CARDCAPTOR SAKURA: MASTER OF THE CLOW*
CLAMP SCHOOL DETECTIVES*
CHOBITS*
CHRONICLES OF THE CURSED SWORD (July 2003)
CLOVER
CONFIDENTIAL CONFESSIONS* (July 2003)
CORRECTOR YUI
COWBOY BEBOP*
COWBOY BEBOP: SHOOTING STAR* (June 2003)
DEMON DIARY (May 2003)
DIGIMON
DRAGON HUNTER (June 2003)
DRAGON KNIGHTS*
DUKLYON: CLAMP SCHOOL DEFENDERS* (September 2003)
ERICA SAKURAZAWA* (May 2003)
ESCAFLOWNE* (July 2003)
FAKE*(May 2003)
FLCL* (September 2003)
FORBIDDEN DANCE* (August 2003)
GATE KEEPERS*
G-GUNDAM* (June 2003)
GRAVITATION* (June 2003)
GTO*
GUNDAM WING
GUNDAM WING: ENDLESS WALTZ*
GUNDAM: THE LAST OUTPOST*
HAPPY MANIA*
HARLEM BEAT
INITIAL D*
I.N.V.U.
ISLAND
JING: KING OF BANDITS* (June 2003)
JULINE
KARE KANO*
KINDAICHI CASE FILES* (June 2003)
KING OF HELL (June 2003)

KODOCHA*
LOVE HINA*
LUPIN III*
MAGIC KNIGHT RAYEARTH* (August 2003)
MAN OF MANY FACES* (May 2003)
MARMALADE BOY*
MARS*
MIRACLE GIRLS
MIYUKI-CHAN IN WONDERLAND* (October 2003)
MONSTERS, INC.
NIEA_7* (August 2003)
PARADISE KISS*
PARASYTE
PEACH GIRL
PEACH GIRL: CHANGE OF HEART*
PET SHOP OF HORRORS* (June 2003)
PLANET LADDER
PLANETS* (October 2003)
PRIEST
RAGNAROK
RAVE MASTER*
REAL BOUT HIGH SCHOOL*
REALITY CHECK
REBIRTH
REBOUND*
SABER MARIONETTE J* (July 2003)
SAILOR MOON
SAINT TAIL
SAMURAI DEEPER KYO* (June 2003)
SCRYED*
SHAOLIN SISTERS*
SHIRAHIME-SYO* (December 2003)
THE SKULL MAN*
SORCERER HUNTERS
TOKYO MEW MEW*
UNDER THE GLASS MOON (June 2003)
VAMPIRE GAME* (June 2003)
WILD ACT* (July 2003)
WISH*
X-DAY* (August 2003)
ZODIAC P.I.* (July 2003)

CINE-MANGA™

AKIRA*
CARDCAPTORS
JIMMY NEUTRON (COMING SOON)
KIM POSSIBLE
LIZZIE McGUIRE
SPONGEBOB SQUAREPANTS (COMING SOON)
SPY KIDS 2

NOVELS

SAILOR MOON
KARMA CLUB (COMING SOON)

TOKYOPOP KIDS

STRAY SHEEP (September 2003)

ART BOOKS

CARDCAPTOR SAKURA*
MAGIC KNIGHT RAYEARTH*

ANIME GUIDES

GUNDAM TECHNICAL MANUALS
COWBOY BEBOP
SAILOR MOON SCOUT GUIDES

It is a difficult time for the Earth—social unrest, war, wide-spread division among the peoples of the planet... a time ripe for extra-terrestrial invaders to strike.

To protect us against this otherworldly threat, Earth's leaders have formed the top-secret international defense organization A.E.G.I.S.— The Alien Extermination Global Intercept System.

A.E.G.I.S.'s secret weapon in this trans-world clash are the Gate Keepers, special humans who have the ability to summon colossal power from other dimensions. The leader of the Gate Keepers is the brash and cocky Shun, the one boy on a team of beautiful girls. But the aliens also have a powerful human in their ranks, the equally cocky but not nearly as brash Reiji. So the battle to save mankind from aliens has boiled down to a grudge match between two humans.

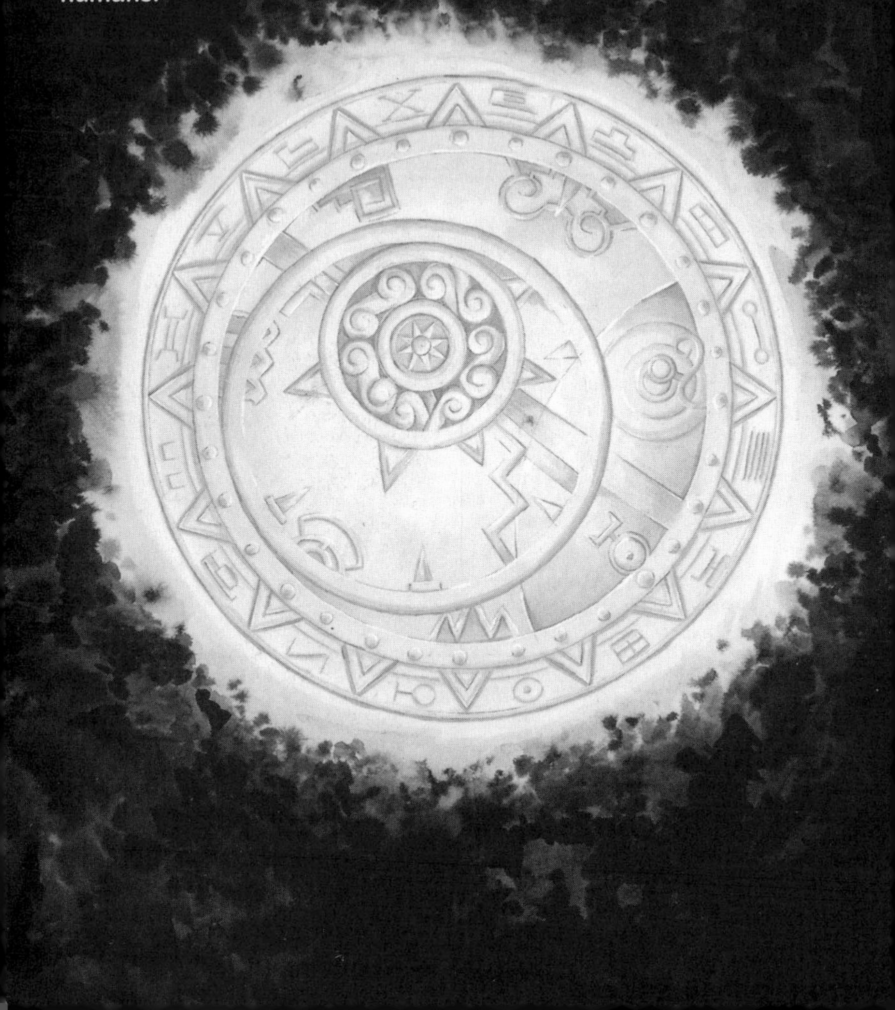

Translator - Yuki Nakamura
English Adaption - Nathan Johnson
Retouch and Lettering - Ronnel Papa
Cover Layout - Gary Shum
Graphic Retouch - Anna Kernbaum

Senior Editor - Luis Reyes
Managing Editor - Jill Freshney
Production Coordinator - Antonio DePietro
Production Manager - Jennifer Miller
Art Director - Matthew Alford
VP of Production & Manufacturing - Ron Klamert
President & C.O.O. - John Parker
Publisher - Stuart Levy

Email: editor@TOKYOPOP.com
Come visit us online at www.TOKYOPOP.com

A ⊙ **TOKYOPOP**® Manga

TOKYOPOP® is an imprint of Mixx Entertainment, Inc.
5900 Wilshire Blvd. Suite 2000, Los Angeles, CA 90036

Gate Keepers Volume 2 © 1999 KEIJI GOTO © GONZO 1987
First published in 2001 by KADOKAWA SHOTEN PUBLISHING CO., LTD., Tokyo.
English translation rights arranged with KADOKAWA SHOTEN PUBLISHING CO., LTD., Tokyo
through TUTTLE-MORI AGENCY, INC., Tokyo.

English text © 2003 by Mixx Entertainment, Inc.
TOKYOPOP is a registered trademark of Mixx Entertainment, Inc.

ISBN: 1-59182-165-7

First TOKYOPOP® printing: May 2003

10 9 8 7 6 5 4 3 2 1
Printed in the USA

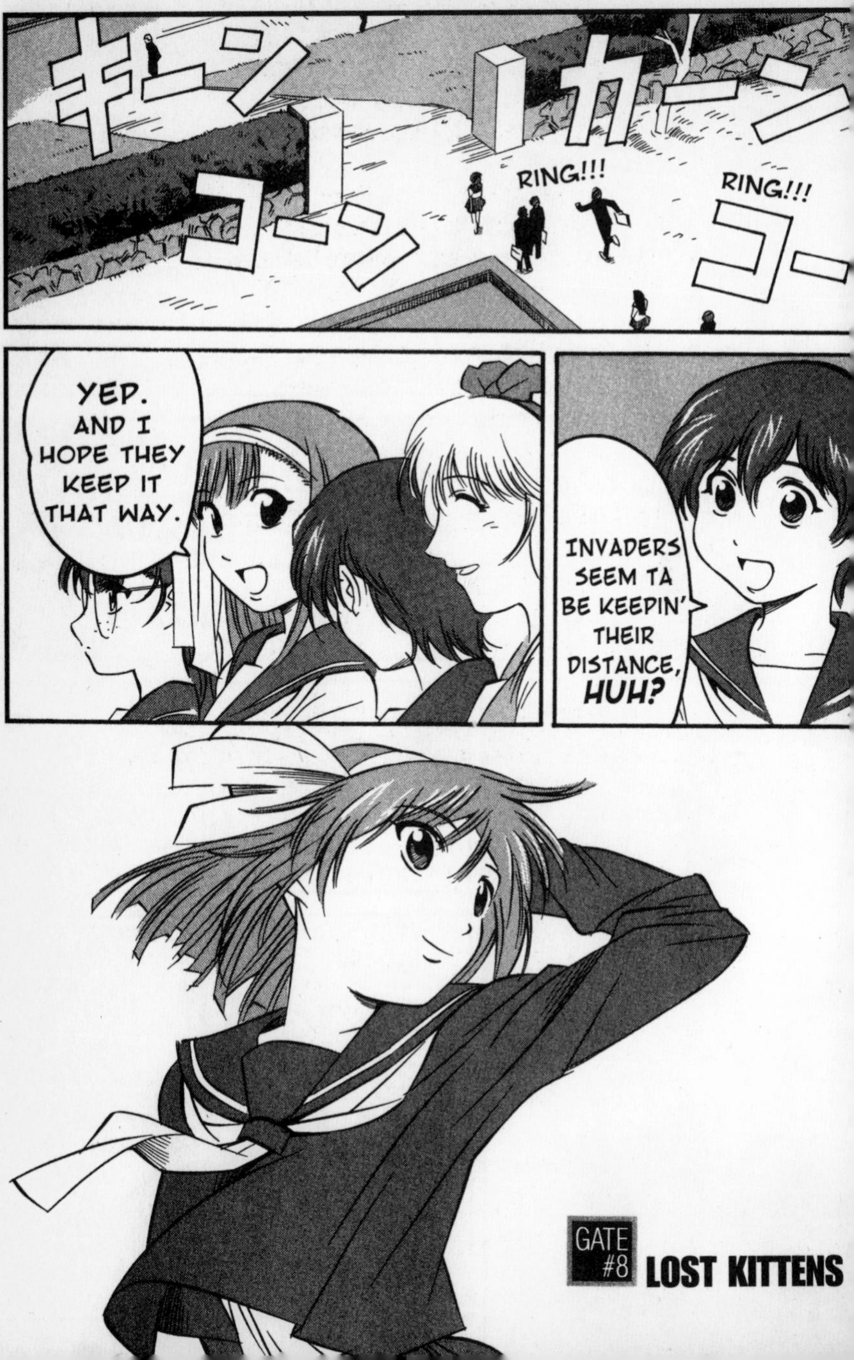
RING!!!
RING!!!
キーン
コーン
カーン
コー
INVADERS SEEM TA BE KEEPIN' THEIR DISTANCE, HUH?
YEP. AND I HOPE THEY KEEP IT THAT WAY.
GATE #8
LOST KITTENS

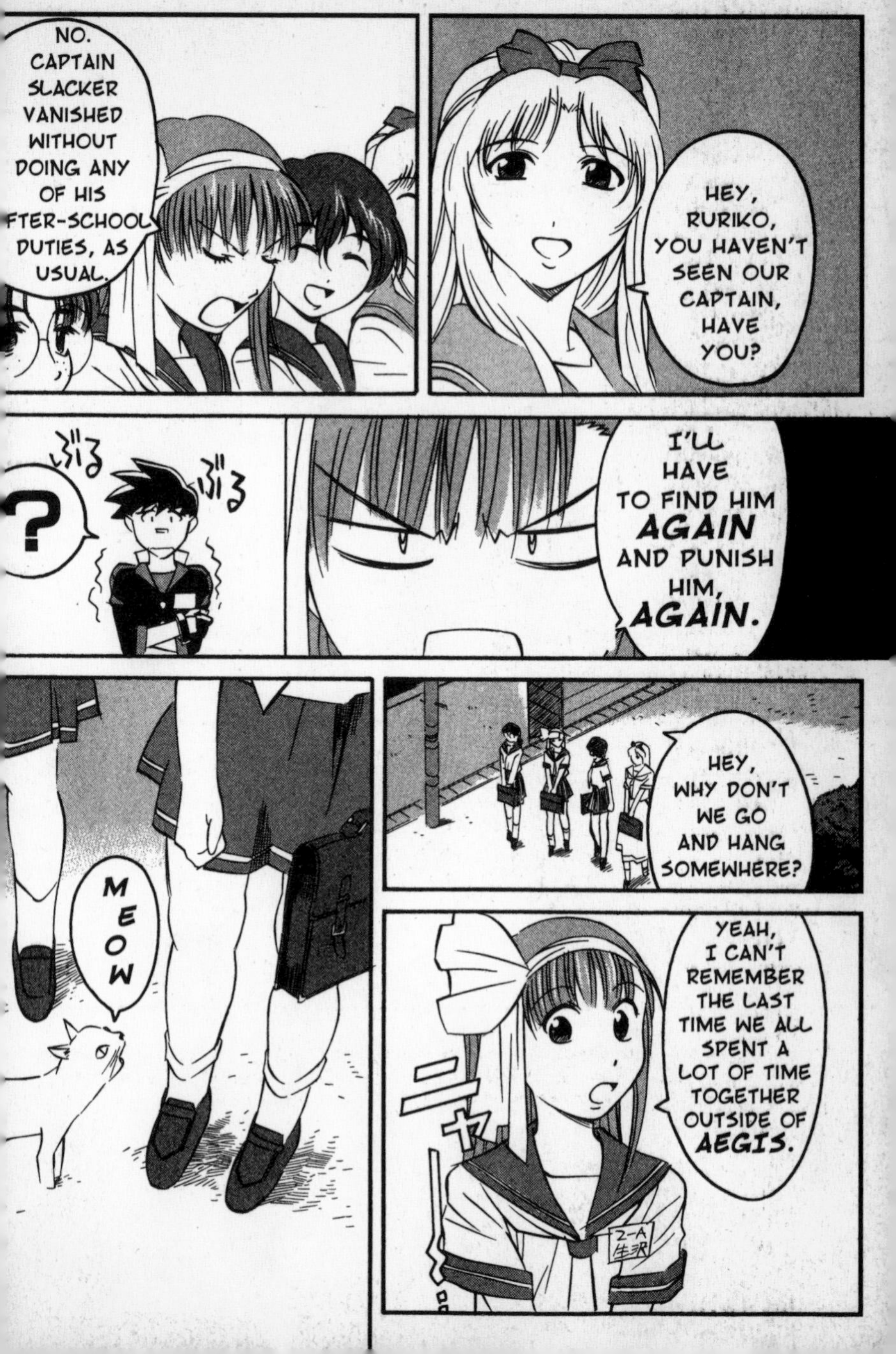
HEY, RURIKO, YOU HAVEN'T SEEN OUR CAPTAIN, HAVE YOU?
NO. CAPTAIN SLACKER VANISHED WITHOUT DOING ANY OF HIS FTER-SCHOOL DUTIES, AS USUAL.
I'LL HAVE TO FIND HIM AGAIN AND PUNISH HIM, AGAIN.
ぶる
ぶる
?
HEY, WHY DON'T WE GO AND HANG SOMEWHERE?
YEAH, I CAN'T REMEMBER THE LAST TIME WE ALL SPENT A LOT OF TIME TOGETHER OUTSIDE OF AEGIS.
ニャ
MEOW

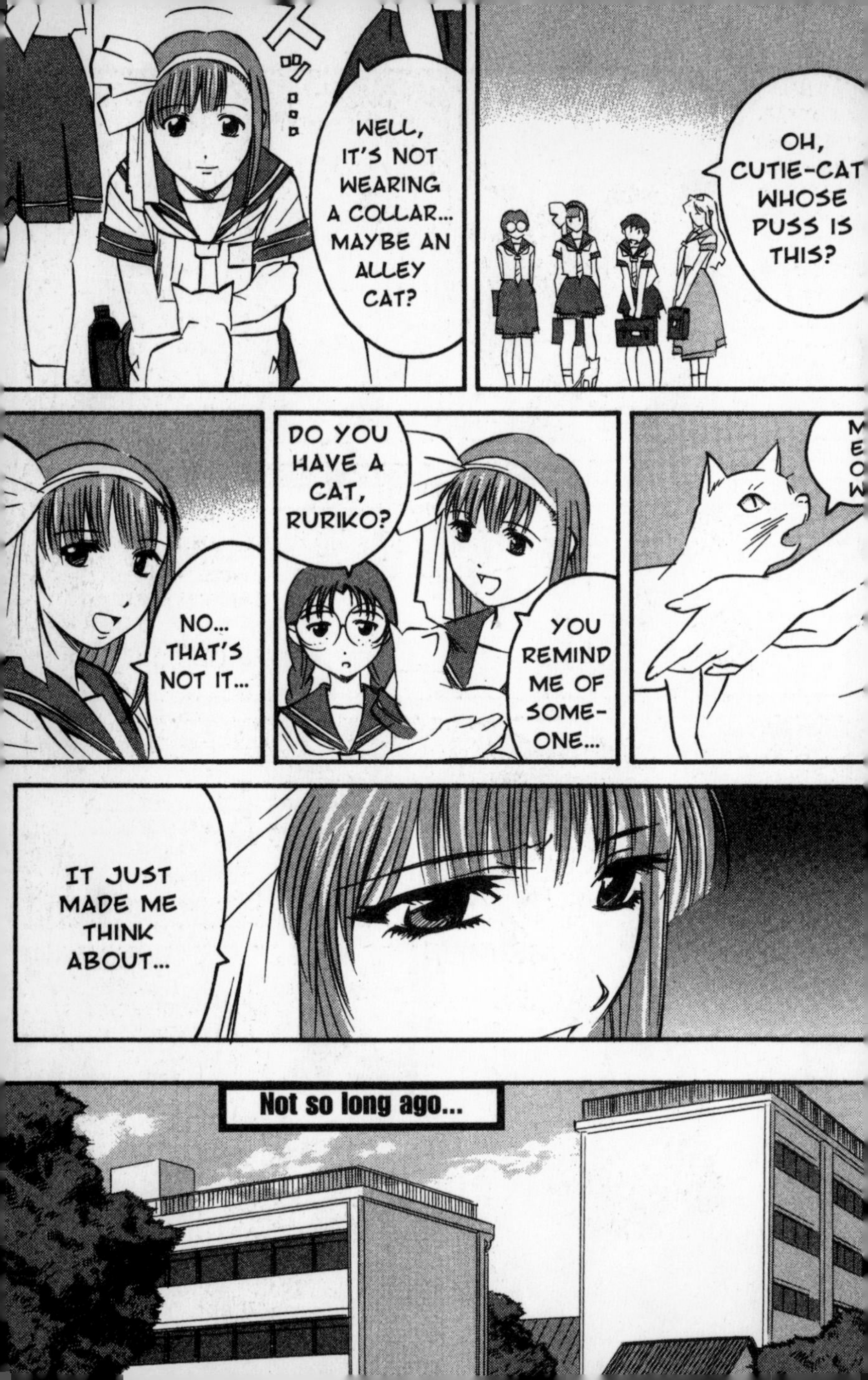
OH, CUTIE-CAT WHOSE PUSS IS THIS?
WELL, IT'S NOT WEARING A COLLAR... MAYBE AN ALLEY CAT?
MEOW
YOU REMIND ME OF SOME-ONE...
DO YOU HAVE A CAT, RURIKO?
NO... THAT'S NOT IT...
IT JUST MADE ME THINK ABOUT...
Not so long ago...

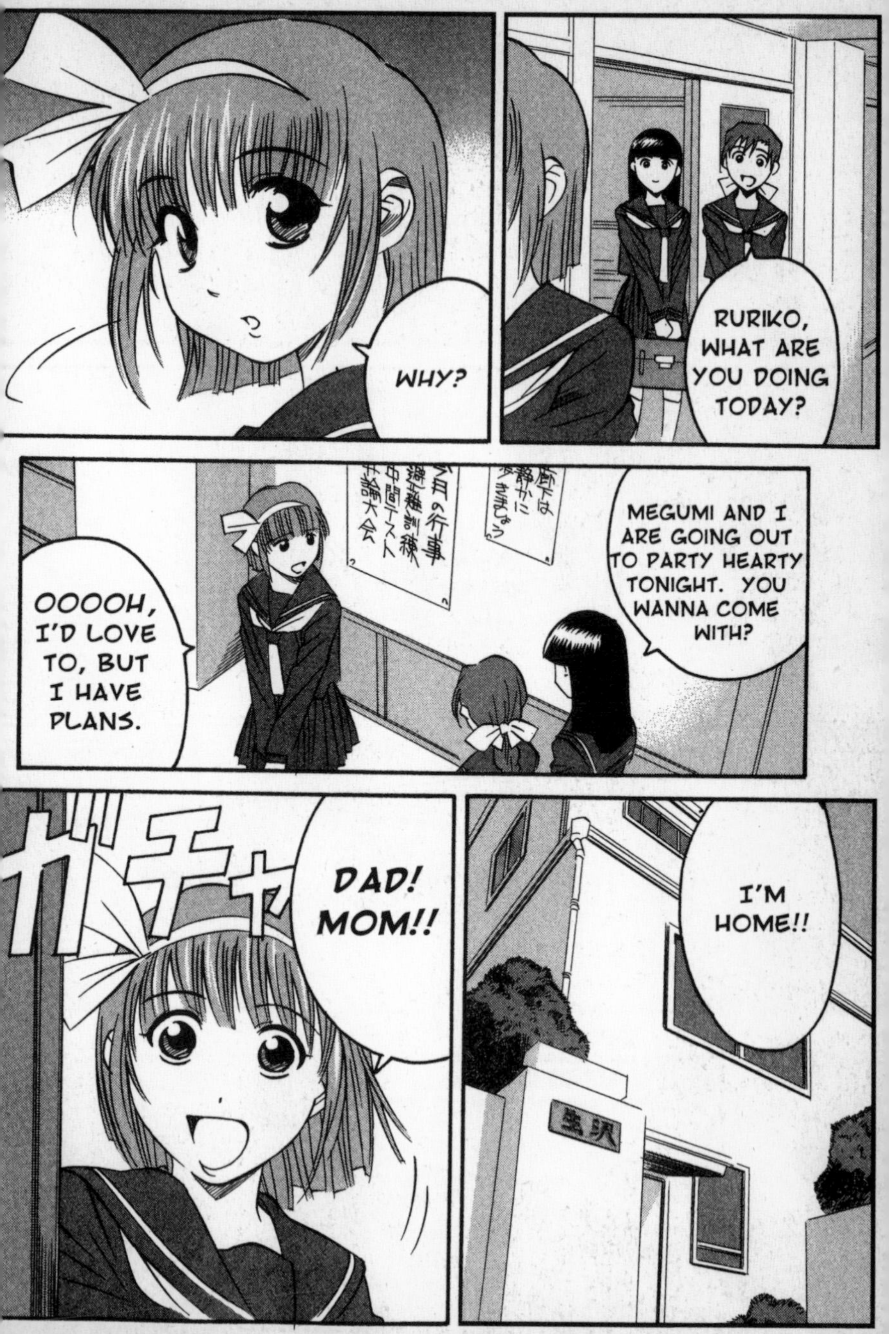
RURIKO, WHAT ARE YOU DOING TODAY?
WHY?
廊下は静かに歩きましょう
今月の行事 避難訓練 中間テスト 弁論大会
MEGUMI AND I ARE GOING OUT TO PARTY HEARTY TONIGHT. YOU WANNA COME WITH?
OOOOH, I'D LOVE TO, BUT I HAVE PLANS.
I'M HOME!!
ガチャ
DAD! MOM!!

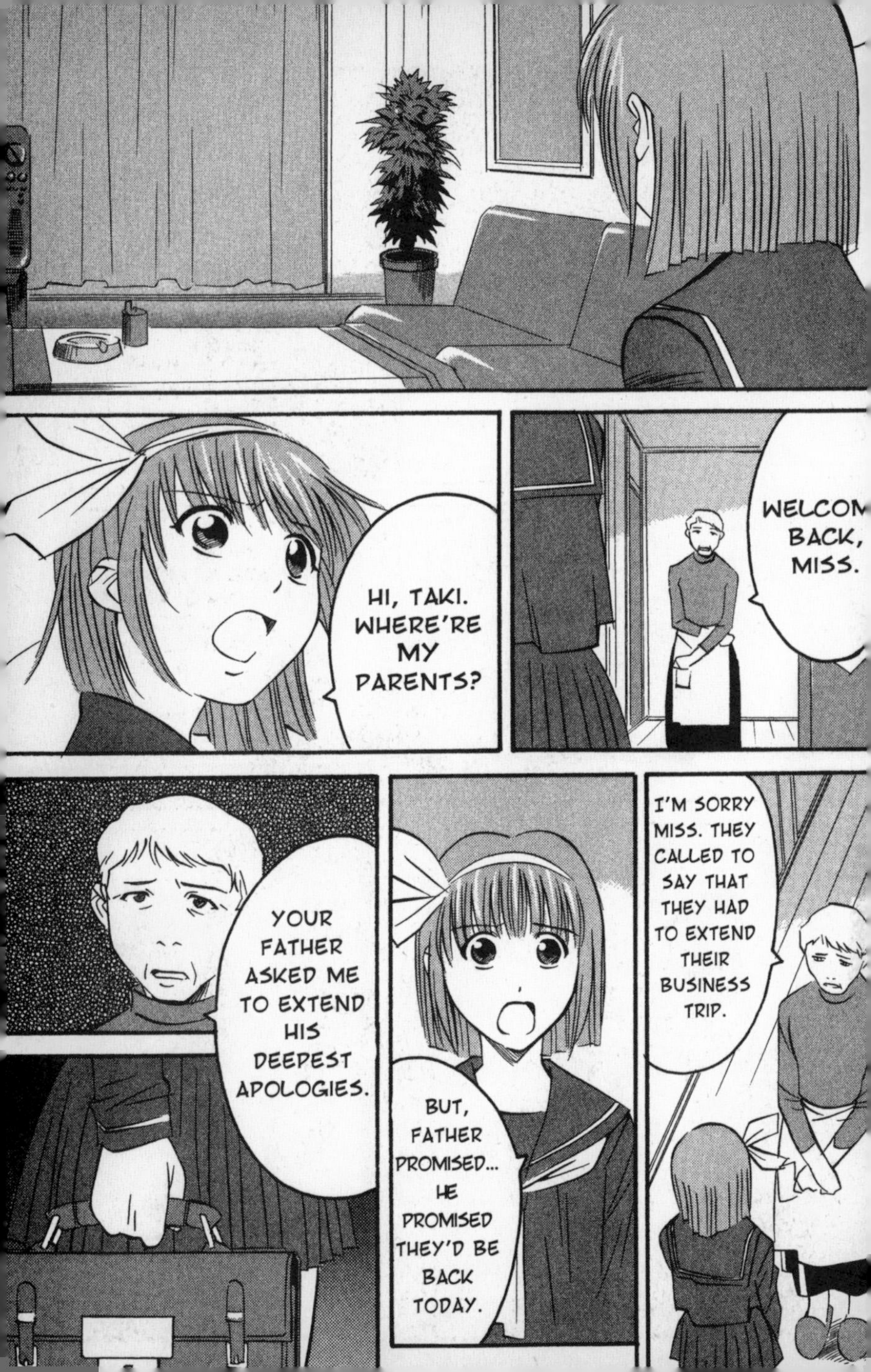
WELCOM BACK, MISS.
HI, TAKI. WHERE'RE MY PARENTS?
I'M SORRY MISS. THEY CALLED TO SAY THAT THEY HAD TO EXTEND THEIR BUSINESS TRIP.
BUT, FATHER PROMISED... HE PROMISED THEY'D BE BACK TODAY.
YOUR FATHER ASKED ME TO EXTEND HIS DEEPEST APOLOGIES.

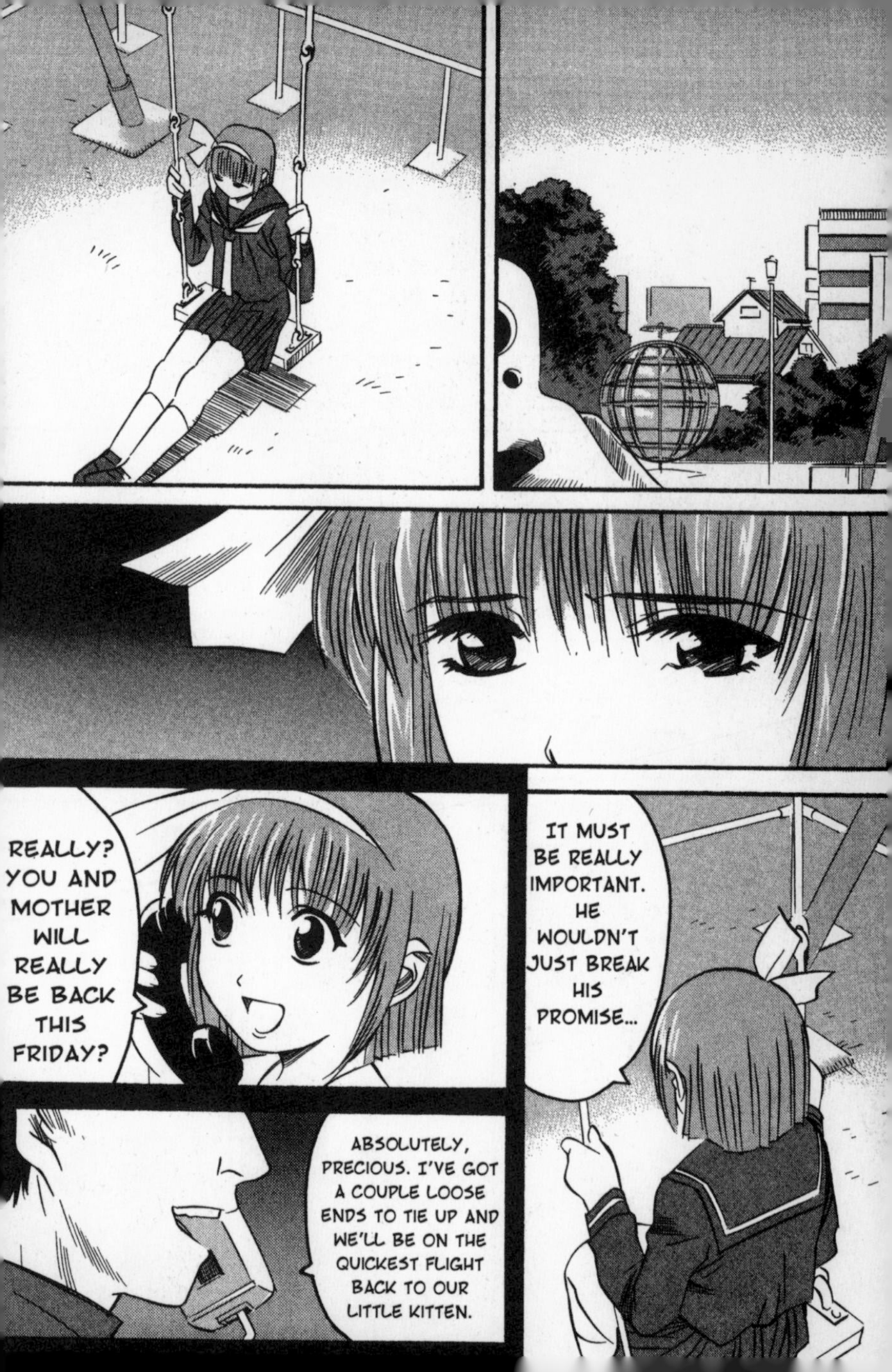
IT MUST BE REALLY IMPORTANT. HE WOULDN'T JUST BREAK HIS PROMISE...
REALLY? YOU AND MOTHER WILL REALLY BE BACK THIS FRIDAY?
ABSOLUTELY, PRECIOUS. I'VE GOT A COUPLE LOOSE ENDS TO TIE UP AND WE'LL BE ON THE QUICKEST FLIGHT BACK TO OUR LITTLE KITTEN.

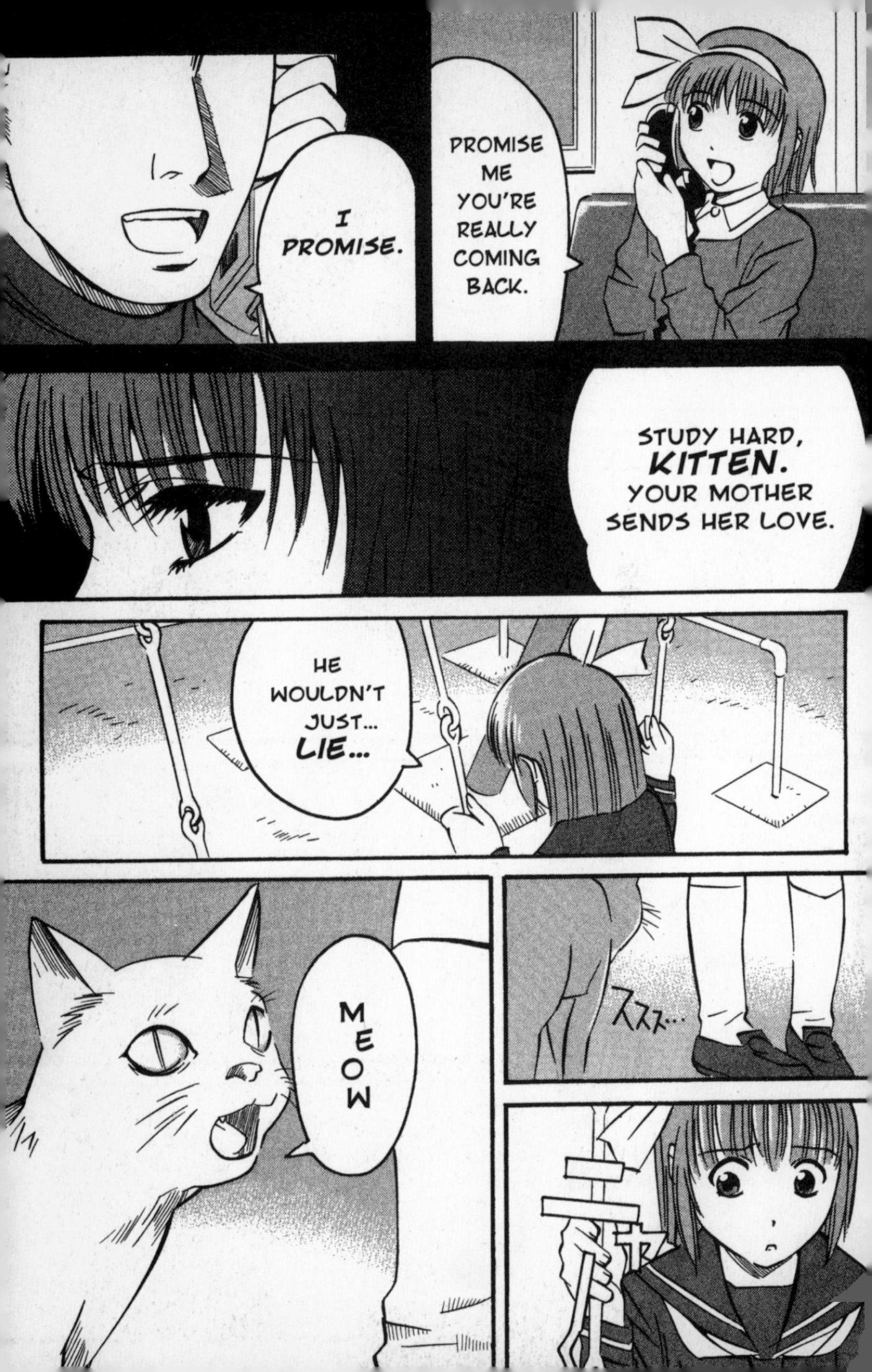
PROMISE ME YOU'RE REALLY COMING BACK.
I PROMISE.
STUDY HARD, **KITTEN.** YOUR MOTHER SENDS HER LOVE.
HE WOULDN'T JUST... **LIE...**
ススス…
MEOW

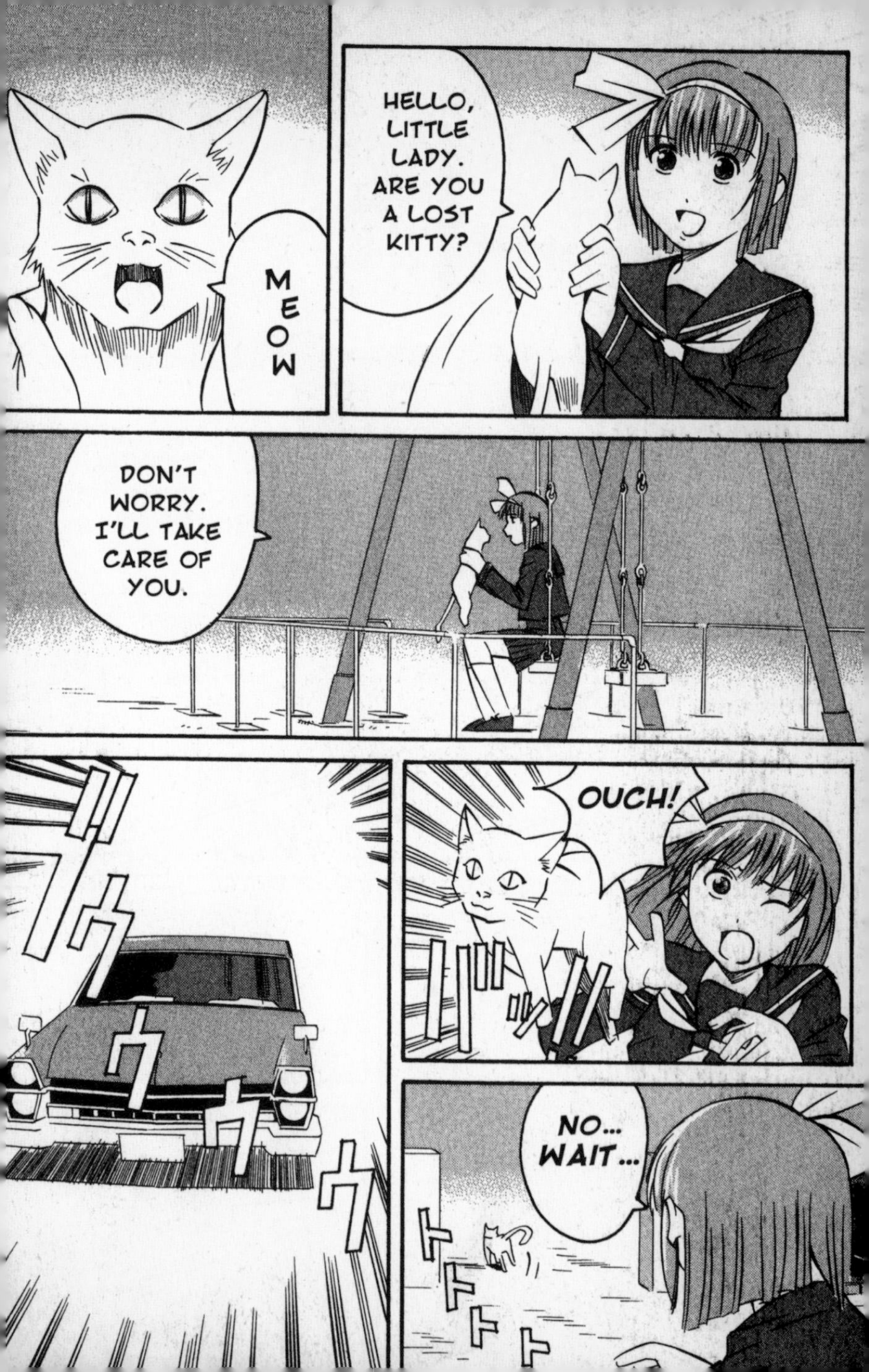
HELLO, LITTLE LADY. ARE YOU A LOST KITTY?
MEOW
DON'T WORRY. I'LL TAKE CARE OF YOU.
OUCH!
NO... WAIT...

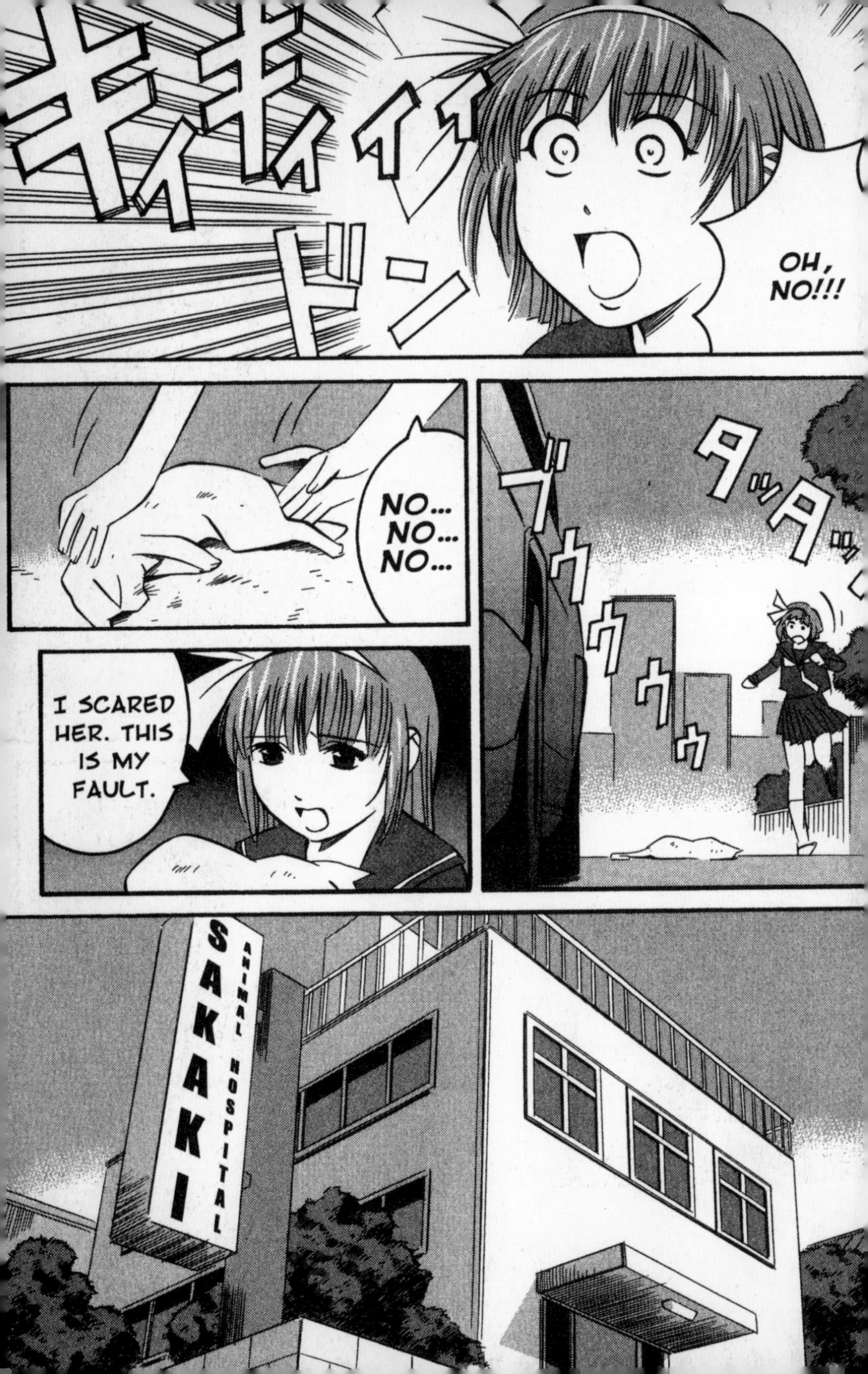
OH, NO!!!
タッタッ
NO... NO... NO...
I SCARED HER. THIS IS MY FAULT.
SAKAKI
ANIMAL HOSPITAL

BUT IT'S ONLY FIVE 'TIL FIVE! YOU HAVE TO BE OPEN!

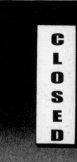

CLOSED

GOTTA BE SOME PLACE OPEN...

I'M SORRY. WE'RE ALREADY CLOSING UP.

DUE TO RENOVATIONS, WE WILL BE CLOSING AT 2PM TODAY. KIMURA ANIMAL HOSPITAL

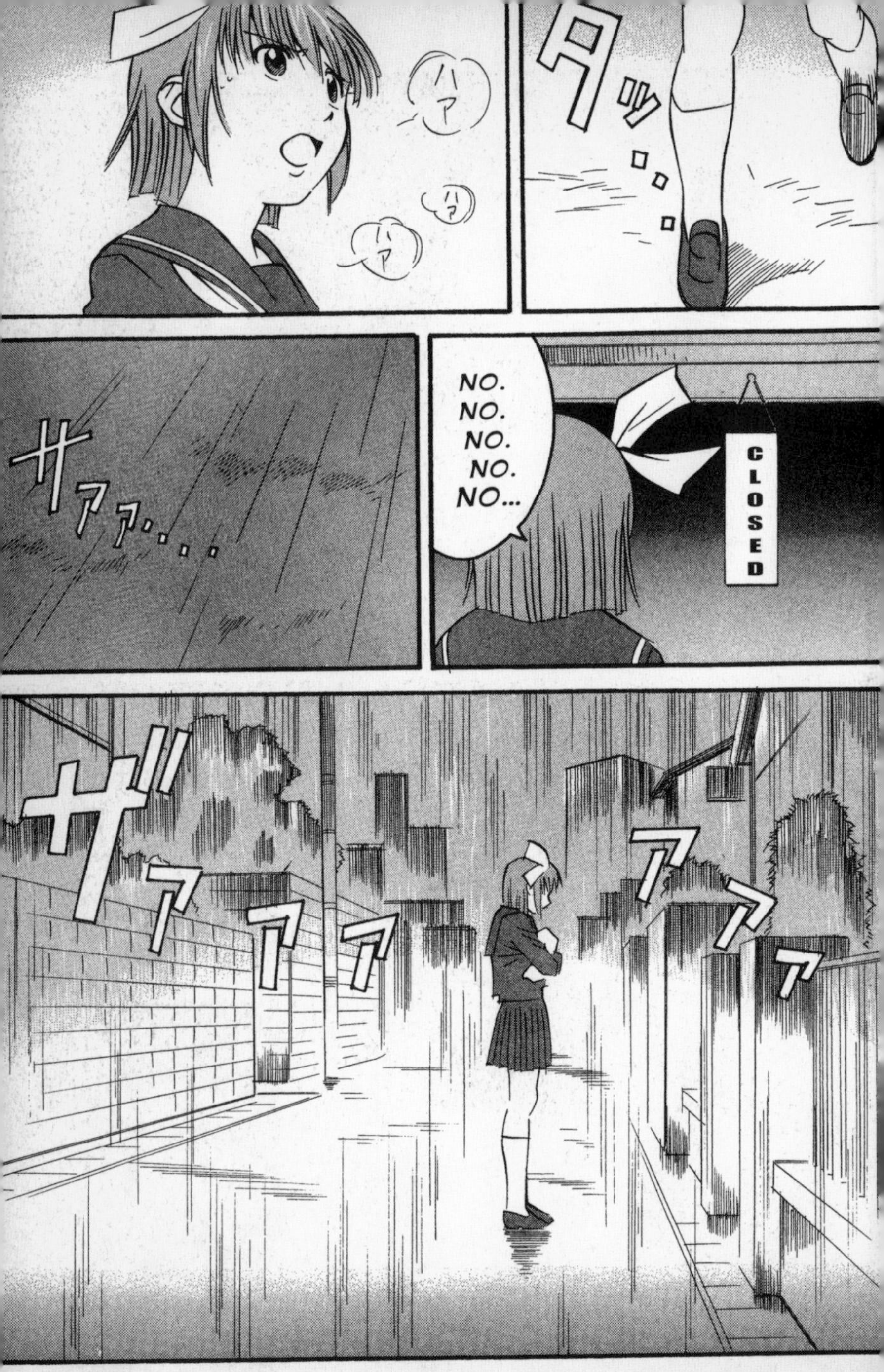
タッ...
ハァ
ハァ
ハァ
NO. NO. NO. NO. NO...
CLOSED
サァァ....
ザァアア
アァァ

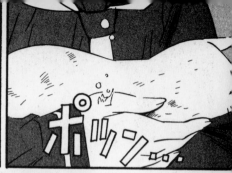

I CAN'T LET YOU DIE.

...AND LOVE YOU...

IT'S MY FAULT AND I WON'T LET YOU DIE. I'M GONNA HOLD YOU...

...AND SAVE YOU...

WHAT?

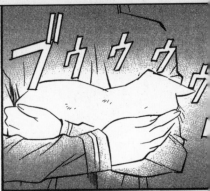

YOU'RE GLOWING! WHY ARE YOU GLOWING?

OH MY GOSH, WHAT...!

MEOW

YOUR POWER HAS REVEALED YOU, GATE KEEPER.

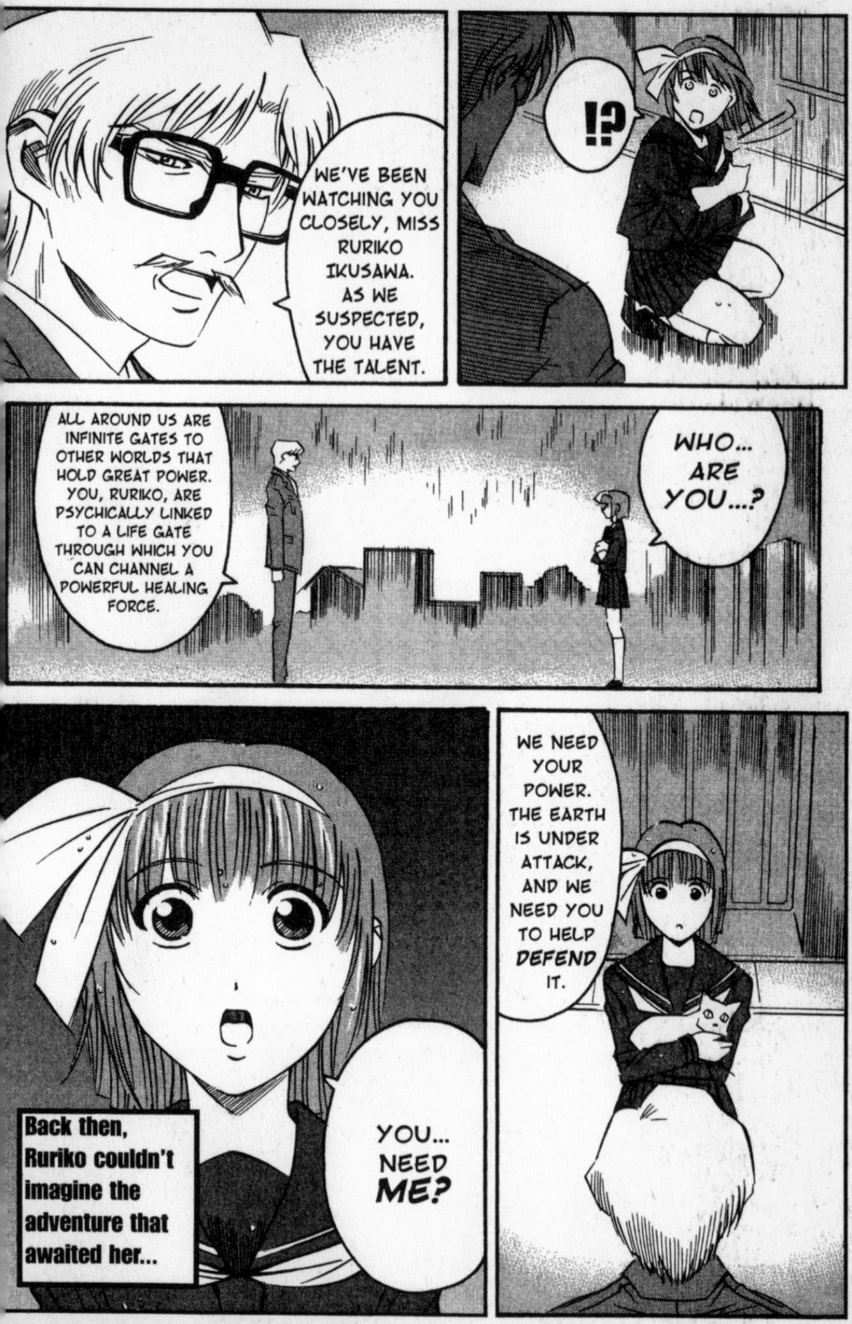
!?
WE'VE BEEN WATCHING YOU CLOSELY, MISS RURIKO IKUSAWA. AS WE SUSPECTED, YOU HAVE THE TALENT.
WHO... ARE YOU...?
ALL AROUND US ARE INFINITE GATES TO OTHER WORLDS THAT HOLD GREAT POWER. YOU, RURIKO, ARE PSYCHICALLY LINKED TO A LIFE GATE THROUGH WHICH YOU CAN CHANNEL A POWERFUL HEALING FORCE.
WE NEED YOUR POWER. THE EARTH IS UNDER ATTACK, AND WE NEED YOU TO HELP DEFEND IT.
YOU... NEED ME?
Back then, Ruriko couldn't imagine the adventure that awaited her...

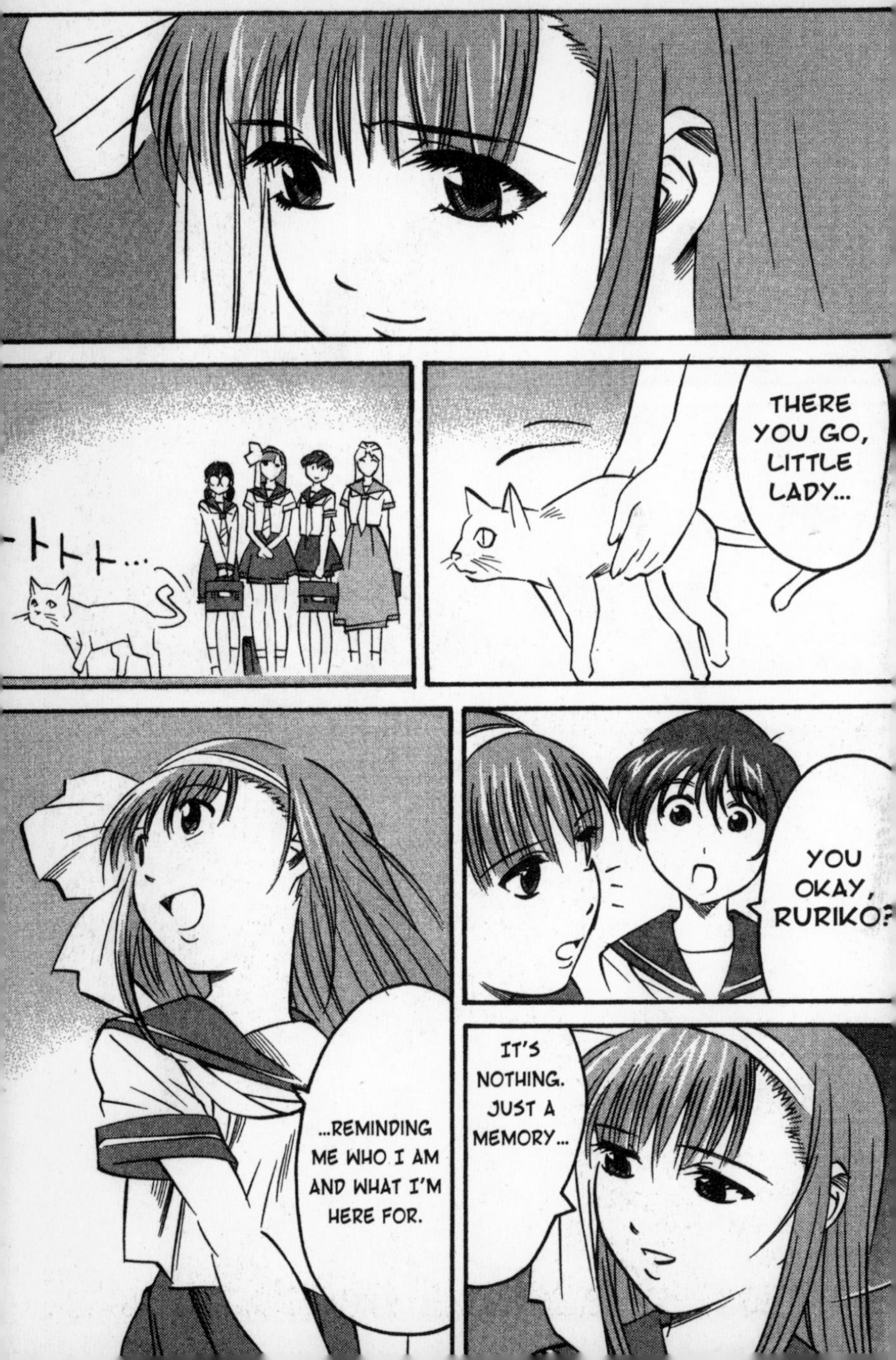
THERE YOU GO, LITTLE LADY...
トトト...
YOU OKAY, RURIKO?
IT'S NOTHING. JUST A MEMORY...
...REMINDING ME WHO I AM AND WHAT I'M HERE FOR.

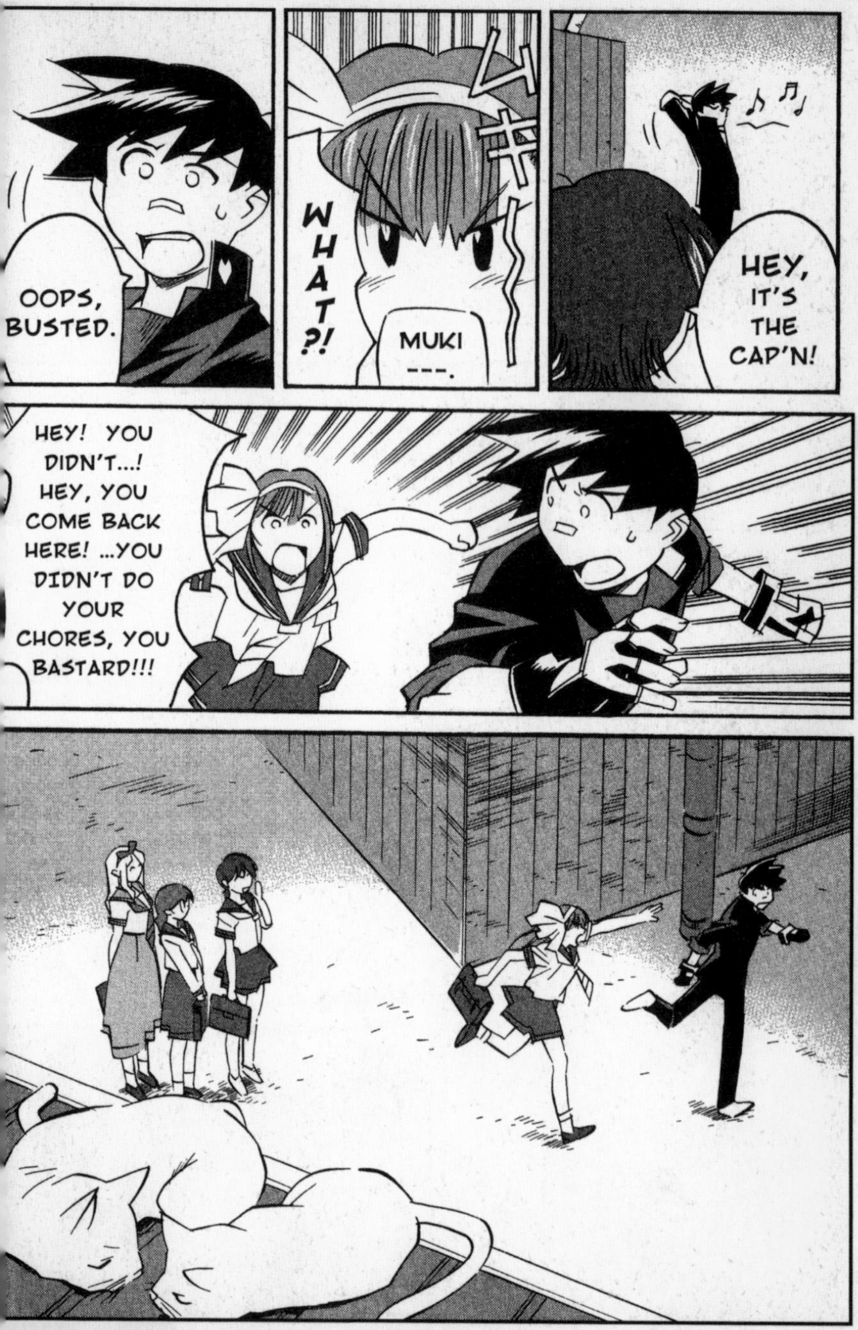
HEY, IT'S THE CAP'N!
WHAT?!
MUKI ---.
OOPS, BUSTED.
HEY! YOU DIDN'T...! HEY, YOU COME BACK HERE! ...YOU DIDN'T DO YOUR CHORES, YOU BASTARD!!!

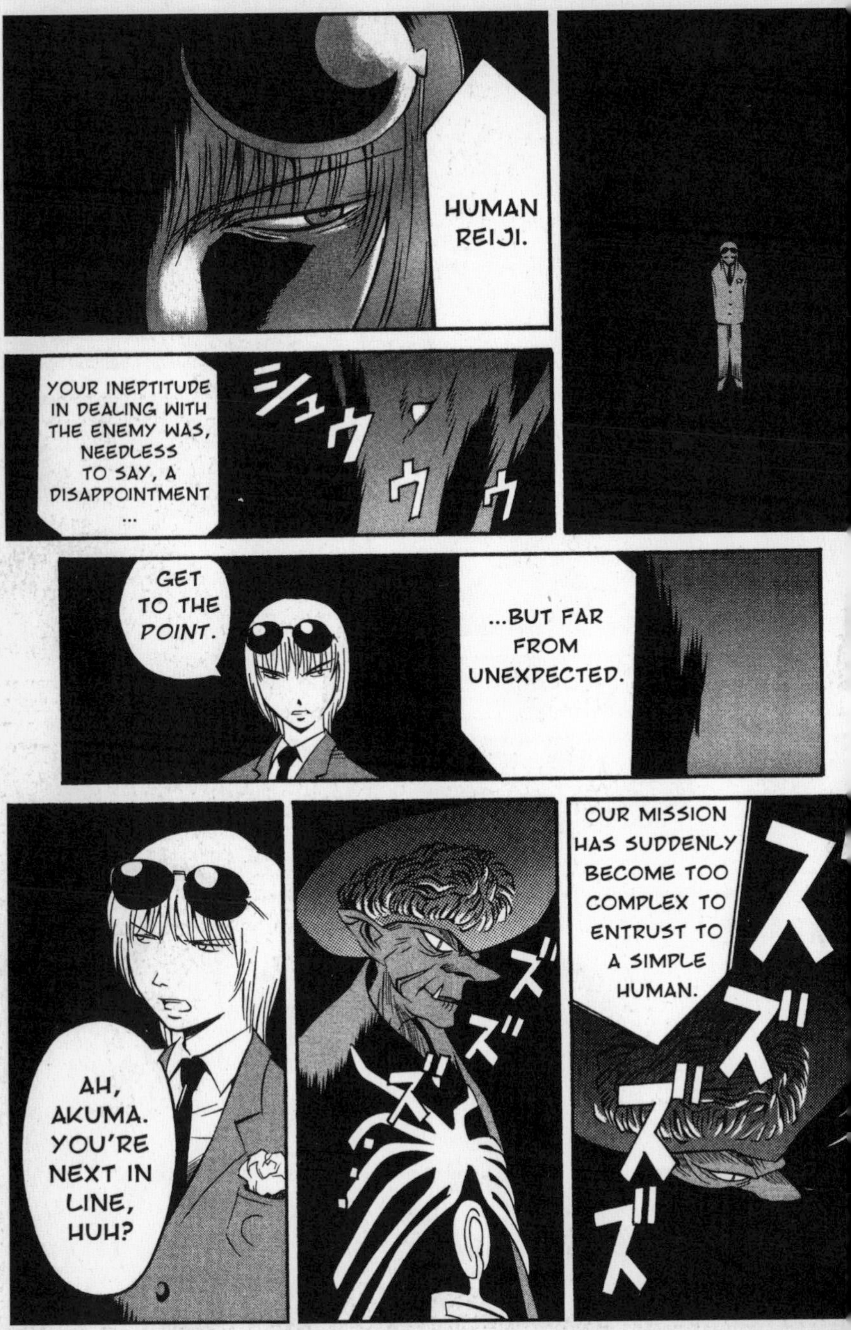
HUMAN REIJI.
シュウウウ
YOUR INEPTITUDE IN DEALING WITH THE ENEMY WAS, NEEDLESS TO SAY, A DISAPPOINTMENT ...
...BUT FAR FROM UNEXPECTED.
GET TO THE POINT.
OUR MISSION HAS SUDDENLY BECOME TOO COMPLEX TO ENTRUST TO A SIMPLE HUMAN.
ズズズズズズ
ズズズズ
AH, AKUMA. YOU'RE NEXT IN LINE, HUH?

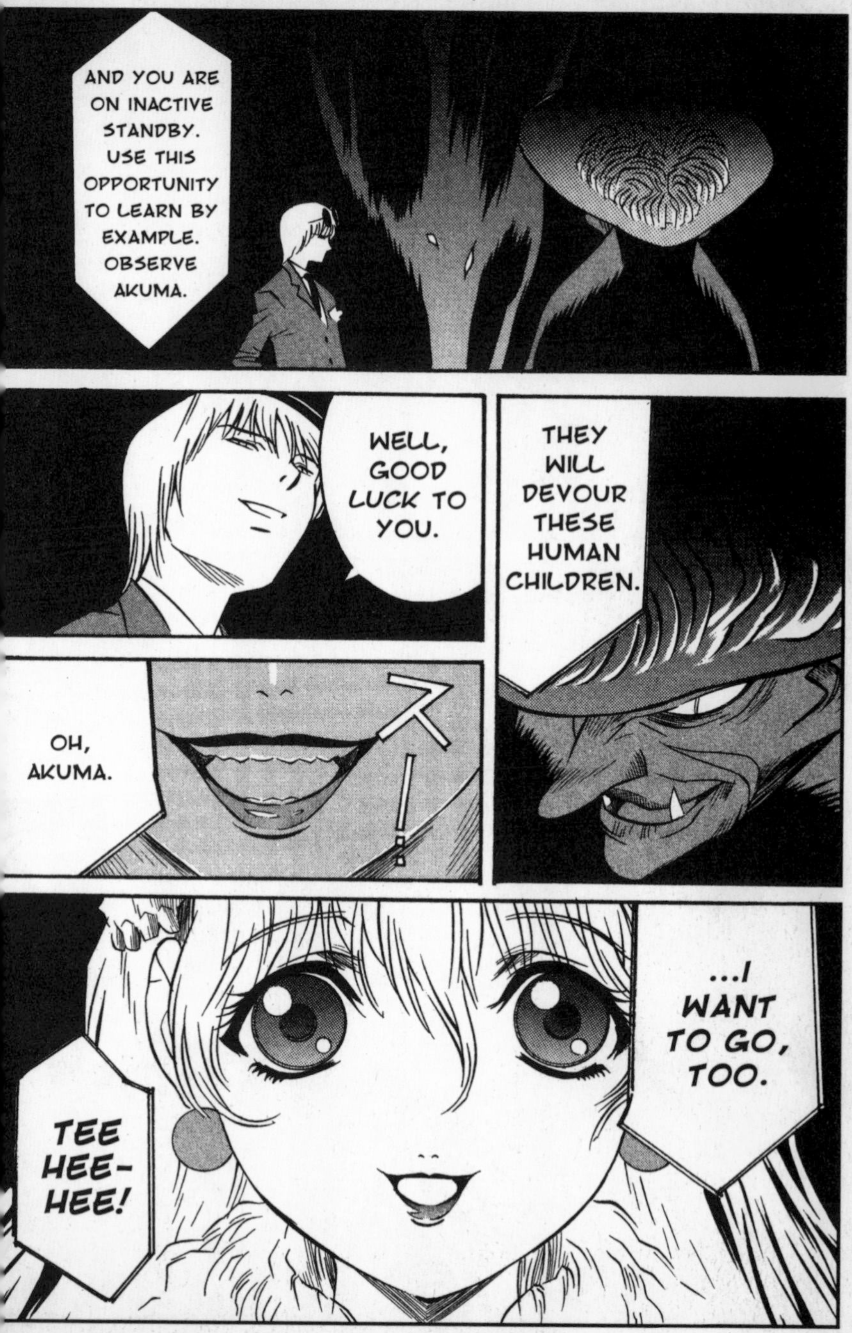

AND YOU ARE ON INACTIVE STANDBY. USE THIS OPPORTUNITY TO LEARN BY EXAMPLE. OBSERVE AKUMA.
THEY WILL DEVOUR THESE HUMAN CHILDREN.
WELL, GOOD LUCK TO YOU.
ス!
OH, AKUMA.
...I WANT TO GO, TOO.
TEE HEE-HEE!

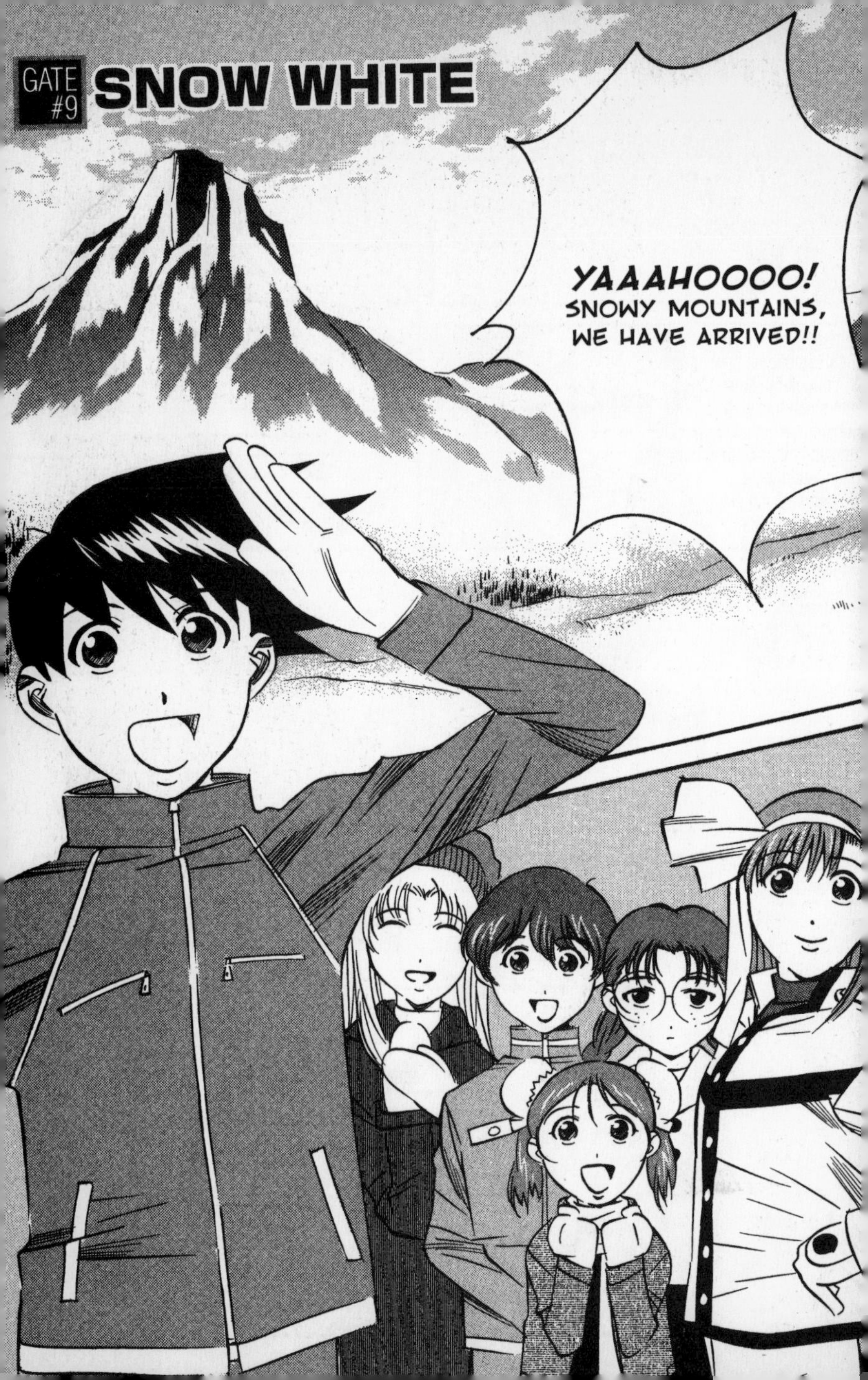
GATE #9 SNOW WHITE
YAAAHOOOO! SNOWY MOUNTAINS, WE HAVE ARRIVED!!

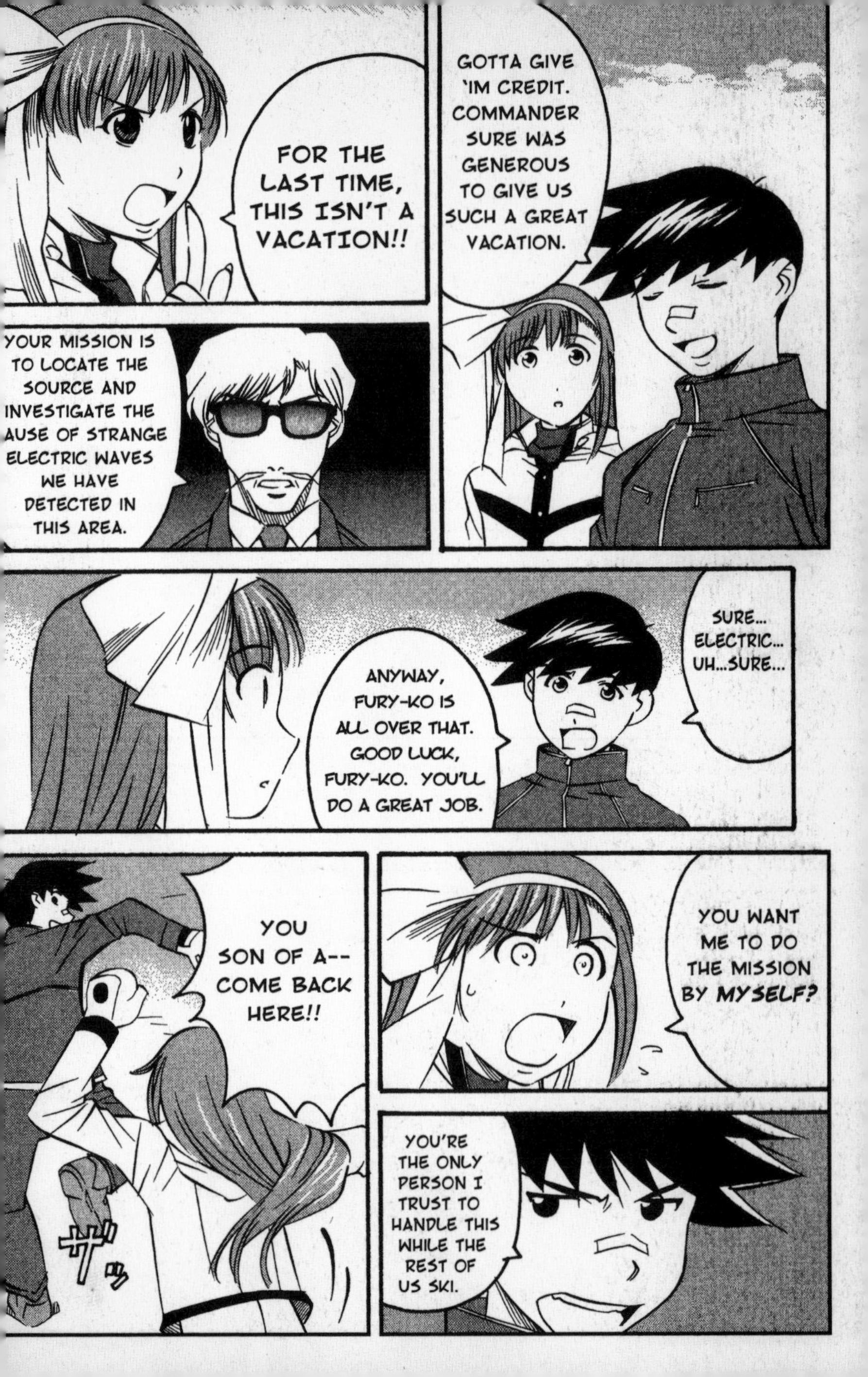
GOTTA GIVE 'IM CREDIT. COMMANDER SURE WAS GENEROUS TO GIVE US SUCH A GREAT VACATION.
FOR THE LAST TIME, THIS ISN'T A VACATION!!
YOUR MISSION IS TO LOCATE THE SOURCE AND INVESTIGATE THE AUSE OF STRANGE ELECTRIC WAVES WE HAVE DETECTED IN THIS AREA.
SURE... ELECTRIC... UH...SURE...
ANYWAY, FURY-KO IS ALL OVER THAT. GOOD LUCK, FURY-KO. YOU'LL DO A GREAT JOB.
YOU WANT ME TO DO THE MISSION BY MYSELF?
YOU'RE THE ONLY PERSON I TRUST TO HANDLE THIS WHILE THE REST OF US SKI.
YOU SON OF A-- COME BACK HERE!!
ザッ

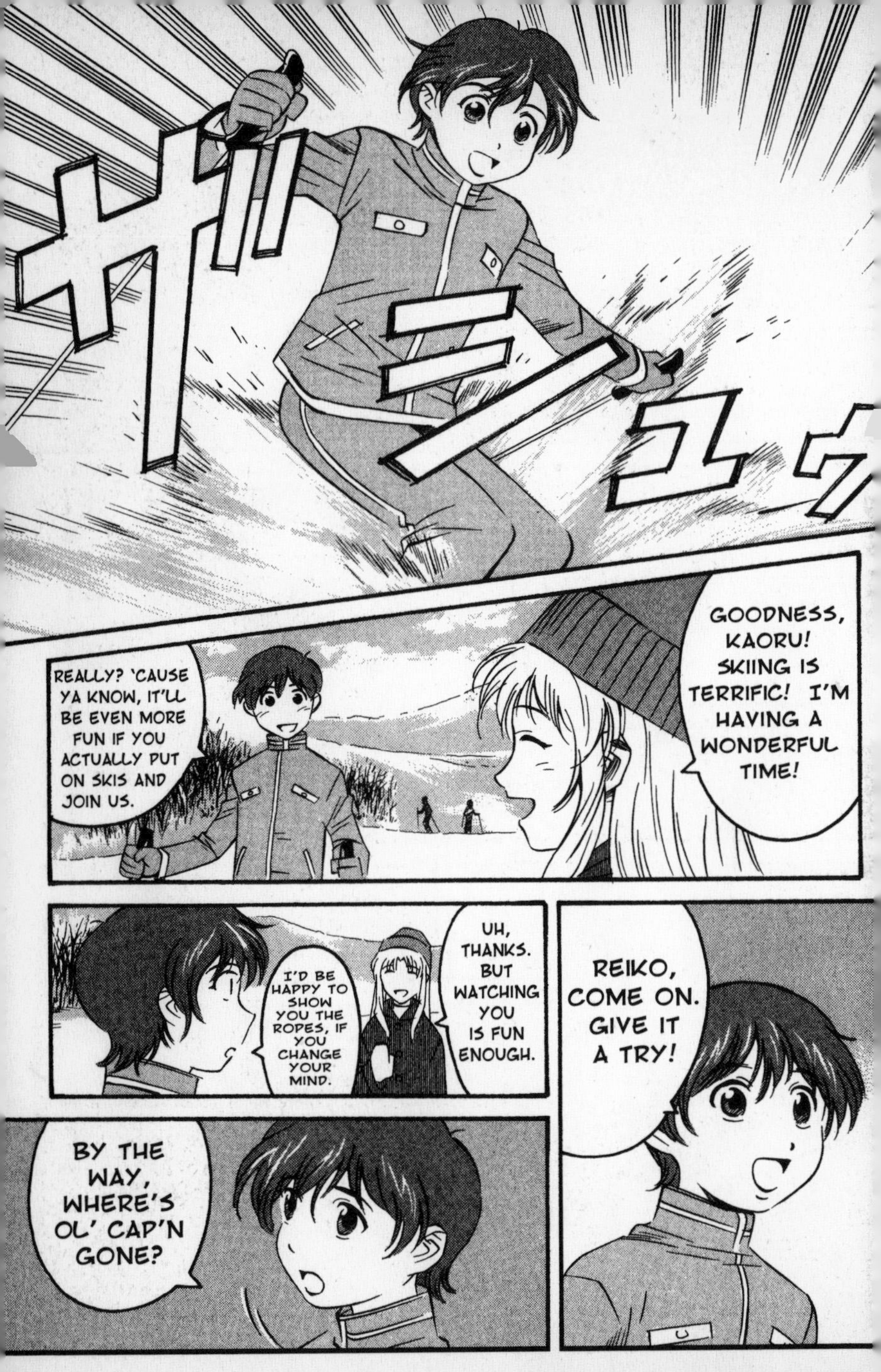
GOODNESS, KAORU! SKIING IS TERRIFIC! I'M HAVING A WONDERFUL TIME!
REALLY? 'CAUSE YA KNOW, IT'LL BE EVEN MORE FUN IF YOU ACTUALLY PUT ON SKIS AND JOIN US.
REIKO, COME ON. GIVE IT A TRY!
UH, THANKS. BUT WATCHING YOU IS FUN ENOUGH.
I'D BE HAPPY TO SHOW YOU THE ROPES, IF YOU CHANGE YOUR MIND.
BY THE WAY, WHERE'S OL' CAP'N GONE?

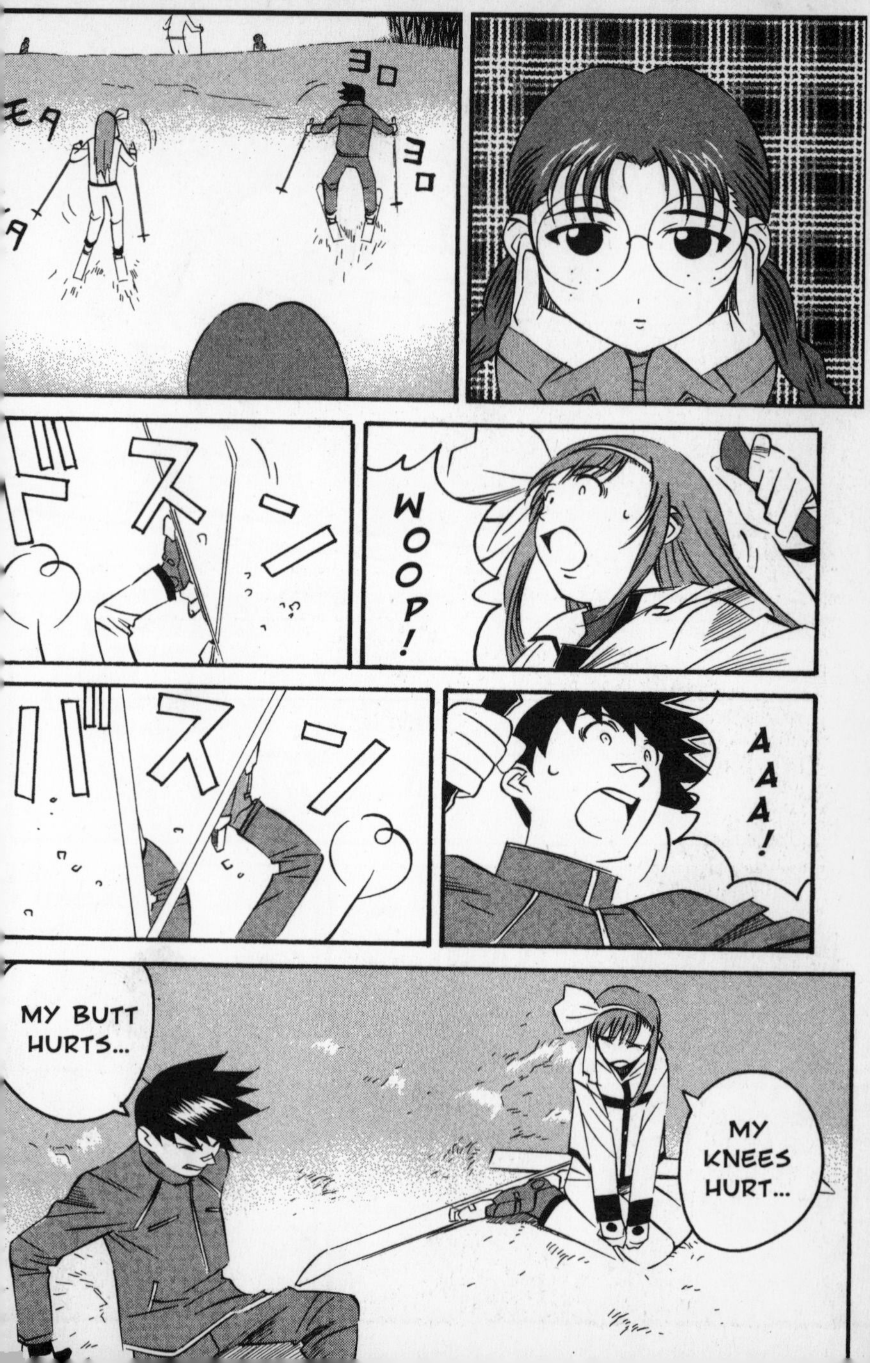
ヨロ
ヨロ
モタ
タ
WOOOP!
ドスーン
AAA!
バスーン
MY KNEES HURT...
MY BUTT HURTS...

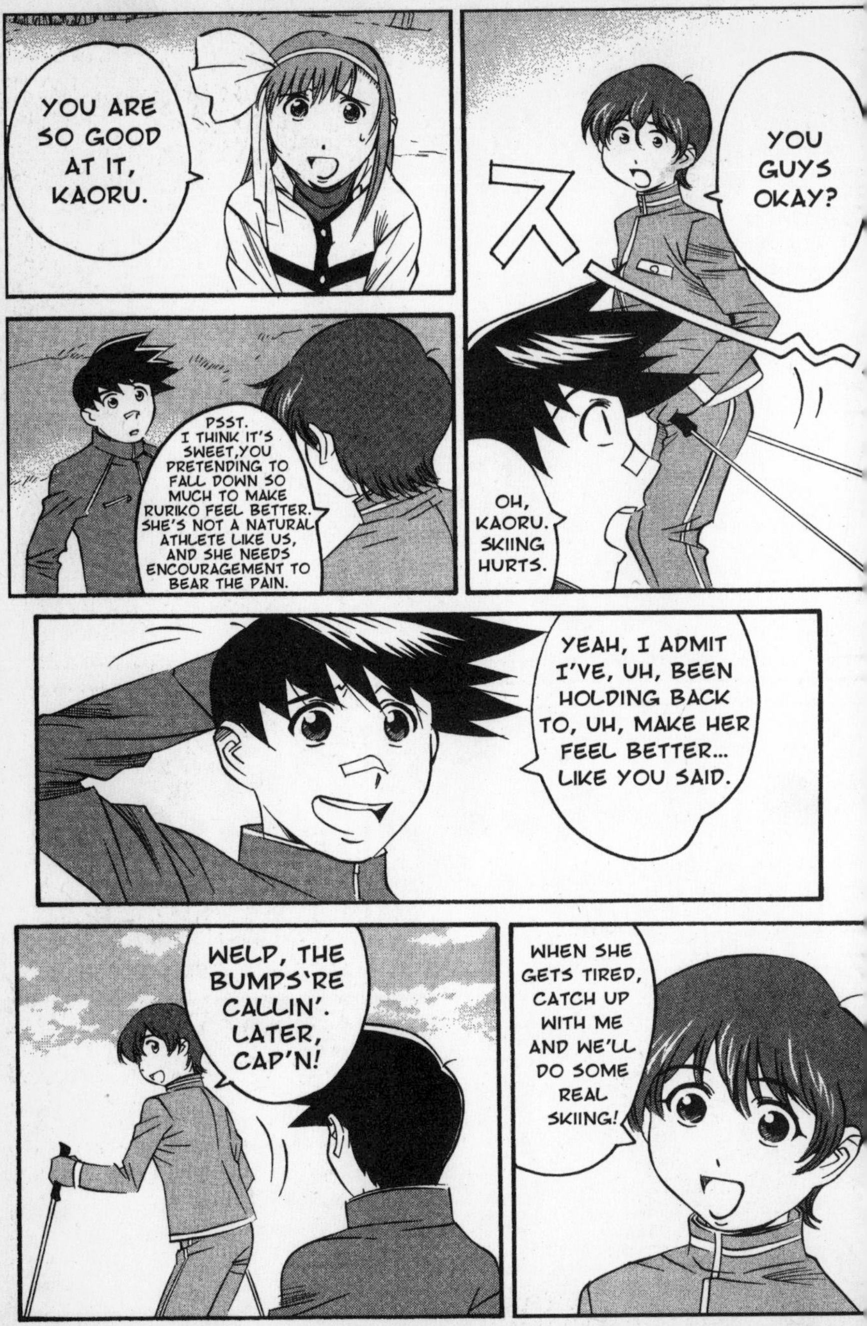

ス
YOU GUYS OKAY?
OH, KAORU. SKIING HURTS.
YOU ARE SO GOOD AT IT, KAORU.
PSST. I THINK IT'S SWEET,YOU PRETENDING TO FALL DOWN SO MUCH TO MAKE RURIKO FEEL BETTER. SHE'S NOT A NATURAL ATHLETE LIKE US, AND SHE NEEDS ENCOURAGEMENT TO BEAR THE PAIN.
YEAH, I ADMIT I'VE, UH, BEEN HOLDING BACK TO, UH, MAKE HER FEEL BETTER... LIKE YOU SAID.
WHEN SHE GETS TIRED, CATCH UP WITH ME AND WE'LL DO SOME REAL SKIING!
WELP, THE BUMPS'RE CALLIN'. LATER, CAP'N!

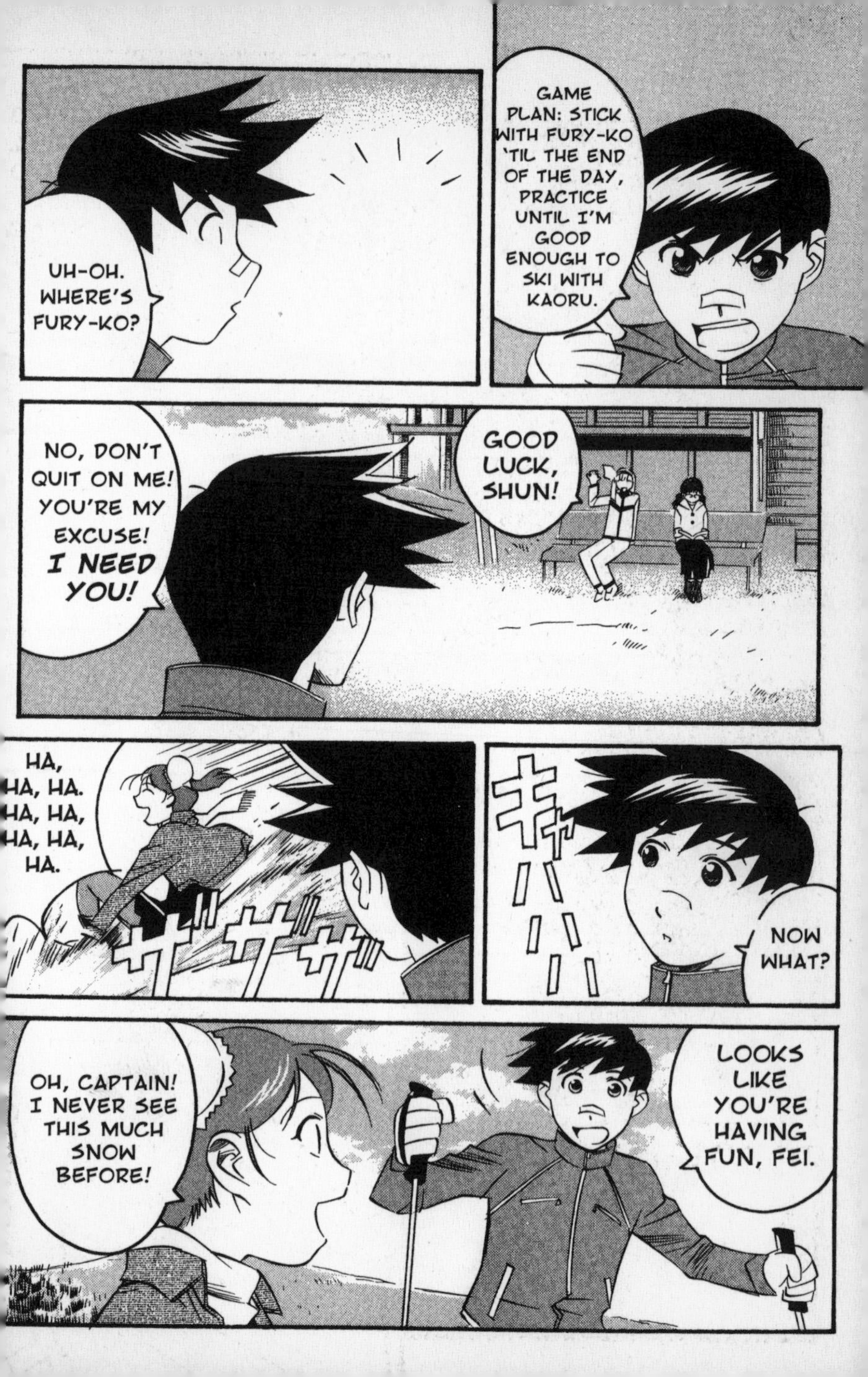
GAME PLAN: STICK WITH FURY-KO 'TIL THE END OF THE DAY, PRACTICE UNTIL I'M GOOD ENOUGH TO SKI WITH KAORU.
UH-OH. WHERE'S FURY-KO?
GOOD LUCK, SHUN!
NO, DON'T QUIT ON ME! YOU'RE MY EXCUSE! ***I NEED YOU!***
キャハハ
NOW WHAT?
HA, HA, HA. HA, HA, HA, HA, HA.
ザザザ
LOOKS LIKE YOU'RE HAVING FUN, FEI.
OH, CAPTAIN! I NEVER SEE THIS MUCH SNOW BEFORE!

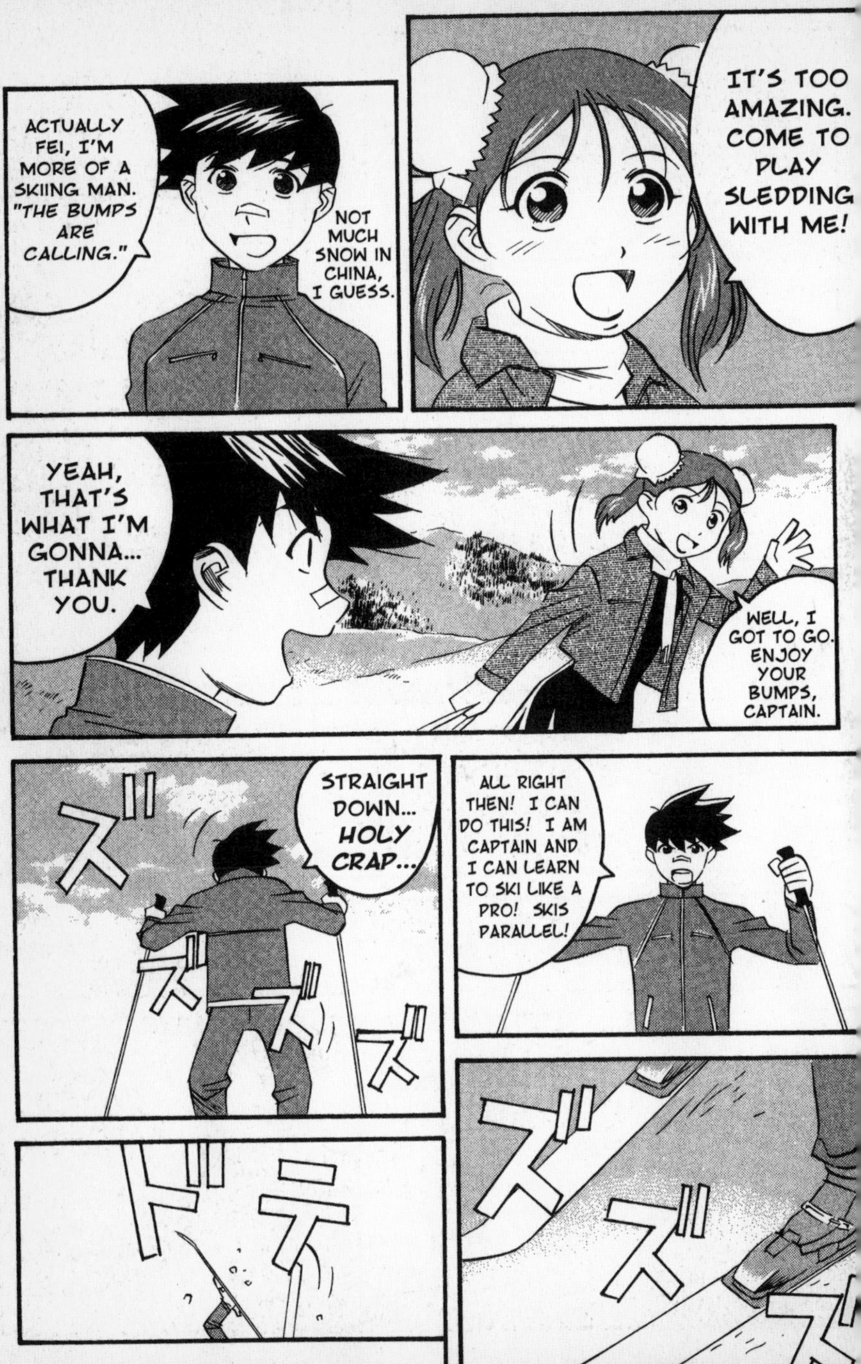
IT'S TOO AMAZING. COME TO PLAY SLEDDING WITH ME!
ACTUALLY FEI, I'M MORE OF A SKIING MAN. "THE BUMPS ARE CALLING."
NOT MUCH SNOW IN CHINA, I GUESS.
WELL, I GOT TO GO. ENJOY YOUR BUMPS, CAPTAIN.
YEAH, THAT'S WHAT I'M GONNA... THANK YOU.
ALL RIGHT THEN! I CAN DO THIS! I AM CAPTAIN AND I CAN LEARN TO SKI LIKE A PRO! SKIS PARALLEL!
ズ
STRAIGHT DOWN... HOLY CRAP...
ズ
ズ
ズ
ズ
ズ
ズ
ドテ

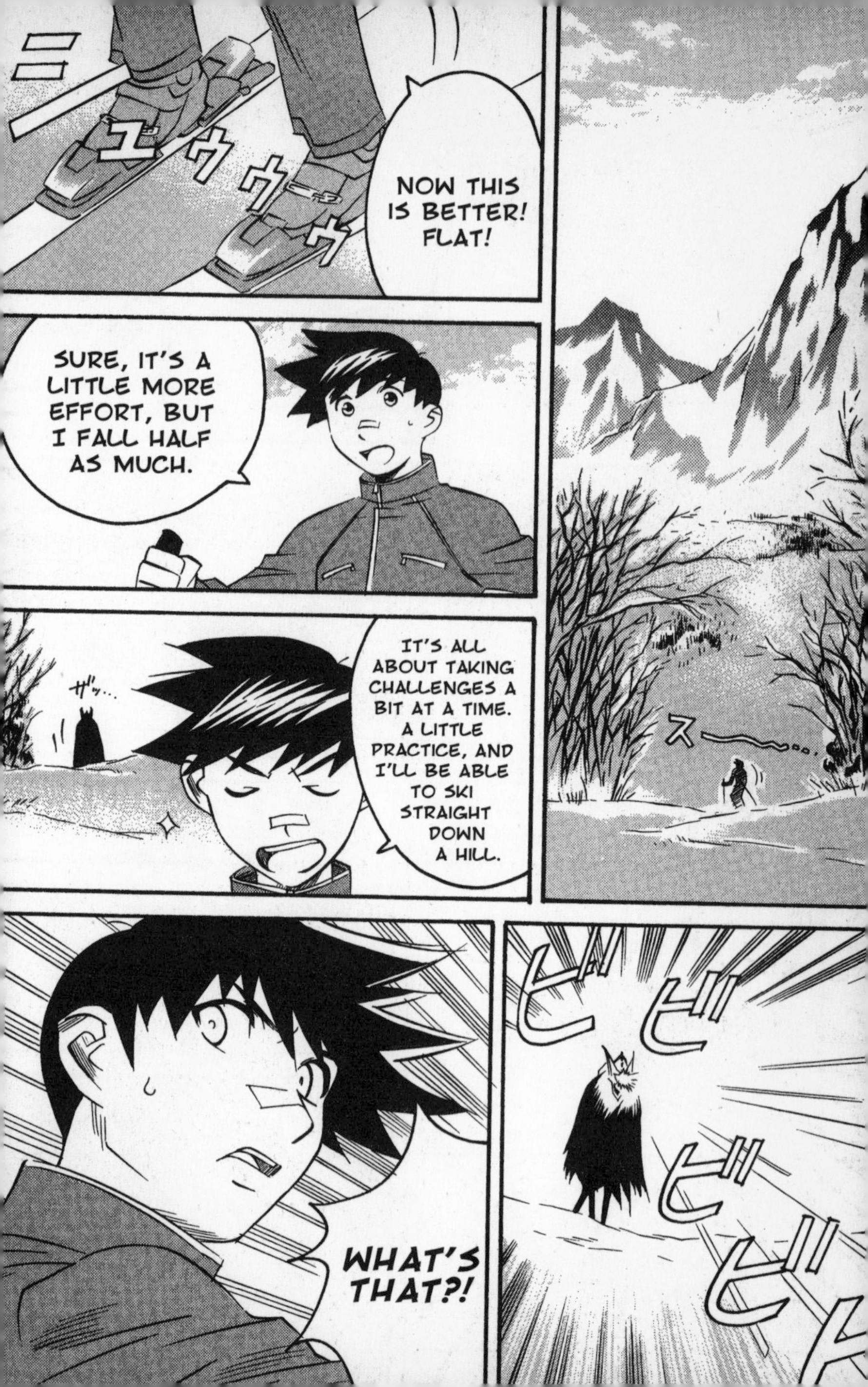
スー…
ニュウウーウ
NOW THIS IS BETTER! FLAT!
SURE, IT'S A LITTLE MORE EFFORT, BUT I FALL HALF AS MUCH.
ザッ…
IT'S ALL ABOUT TAKING CHALLENGES A BIT AT A TIME. A LITTLE PRACTICE, AND I'LL BE ABLE TO SKI STRAIGHT DOWN A HILL.
WHAT'S THAT?!

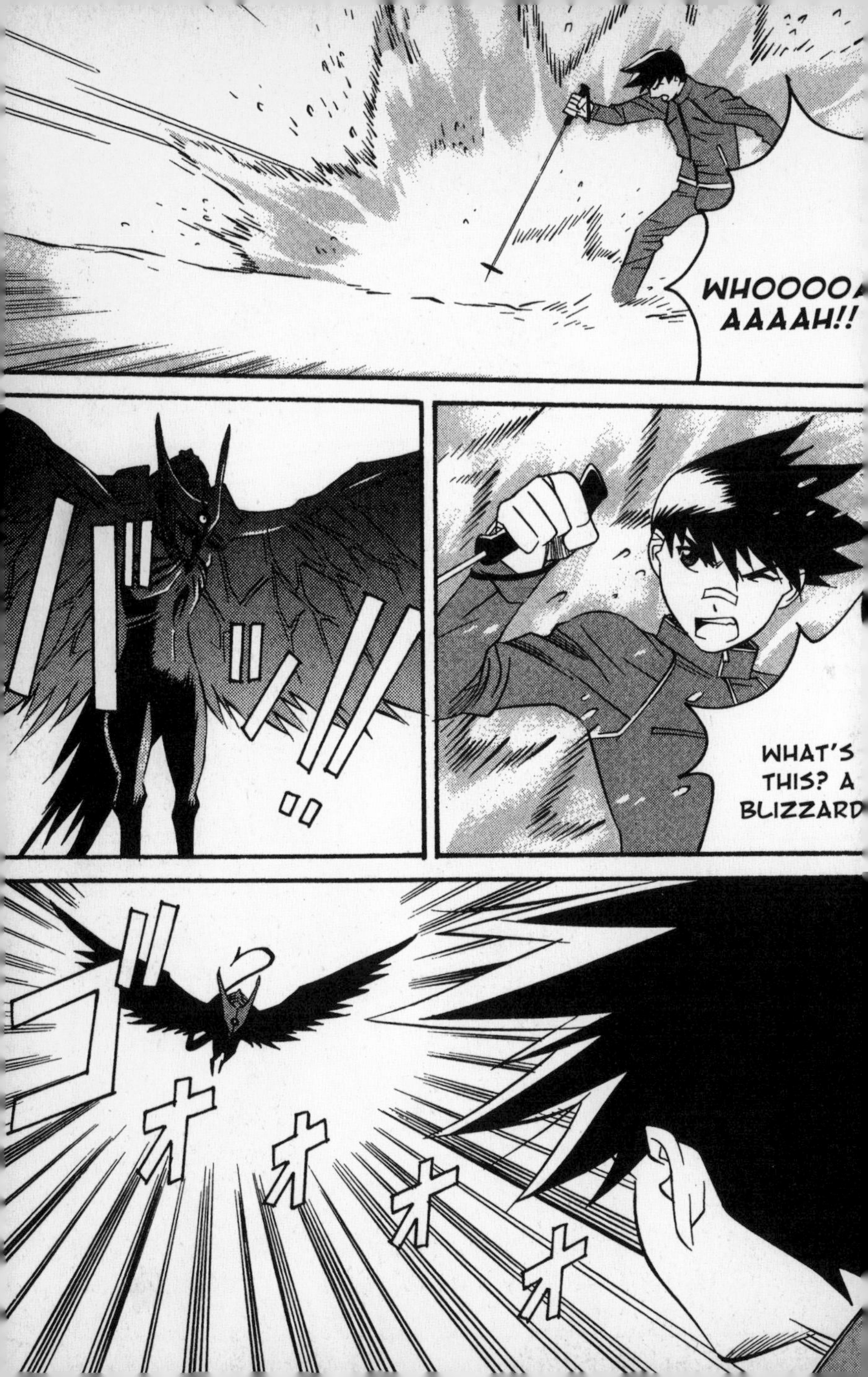
WHOOOOA AAAAH!!
WHAT'S THIS? A BLIZZARD
ゴオオオオ

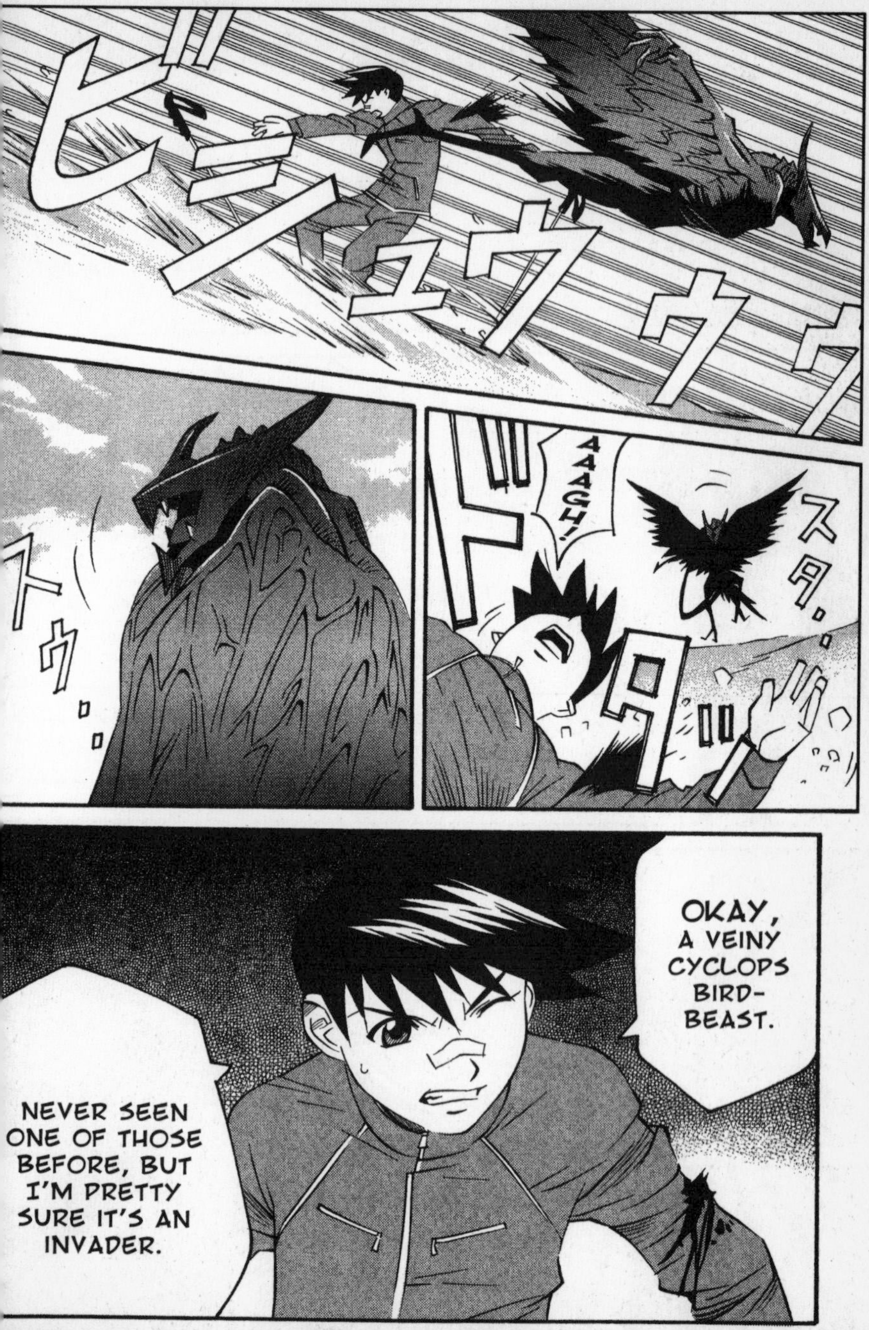
ビジュウウウ
AAAGH!
ドサ
スタッ
スタッ
トゥ
OKAY, A VEINY CYCLOPS BIRD-BEAST.
NEVER SEEN ONE OF THOSE BEFORE, BUT I'M PRETTY SURE IT'S AN INVADER.

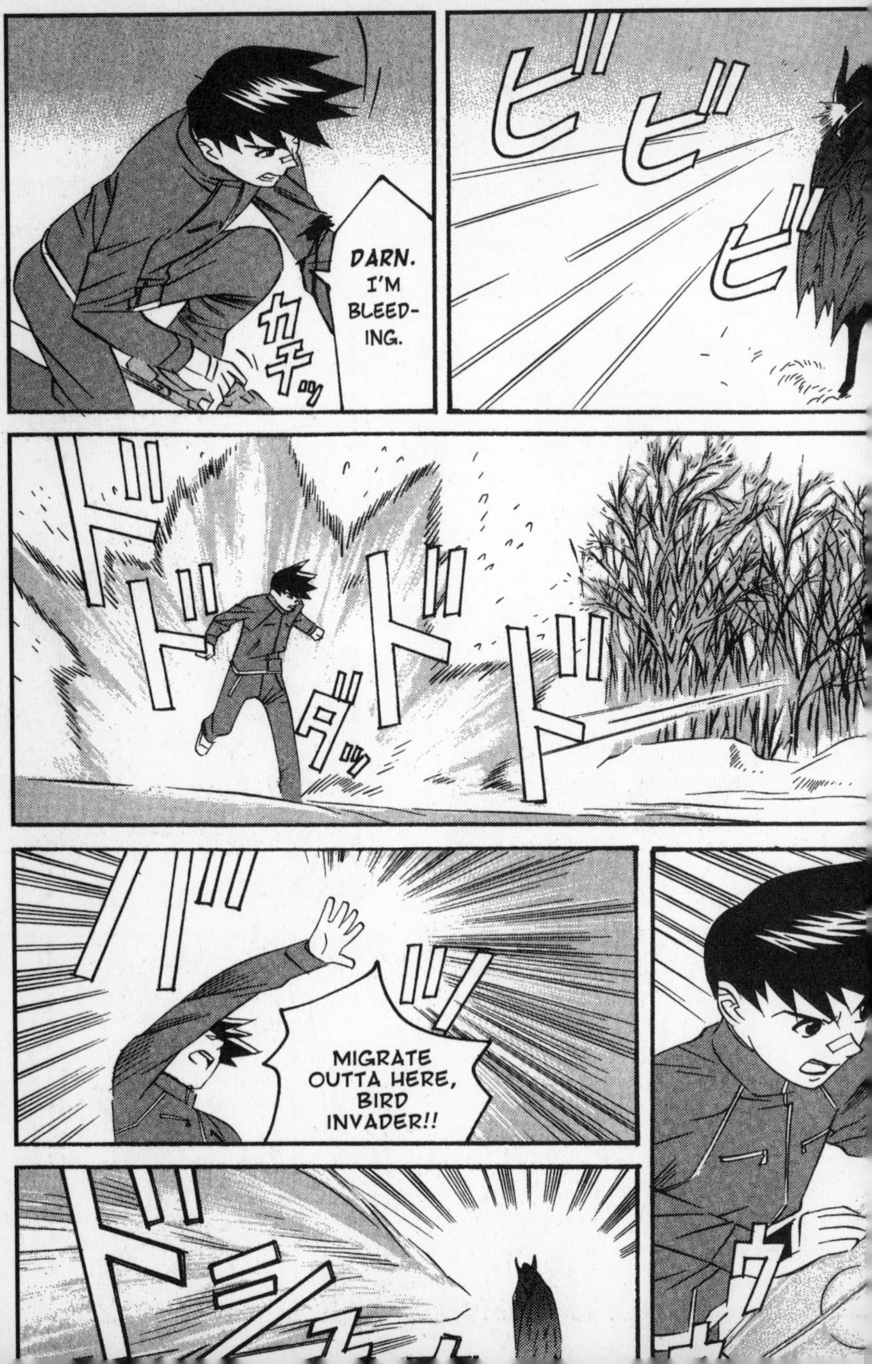
DARN. I'M BLEED-ING.
MIGRATE OUTTA HERE, BIRD INVADER!!

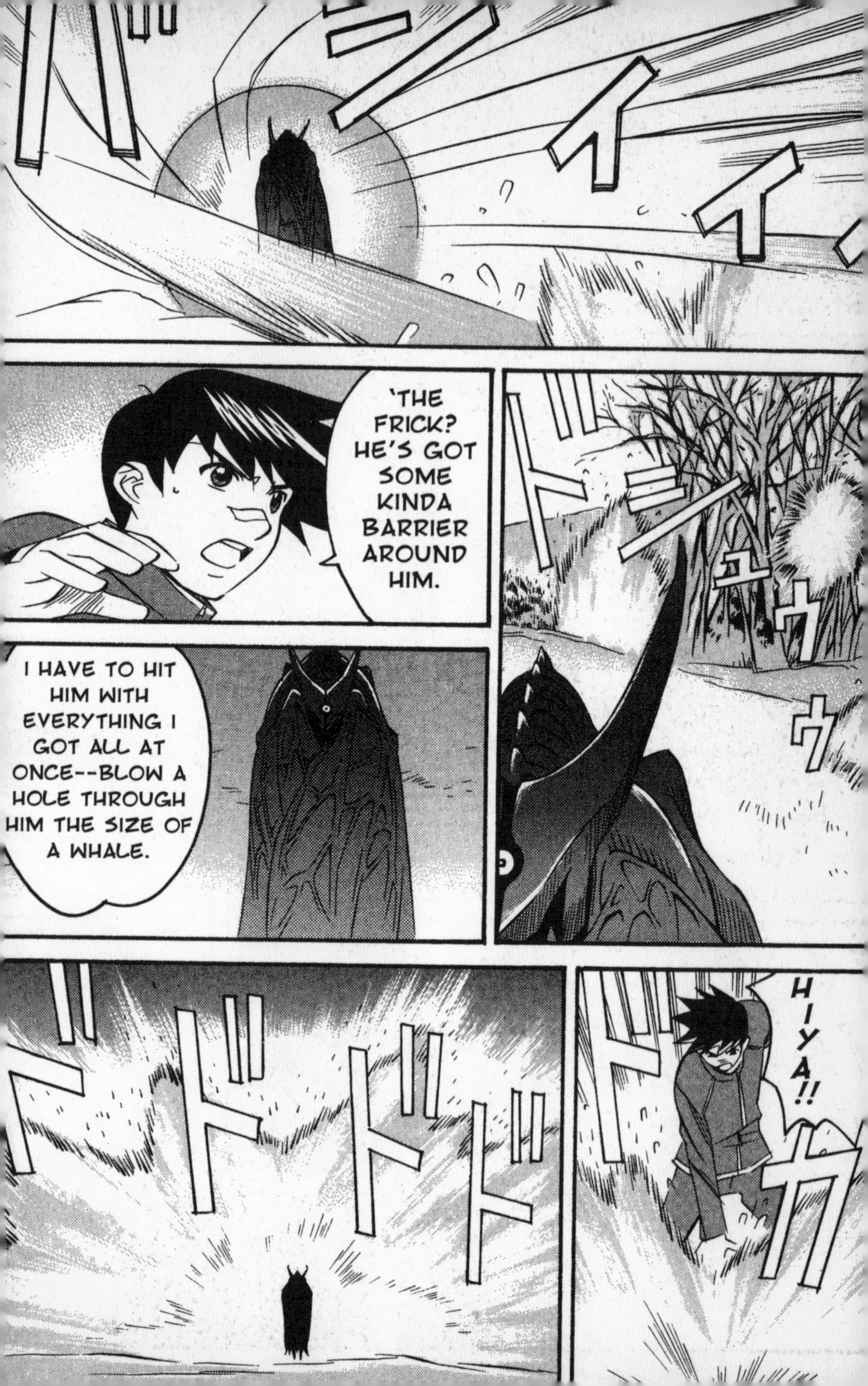

バシイイ
ドシュウウ
'THE FRICK? HE'S GOT SOME KINDA BARRIER AROUND HIM.
I HAVE TO HIT HIM WITH EVERYTHING I GOT ALL AT ONCE--BLOW A HOLE THROUGH HIM THE SIZE OF A WHALE.
HIYA!!

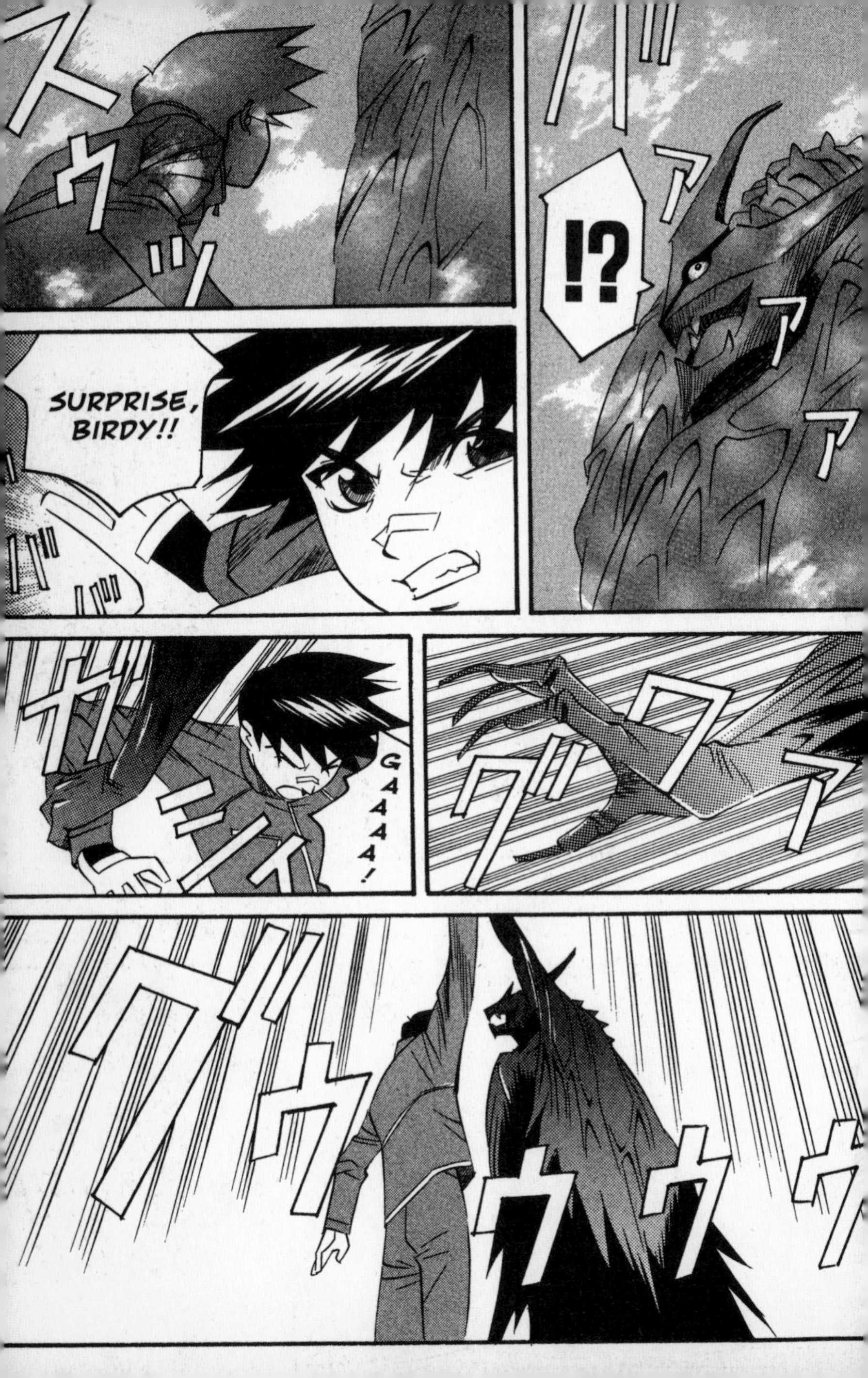
!?
SURPRISE, BIRDY!!
GAAAAA!

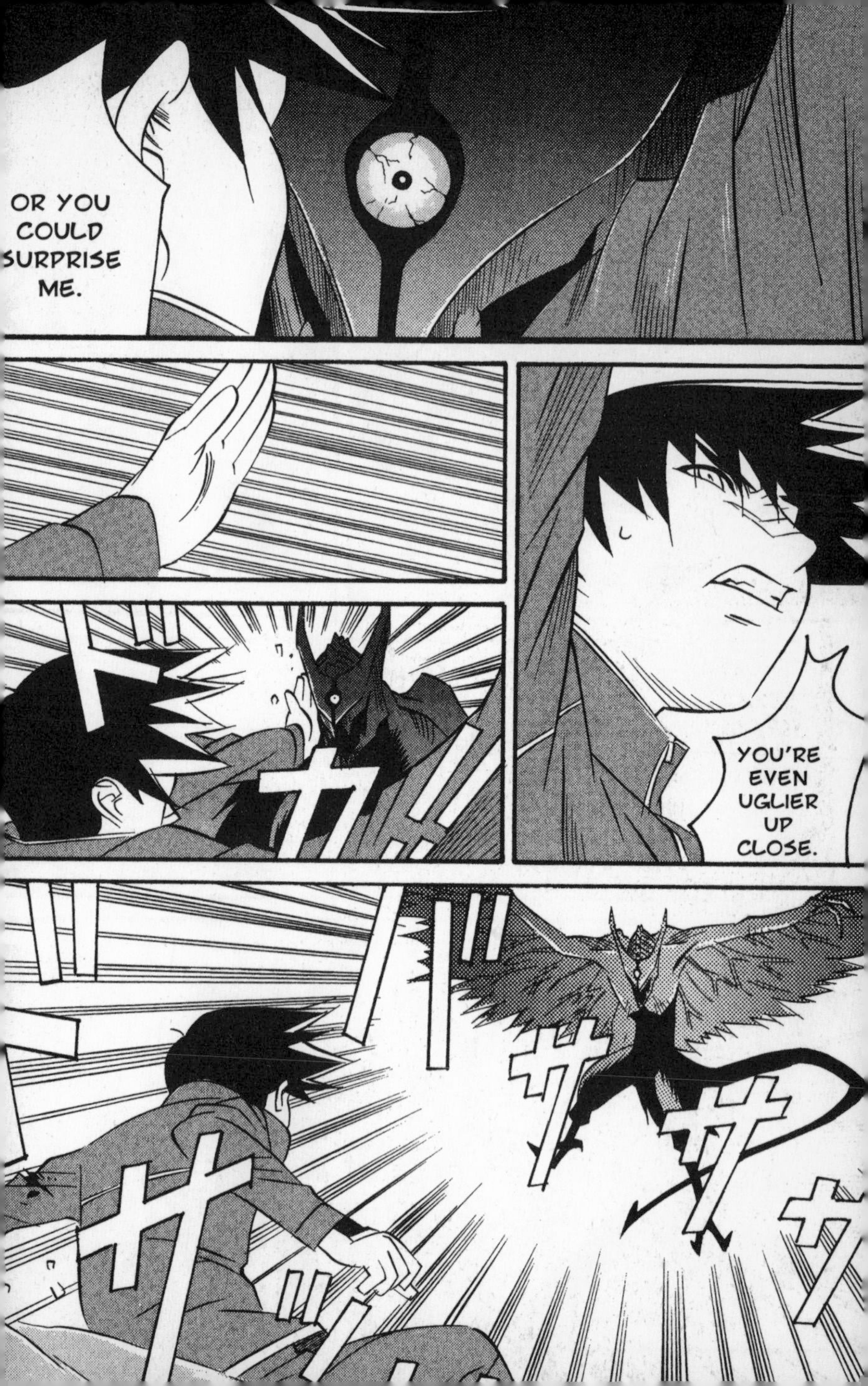
OR YOU COULD SURPRISE ME.
YOU'RE EVEN UGLIER UP CLOSE.

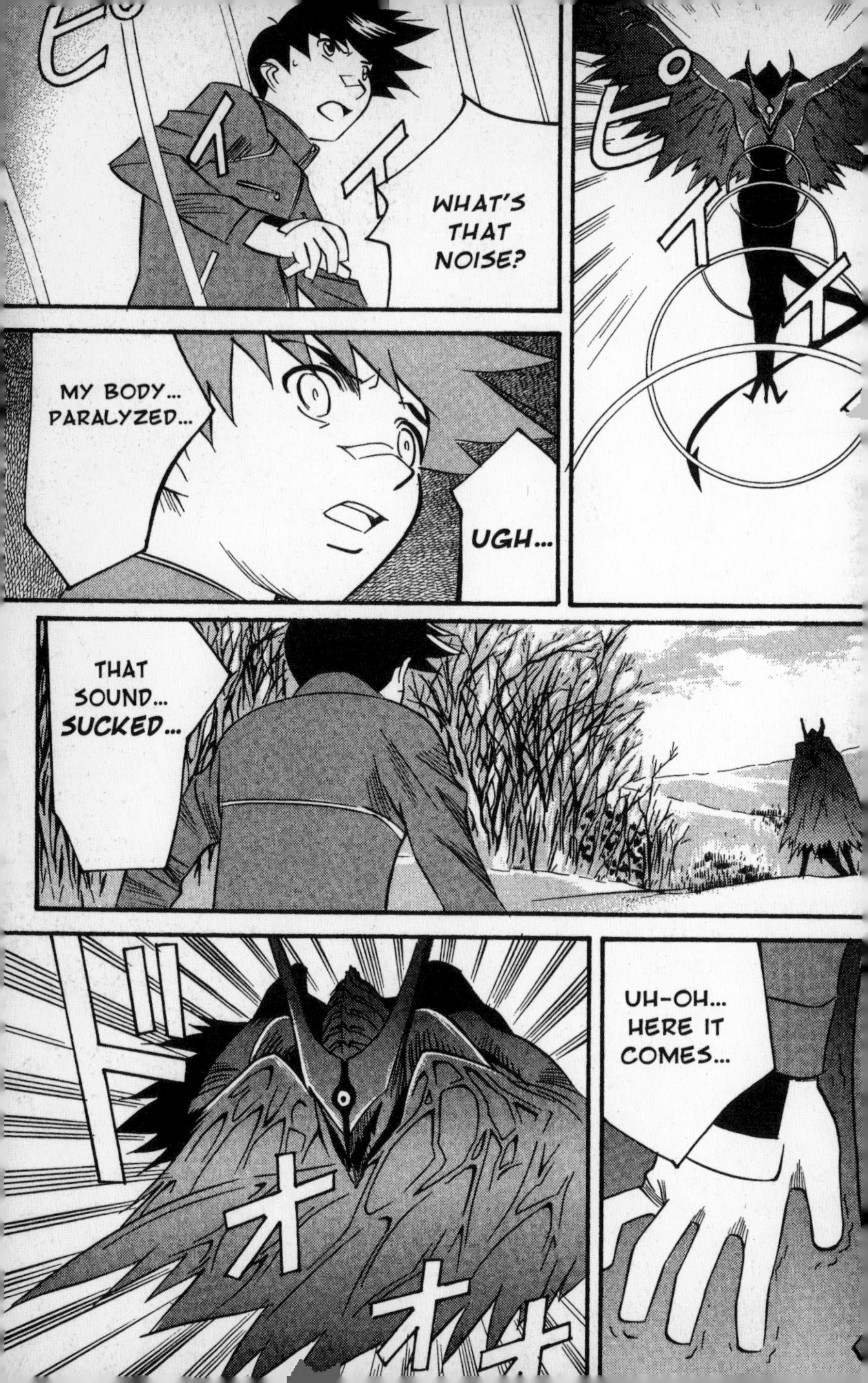
WHAT'S THAT NOISE?
MY BODY... PARALYZED...
UGH...
THAT SOUND... SUCKED...
UH-OH... HERE IT COMES...

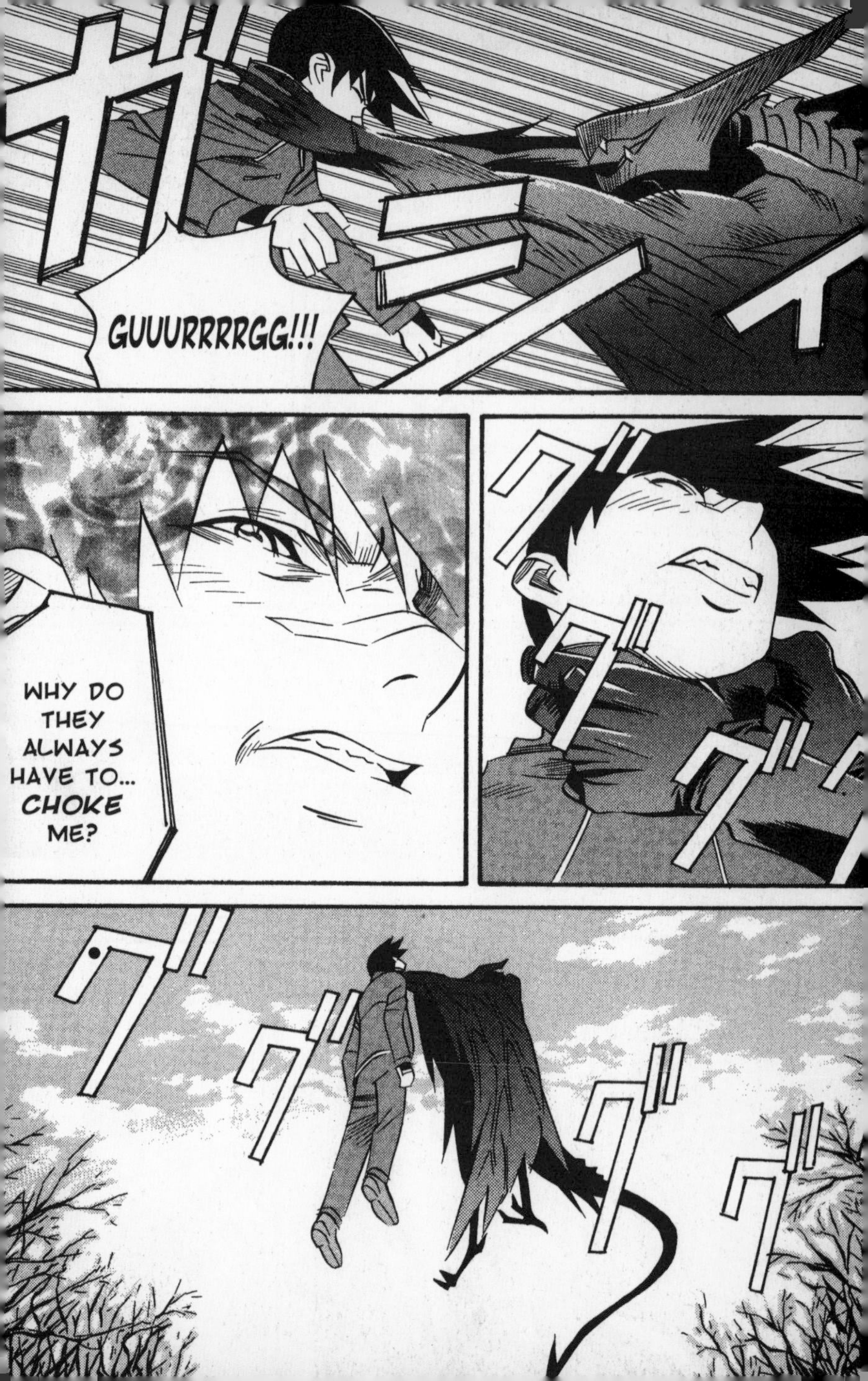
GUUURRRRGG!!!
WHY DO THEY ALWAYS HAVE TO... CHOKE ME?

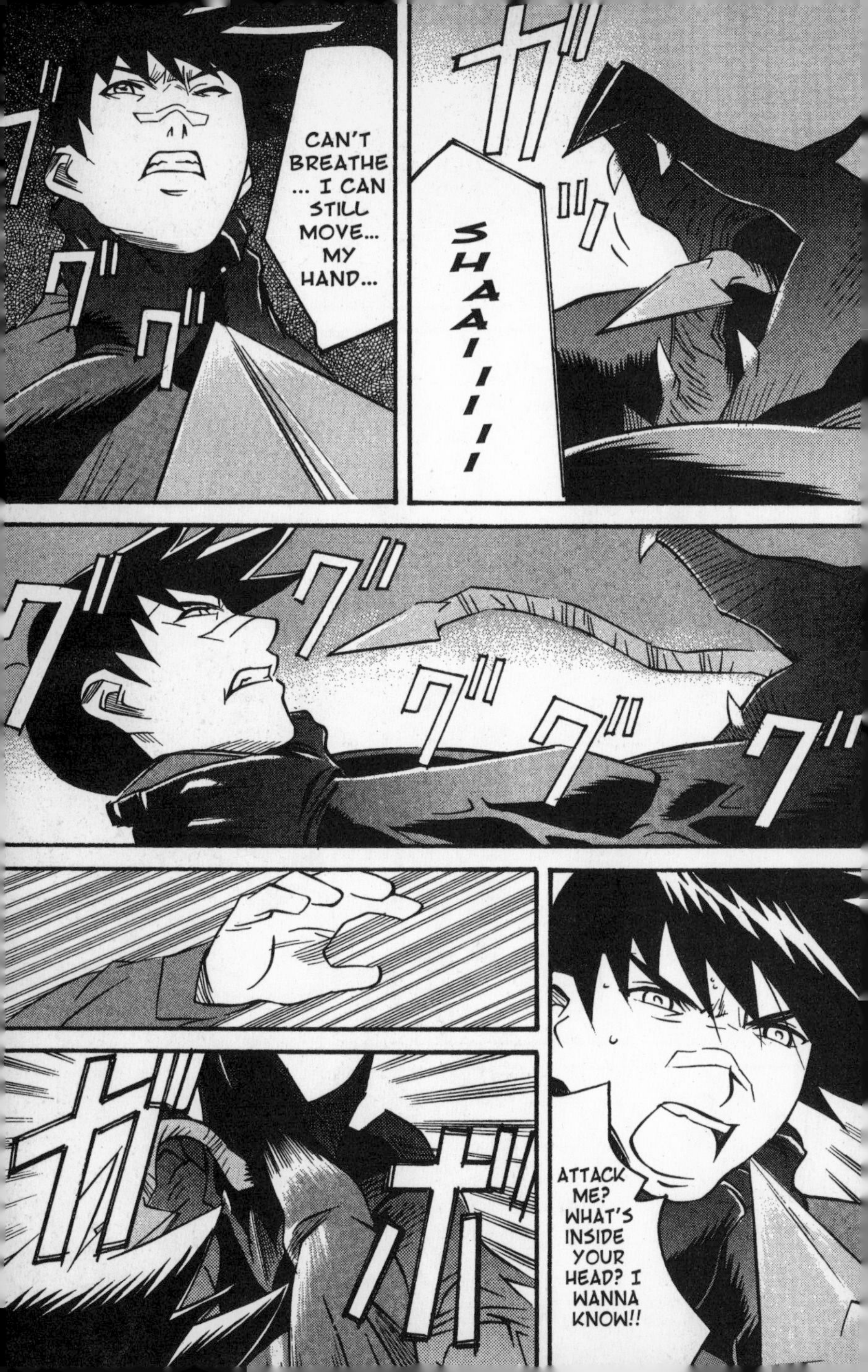
SHAAIIIII
CAN'T BREATHE ... I CAN STILL MOVE... MY HAND...
ATTACK ME? WHAT'S INSIDE YOUR HEAD? I WANNA KNOW!!

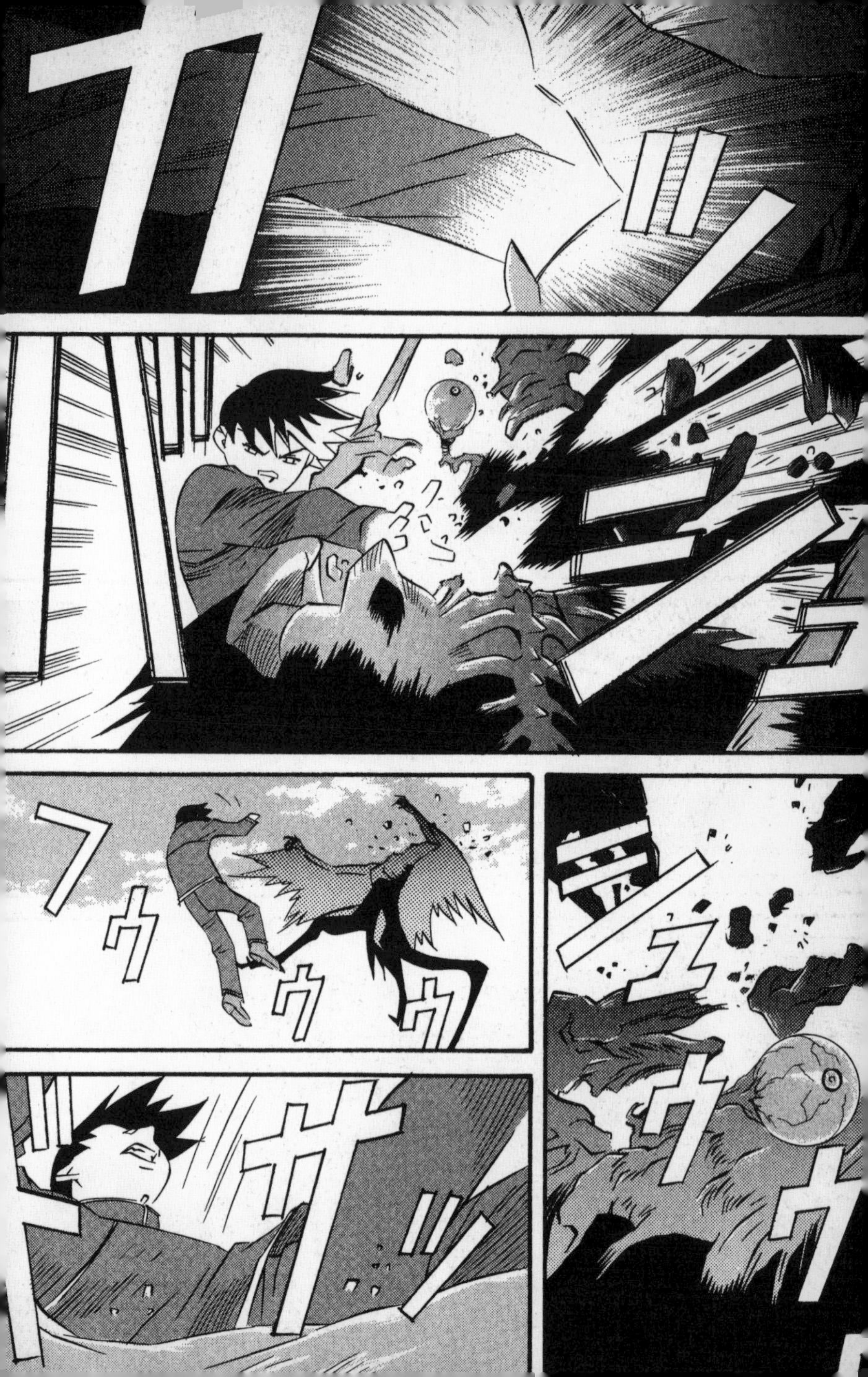

フゥゥゥ
ザッ

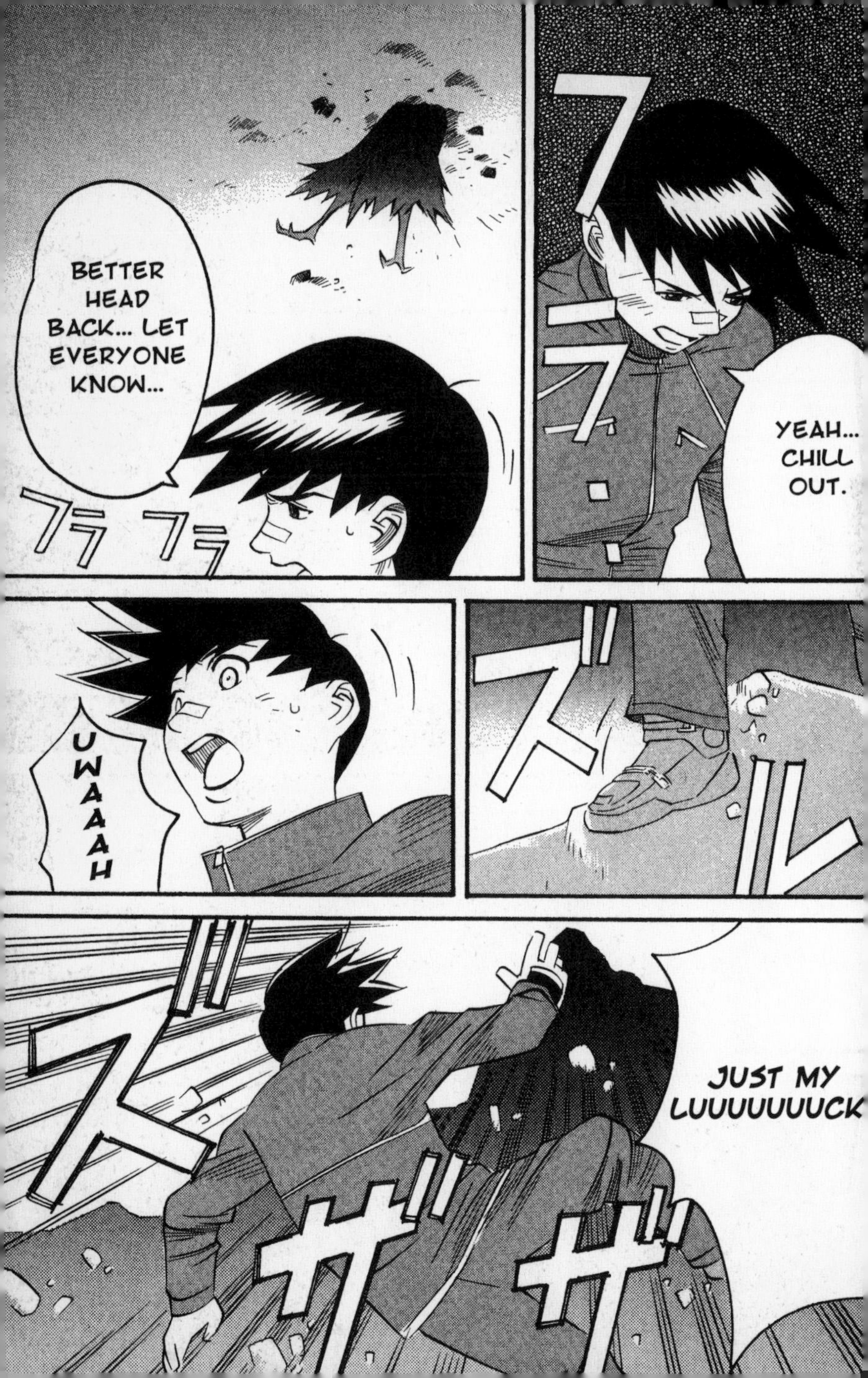
YEAH... CHILL OUT.
BETTER HEAD BACK... LET EVERYONE KNOW...
フラ フラ
UWAAAAH
JUST MY LUUUUUUUCK

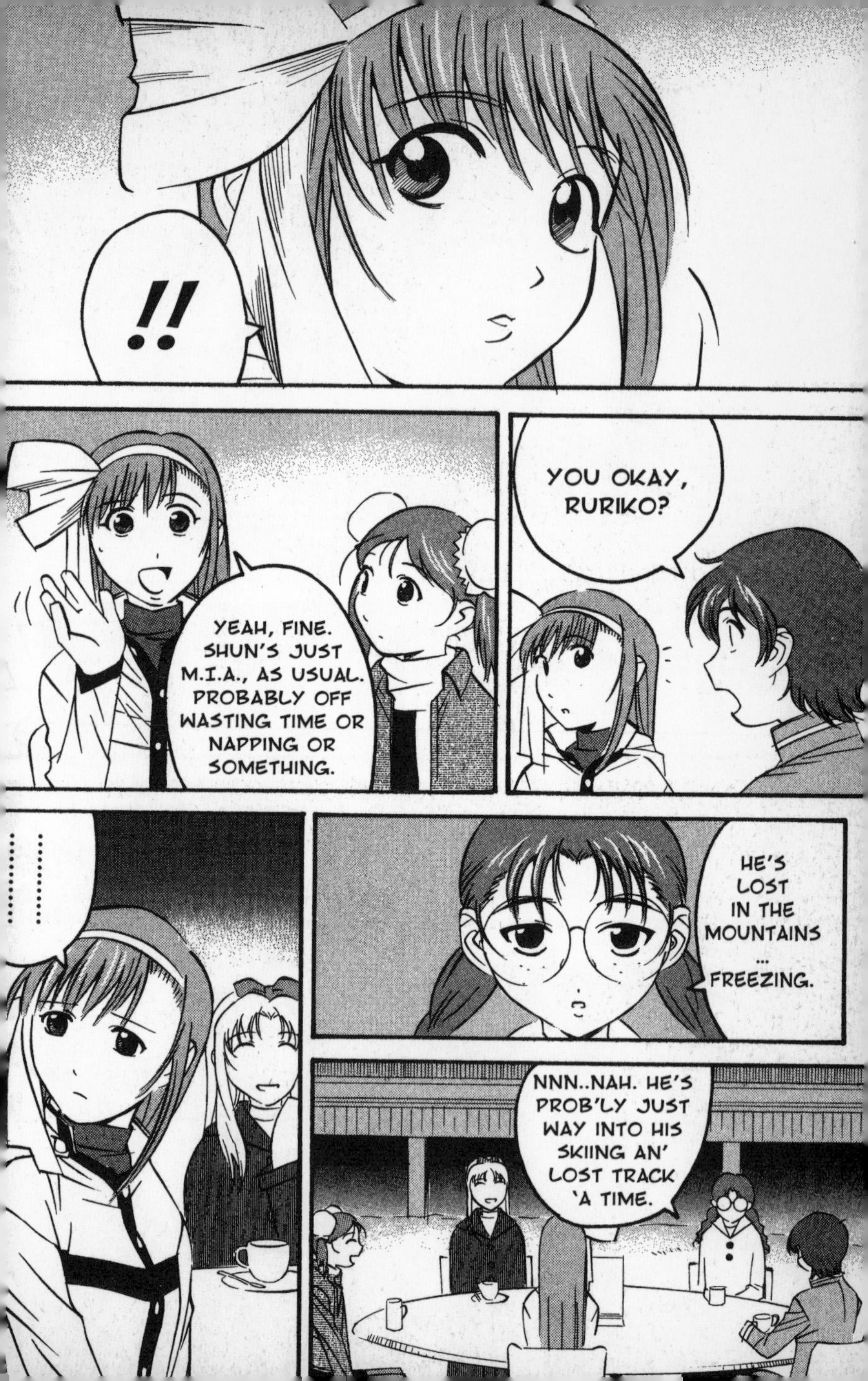
!!
YOU OKAY, RURIKO?
YEAH, FINE. SHUN'S JUST M.I.A., AS USUAL. PROBABLY OFF WASTING TIME OR NAPPING OR SOMETHING.
HE'S LOST IN THE MOUNTAINS ... FREEZING.
NNN..NAH. HE'S PROB'LY JUST WAY INTO HIS SKIING AN' LOST TRACK 'A TIME.
......

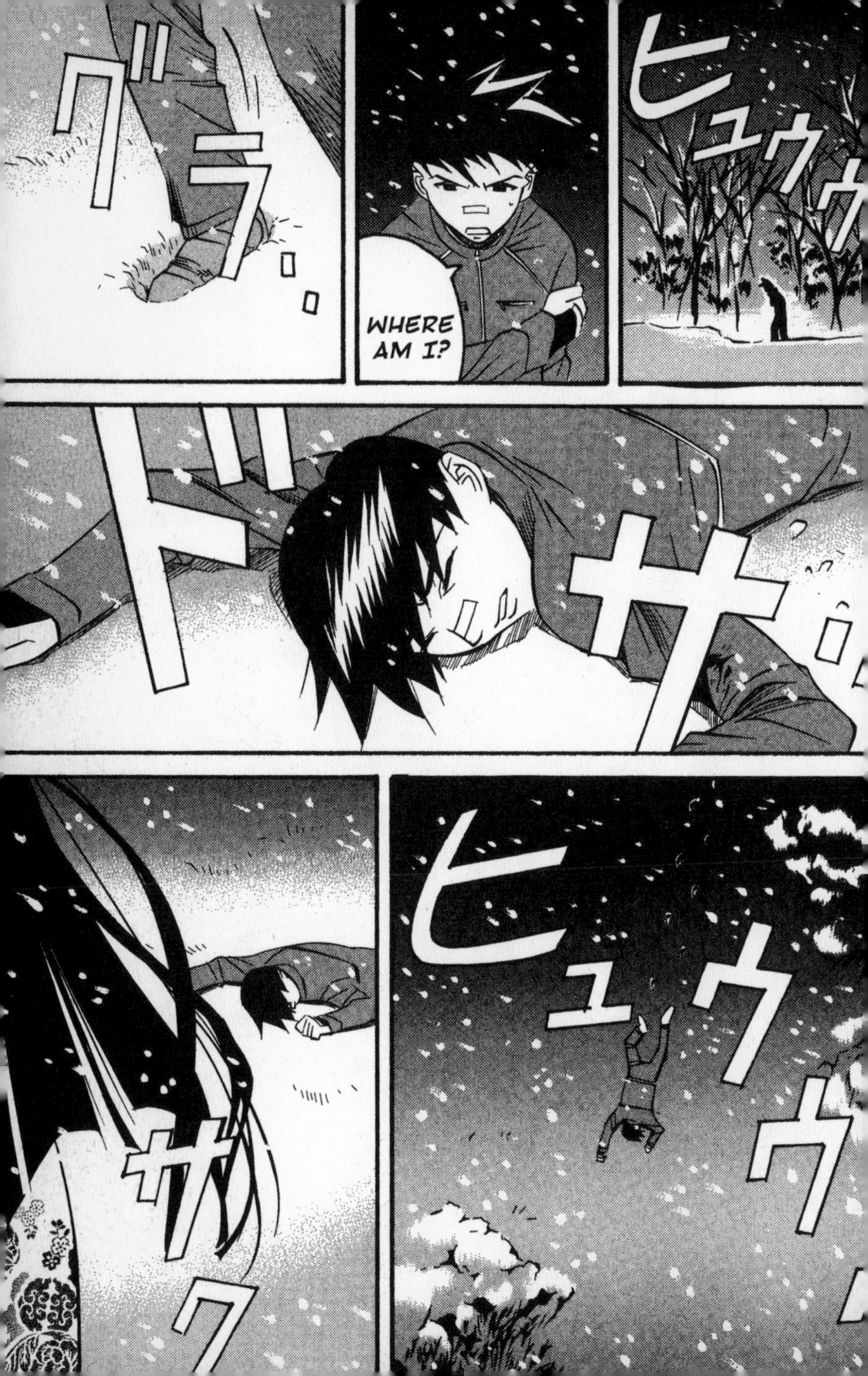
ヒュウウ
WHERE AM I?
グラ
ドサッ
ヒュウウ
ザク

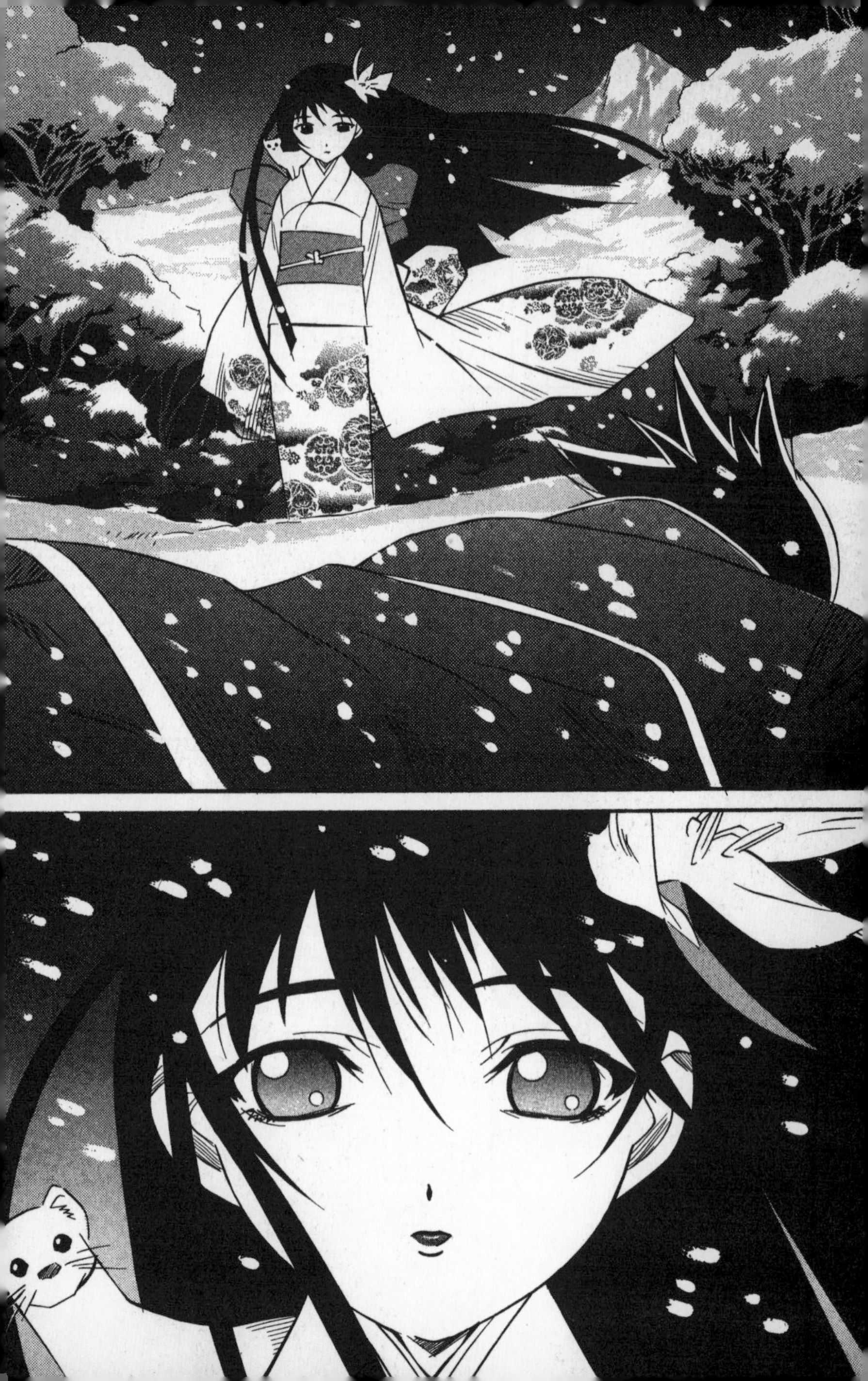

GATE #10 SNOW WHITE 2

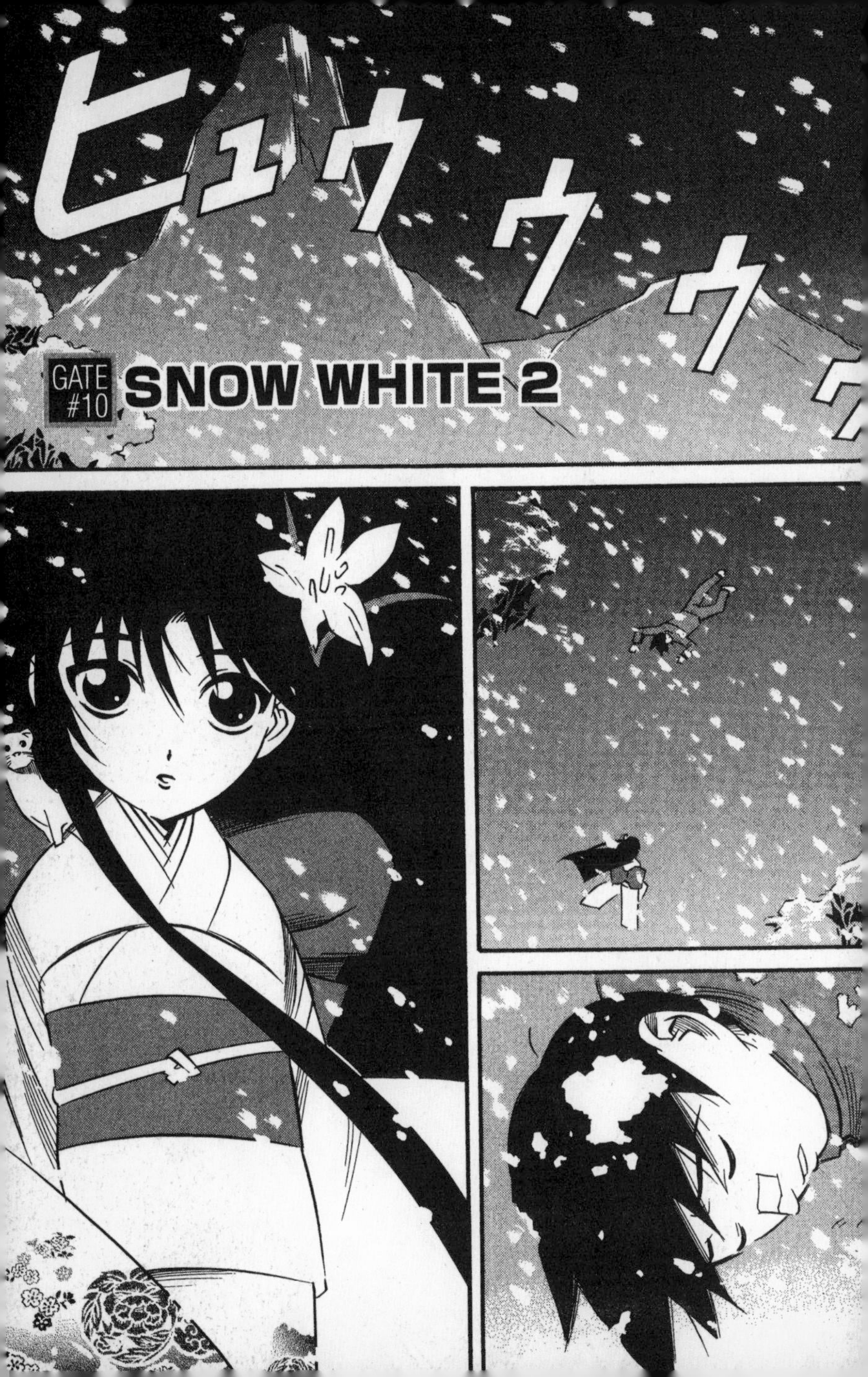
ヒュウウウウ

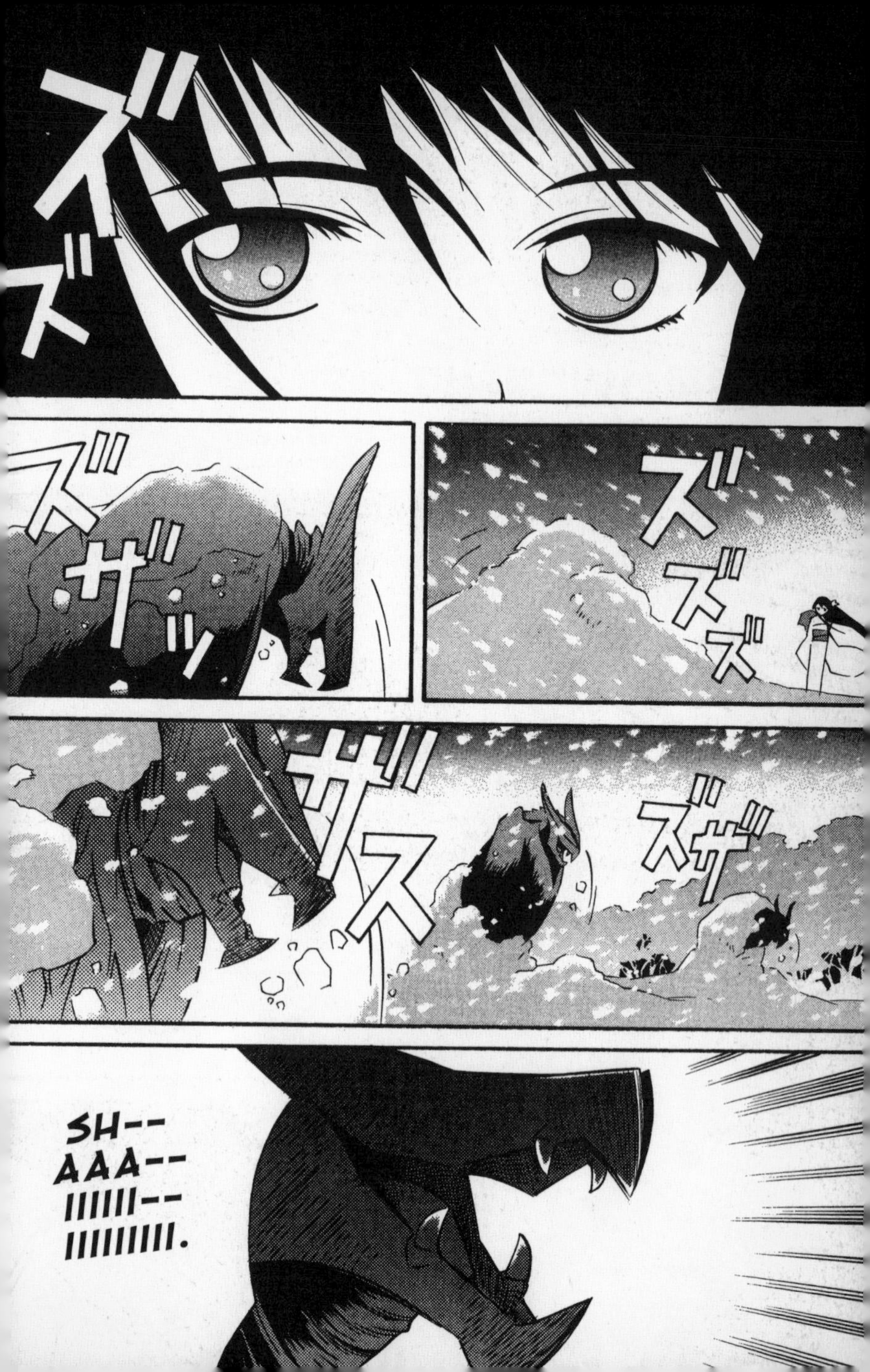
ズズ
ズズズ
ズザッ
ズザ
ザス
SH--
AAA--
IIIIII--
IIIIIIIII.

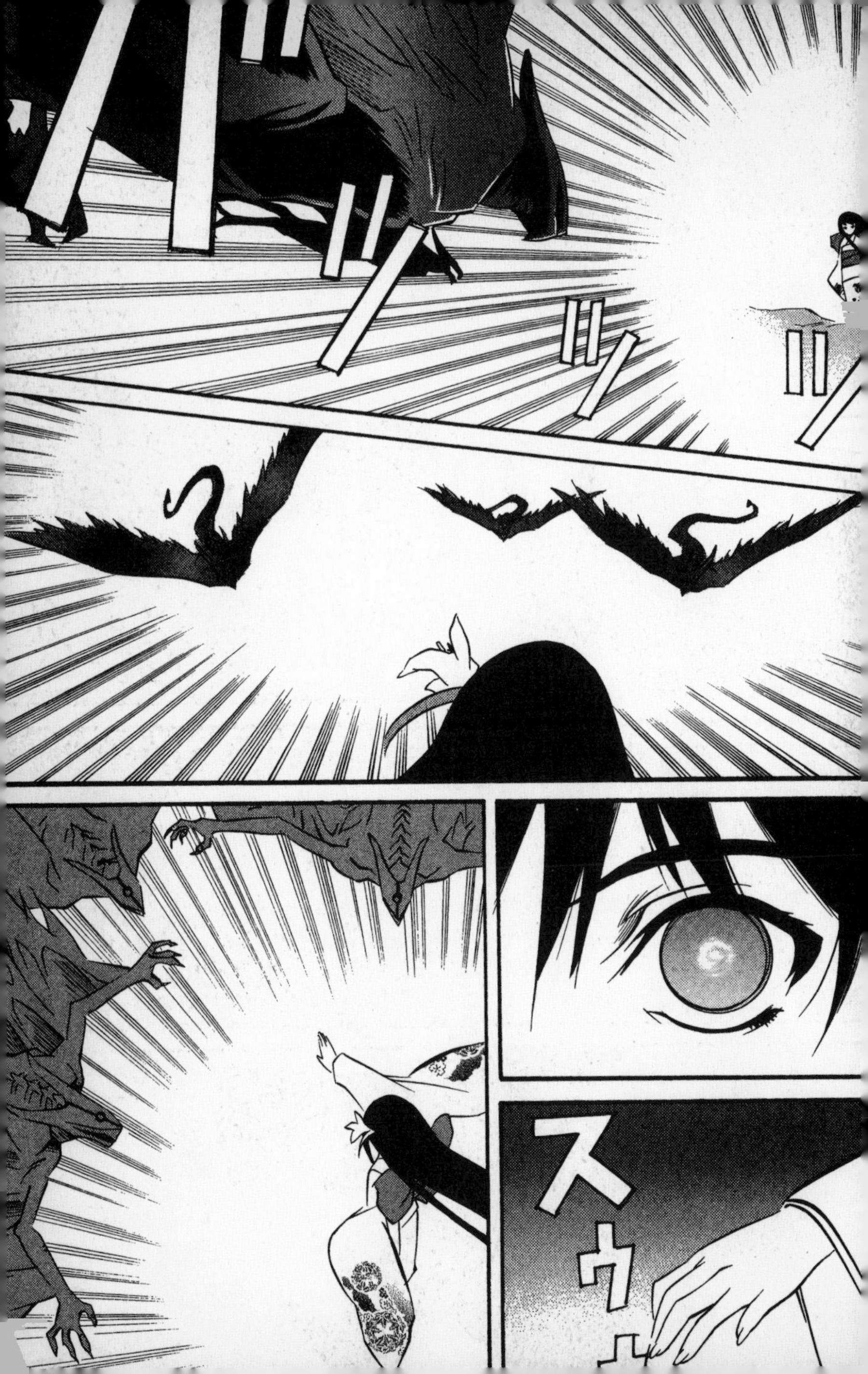
スウ

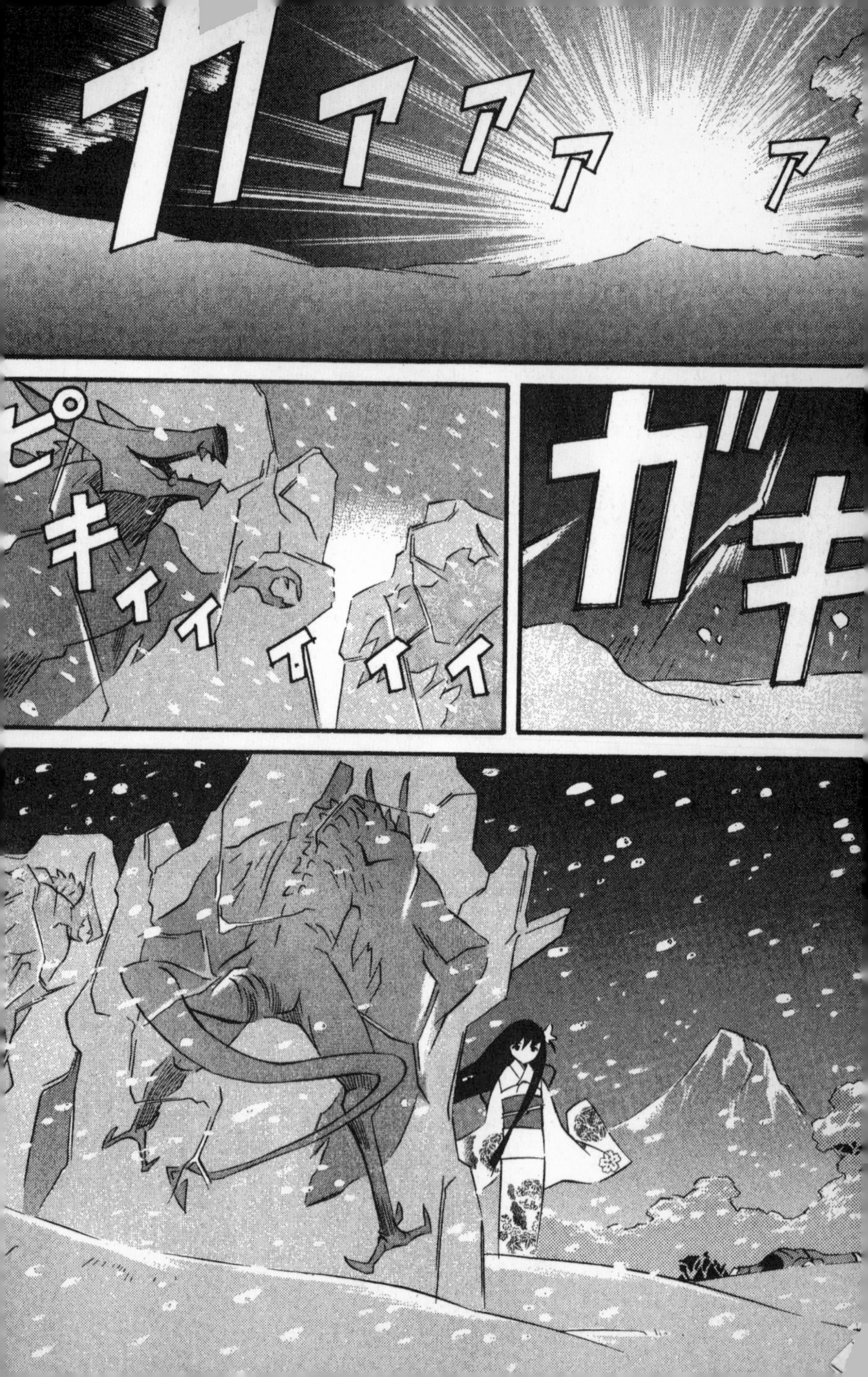
カアアアア
ガキ
ピキイイイイイ

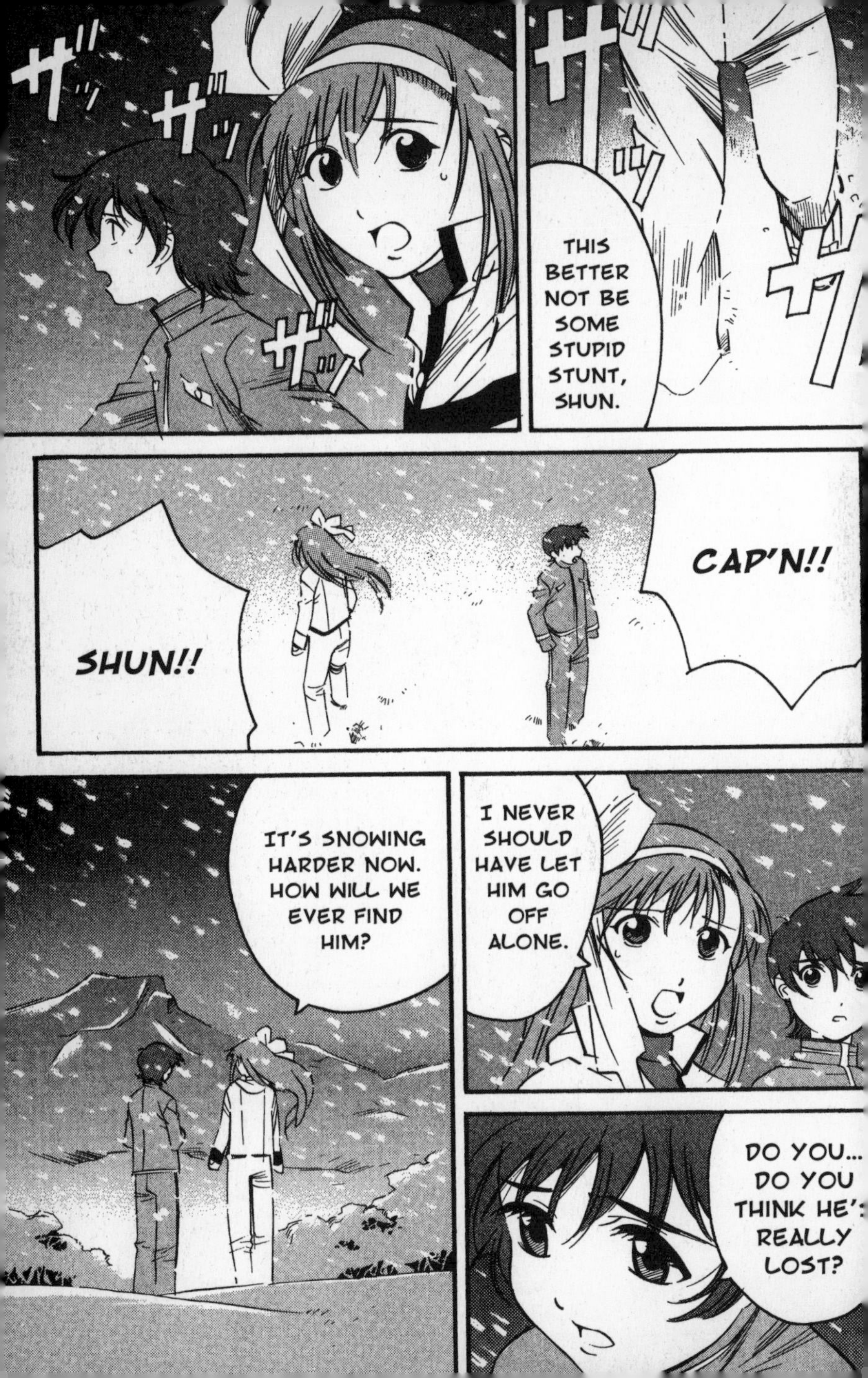
THIS BETTER NOT BE SOME STUPID STUNT, SHUN.
CAP'N!!
SHUN!!
I NEVER SHOULD HAVE LET HIM GO OFF ALONE.
DO YOU... DO YOU THINK HE'S REALLY LOST?
IT'S SNOWING HARDER NOW. HOW WILL WE EVER FIND HIM?

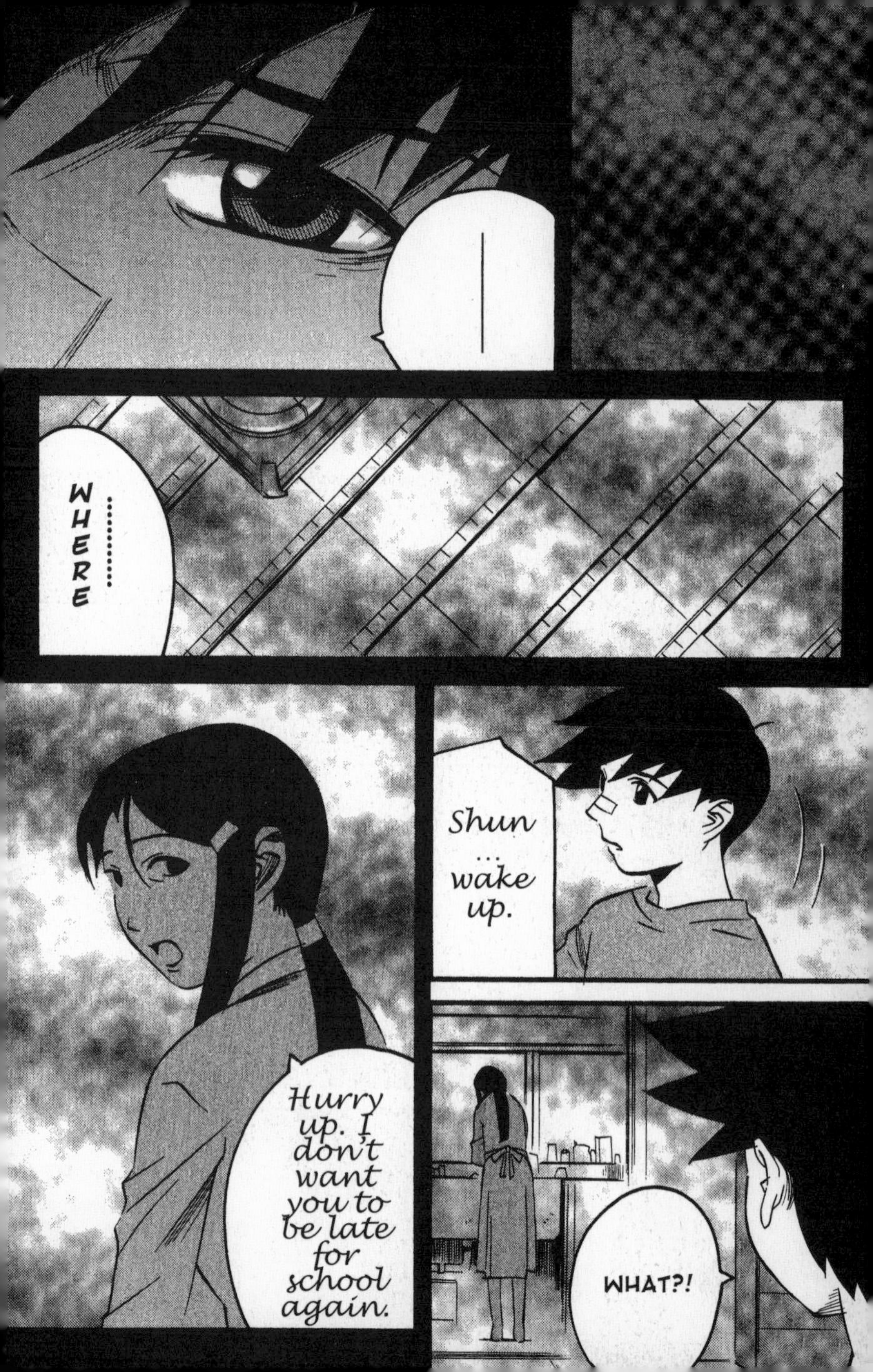
WHERE......
Shun ... wake up.
WHAT?!
Hurry up. I don't want you to be late for school again.

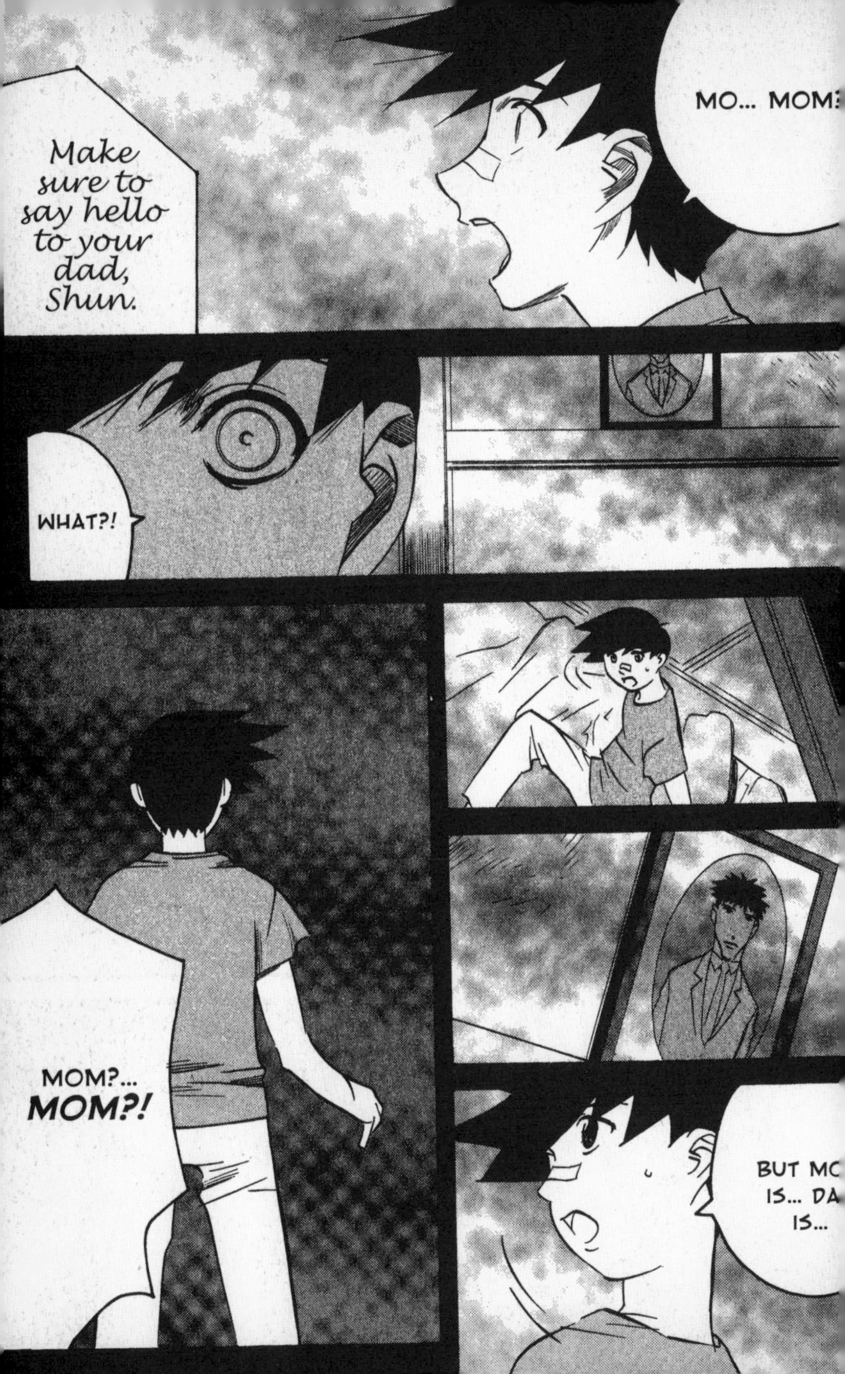
MO... MOM?
Make sure to say hello to your dad, Shun.
WHAT?!
BUT MO IS... DA IS...
MOM?... MOM?!

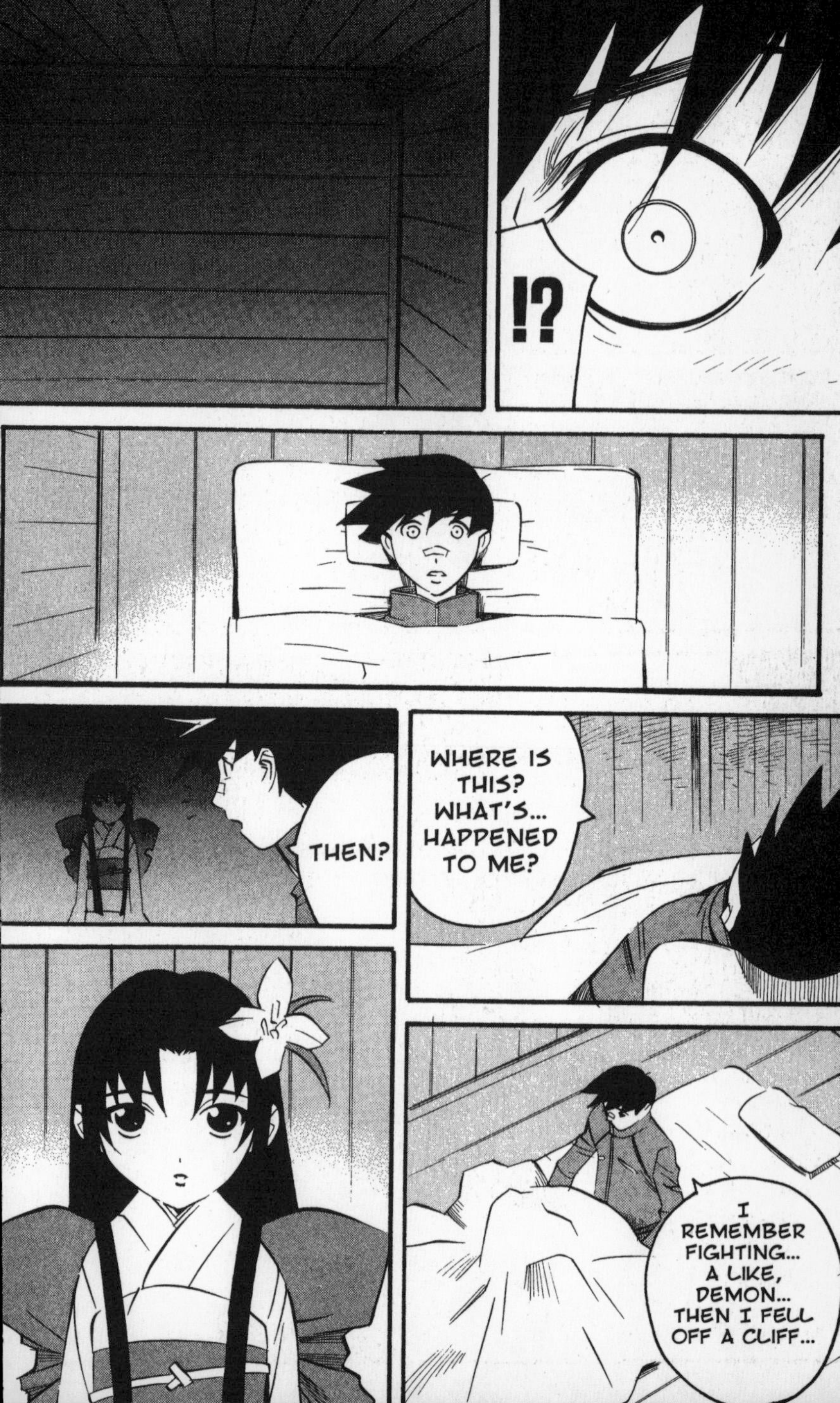
!?
WHERE IS THIS? WHAT'S... HAPPENED TO ME?
THEN?
I REMEMBER FIGHTING... A LIKE, DEMON... THEN I FELL OFF A CLIFF...

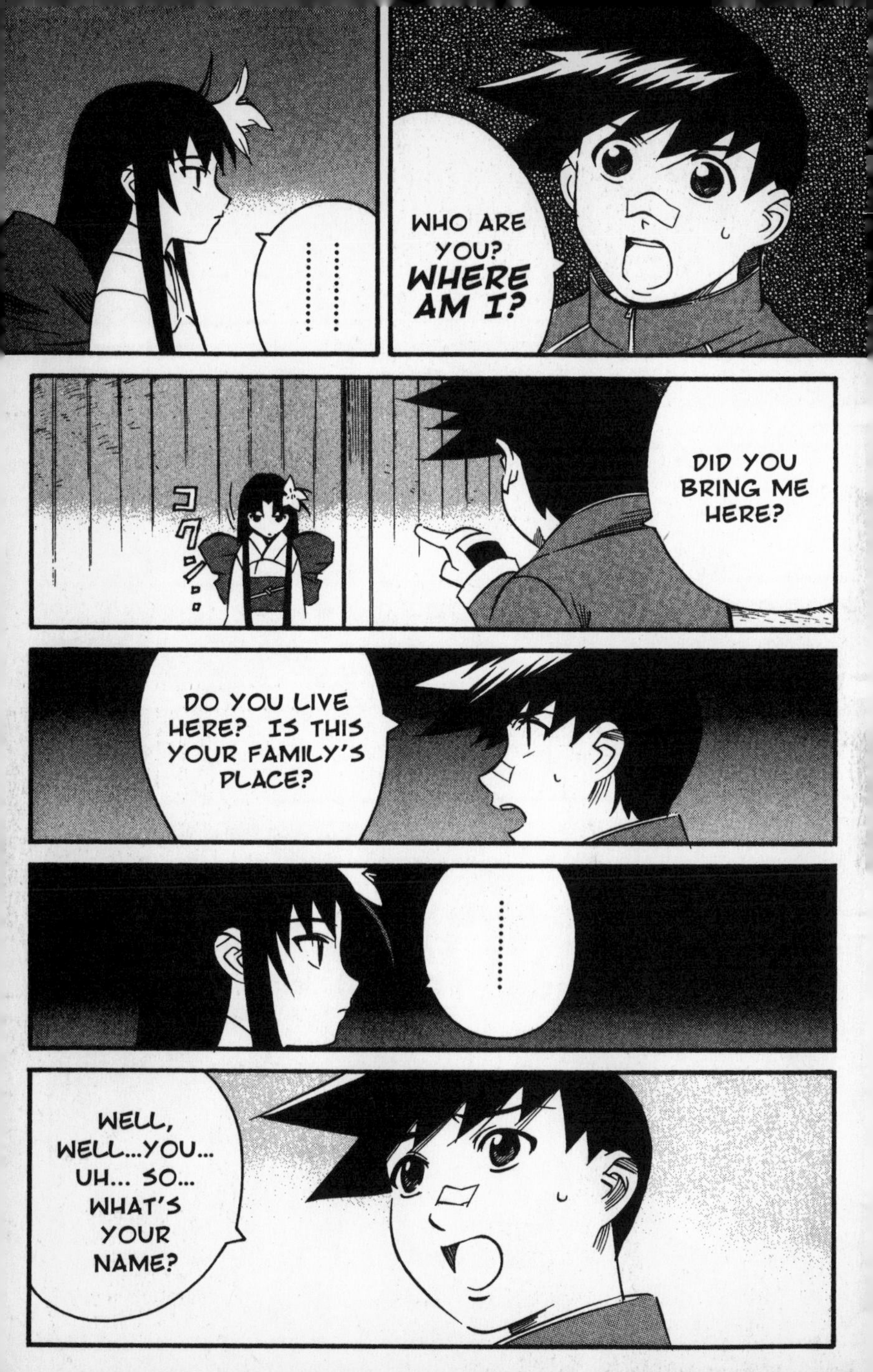
WHO ARE YOU? WHERE AM I?
......
DID YOU BRING ME HERE?
コクン。。
DO YOU LIVE HERE? IS THIS YOUR FAMILY'S PLACE?
......
WELL, WELL...YOU... UH... SO... WHAT'S YOUR NAME?

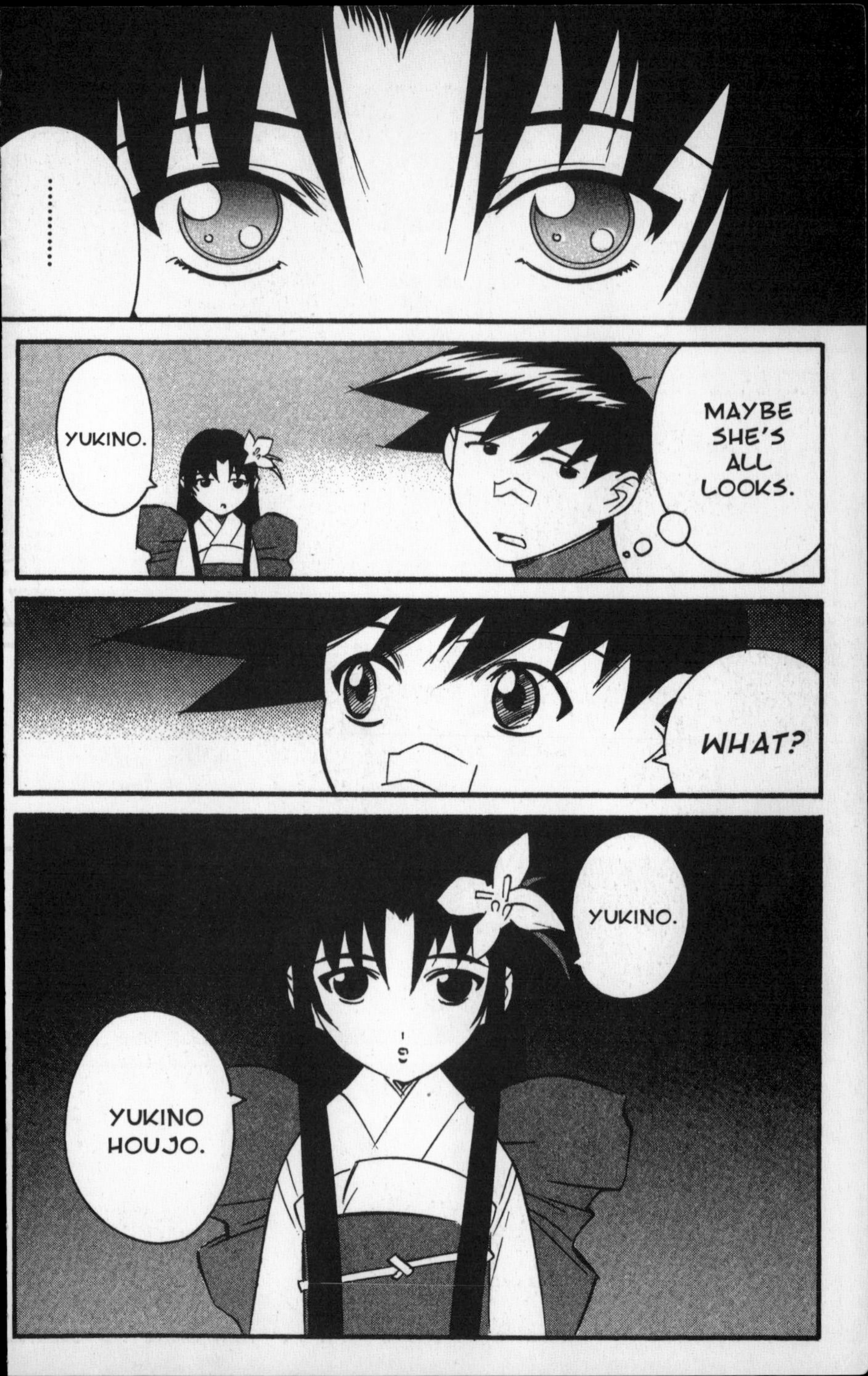
....
MAYBE SHE'S ALL LOOKS.
YUKINO.
WHAT?
YUKINO.
YUKINO HOUJO.

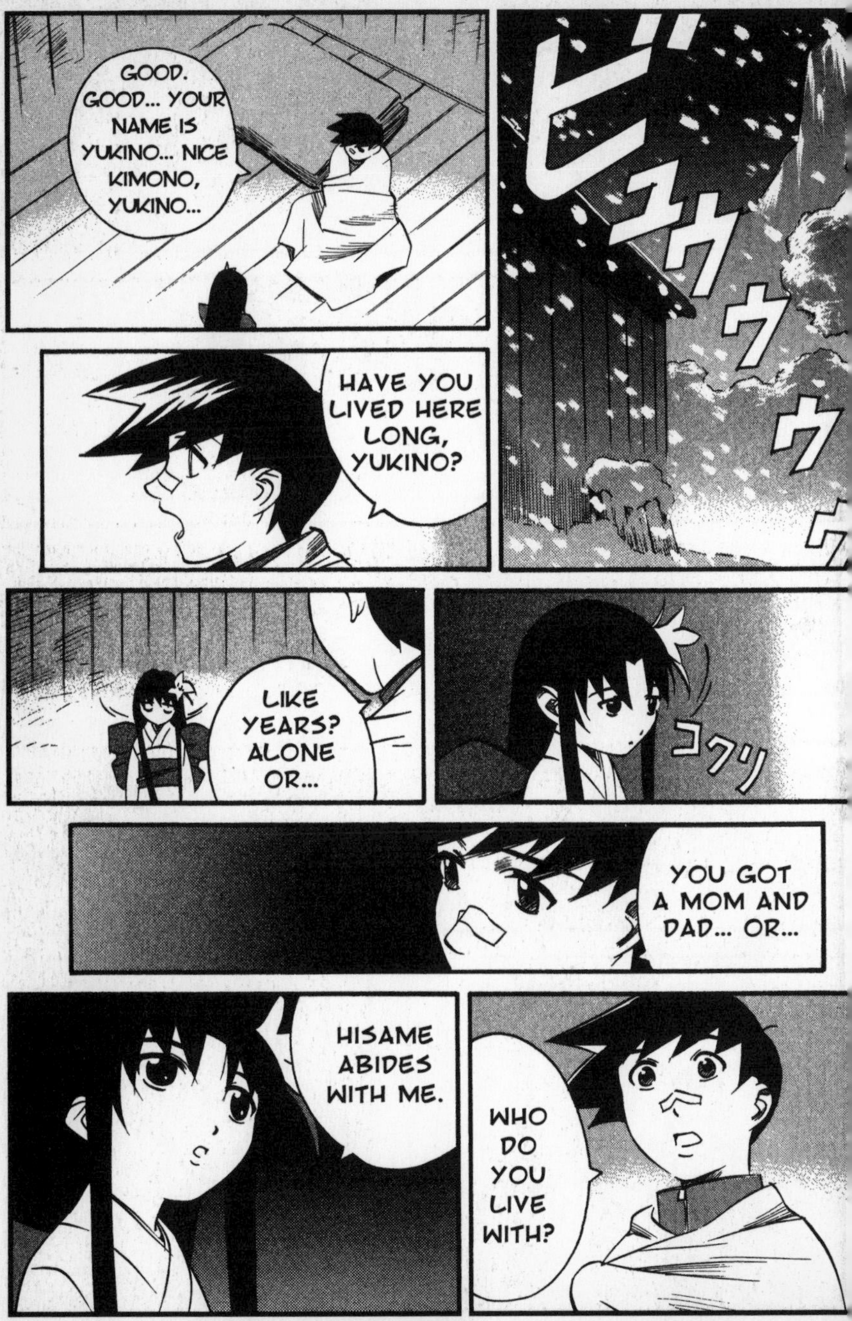
ビュウウウウ
GOOD. GOOD... YOUR NAME IS YUKINO... NICE KIMONO, YUKINO...
HAVE YOU LIVED HERE LONG, YUKINO?
コクリ
LIKE YEARS? ALONE OR...
YOU GOT A MOM AND DAD... OR...
WHO DO YOU LIVE WITH?
HISAME ABIDES WITH ME.

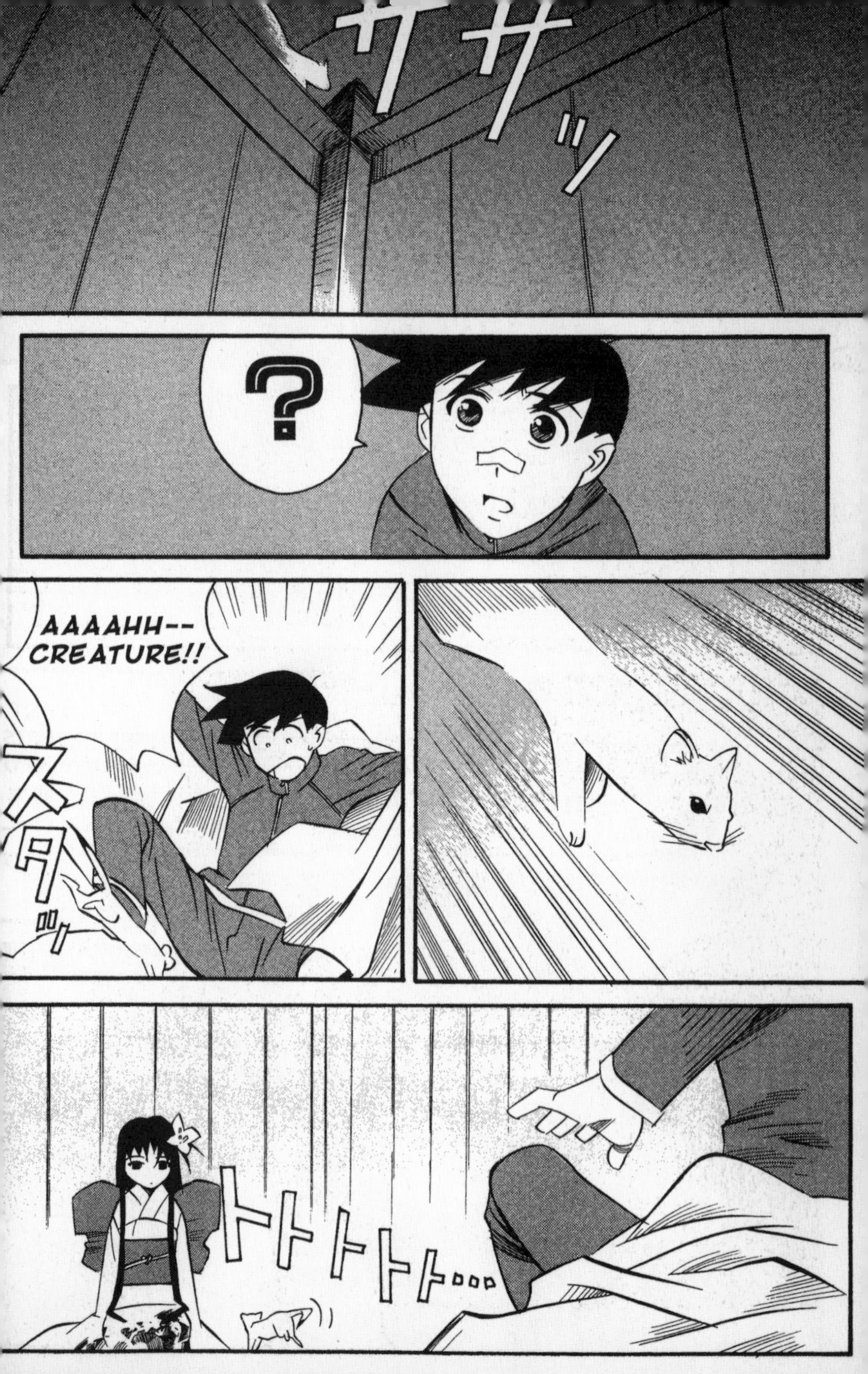
サザッ
?
AAAAHH-- CREATURE!!
スタッ
トトトトト…

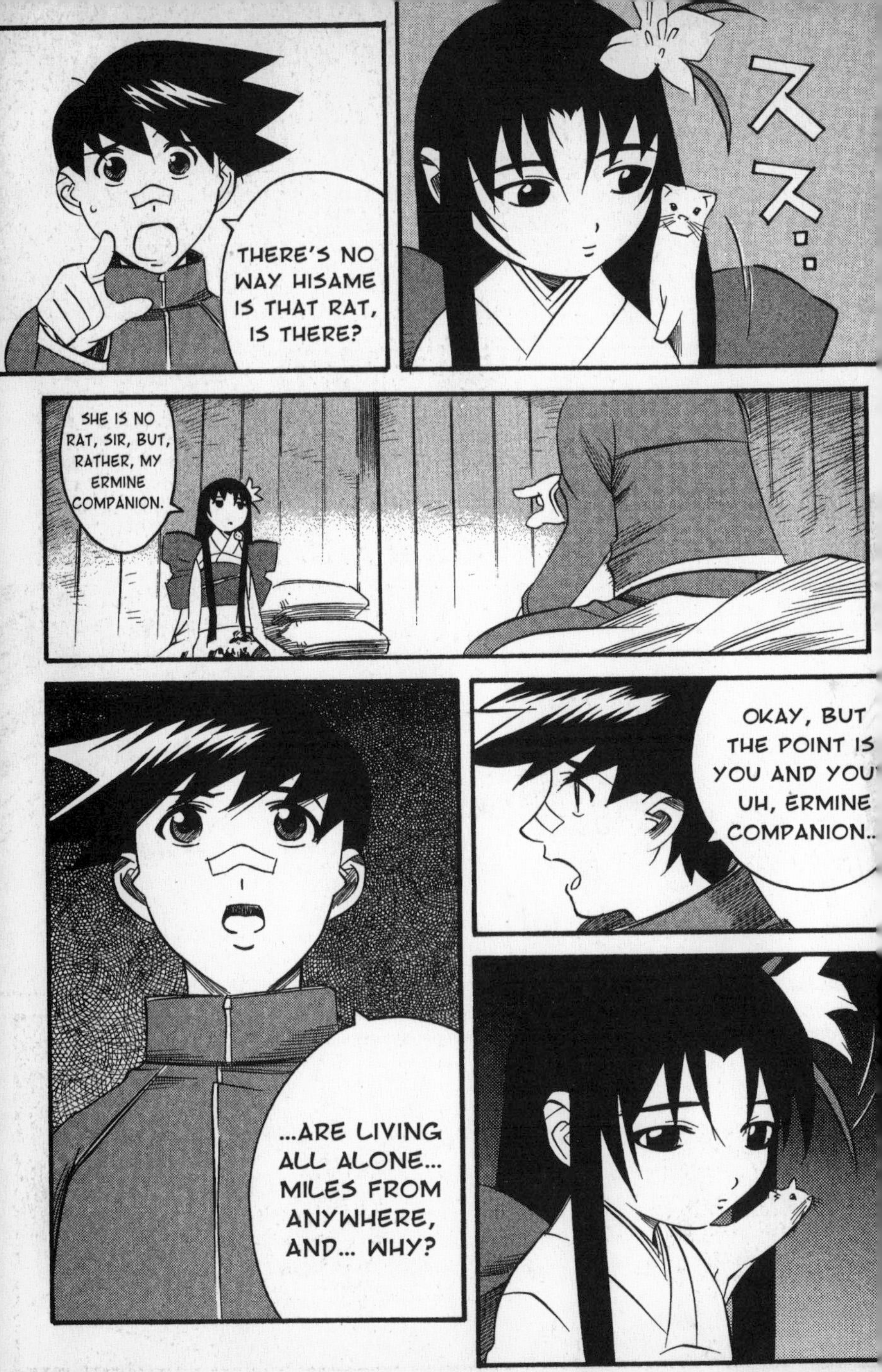
スス..
THERE'S NO WAY HISAME IS THAT RAT, IS THERE?
SHE IS NO RAT, SIR, BUT, RATHER, MY ERMINE COMPANION.
OKAY, BUT THE POINT IS YOU AND YOU UH, ERMINE COMPANION..
...ARE LIVING ALL ALONE... MILES FROM ANYWHERE, AND... WHY?

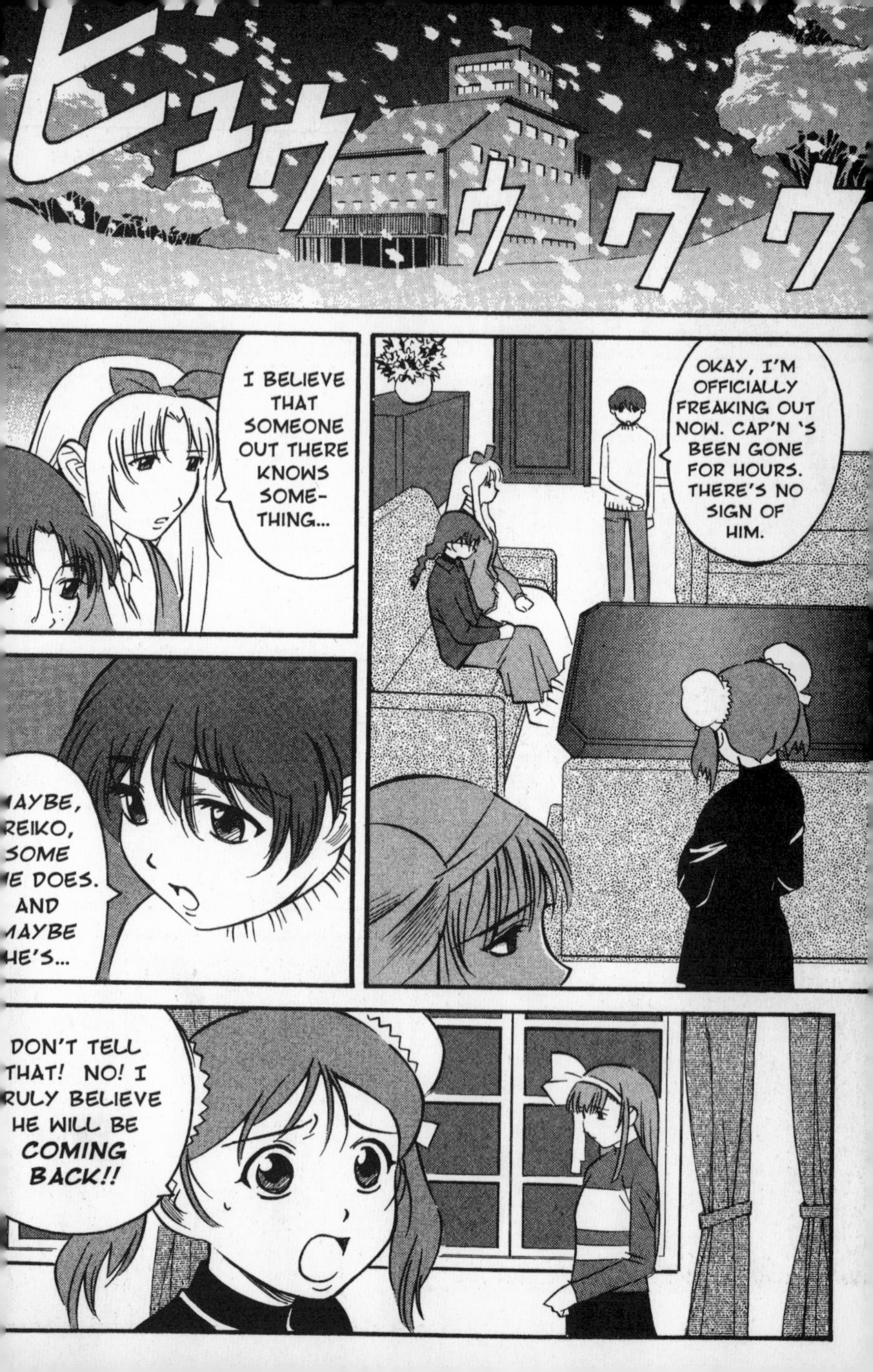
ヒュウウウウ
OKAY, I'M OFFICIALLY FREAKING OUT NOW. CAP'N 'S BEEN GONE FOR HOURS. THERE'S NO SIGN OF HIM.
I BELIEVE THAT SOMEONE OUT THERE KNOWS SOME-THING...
AYBE, REIKO, SOME E DOES. AND AYBE HE'S...
DON'T TELL THAT! NO! I RULY BELIEVE HE WILL BE COMING BACK!!

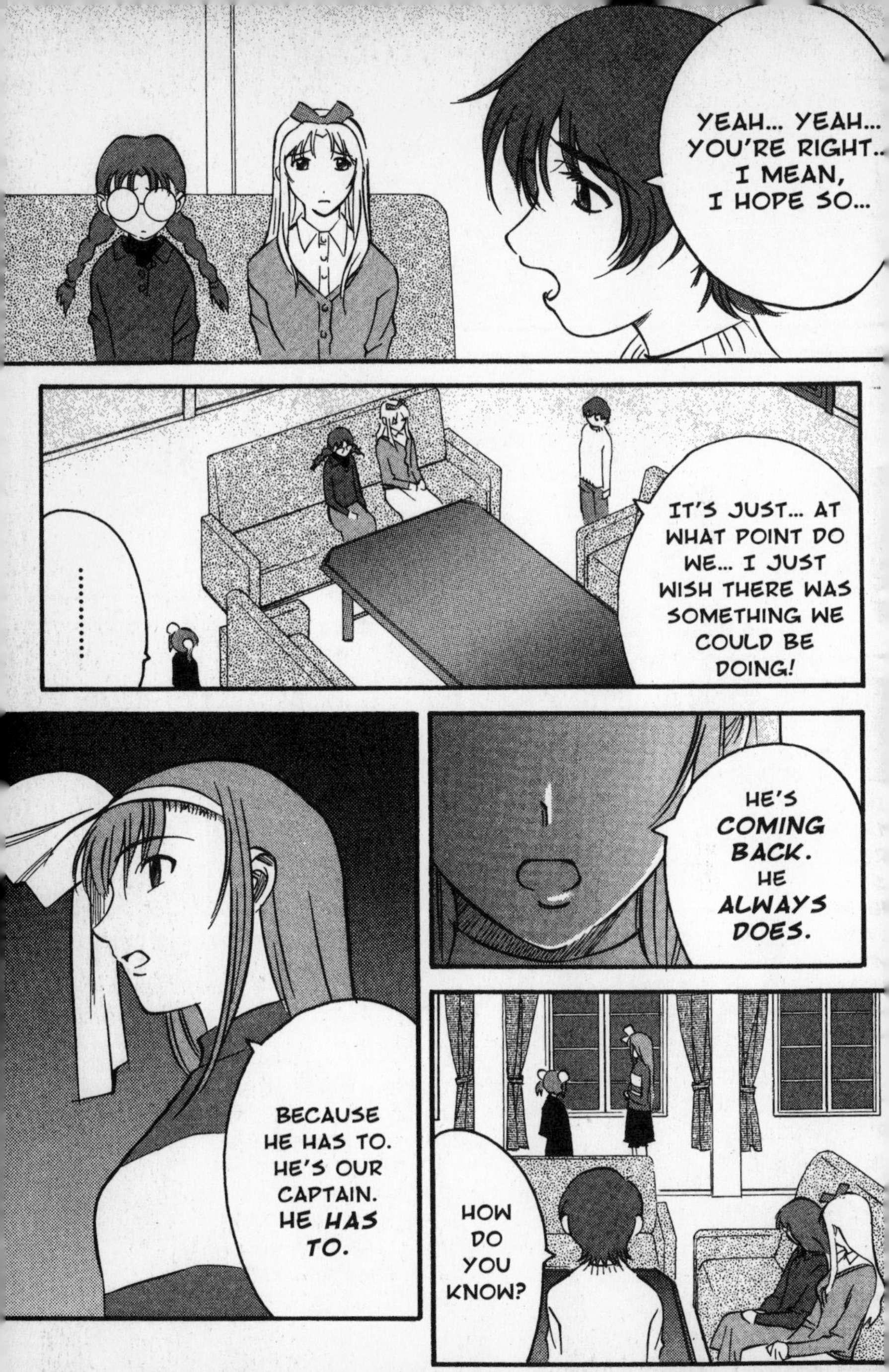
YEAH... YEAH... YOU'RE RIGHT.. I MEAN, I HOPE SO...
IT'S JUST... AT WHAT POINT DO WE... I JUST WISH THERE WAS SOMETHING WE COULD BE DOING!
....
HE'S **COMING BACK.** HE **ALWAYS DOES.**
HOW DO YOU KNOW?
BECAUSE HE HAS TO. HE'S OUR CAPTAIN. **HE *HAS* TO.**

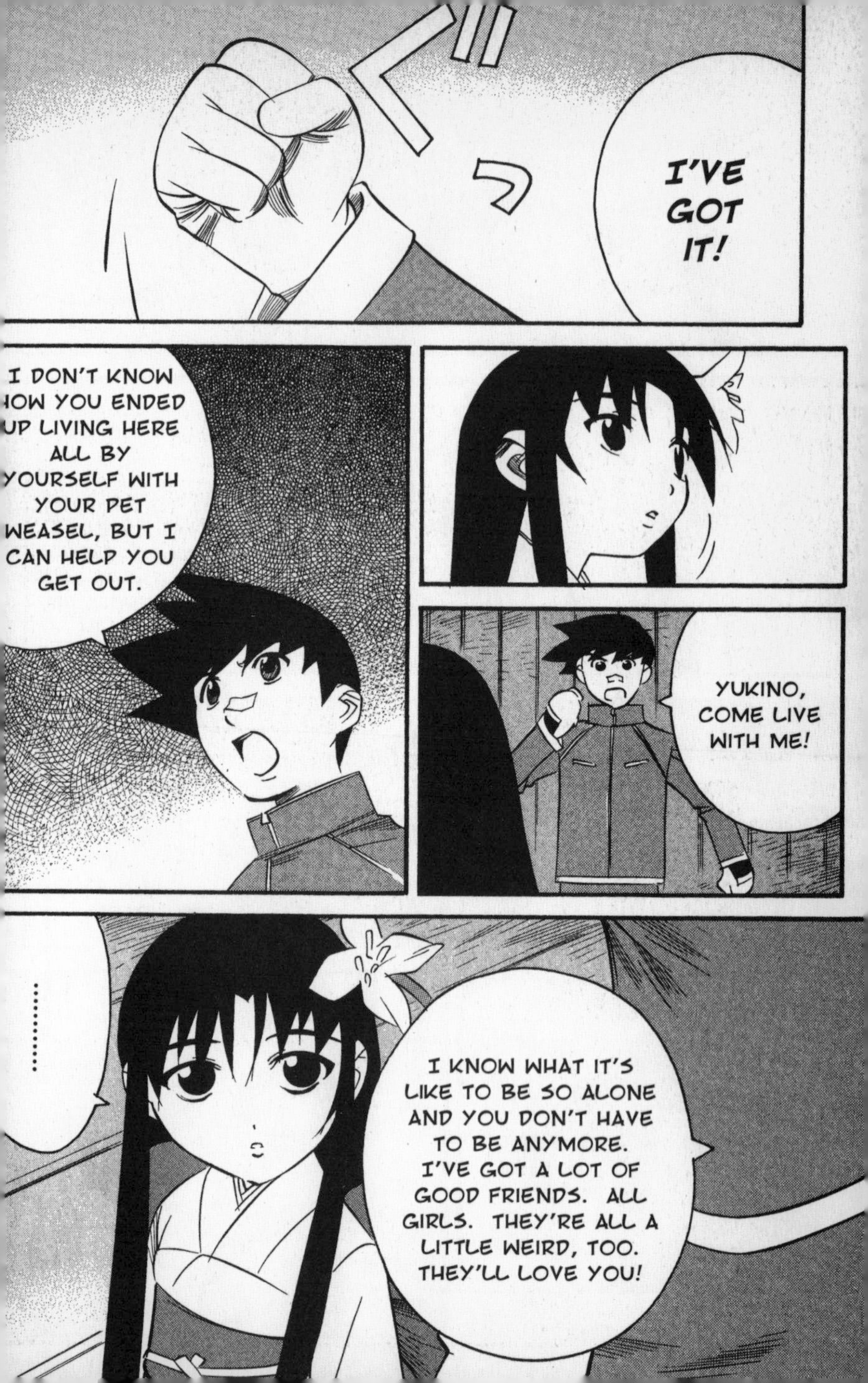
I'VE GOT IT!
YUKINO, COME LIVE WITH ME!
I DON'T KNOW HOW YOU ENDED UP LIVING HERE ALL BY YOURSELF WITH YOUR PET WEASEL, BUT I CAN HELP YOU GET OUT.
I KNOW WHAT IT'S LIKE TO BE SO ALONE AND YOU DON'T HAVE TO BE ANYMORE. I'VE GOT A LOT OF GOOD FRIENDS. ALL GIRLS. THEY'RE ALL A LITTLE WEIRD, TOO. THEY'LL LOVE YOU!
....

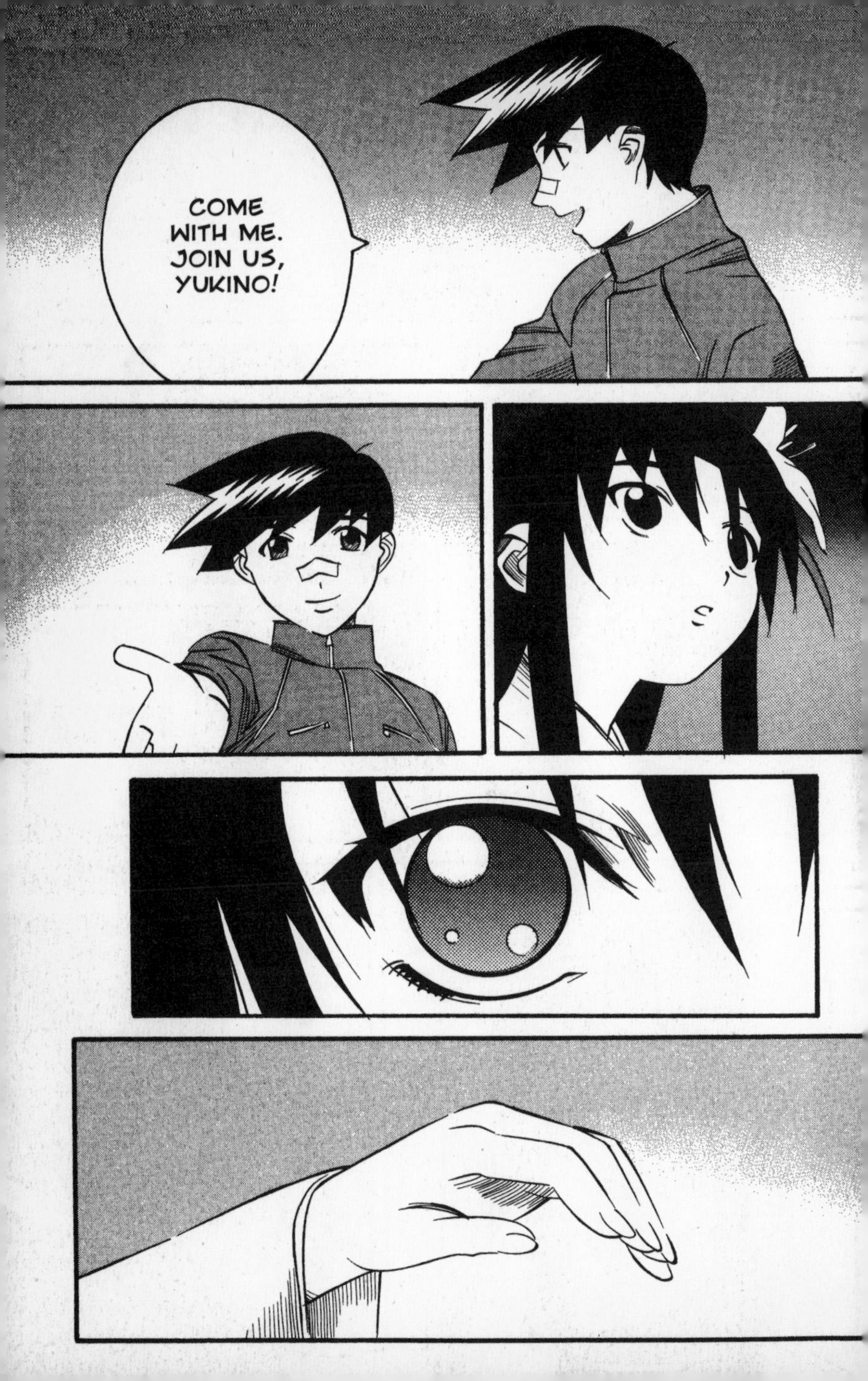
COME WITH ME. JOIN US, YUKINO!

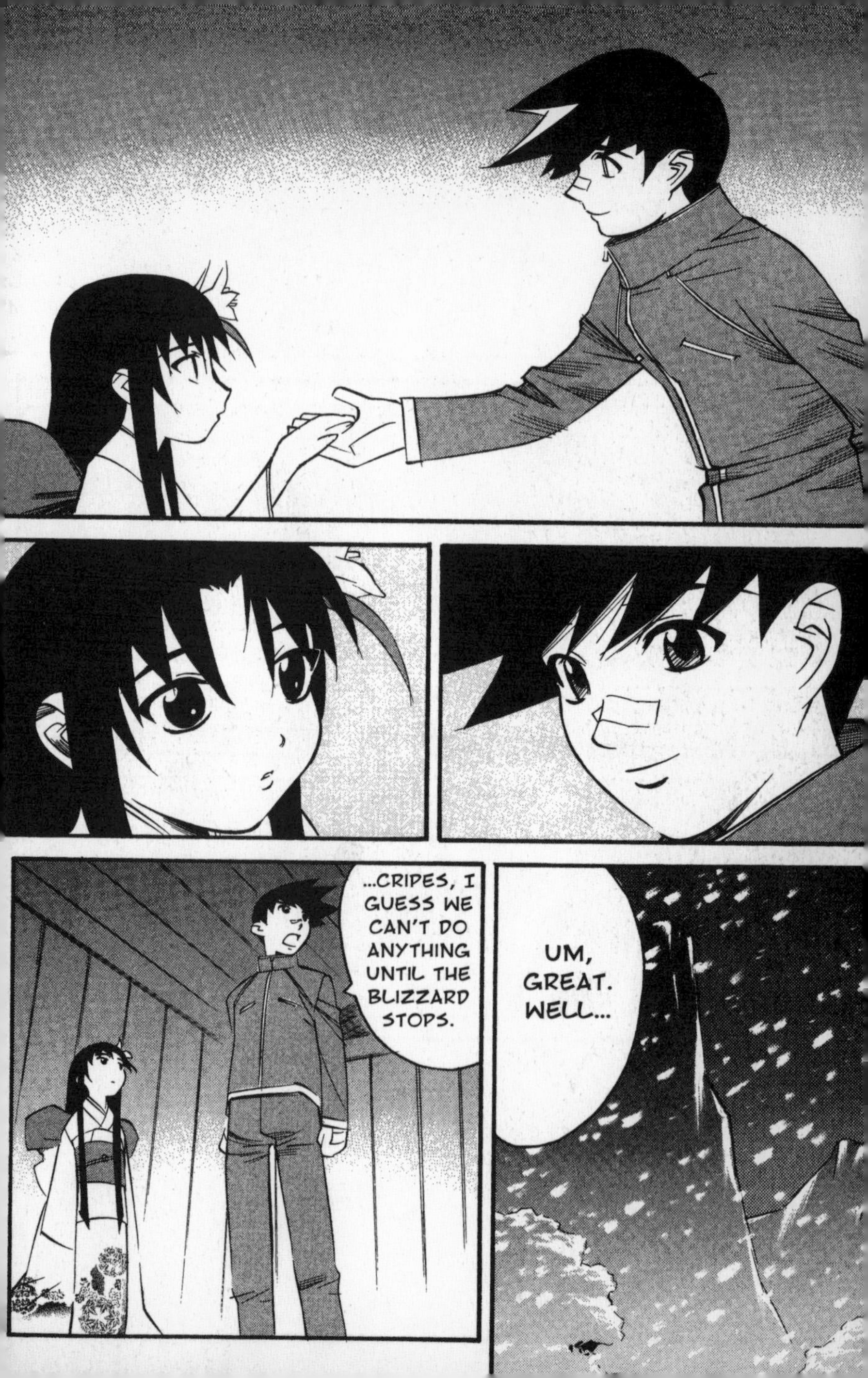
UM, GREAT. WELL...
...CRIPES, I GUESS WE CAN'T DO ANYTHING UNTIL THE BLIZZARD STOPS.

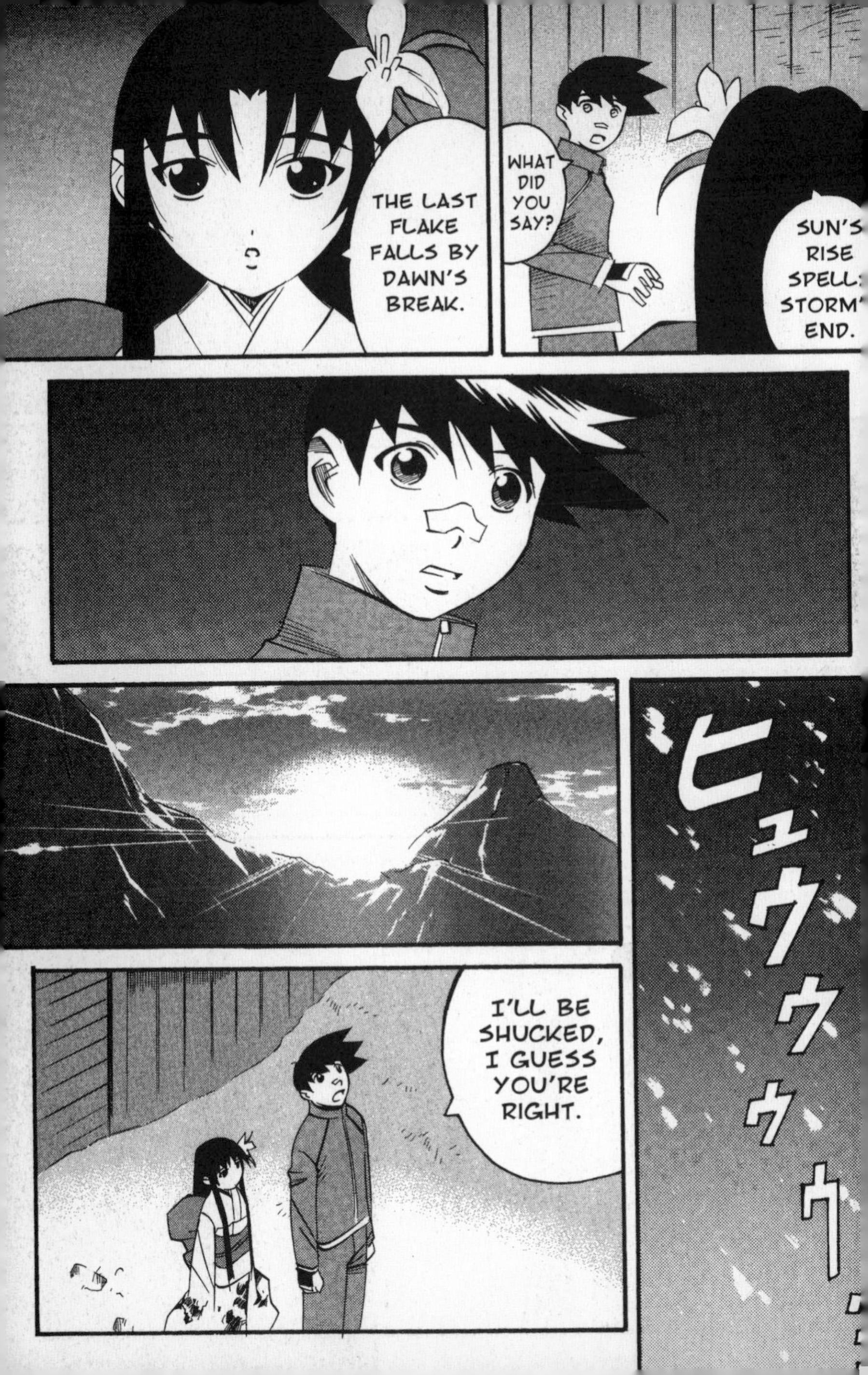
SUN'S RISE SPELL: STORM' END.
WHAT DID YOU SAY?
THE LAST FLAKE FALLS BY DAWN'S BREAK.
ヒュウウウウー
I'LL BE SHUCKED, I GUESS YOU'RE RIGHT.

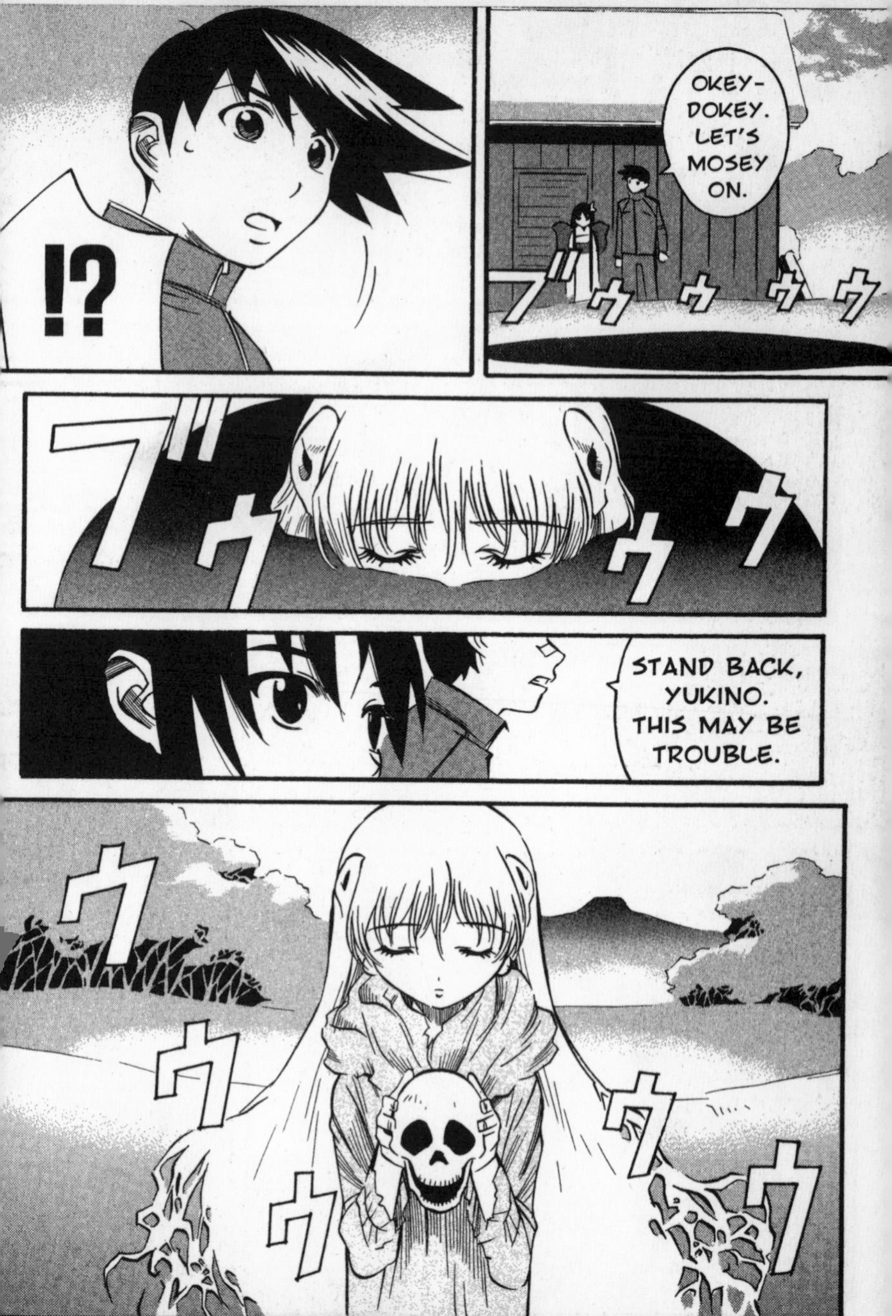
OKEY-DOKEY. LET'S MOSEY ON.
!?
STAND BACK, YUKINO. THIS MAY BE TROUBLE.

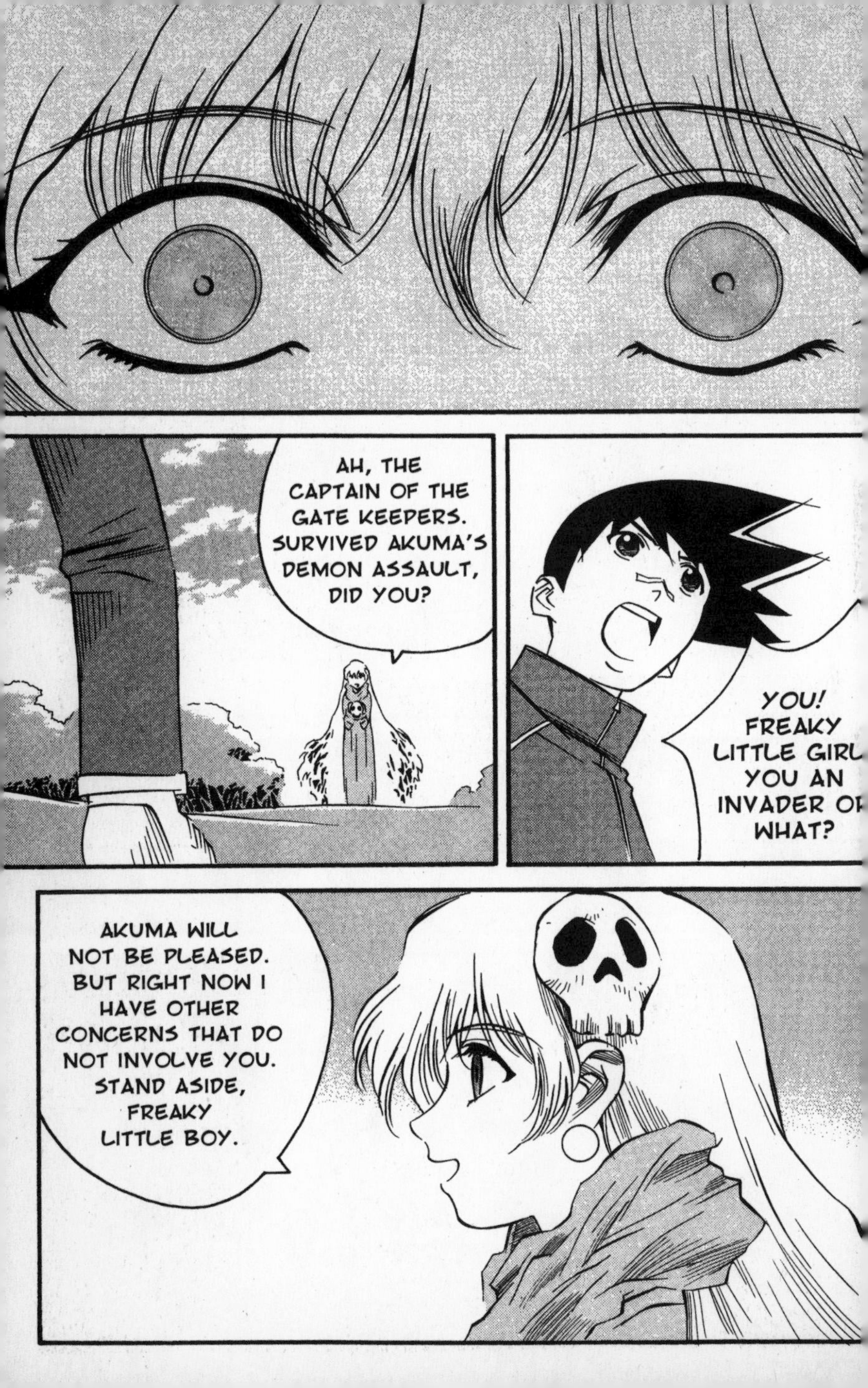

YOU! FREAKY LITTLE GIRL YOU AN INVADER O WHAT?
AH, THE CAPTAIN OF THE GATE KEEPERS. SURVIVED AKUMA'S DEMON ASSAULT, DID YOU?
AKUMA WILL NOT BE PLEASED. BUT RIGHT NOW I HAVE OTHER CONCERNS THAT DO NOT INVOLVE YOU. STAND ASIDE, FREAKY LITTLE BOY.

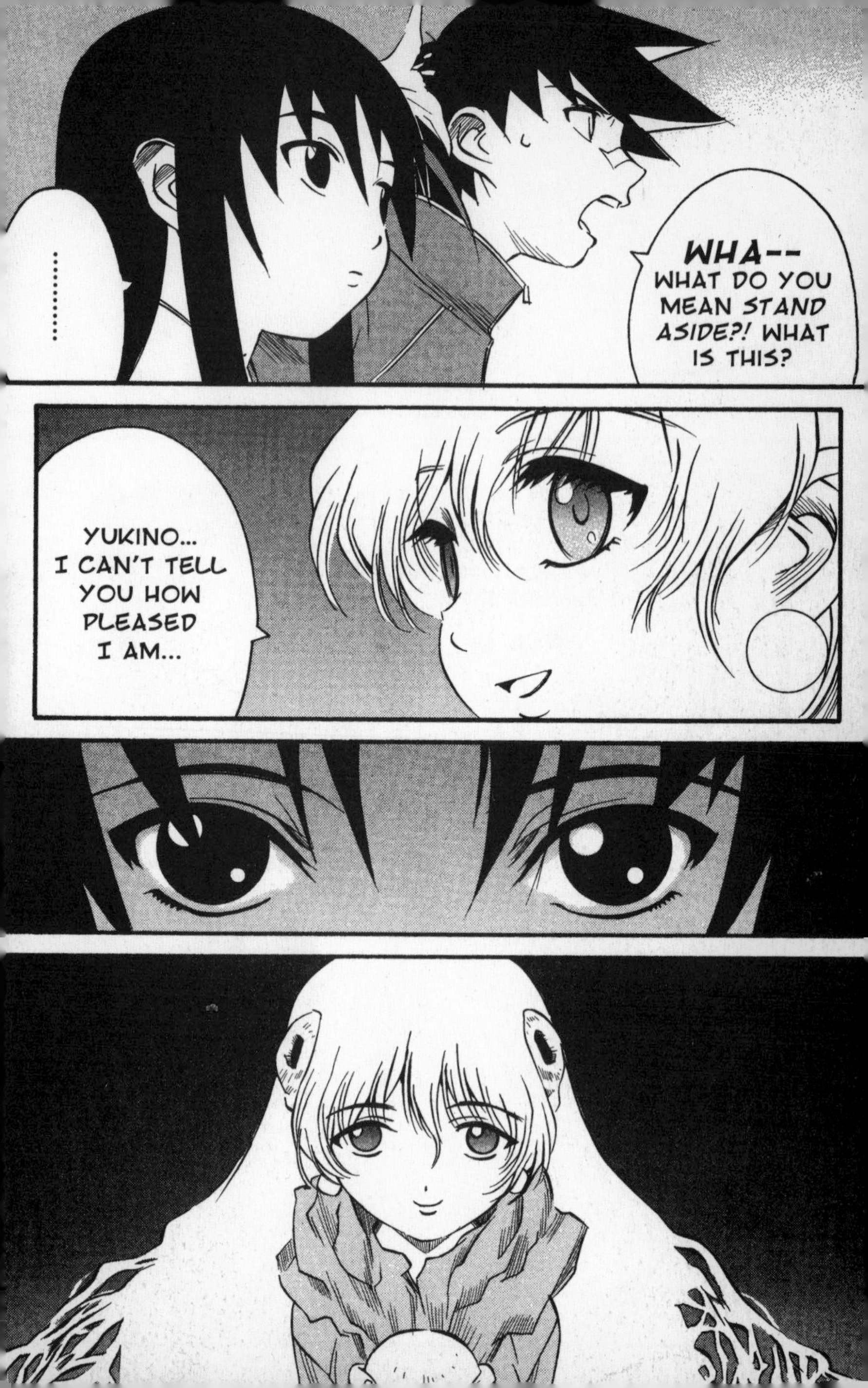
WHA-- WHAT DO YOU MEAN STAND ASIDE?! WHAT IS THIS?
....
YUKINO... I CAN'T TELL YOU HOW PLEASED I AM...

GATE #11 ALICE

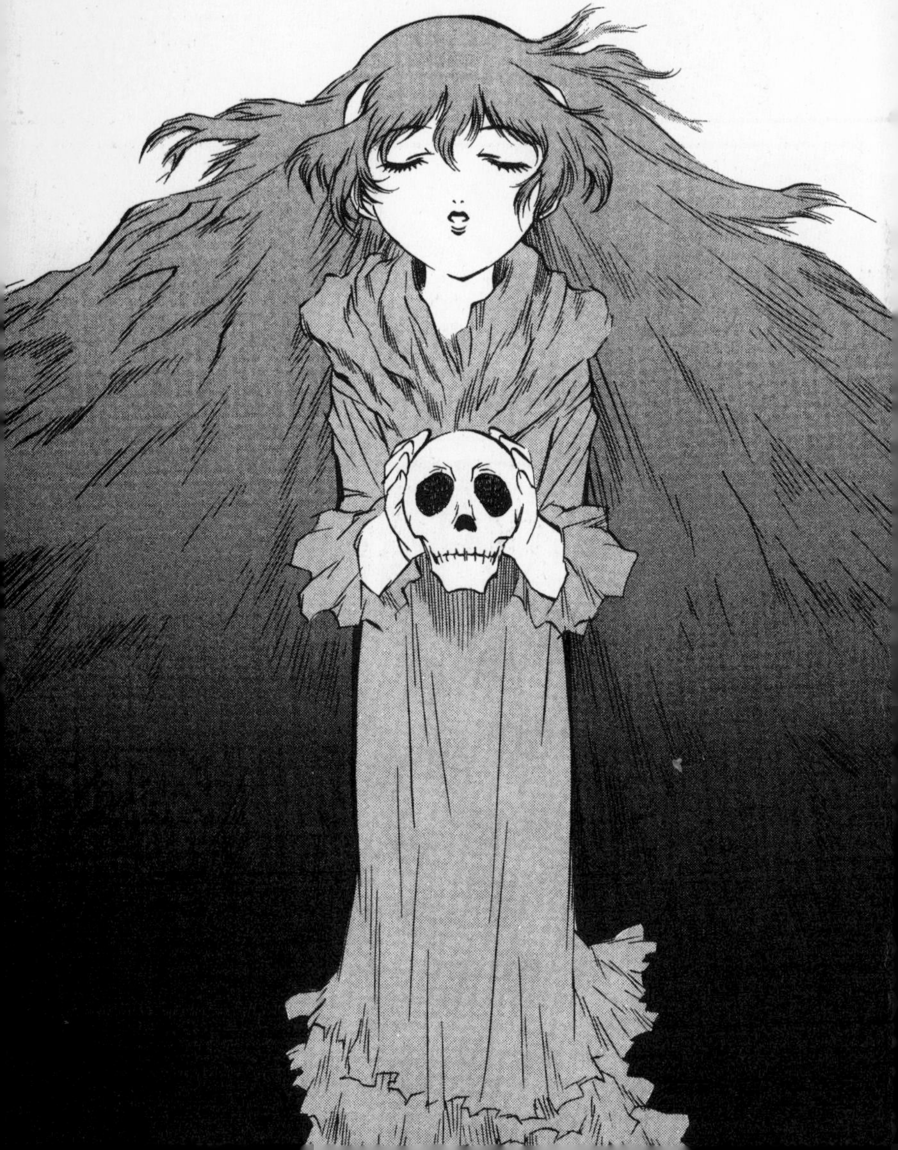

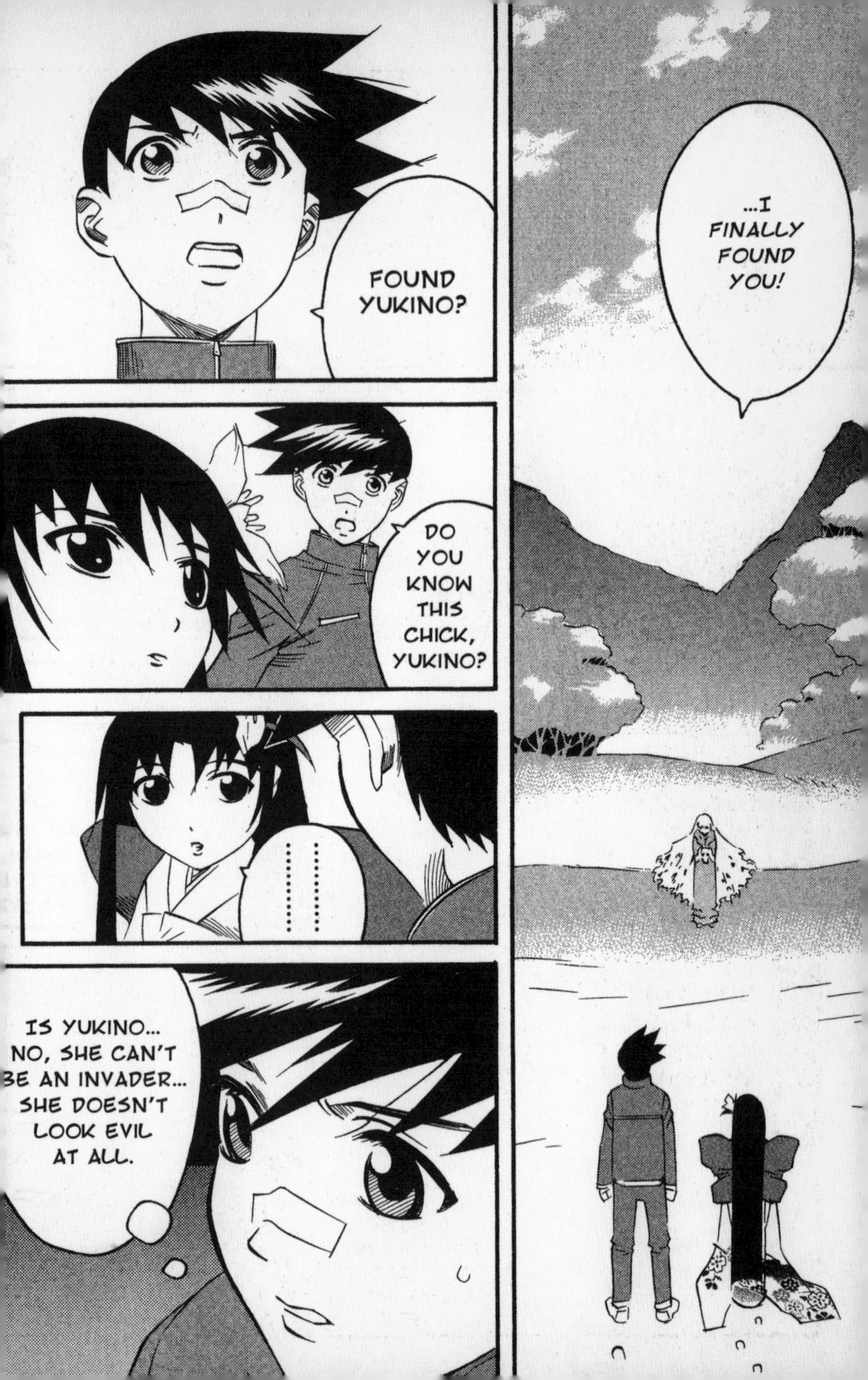
...I FINALLY FOUND YOU!
FOUND YUKINO?
DO YOU KNOW THIS CHICK, YUKINO?
......
IS YUKINO... NO, SHE CAN'T BE AN INVADER... SHE DOESN'T LOOK EVIL AT ALL.

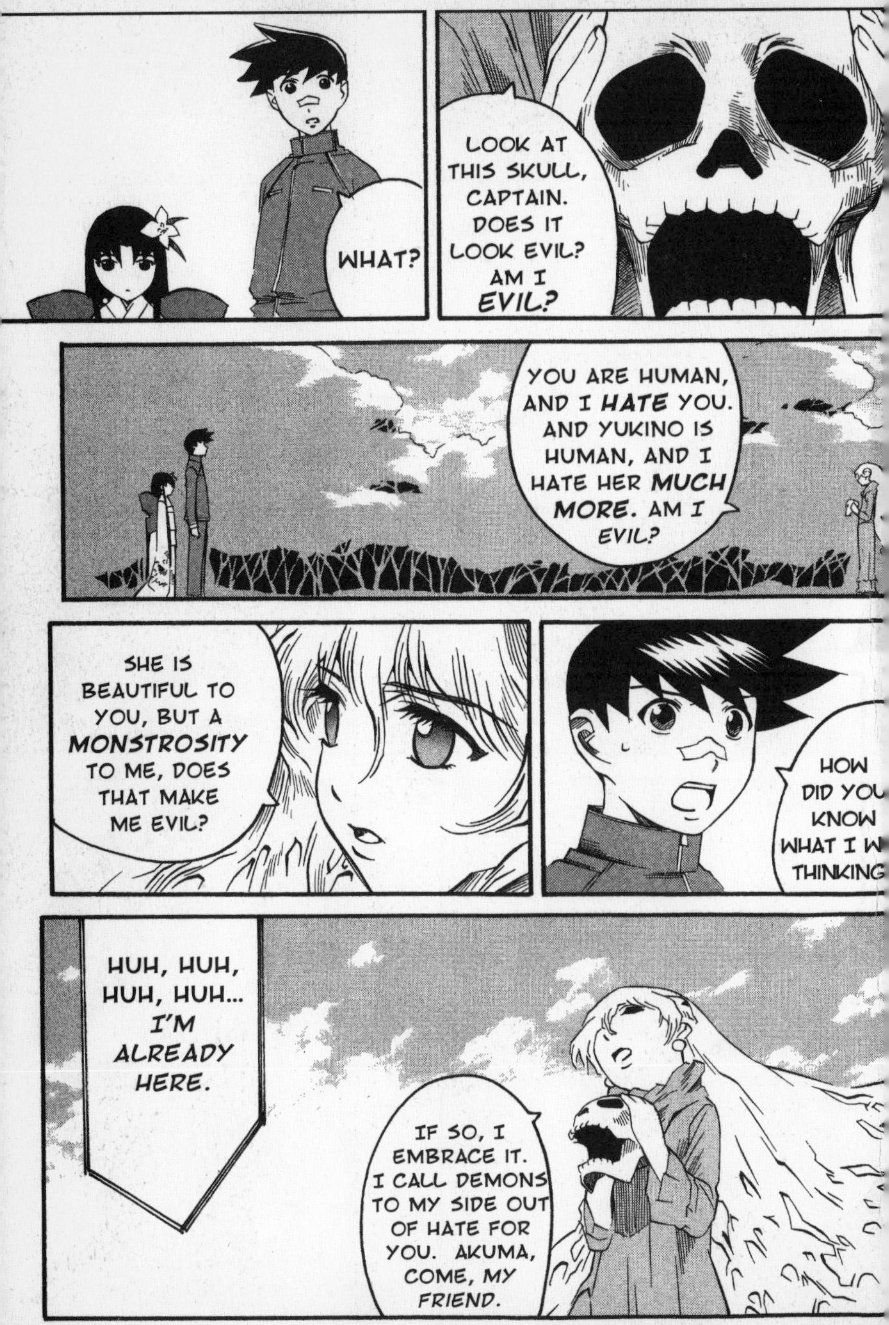
LOOK AT THIS SKULL, CAPTAIN. DOES IT LOOK EVIL? AM I EVIL?
WHAT?
YOU ARE HUMAN, AND I HATE YOU. AND YUKINO IS HUMAN, AND I HATE HER MUCH MORE. AM I EVIL?
HOW DID YOU KNOW WHAT I W THINKING
SHE IS BEAUTIFUL TO YOU, BUT A MONSTROSITY TO ME, DOES THAT MAKE ME EVIL?
IF SO, I EMBRACE IT. I CALL DEMONS TO MY SIDE OUT OF HATE FOR YOU. AKUMA, COME, MY FRIEND.
HUH, HUH, HUH, HUH... I'M ALREADY HERE.

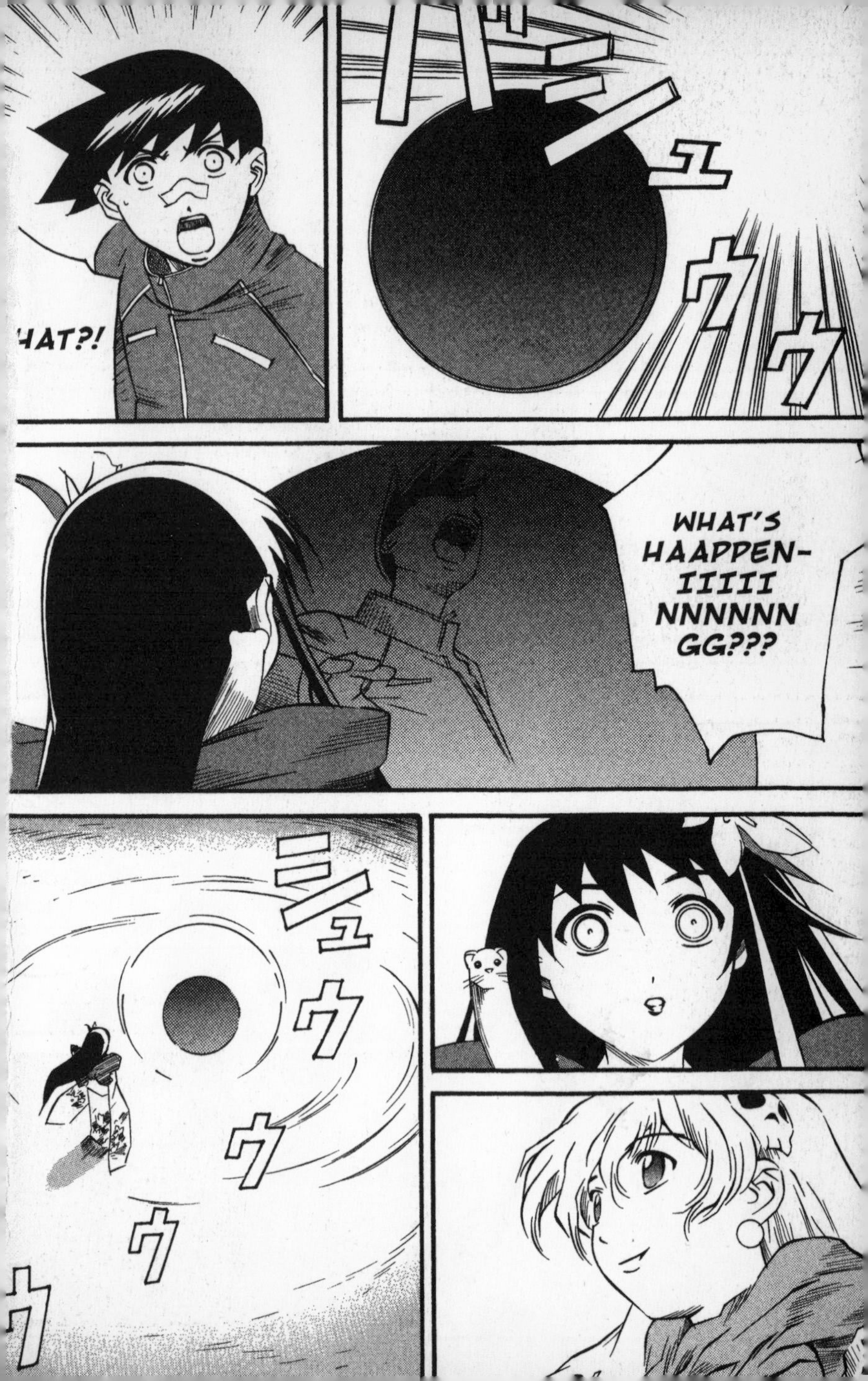
バシュウウ
HAT?!
WHAT'S HAAPPEN- IIIII NNNNNN GG???
シュウウウウ

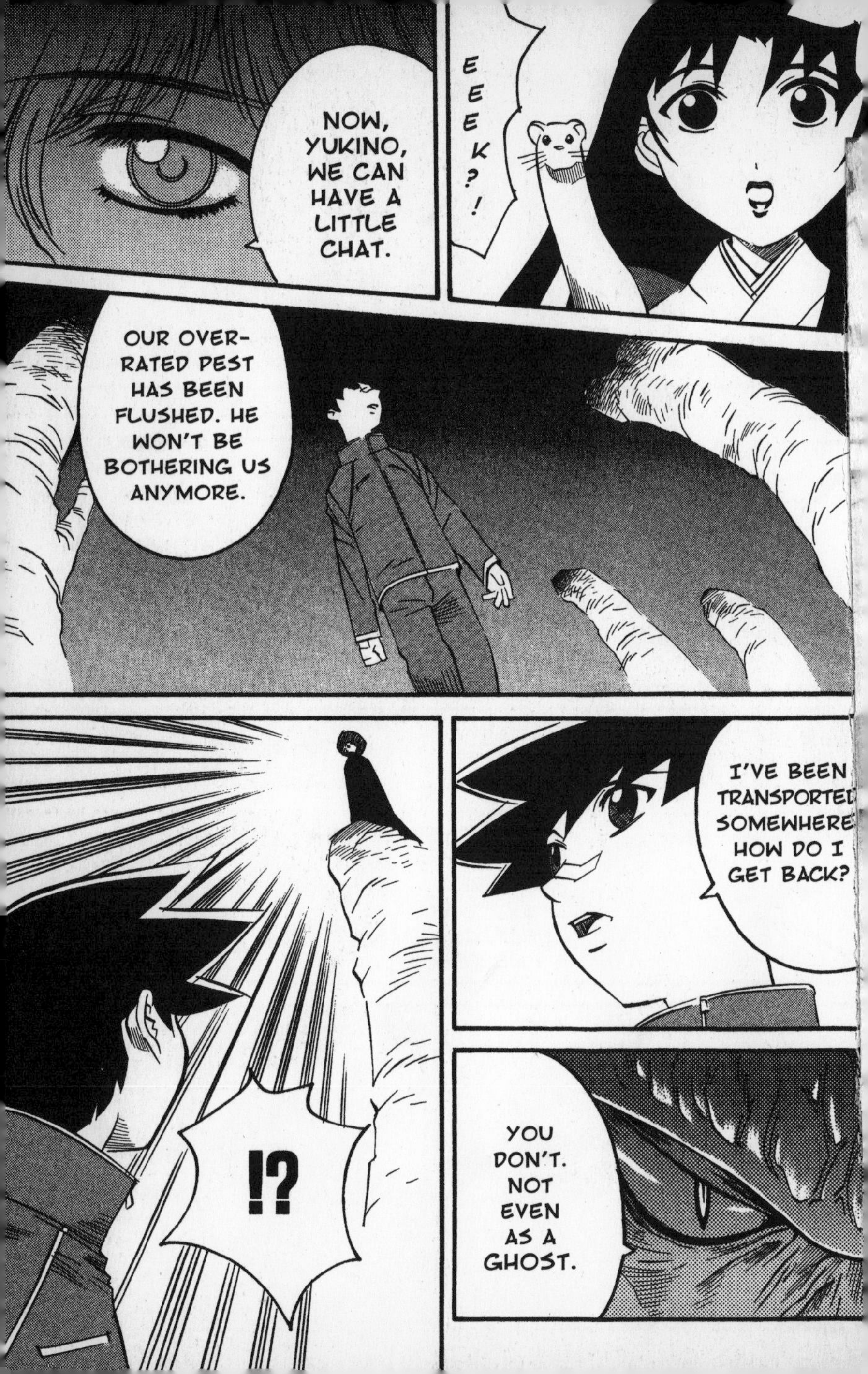
EEEK?!
NOW, YUKINO, WE CAN HAVE A LITTLE CHAT.
OUR OVER-RATED PEST HAS BEEN FLUSHED. HE WON'T BE BOTHERING US ANYMORE.
I'VE BEEN TRANSPORTED SOMEWHERE HOW DO I GET BACK?
YOU DON'T. NOT EVEN AS A GHOST.
!?

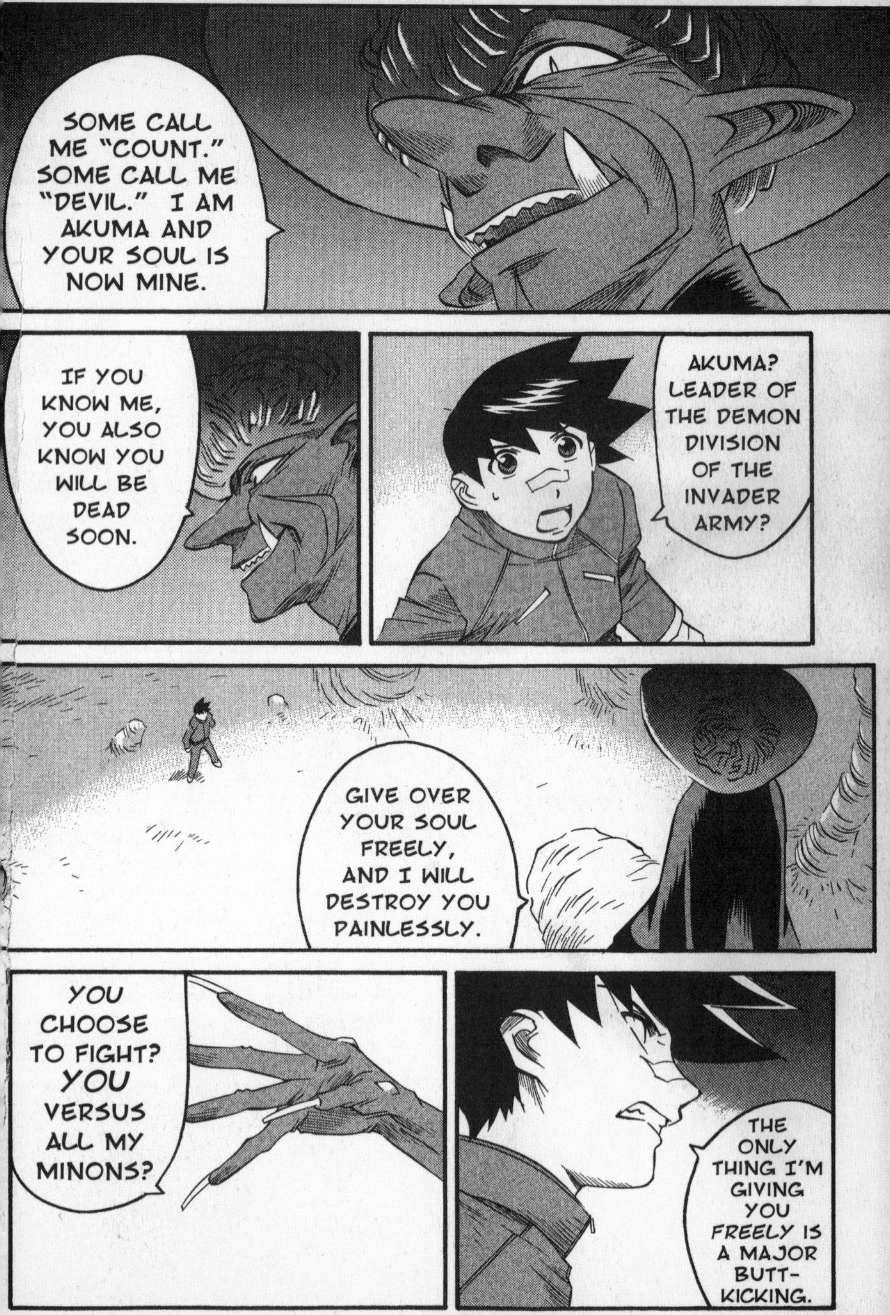
SOME CALL ME "COUNT." SOME CALL ME "DEVIL." I AM AKUMA AND YOUR SOUL IS NOW MINE.
AKUMA? LEADER OF THE DEMON DIVISION OF THE INVADER ARMY?
IF YOU KNOW ME, YOU ALSO KNOW YOU WILL BE DEAD SOON.
GIVE OVER YOUR SOUL FREELY, AND I WILL DESTROY YOU PAINLESSLY.
THE ONLY THING I'M GIVING YOU FREELY IS A MAJOR BUTT-KICKING.
YOU CHOOSE TO FIGHT? YOU VERSUS ALL MY MINONS?

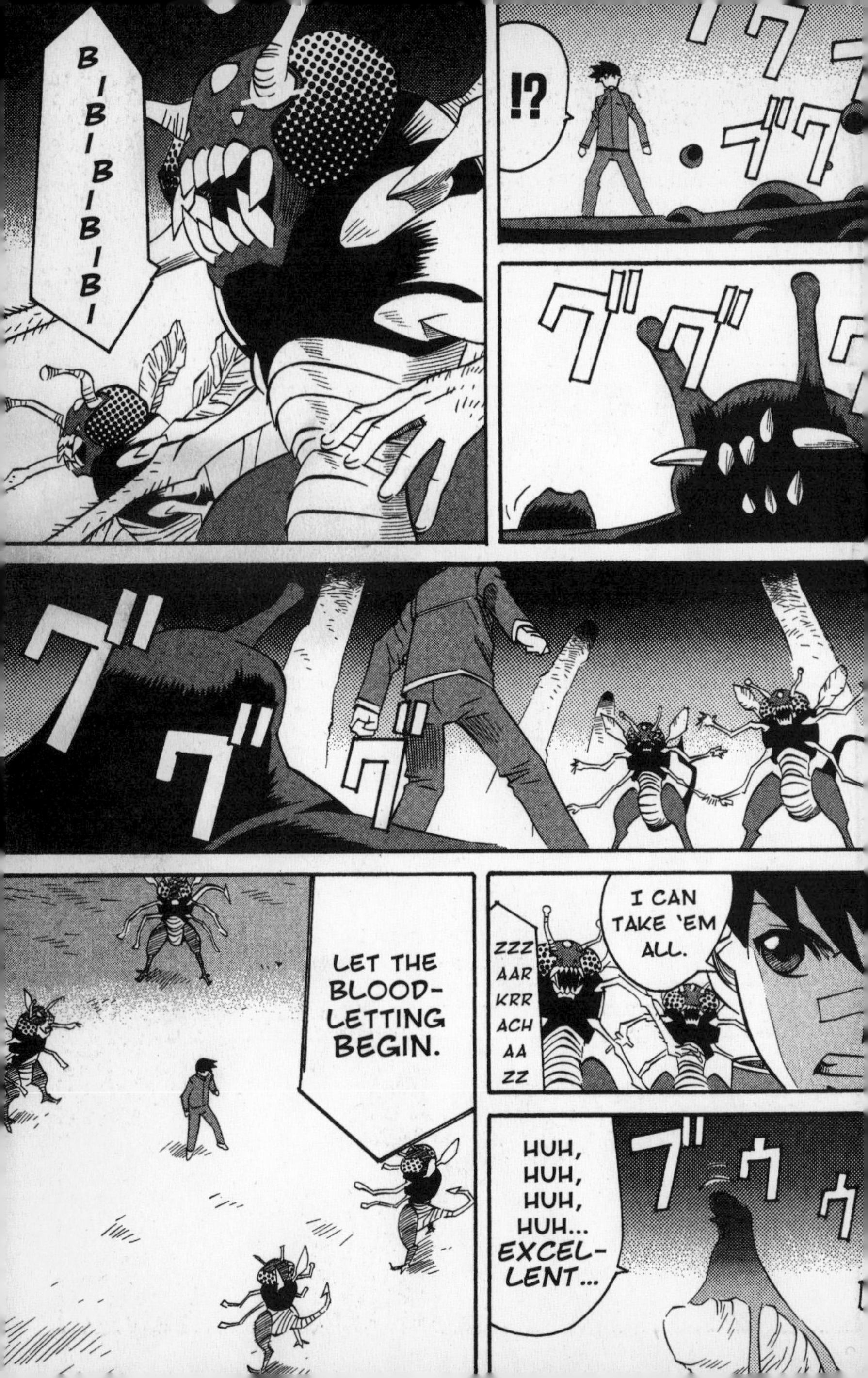
!?
BIBIBIBIBIBI
I CAN TAKE 'EM ALL.
ZZZ AAR KRR ACH AA ZZ
HUH, HUH, HUH, HUH... EXCEL-LENT...
LET THE BLOOD-LETTING BEGIN.

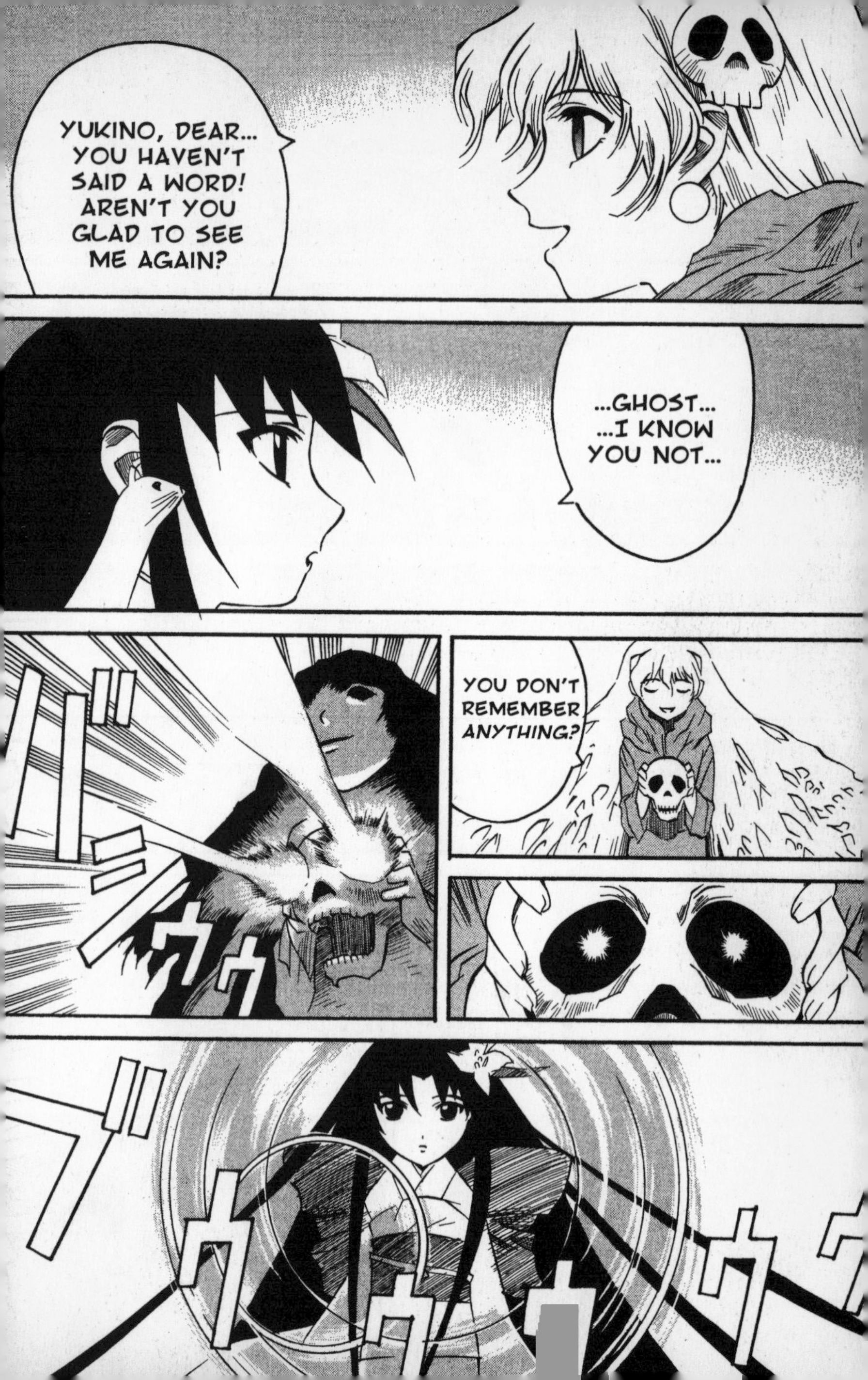
YUKINO, DEAR... YOU HAVEN'T SAID A WORD! AREN'T YOU GLAD TO SEE ME AGAIN?
...GHOST... ...I KNOW YOU NOT...
YOU DON'T REMEMBER ANYTHING?

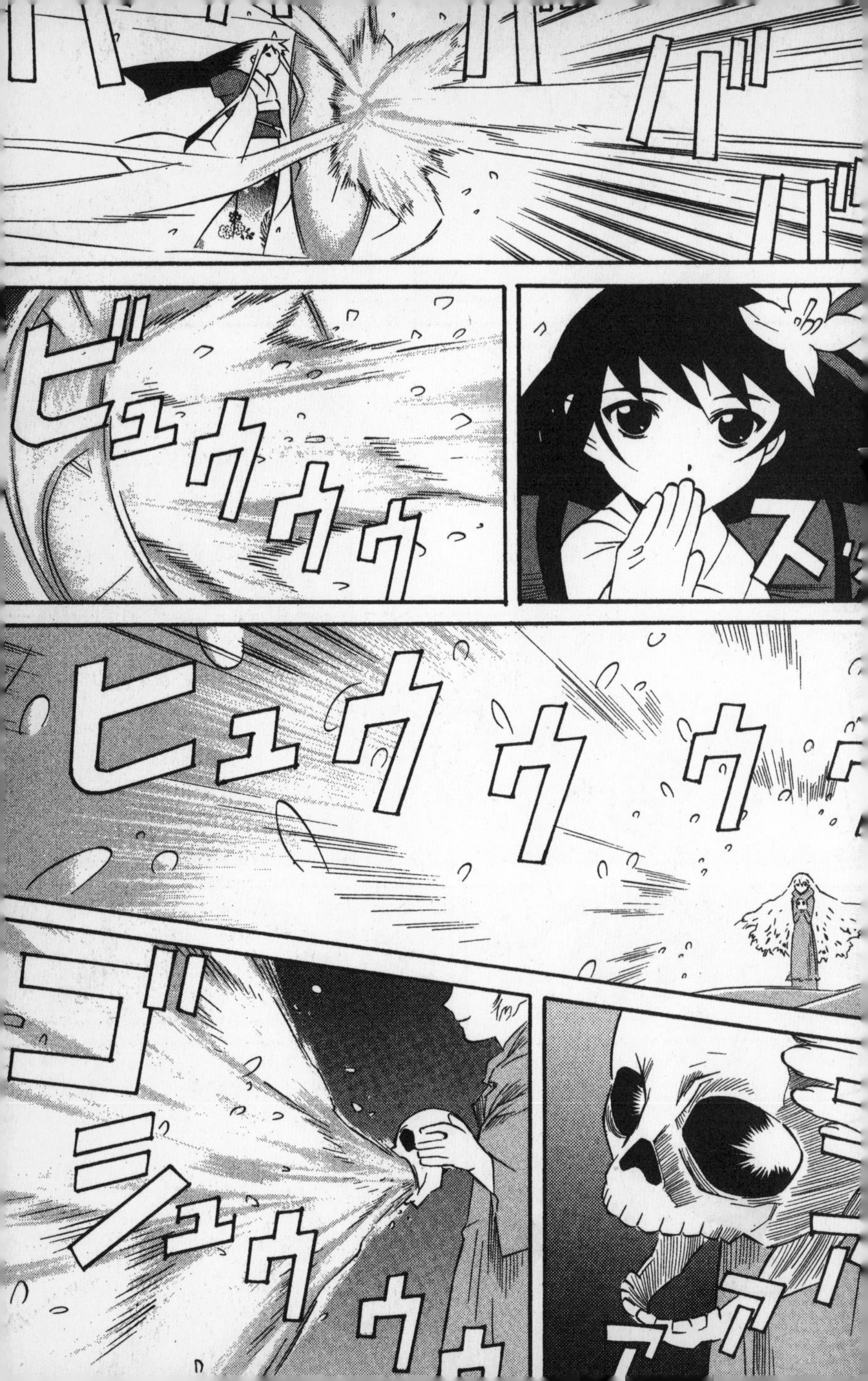
ビュウウウ
ビュウウウウ

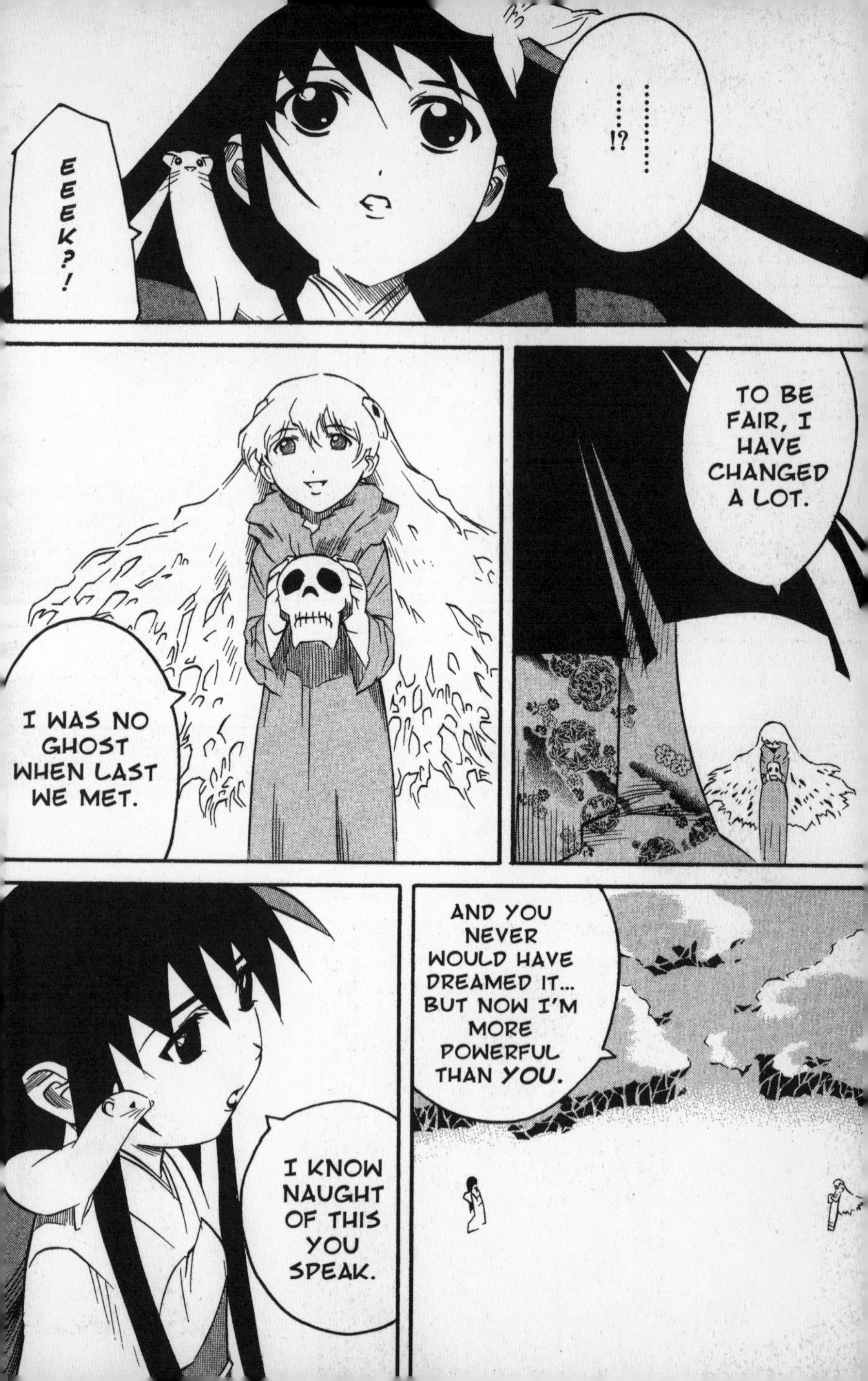
......!?
EEEK?!
TO BE FAIR, I HAVE CHANGED A LOT.
I WAS NO GHOST WHEN LAST WE MET.
AND YOU NEVER WOULD HAVE DREAMED IT... BUT NOW I'M MORE POWERFUL THAN YOU.
I KNOW NAUGHT OF THIS YOU SPEAK.

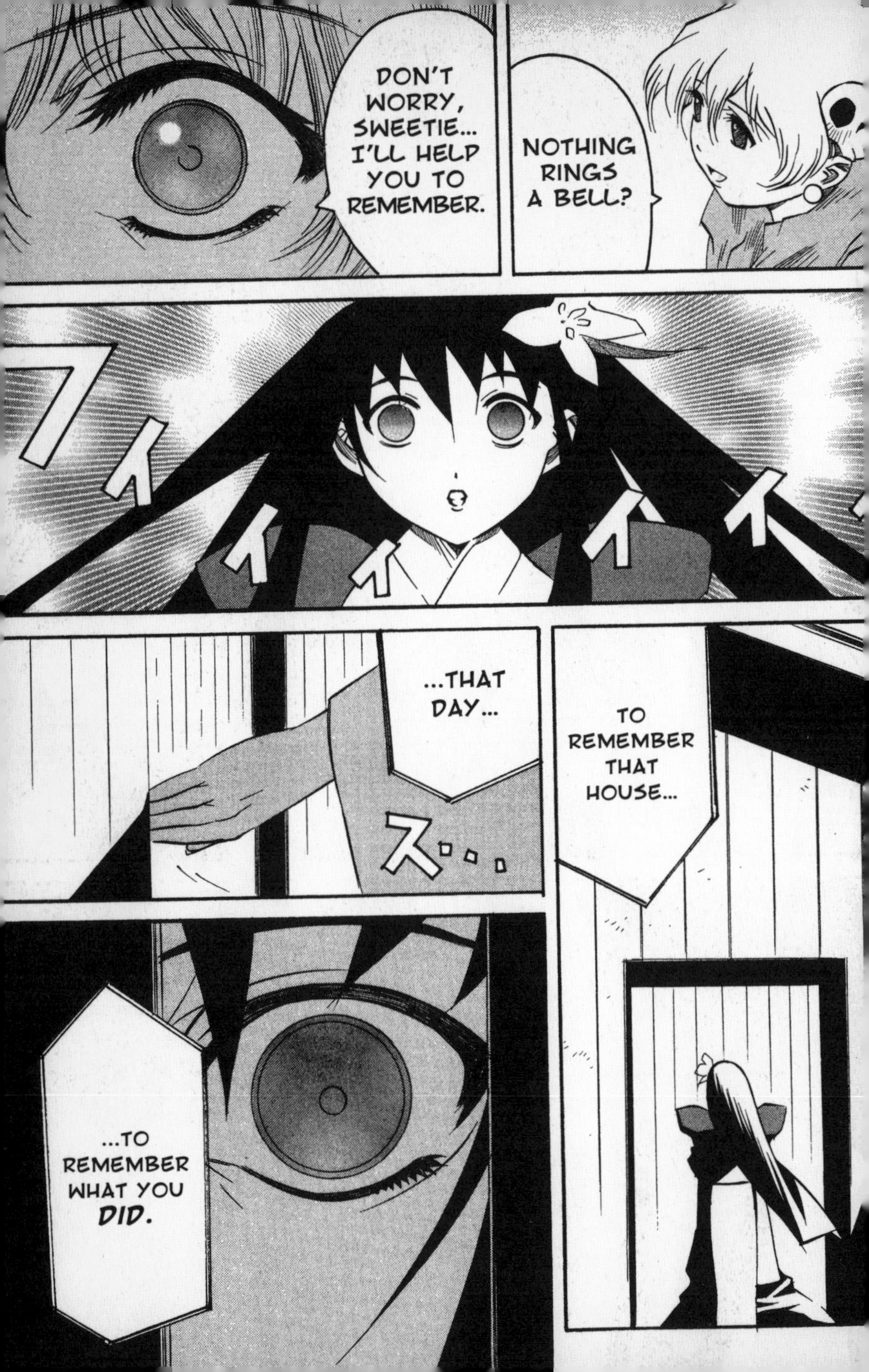
NOTHING RINGS A BELL?
DON'T WORRY, SWEETIE... I'LL HELP YOU TO REMEMBER.
フィイイイ
TO REMEMBER THAT HOUSE...
...THAT DAY...
ス...
...TO REMEMBER WHAT YOU **DID**.

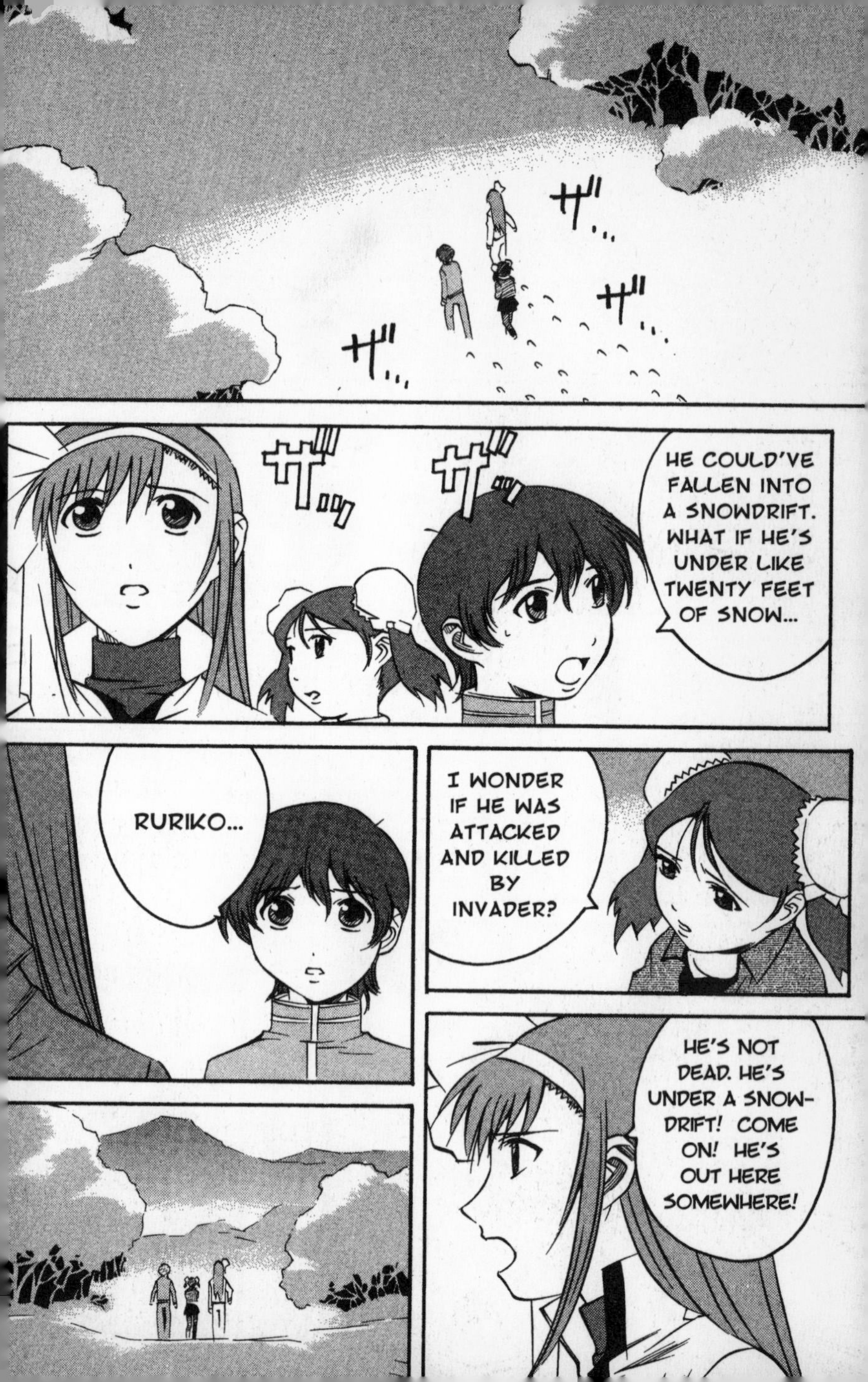
ザ…
ザ…
ザ…
HE COULD'VE FALLEN INTO A SNOWDRIFT. WHAT IF HE'S UNDER LIKE TWENTY FEET OF SNOW...
ザッ
ザッ
I WONDER IF HE WAS ATTACKED AND KILLED BY INVADER?
RURIKO...
HE'S NOT DEAD. HE'S UNDER A SNOW-DRIFT! COME ON! HE'S OUT HERE SOMEWHERE!

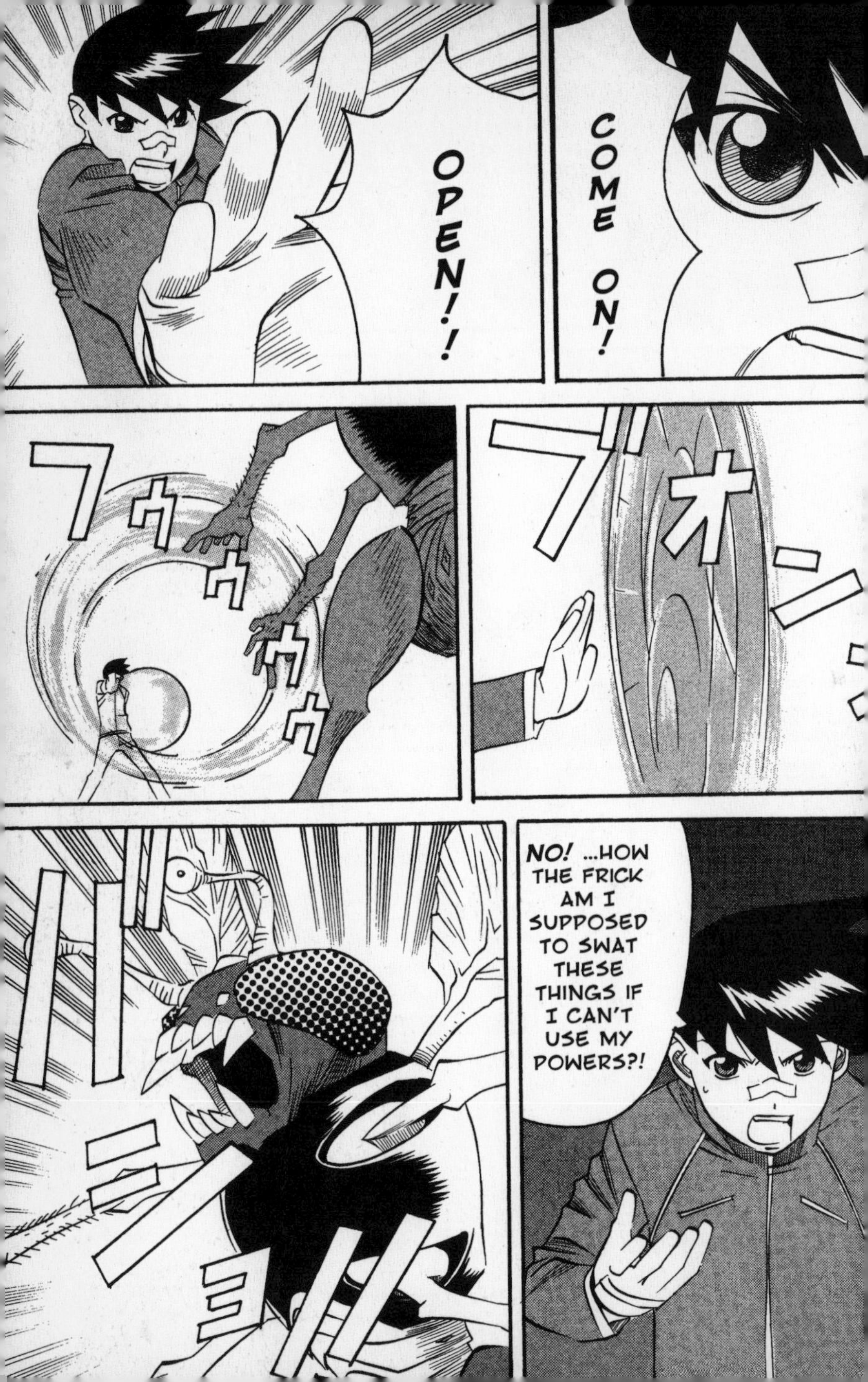
COME ON!
OPEN!!
ブオーン
フゥゥゥゥ
NO! ...HOW THE FRICK AM I SUPPOSED TO SWAT THESE THINGS IF I CAN'T USE MY POWERS?!

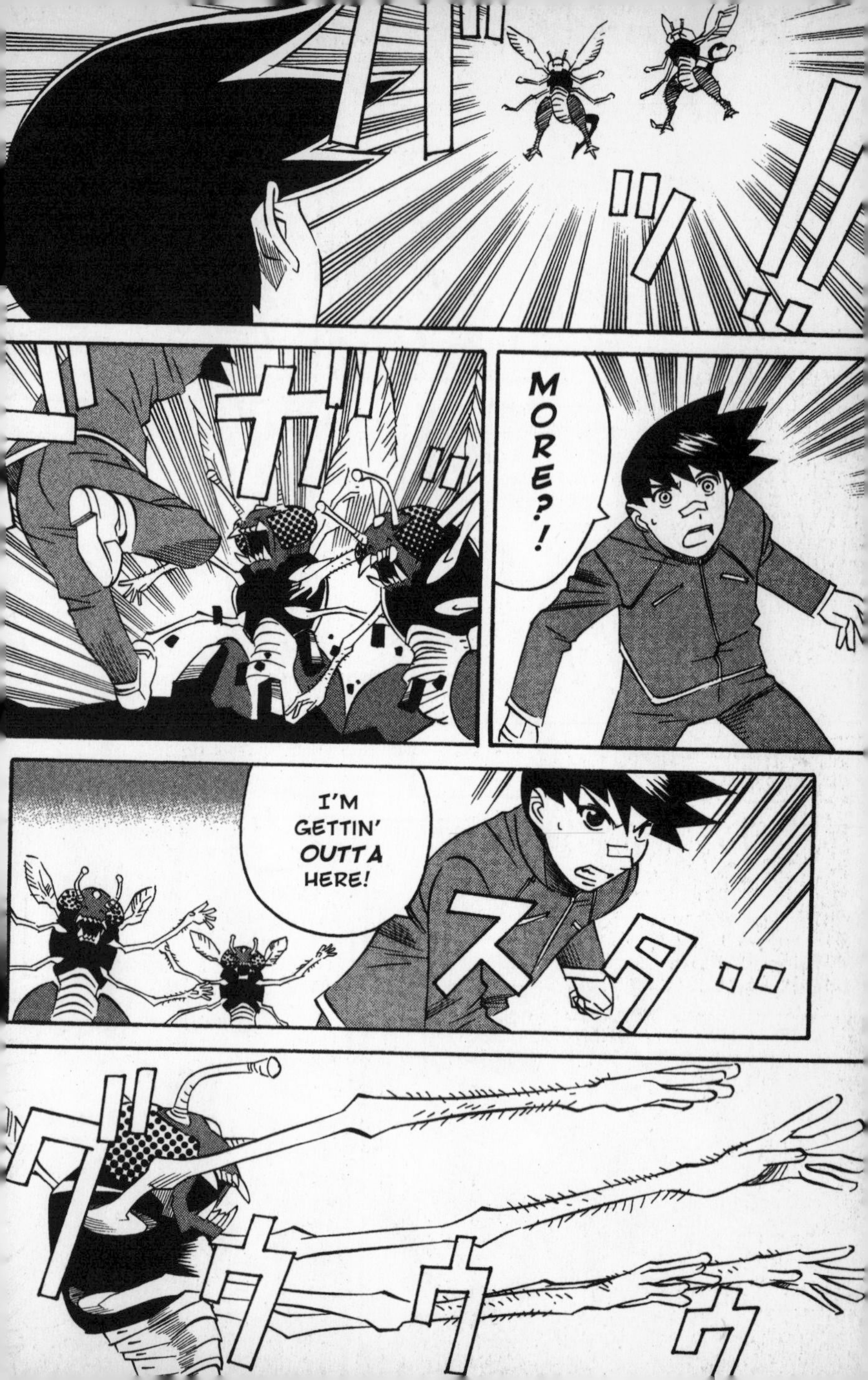
MORE?!
I'M GETTIN' OUTTA HERE!

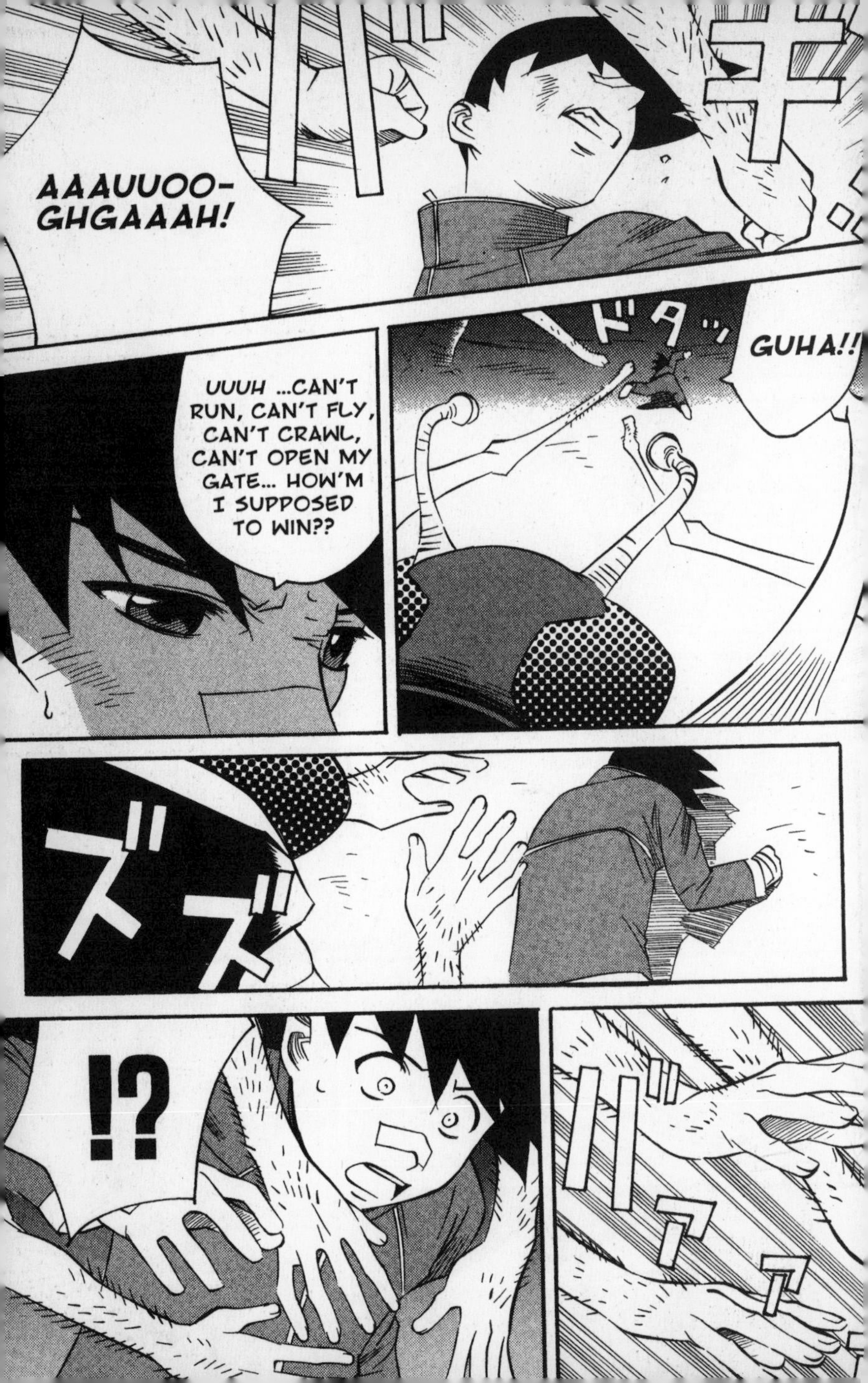

AAAUUOO-GHGAAAH!
ドタッ
GUHA!!
UUUH ...CAN'T RUN, CAN'T FLY, CAN'T CRAWL, CAN'T OPEN MY GATE... HOW'M I SUPPOSED TO WIN??
ズズ
バァァ
!?

GAAA
AAA-
DARN
IT!!

ZZ
AA
URR
GZZ.

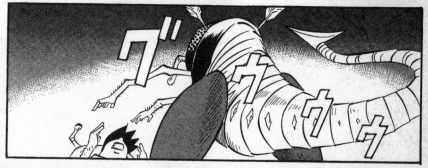

HERE
GOES
NOTHING.

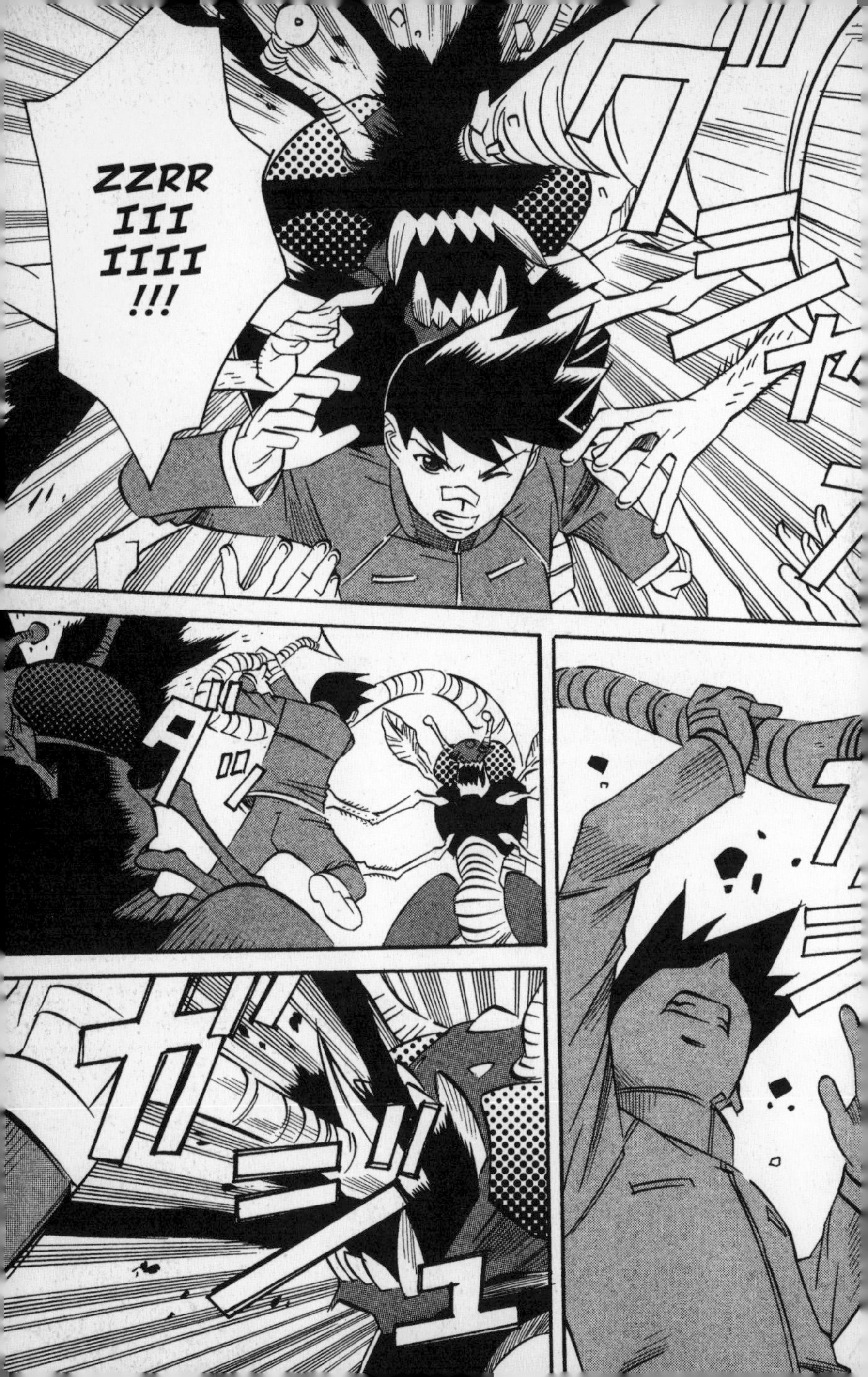
ZZRR
III
IIII
!!!

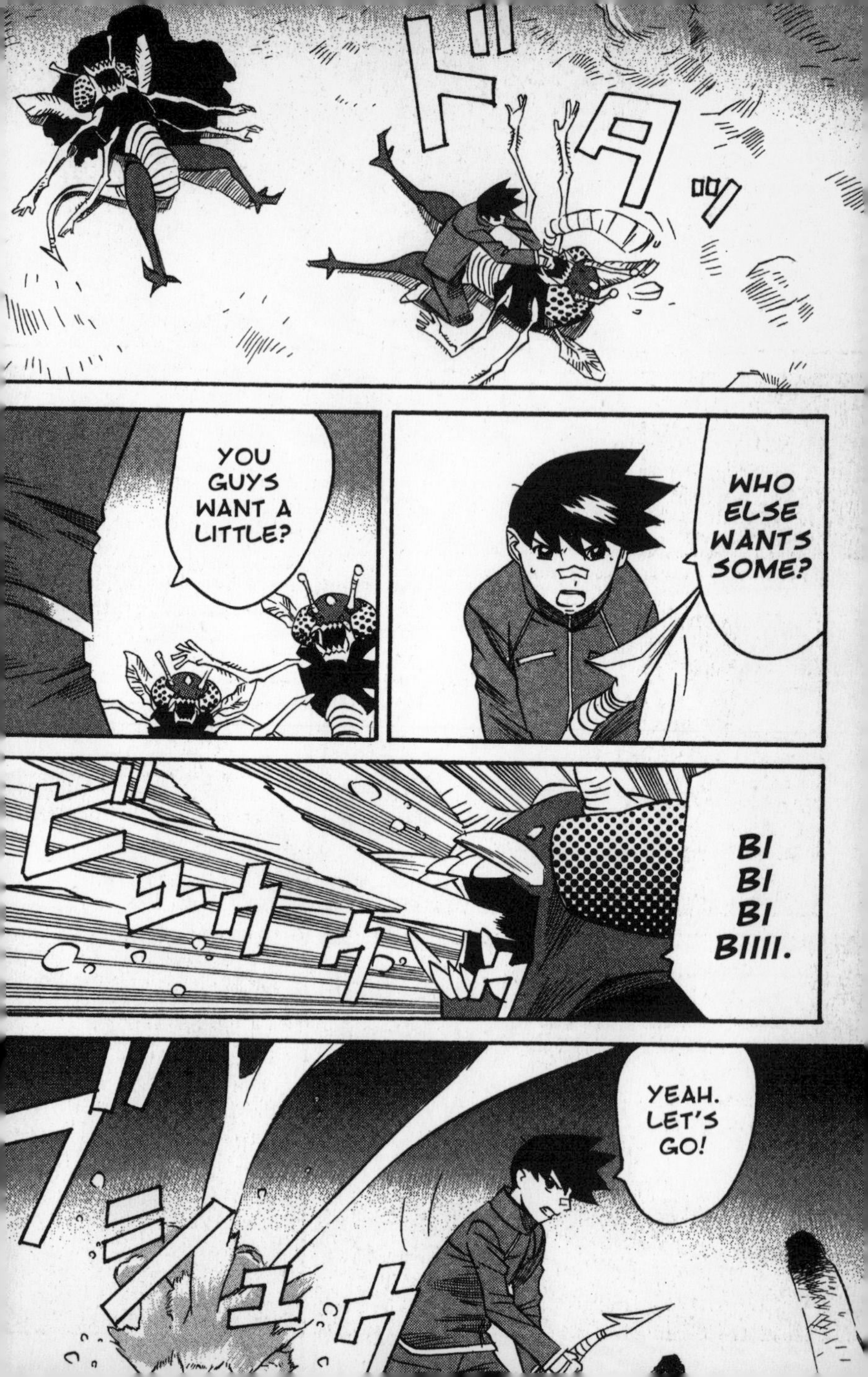
ドタッ
WHO ELSE WANTS SOME?
YOU GUYS WANT A LITTLE?
BI BI BI BIIII.
YEAH. LET'S GO!

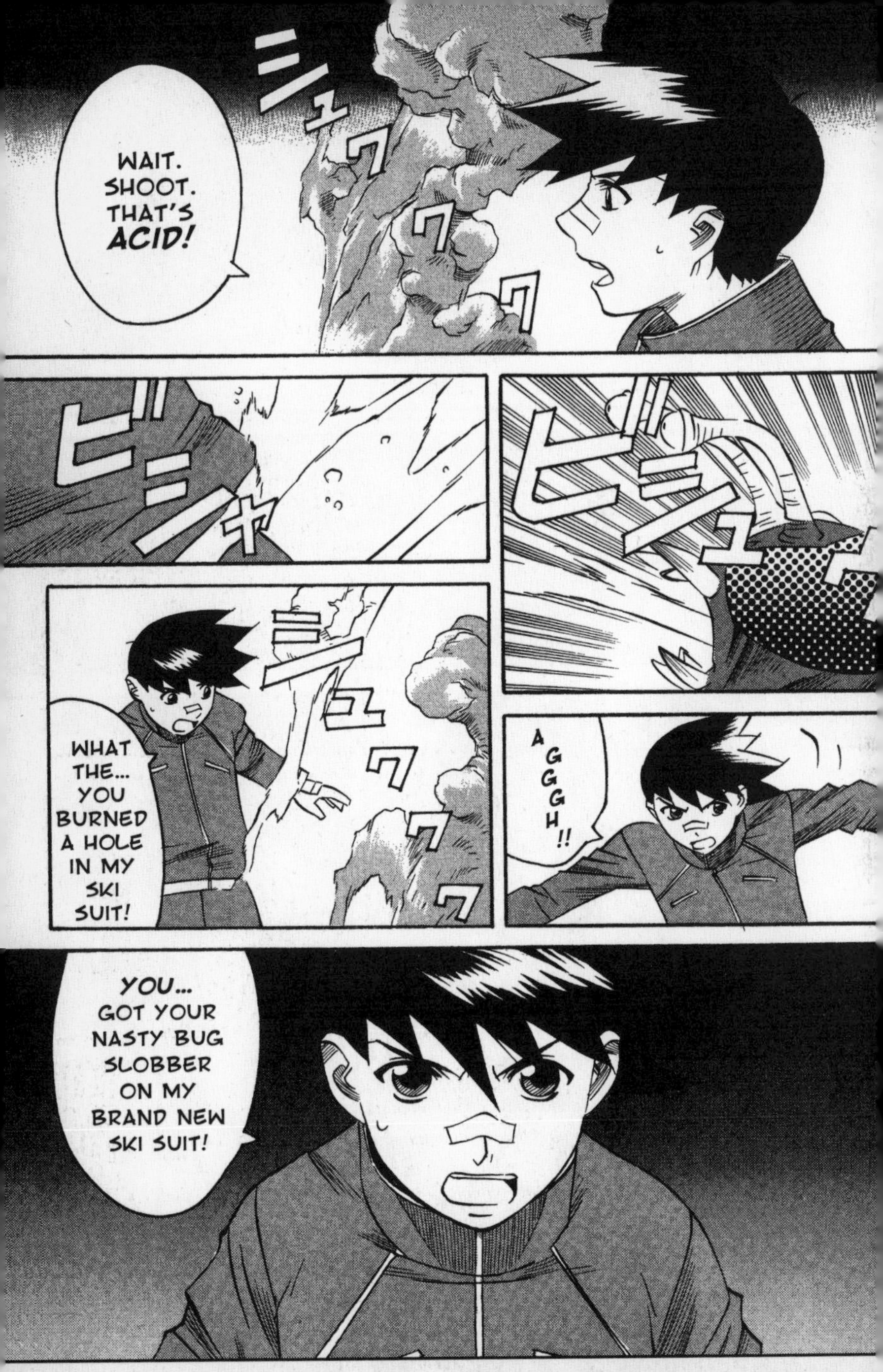
シュワワワ
WAIT. SHOOT. THAT'S **ACID!**
ビシュ
ビシャ
AGGGH!!
シュワワワワ
WHAT THE... YOU BURNED A HOLE IN MY SKI SUIT!
YOU... GOT YOUR NASTY BUG SLOBBER ON MY BRAND NEW SKI SUIT!

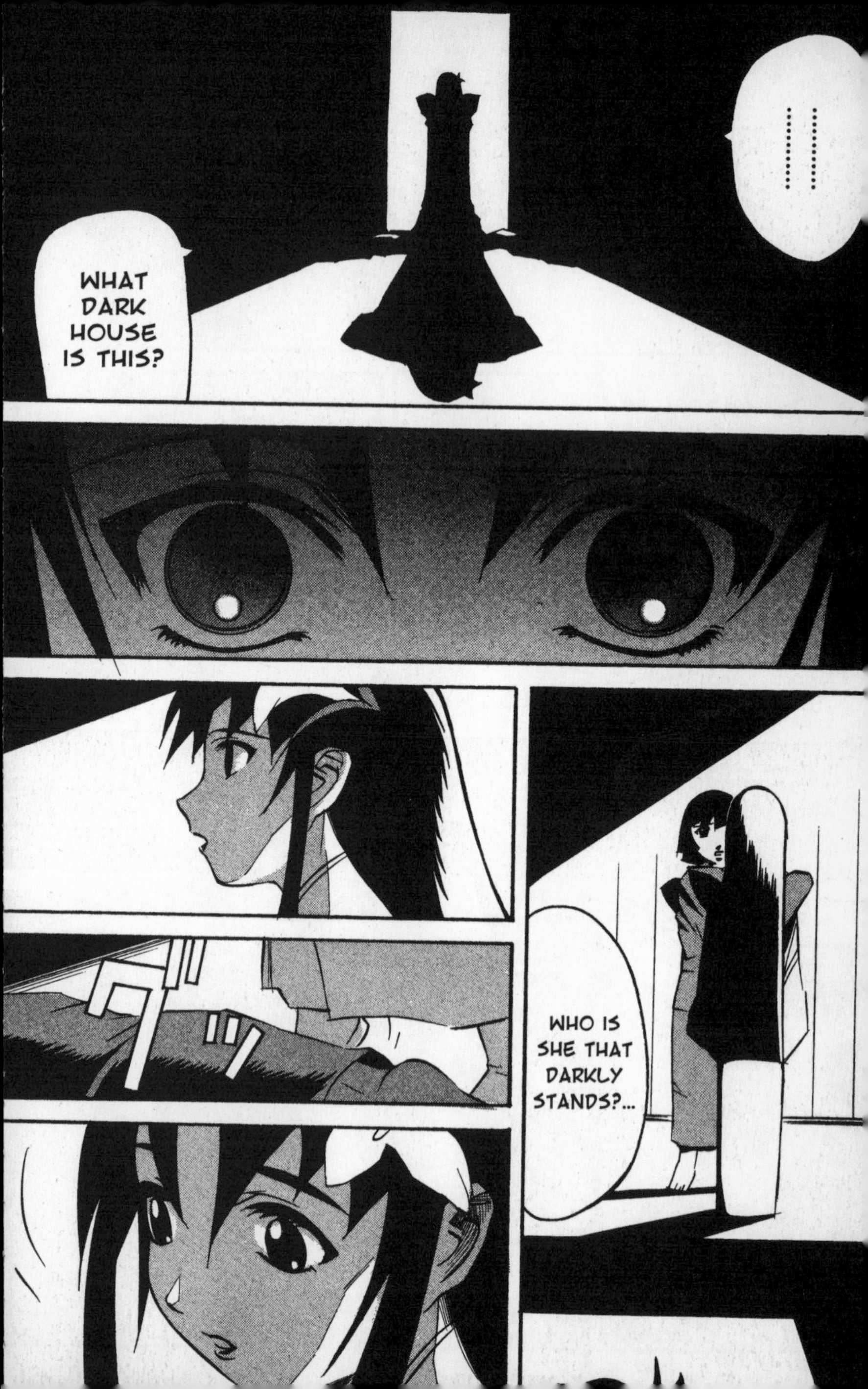
......
WHAT DARK HOUSE IS THIS?
WHO IS SHE THAT DARKLY STANDS?...

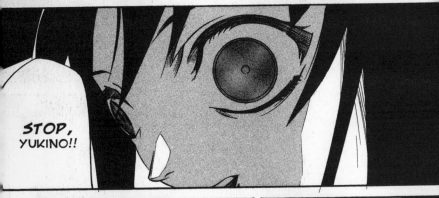

STOP,
YUKINO!!

MY NAME.
MY CLOTHES.
NO.

WHY...
WHY
ARE
YOU
DOING
THIS?

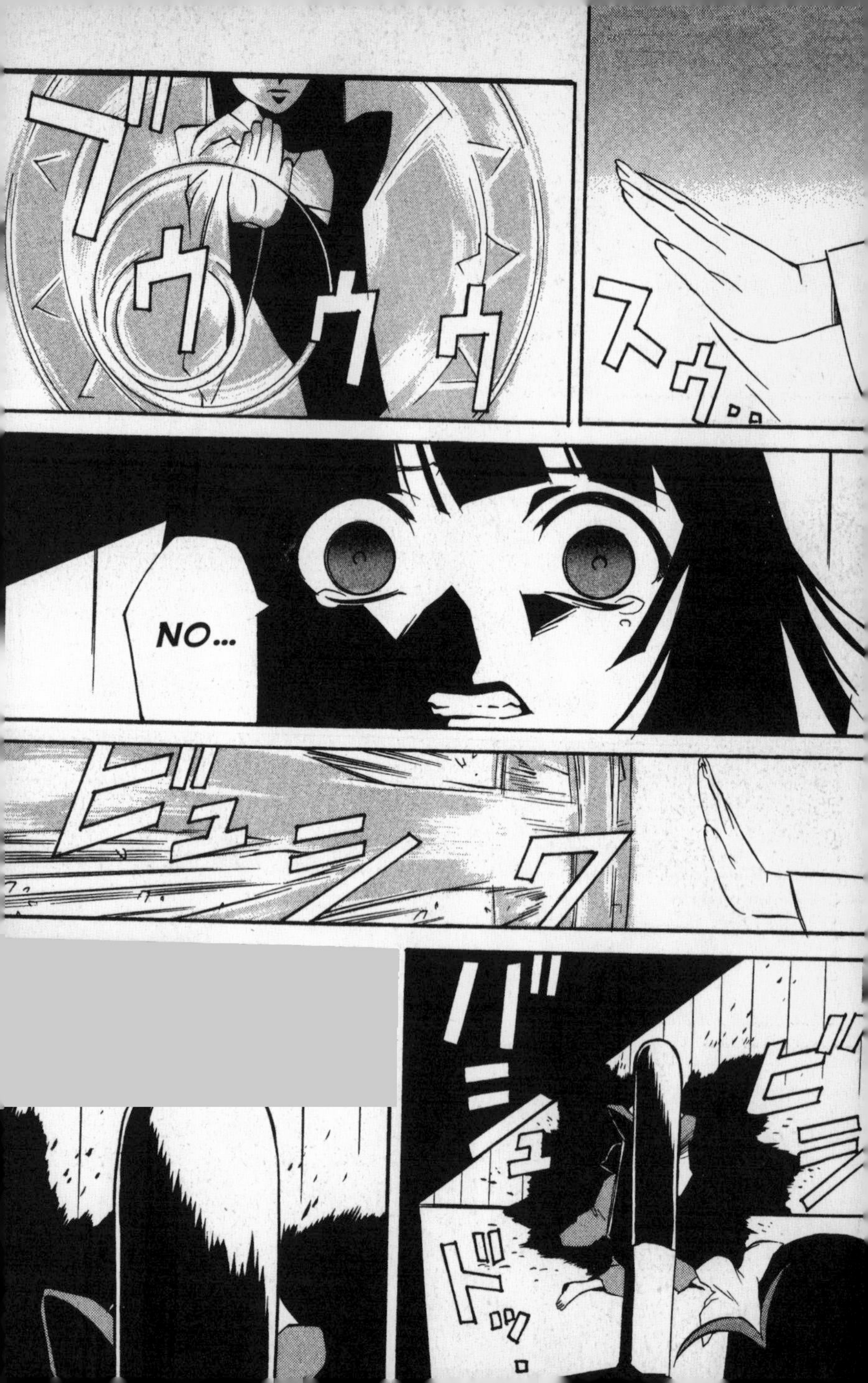
NO...

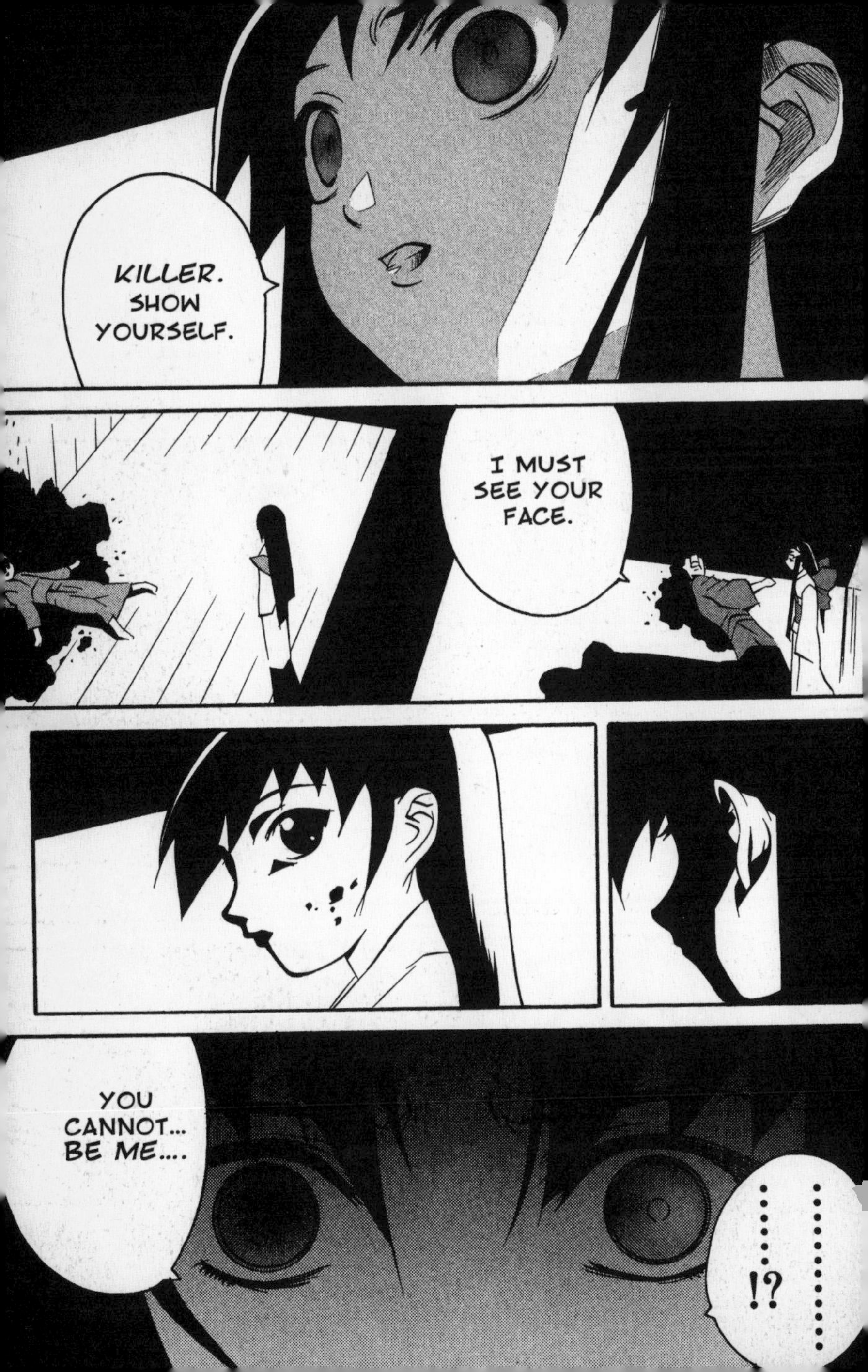
KILLER. SHOW YOURSELF.
I MUST SEE YOUR FACE.
......!?
YOU CANNOT... BE ME....

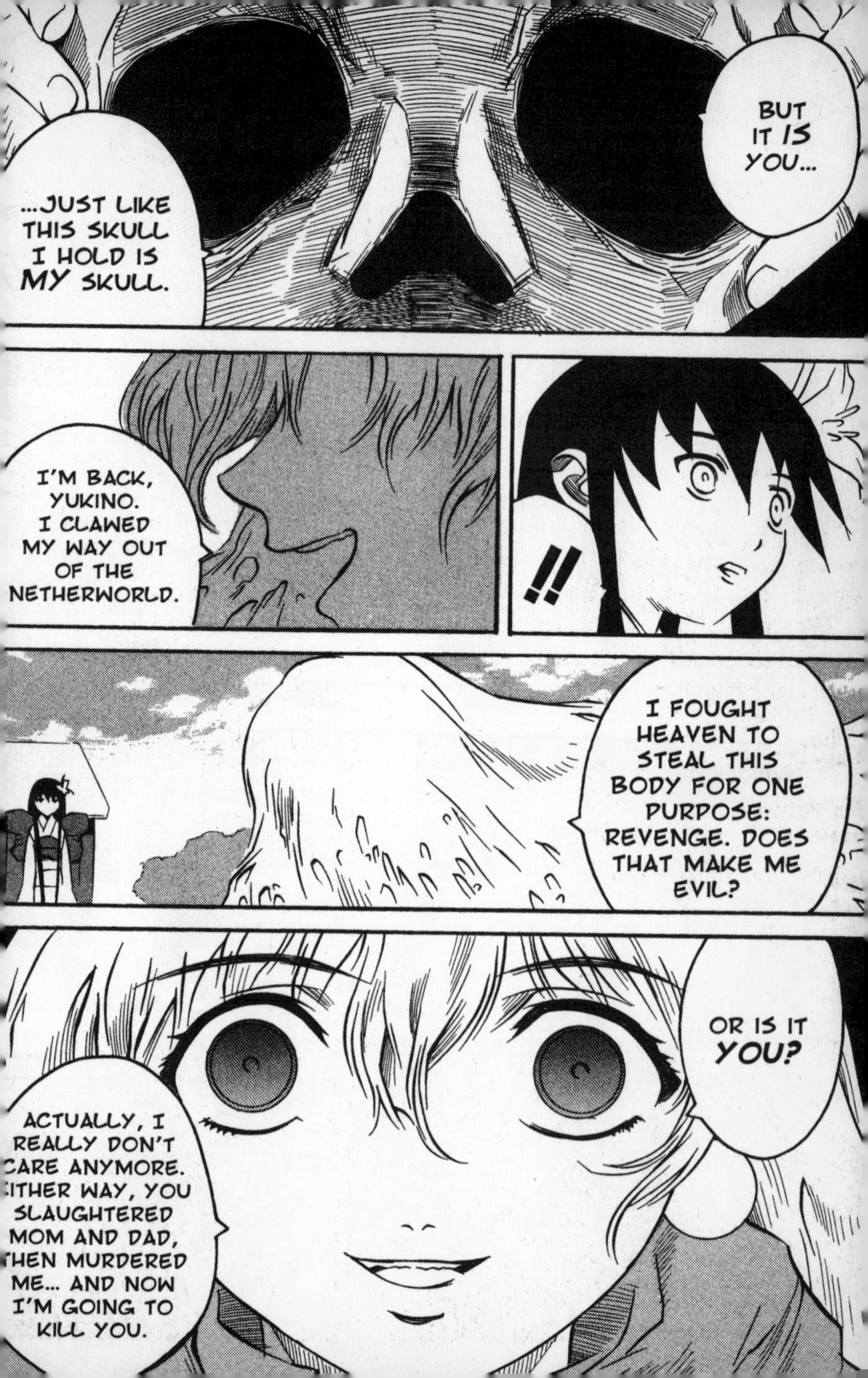
BUT IT IS YOU...
...JUST LIKE THIS SKULL I HOLD IS MY SKULL.
!!
I'M BACK, YUKINO. I CLAWED MY WAY OUT OF THE NETHERWORLD.
I FOUGHT HEAVEN TO STEAL THIS BODY FOR ONE PURPOSE: REVENGE. DOES THAT MAKE ME EVIL?
OR IS IT YOU?
ACTUALLY, I REALLY DON'T CARE ANYMORE. EITHER WAY, YOU SLAUGHTERED MOM AND DAD, THEN MURDERED ME... AND NOW I'M GOING TO KILL YOU.

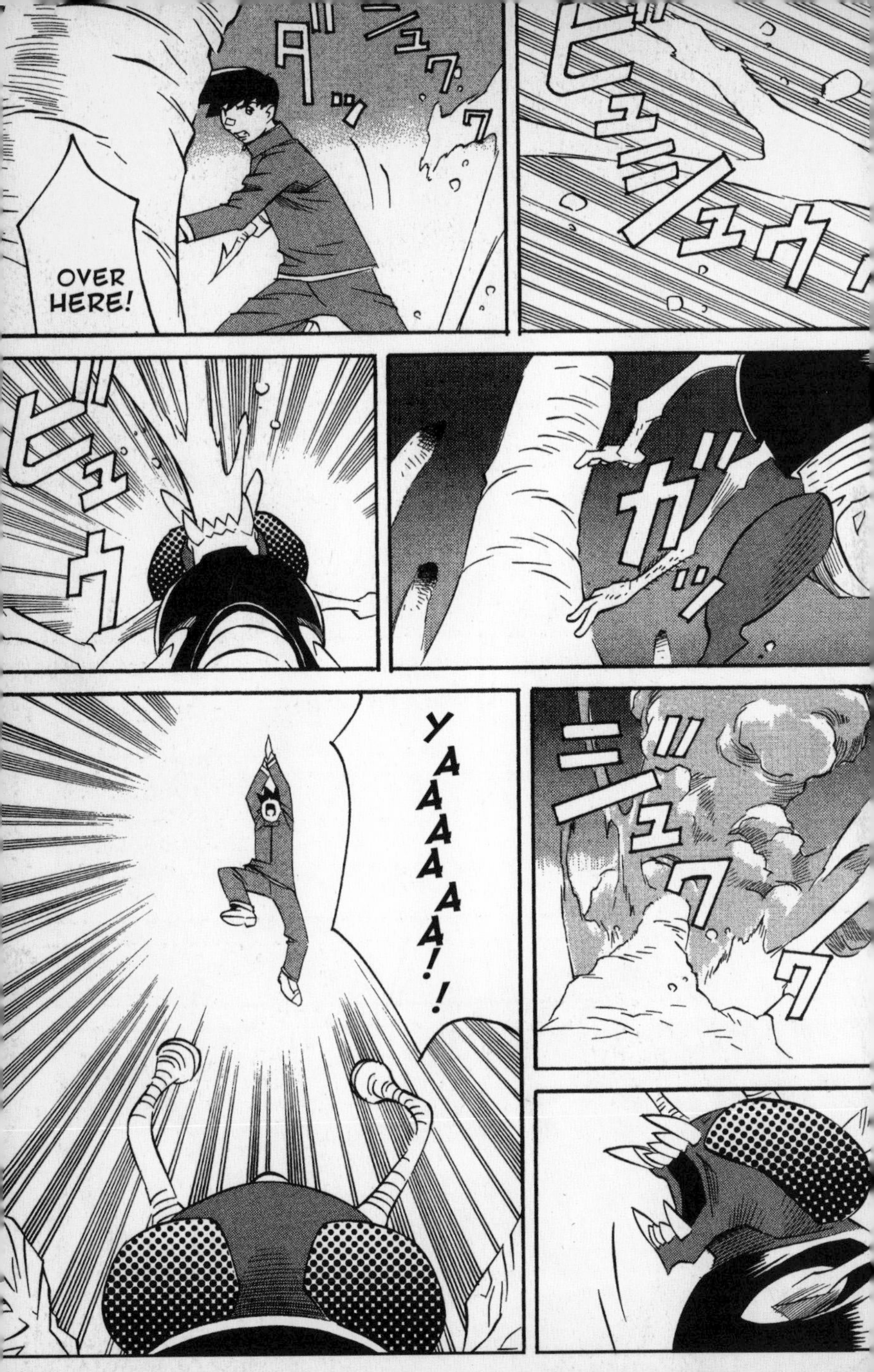
OVER HERE!
YAAAAAA!!

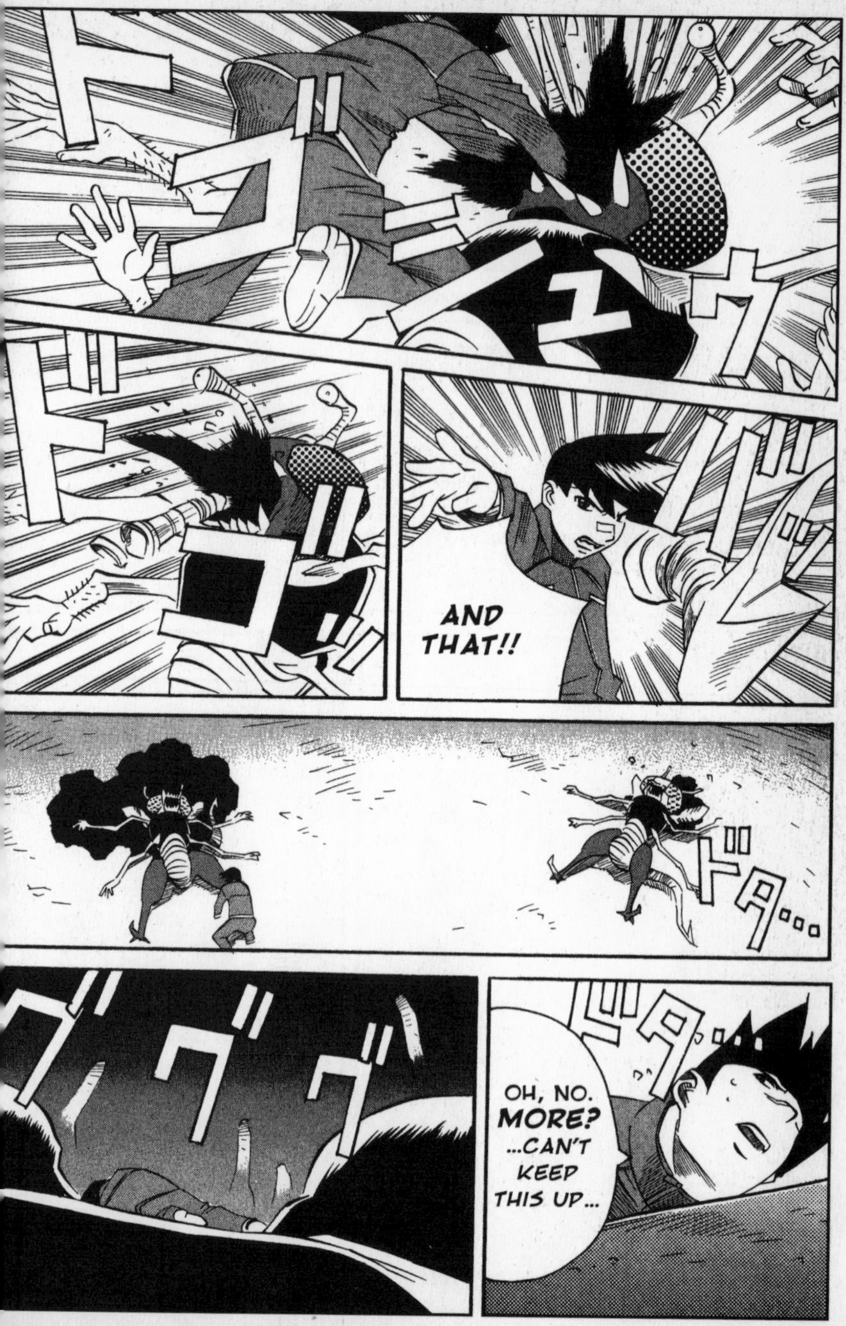
AND THAT!!
OH, NO. MORE? ...CAN'T KEEP THIS UP...

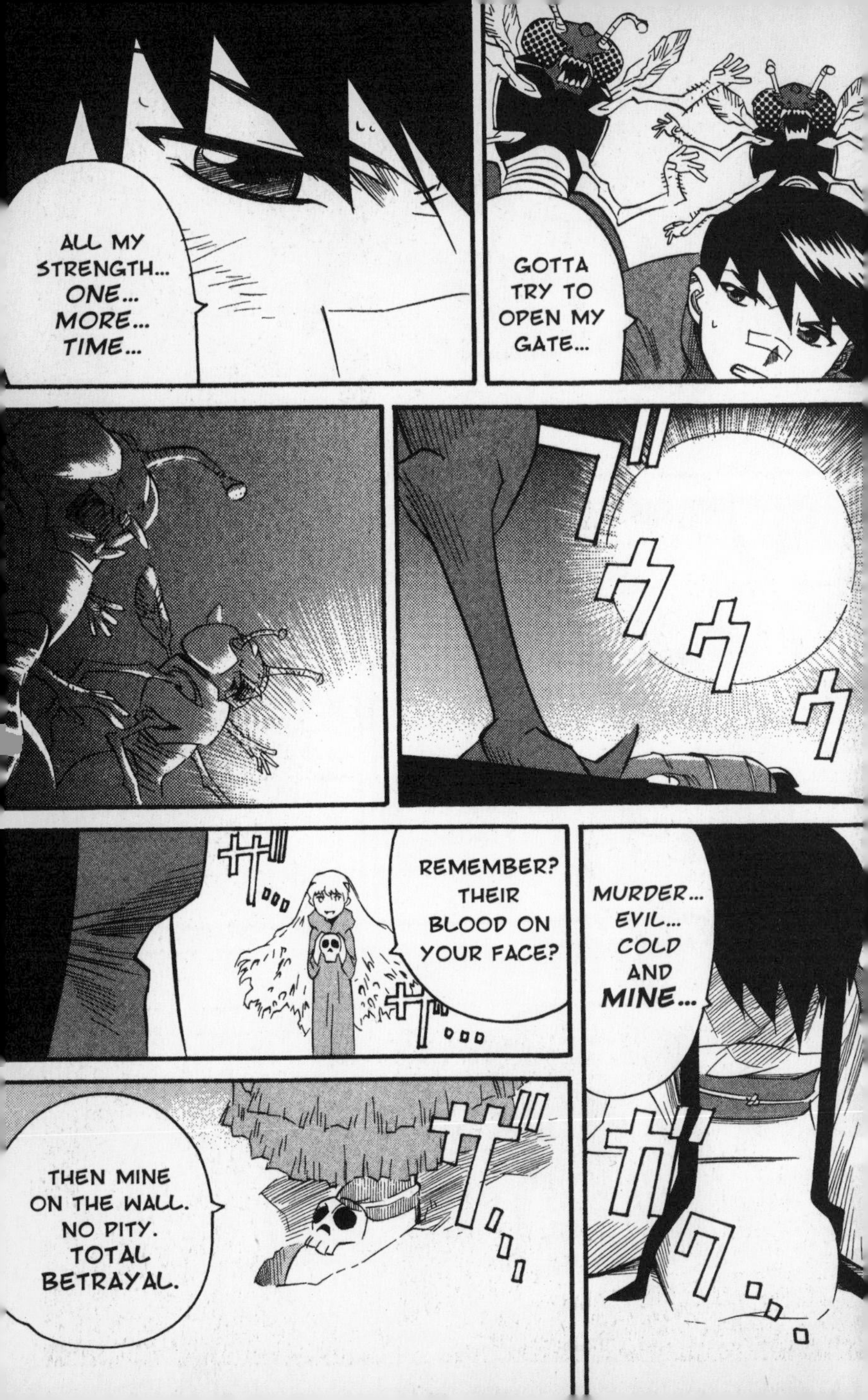
GOTTA TRY TO OPEN MY GATE...
ALL MY STRENGTH... ONE... MORE... TIME...
ブウウウ
MURDER... EVIL... COLD AND **MINE...**
ガク...
ザ...
REMEMBER? THEIR BLOOD ON YOUR FACE?
ザ...
ザ...
THEN MINE ON THE WALL. NO PITY. TOTAL BETRAYAL.

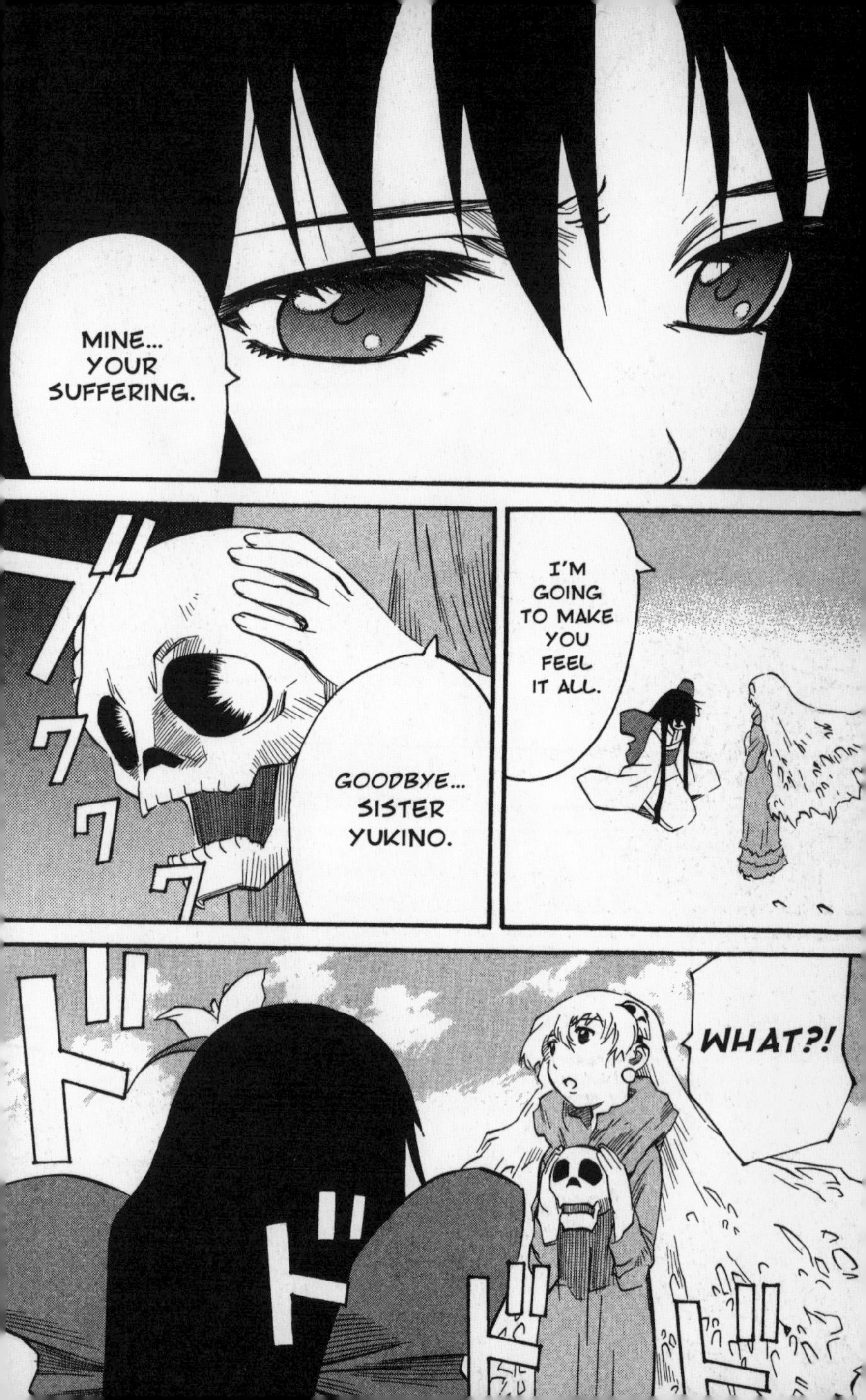
MINE... YOUR SUFFERING.
I'M GOING TO MAKE YOU FEEL IT ALL.
GOODBYE... SISTER YUKINO.
WHAT?!

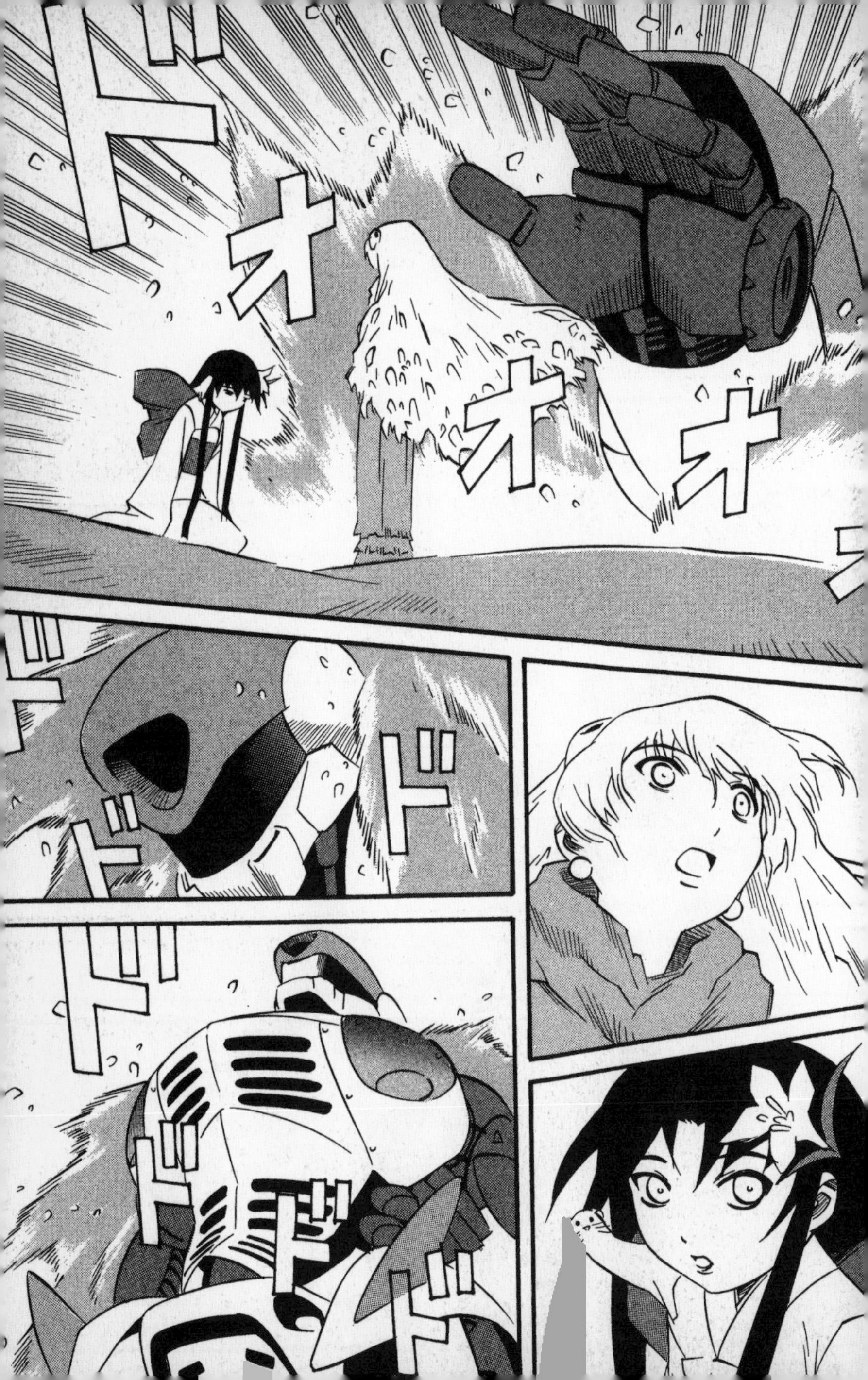
ドオオオ
ドドド
ドドドドド

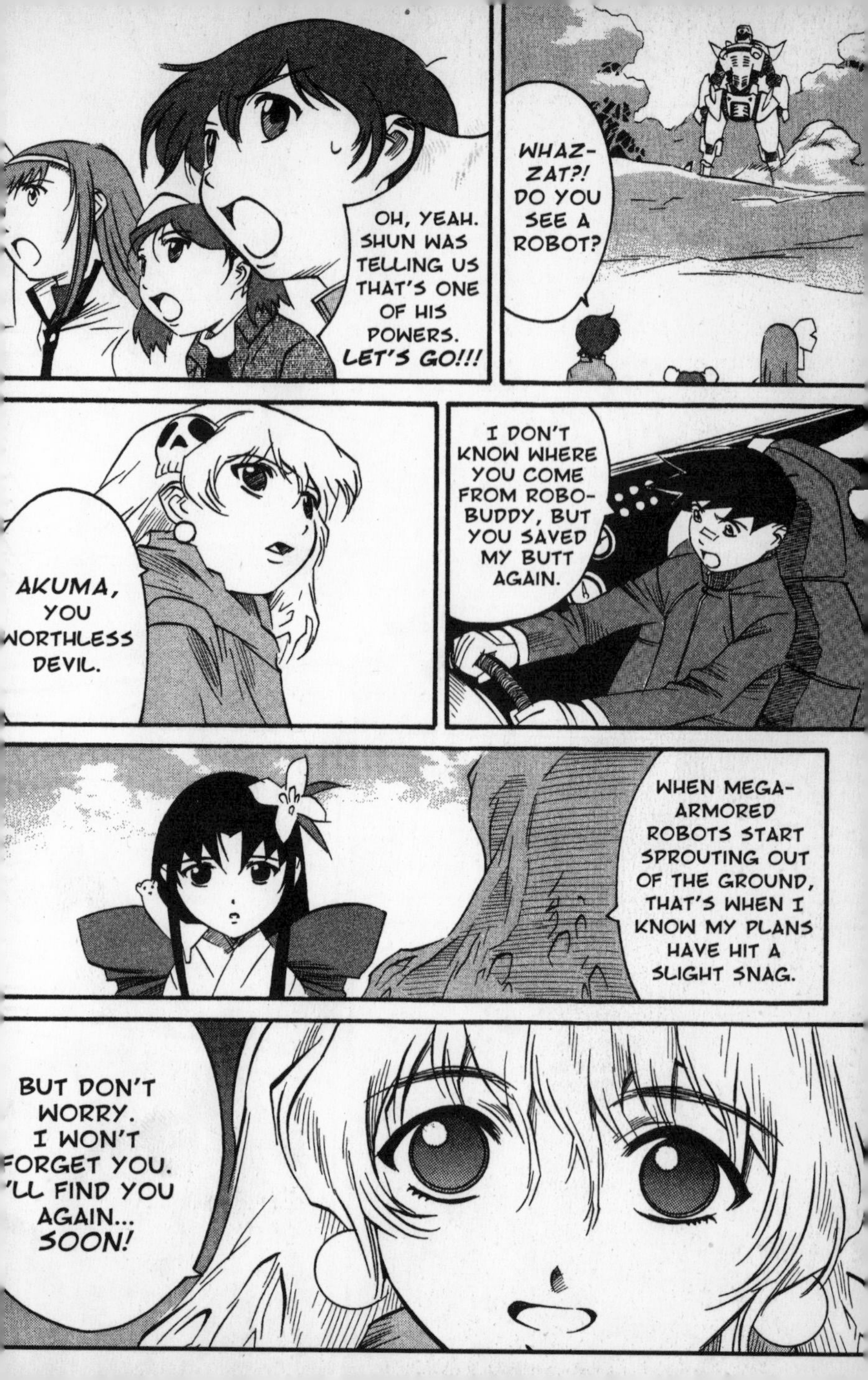
WHAZ-ZAT?! DO YOU SEE A ROBOT?
OH, YEAH. SHUN WAS TELLING US THAT'S ONE OF HIS POWERS. LET'S GO!!!
I DON'T KNOW WHERE YOU COME FROM ROBO-BUDDY, BUT YOU SAVED MY BUTT AGAIN.
AKUMA, YOU WORTHLESS DEVIL.
WHEN MEGA-ARMORED ROBOTS START SPROUTING OUT OF THE GROUND, THAT'S WHEN I KNOW MY PLANS HAVE HIT A SLIGHT SNAG.
BUT DON'T WORRY. I WON'T FORGET YOU. I'LL FIND YOU AGAIN... SOON!

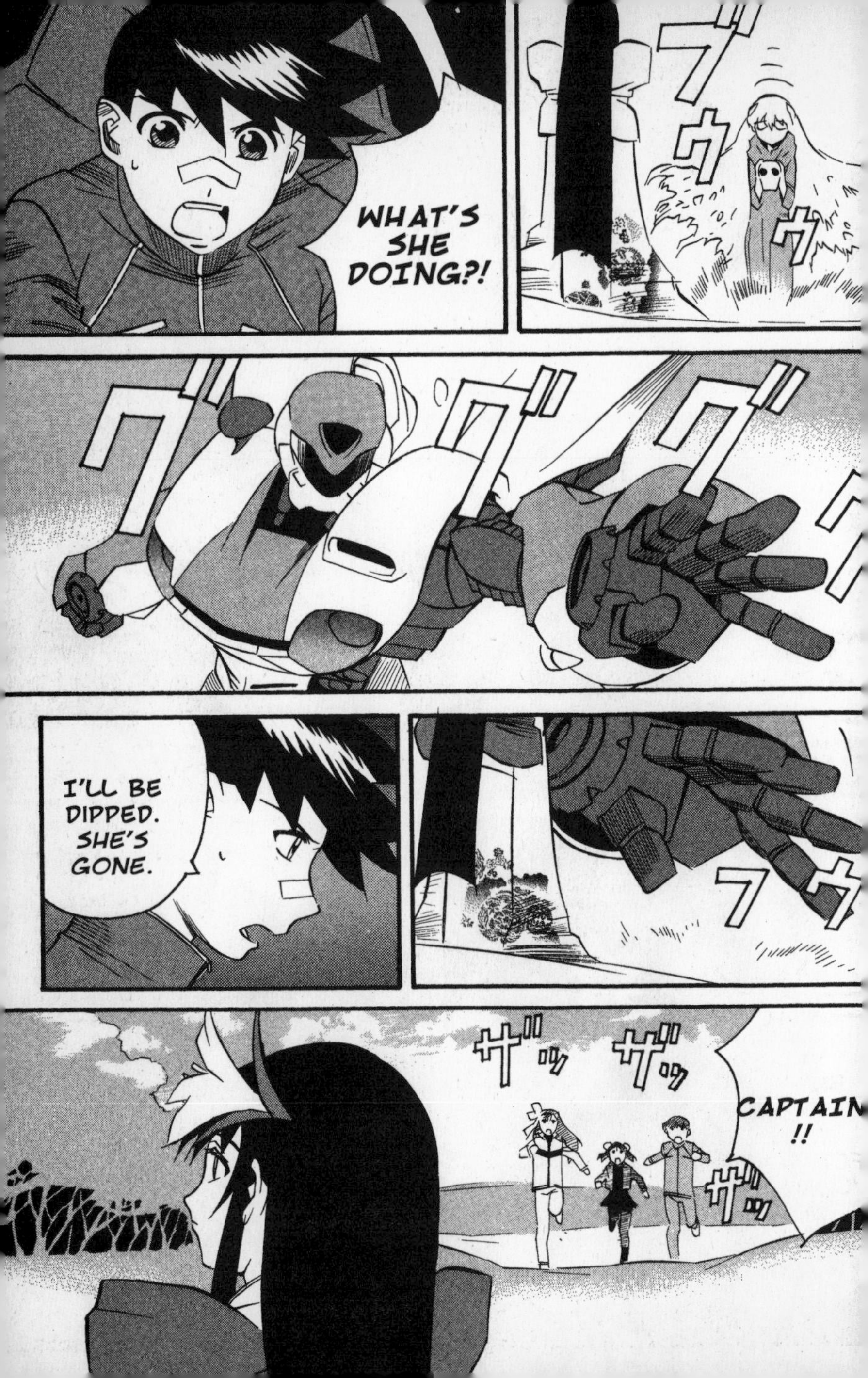
WHAT'S SHE DOING?!
I'LL BE DIPPED. SHE'S GONE.
CAPTAIN !!

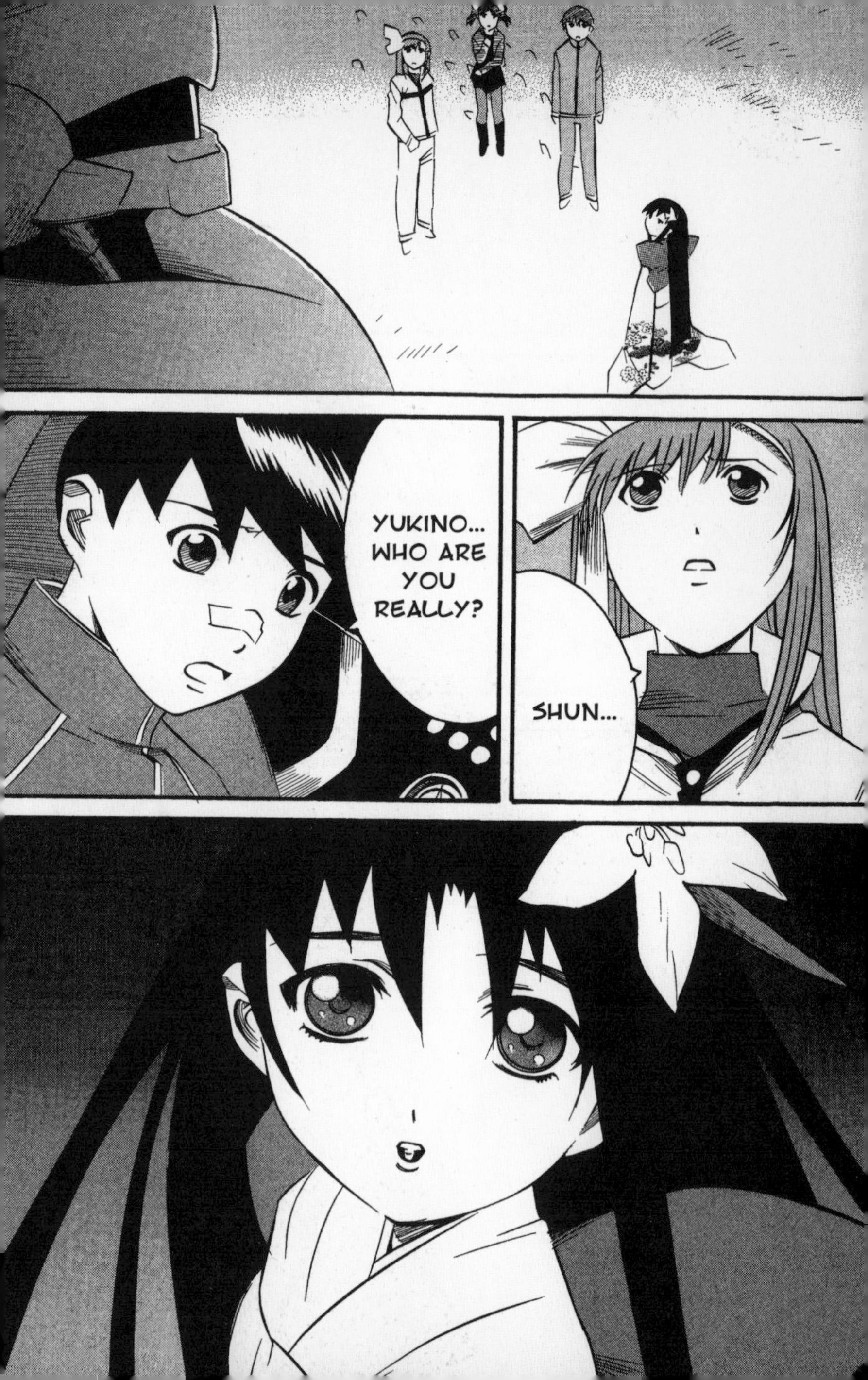
SHUN...
YUKINO... WHO ARE YOU REALLY?

GATE #12

THE PRINCESS AND THE WITCH

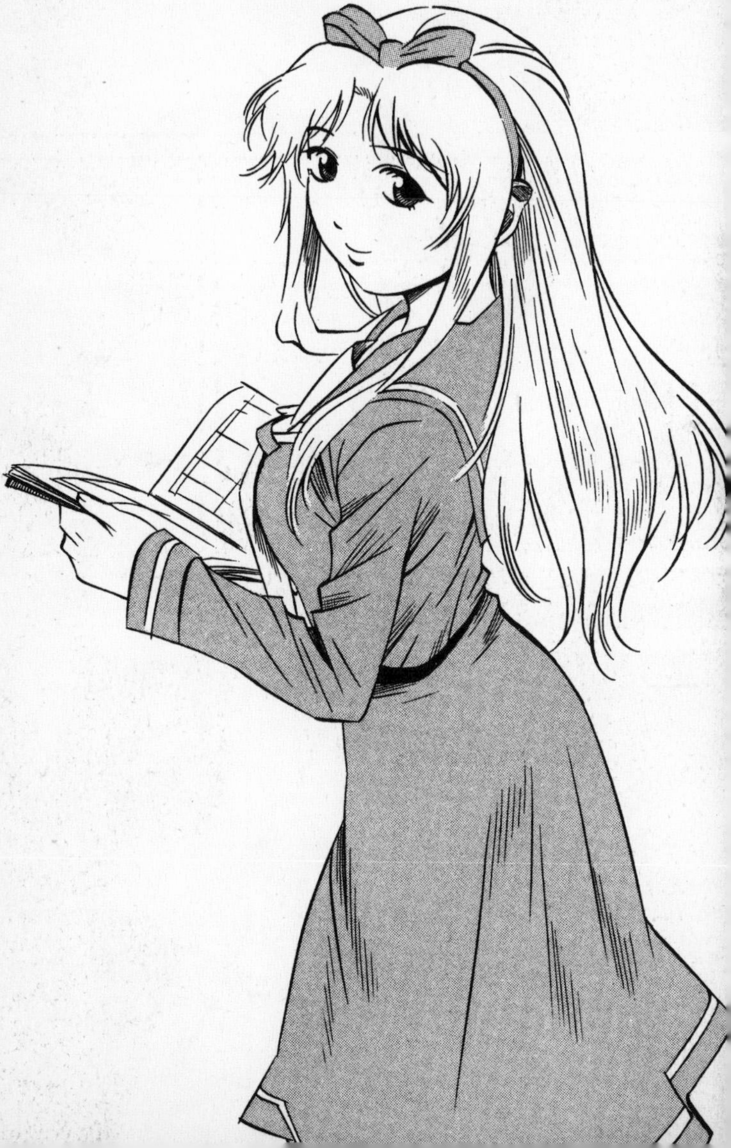

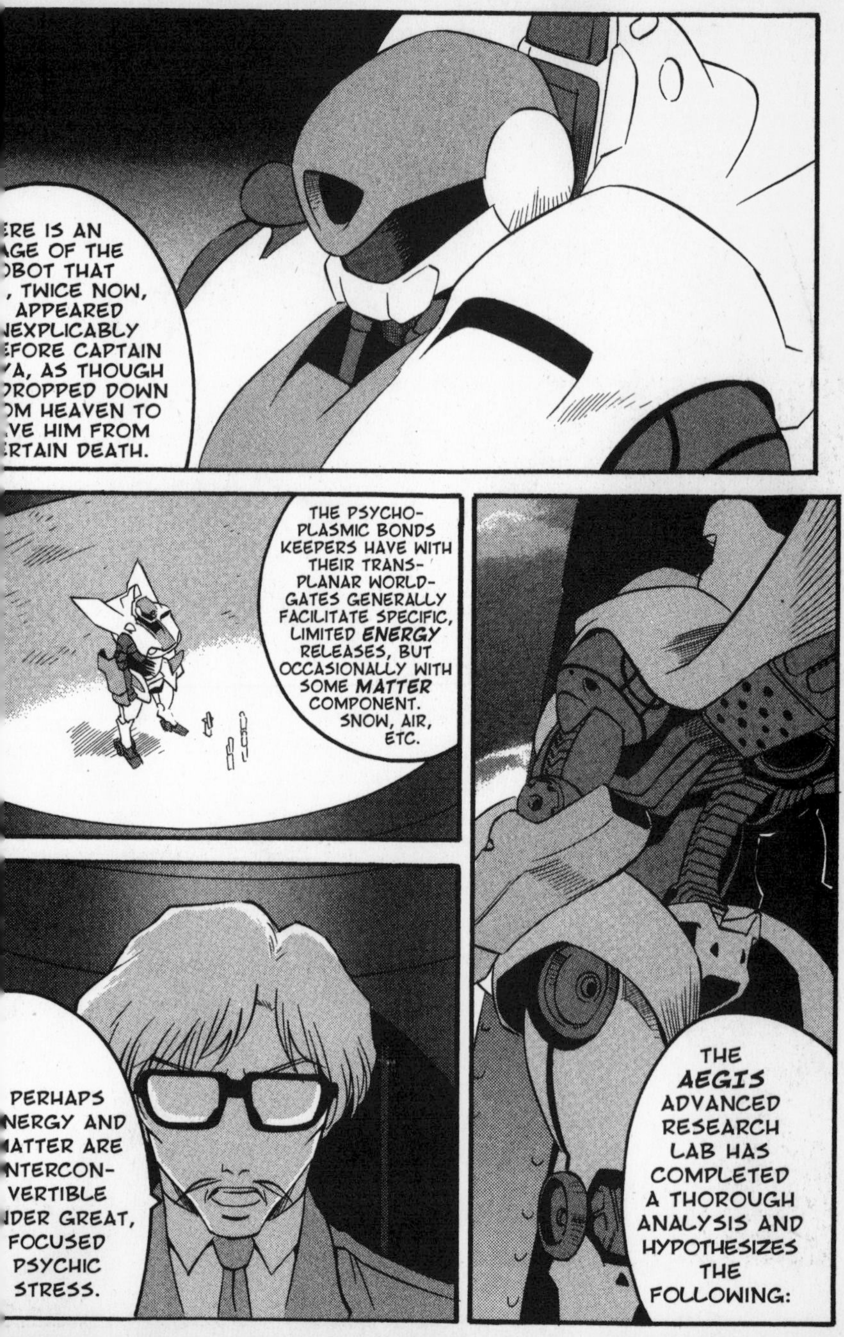
ERE IS AN AGE OF THE OBOT THAT , TWICE NOW, APPEARED NEXPLICABLY EFORE CAPTAIN YA, AS THOUGH DROPPED DOWN OM HEAVEN TO VE HIM FROM RTAIN DEATH.
THE AEGIS ADVANCED RESEARCH LAB HAS COMPLETED A THOROUGH ANALYSIS AND HYPOTHESIZES THE FOLLOWING:
THE PSYCHO-PLASMIC BONDS KEEPERS HAVE WITH THEIR TRANS-PLANAR WORLD-GATES GENERALLY FACILITATE SPECIFIC, LIMITED ENERGY RELEASES, BUT OCCASIONALLY WITH SOME MATTER COMPONENT. SNOW, AIR, ETC.
PERHAPS NERGY AND ATTER ARE NTERCON-VERTIBLE NDER GREAT, FOCUSED PSYCHIC STRESS.

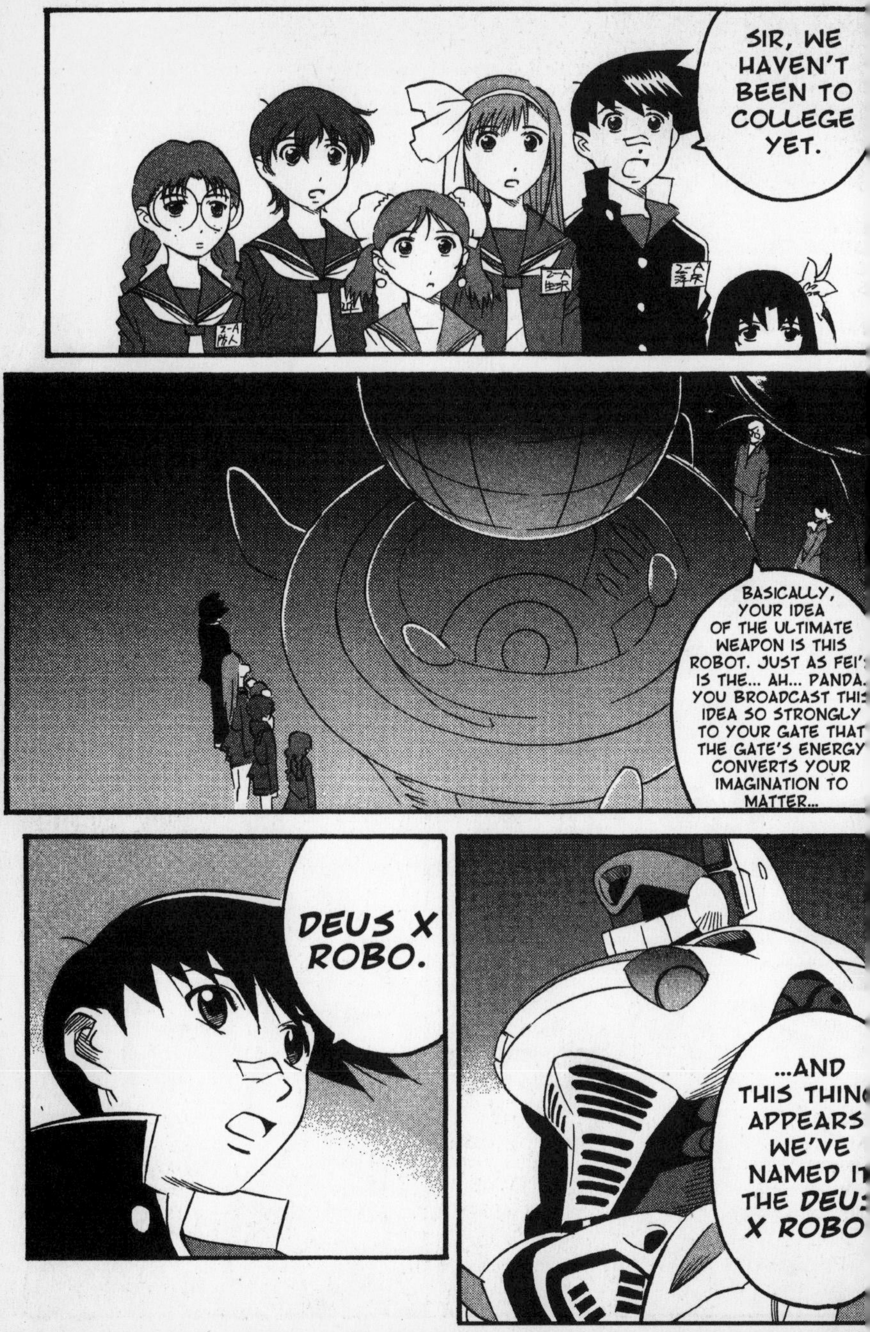
SIR, WE HAVEN'T BEEN TO COLLEGE YET.
BASICALLY, YOUR IDEA OF THE ULTIMATE WEAPON IS THIS ROBOT. JUST AS FEI' IS THE... AH... PANDA. YOU BROADCAST THI IDEA SO STRONGLY TO YOUR GATE THAT THE GATE'S ENERGY CONVERTS YOUR IMAGINATION TO MATTER...
...AND THIS THIN APPEARS WE'VE NAMED IT THE DEU X ROBO
DEUS X ROBO.

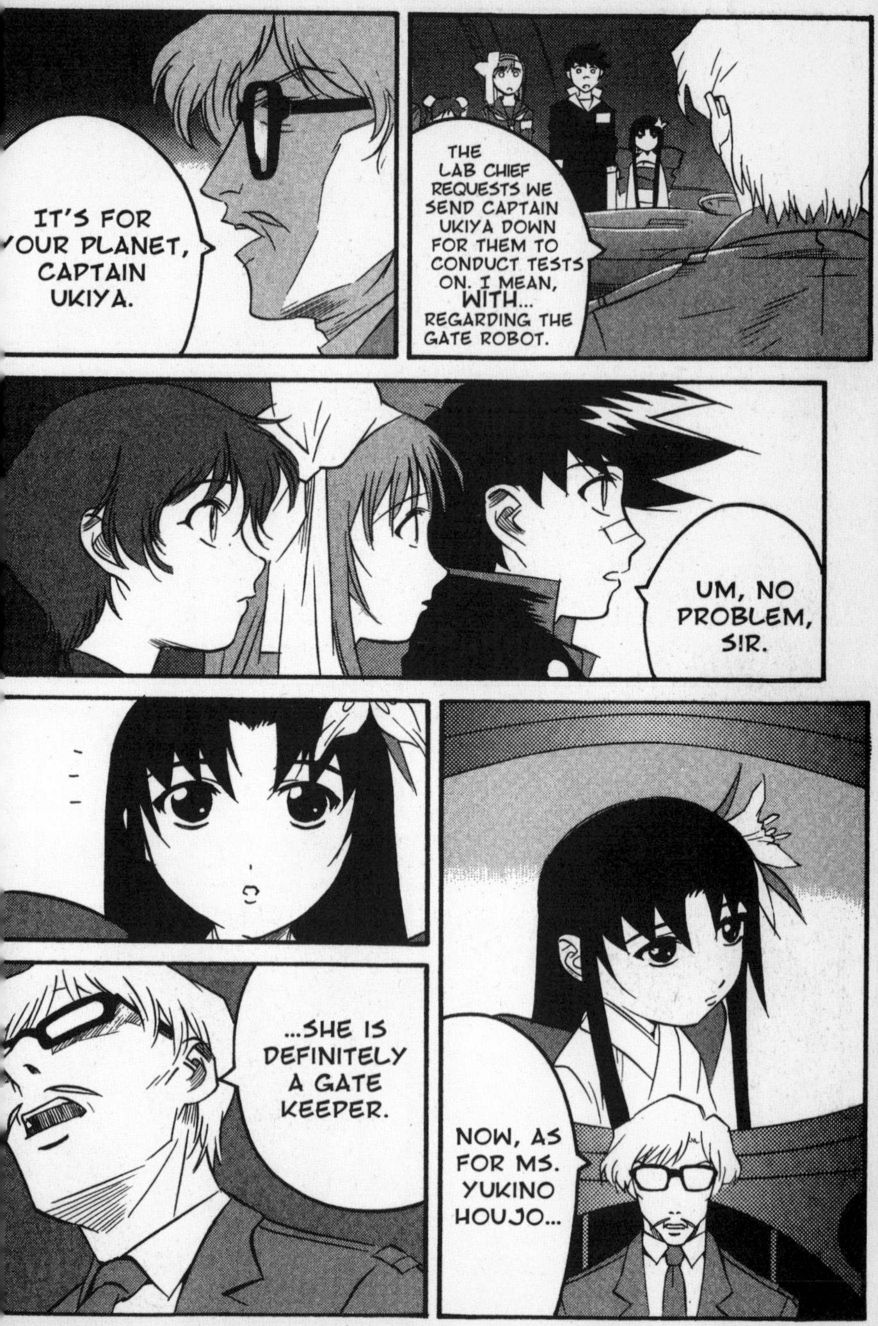
THE LAB CHIEF REQUESTS WE SEND CAPTAIN UKIYA DOWN FOR THEM TO CONDUCT TESTS ON. I MEAN, WITH... REGARDING THE GATE ROBOT.
IT'S FOR YOUR PLANET, CAPTAIN UKIYA.
UM, NO PROBLEM, SIR.
NOW, AS FOR MS. YUKINO HOUJO...
...SHE IS DEFINITELY A GATE KEEPER.

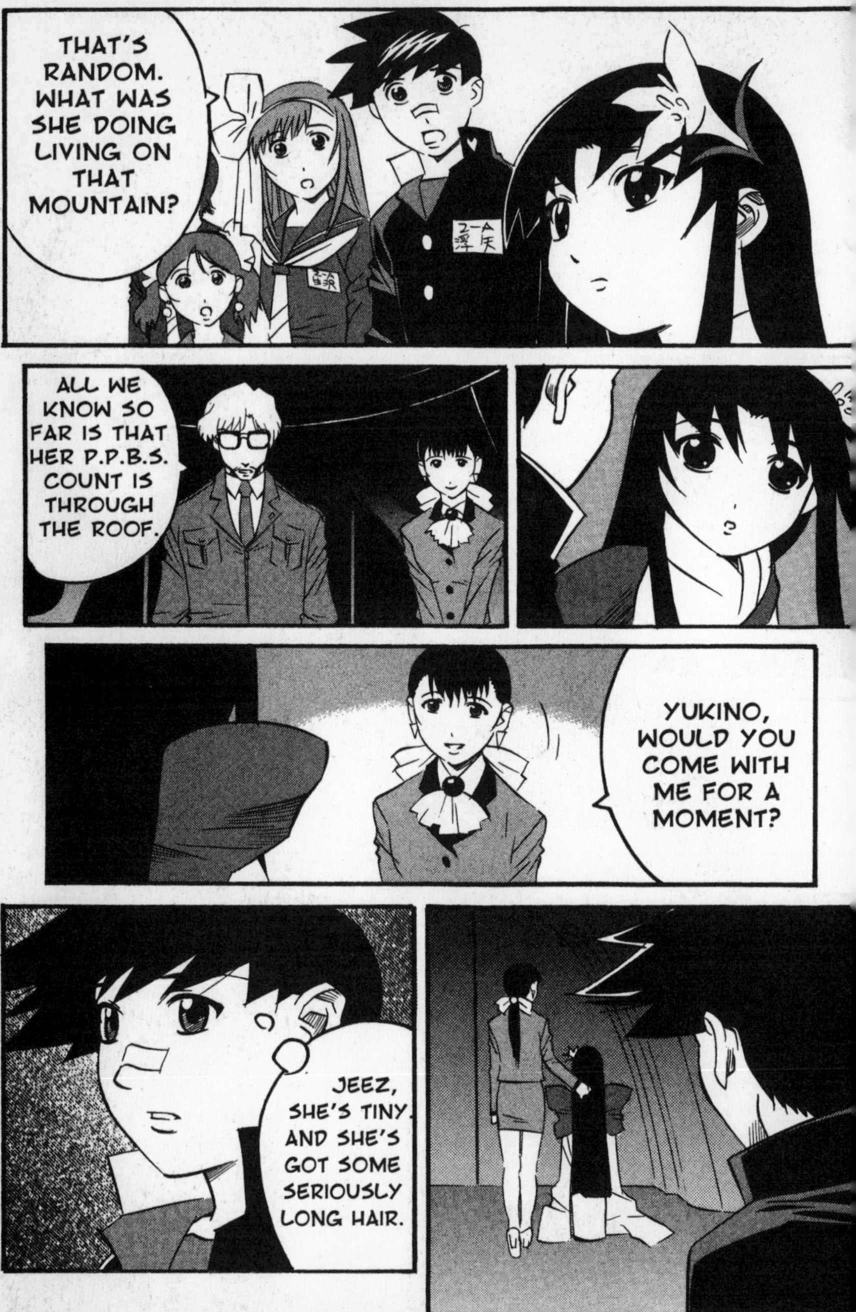
THAT'S RANDOM. WHAT WAS SHE DOING LIVING ON THAT MOUNTAIN?
ALL WE KNOW SO FAR IS THAT HER P.P.B.S. COUNT IS THROUGH THE ROOF.
YUKINO, WOULD YOU COME WITH ME FOR A MOMENT?
JEEZ, SHE'S TINY. AND SHE'S GOT SOME SERIOUSLY LONG HAIR.

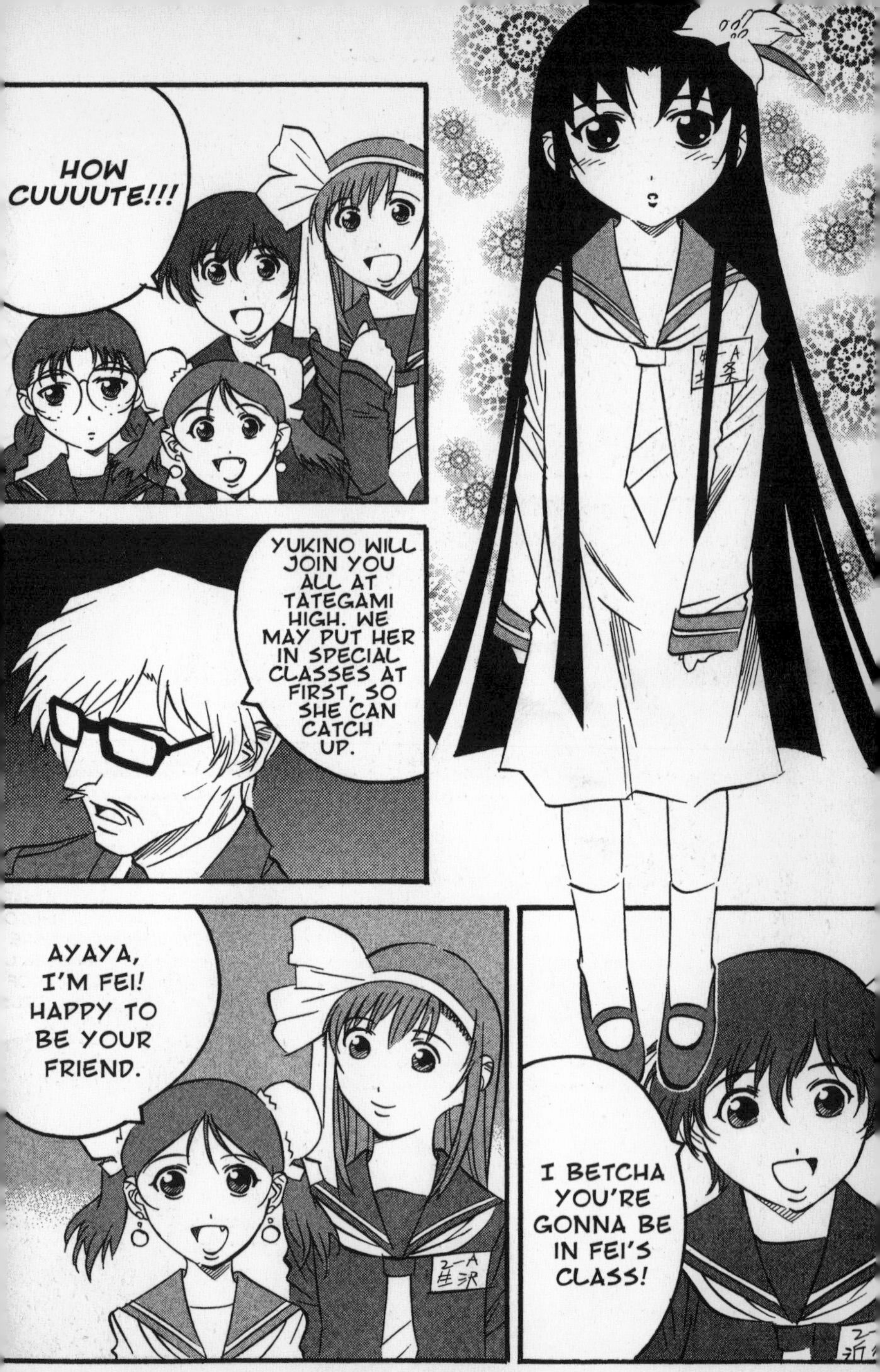
HOW CUUUUTE!!!
YUKINO WILL JOIN YOU ALL AT TATEGAMI HIGH. WE MAY PUT HER IN SPECIAL CLASSES AT FIRST, SO SHE CAN CATCH UP.
I BETCHA YOU'RE GONNA BE IN FEI'S CLASS!
AYAYA, I'M FEI! HAPPY TO BE YOUR FRIEND.

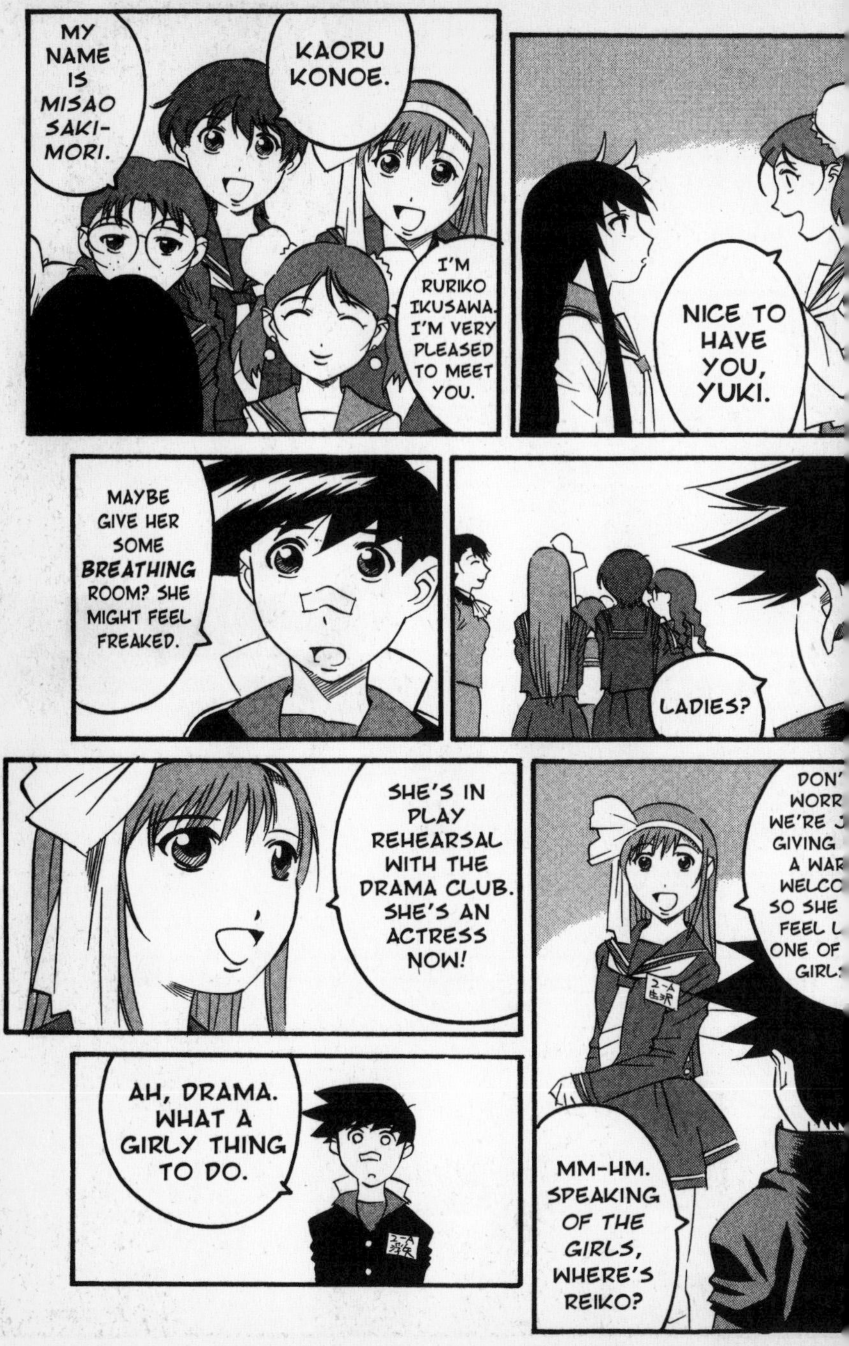
NICE TO HAVE YOU, YUKI.
KAORU KONOE.
MY NAME IS MISAO SAKI-MORI.
I'M RURIKO IKUSAWA. I'M VERY PLEASED TO MEET YOU.
LADIES?
MAYBE GIVE HER SOME BREATHING ROOM? SHE MIGHT FEEL FREAKED.
DON' WORR WE'RE J GIVING A WAR WELCO SO SHE FEEL L ONE OF GIRLS
MM-HM. SPEAKING OF THE GIRLS, WHERE'S REIKO?
SHE'S IN PLAY REHEARSAL WITH THE DRAMA CLUB. SHE'S AN ACTRESS NOW!
AH, DRAMA. WHAT A GIRLY THING TO DO.

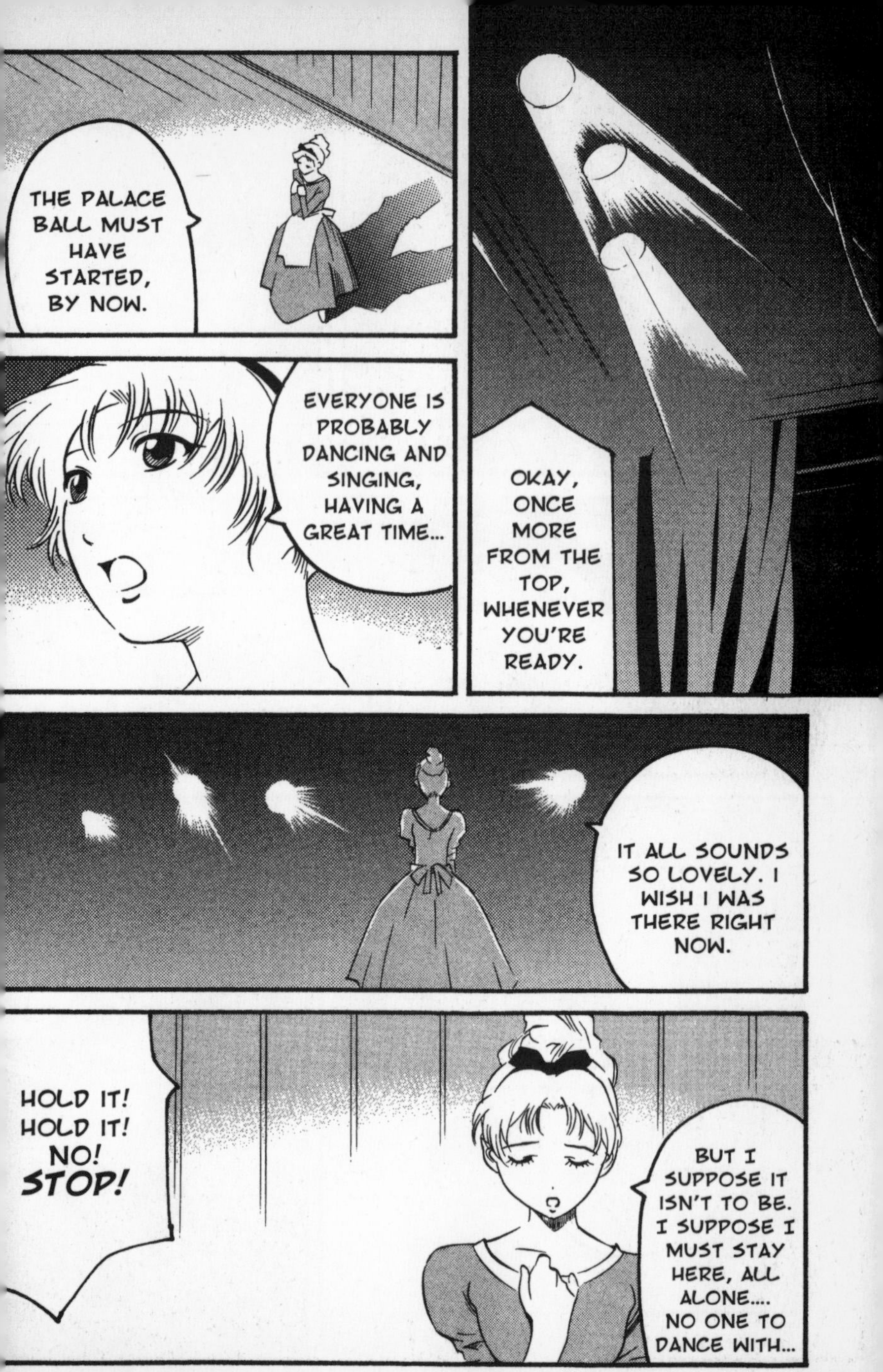
OKAY, ONCE MORE FROM THE TOP, WHENEVER YOU'RE READY.
THE PALACE BALL MUST HAVE STARTED, BY NOW.
EVERYONE IS PROBABLY DANCING AND SINGING, HAVING A GREAT TIME...
IT ALL SOUNDS SO LOVELY. I WISH I WAS THERE RIGHT NOW.
BUT I SUPPOSE IT ISN'T TO BE. I SUPPOSE I MUST STAY HERE, ALL ALONE.... NO ONE TO DANCE WITH...
HOLD IT! HOLD IT! NO! STOP!

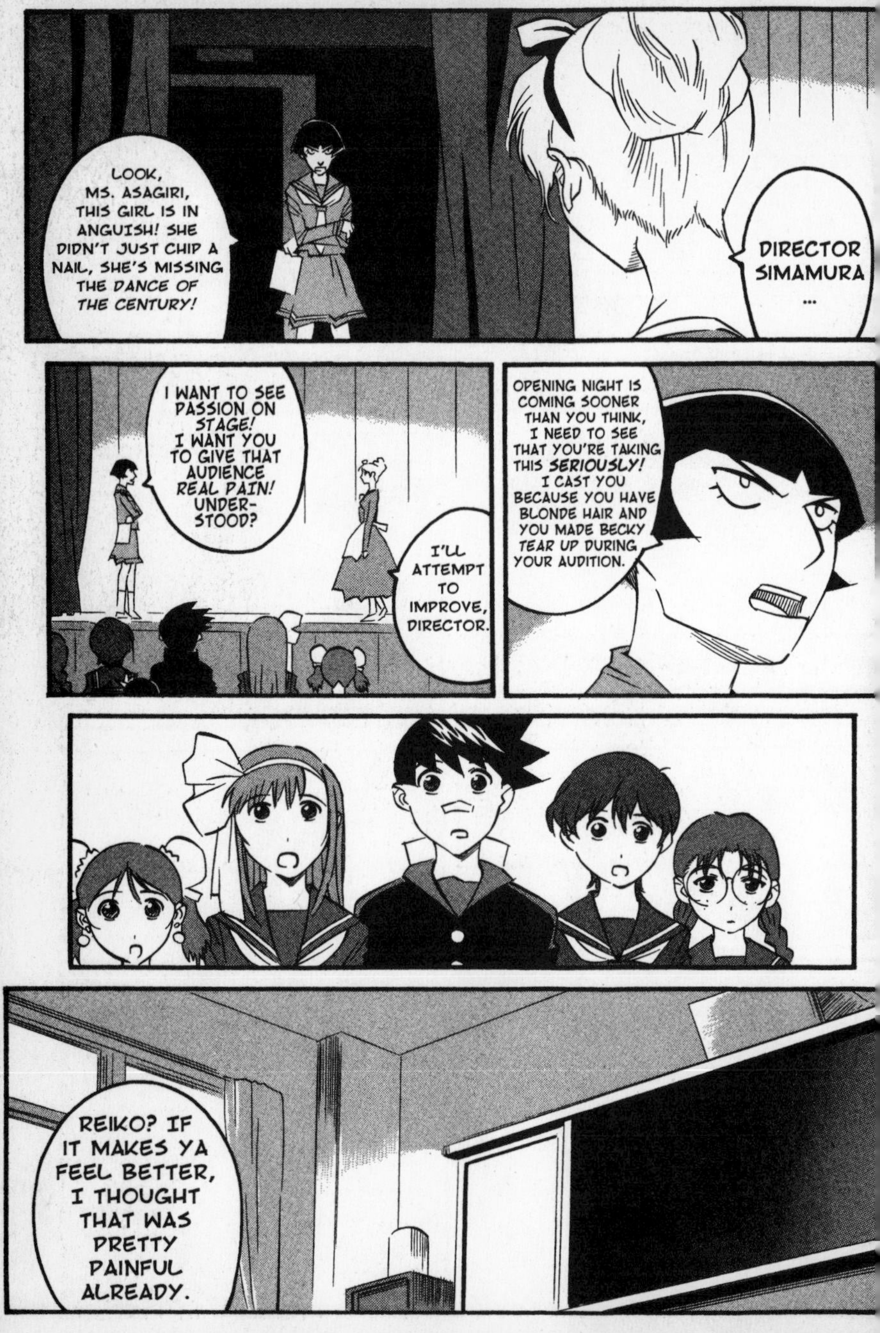
DIRECTOR SIMAMURA ...
LOOK, MS. ASAGIRI, THIS GIRL IS IN ANGUISH! SHE DIDN'T JUST CHIP A NAIL, SHE'S MISSING THE DANCE OF THE CENTURY!
OPENING NIGHT IS COMING SOONER THAN YOU THINK, I NEED TO SEE THAT YOU'RE TAKING THIS SERIOUSLY! I CAST YOU BECAUSE YOU HAVE BLONDE HAIR AND YOU MADE BECKY TEAR UP DURING YOUR AUDITION.
I WANT TO SEE PASSION ON STAGE! I WANT YOU TO GIVE THAT AUDIENCE REAL PAIN! UNDER-STOOD?
I'LL ATTEMPT TO IMPROVE, DIRECTOR.
REIKO? IF IT MAKES YA FEEL BETTER, I THOUGHT THAT WAS PRETTY PAINFUL ALREADY.

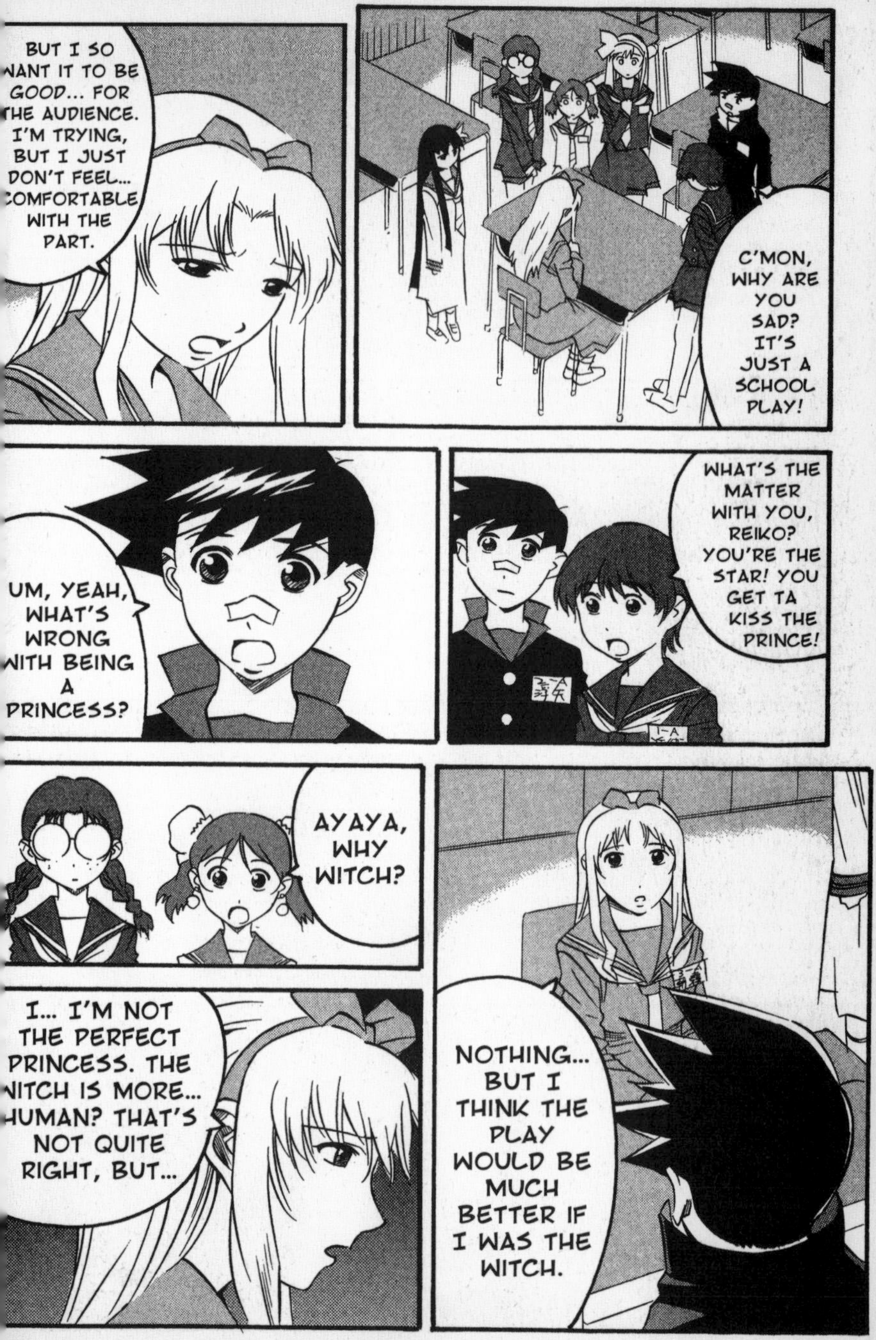
C'MON, WHY ARE YOU SAD? IT'S JUST A SCHOOL PLAY!
BUT I SO WANT IT TO BE GOOD... FOR THE AUDIENCE. I'M TRYING, BUT I JUST DON'T FEEL... COMFORTABLE WITH THE PART.
WHAT'S THE MATTER WITH YOU, REIKO? YOU'RE THE STAR! YOU GET TA KISS THE PRINCE!
UM, YEAH, WHAT'S WRONG WITH BEING A PRINCESS?
NOTHING... BUT I THINK THE PLAY WOULD BE MUCH BETTER IF I WAS THE WITCH.
AYAYA, WHY WITCH?
I... I'M NOT THE PERFECT PRINCESS. THE WITCH IS MORE... HUMAN? THAT'S NOT QUITE RIGHT, BUT...

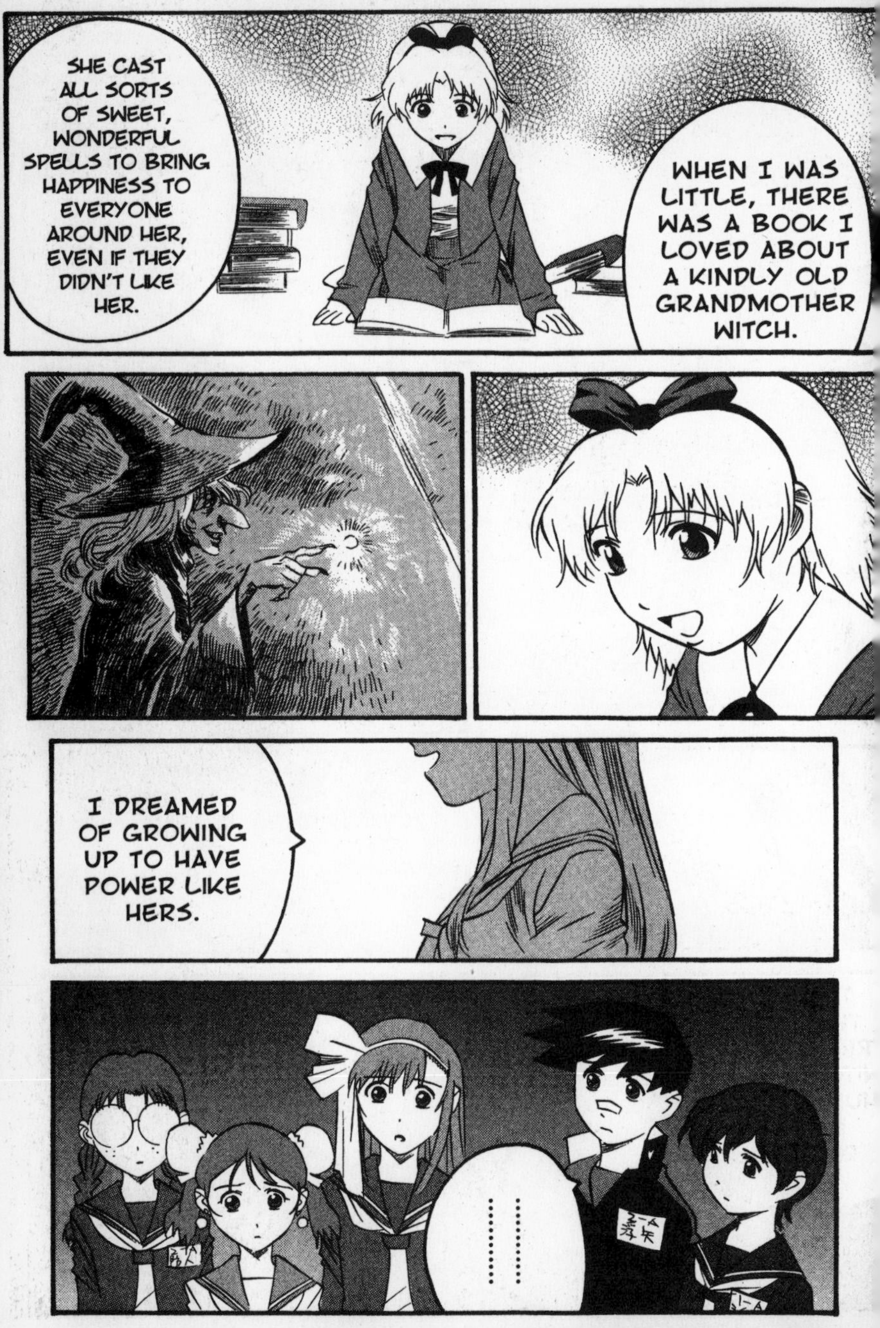
WHEN I WAS LITTLE, THERE WAS A BOOK I LOVED ABOUT A KINDLY OLD GRANDMOTHER WITCH.
SHE CAST ALL SORTS OF SWEET, WONDERFUL SPELLS TO BRING HAPPINESS TO EVERYONE AROUND HER, EVEN IF THEY DIDN'T LIKE HER.
I DREAMED OF GROWING UP TO HAVE POWER LIKE HERS.
......

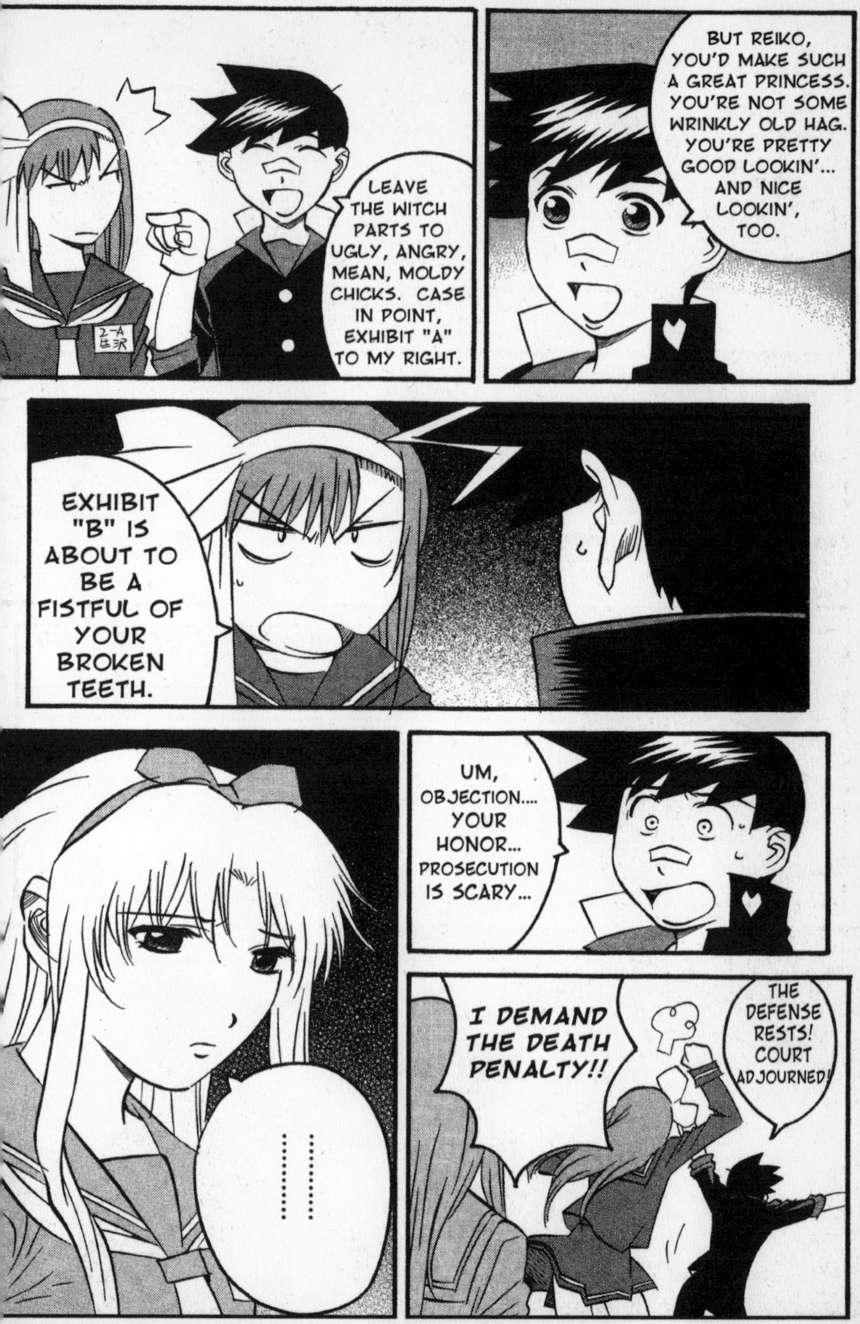
BUT REIKO, YOU'D MAKE SUCH A GREAT PRINCESS. YOU'RE NOT SOME WRINKLY OLD HAG. YOU'RE PRETTY GOOD LOOKIN'... AND NICE LOOKIN', TOO.
LEAVE THE WITCH PARTS TO UGLY, ANGRY, MEAN, MOLDY CHICKS. CASE IN POINT, EXHIBIT "A" TO MY RIGHT.
EXHIBIT "B" IS ABOUT TO BE A FISTFUL OF YOUR BROKEN TEETH.
UM, OBJECTION.... YOUR HONOR... PROSECUTION IS SCARY...
THE DEFENSE RESTS! COURT ADJOURNED!
I DEMAND THE DEATH PENALTY!!
......

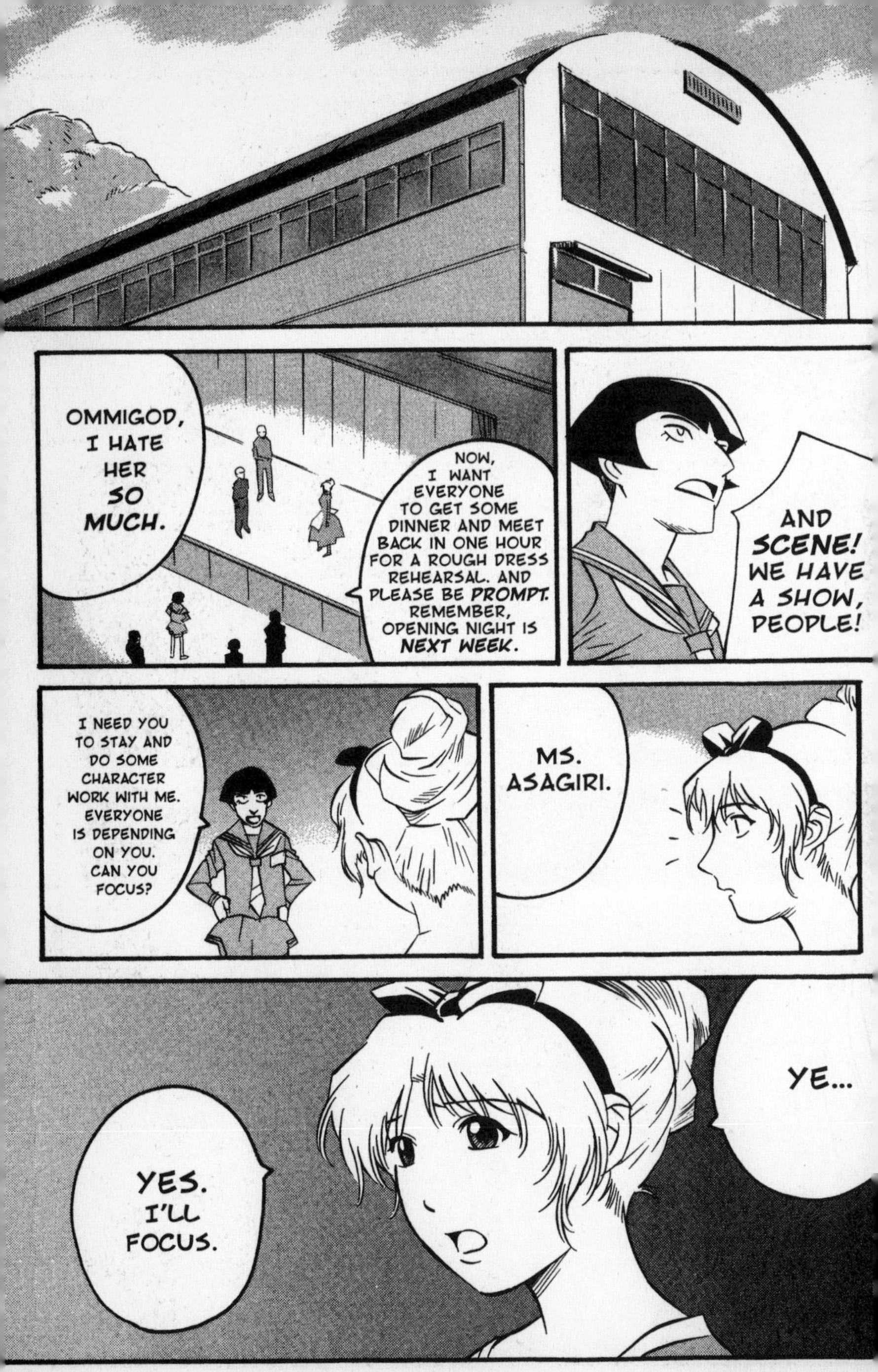
AND SCENE! WE HAVE A SHOW, PEOPLE!
NOW, I WANT EVERYONE TO GET SOME DINNER AND MEET BACK IN ONE HOUR FOR A ROUGH DRESS REHEARSAL. AND PLEASE BE PROMPT. REMEMBER, OPENING NIGHT IS NEXT WEEK.
OMMIGOD, I HATE HER SO MUCH.
MS. ASAGIRI.
I NEED YOU TO STAY AND DO SOME CHARACTER WORK WITH ME. EVERYONE IS DEPENDING ON YOU. CAN YOU FOCUS?
YE...
YES. I'LL FOCUS.

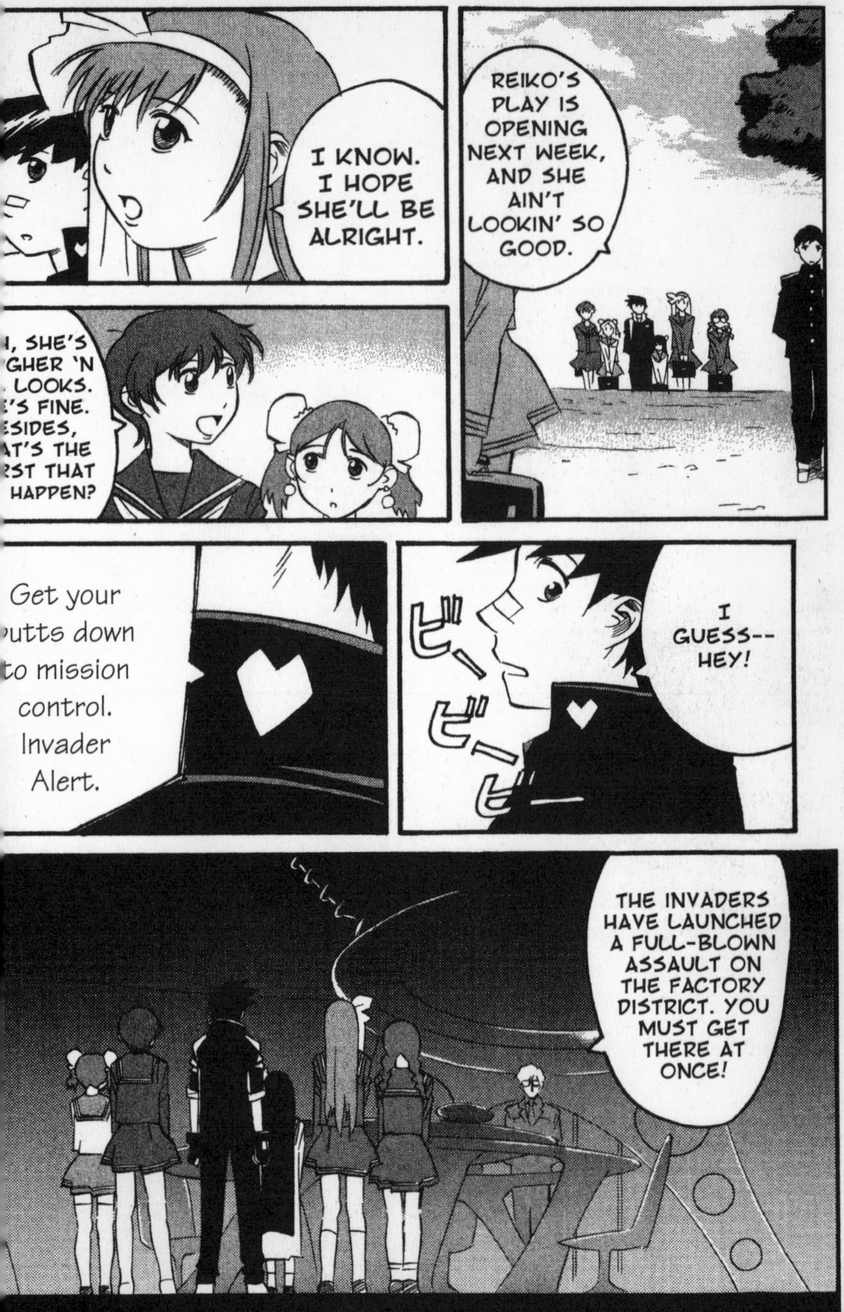
REIKO'S PLAY IS OPENING NEXT WEEK, AND SHE AIN'T LOOKIN' SO GOOD.
I KNOW. I HOPE SHE'LL BE ALRIGHT.
H, SHE'S GHER 'N LOOKS. 'S FINE. ESIDES, AT'S THE RST THAT HAPPEN?
I GUESS-- HEY!
ビー
ビー
ビ
Get your utts down to mission control. Invader Alert.
THE INVADERS HAVE LAUNCHED A FULL-BLOWN ASSAULT ON THE FACTORY DISTRICT. YOU MUST GET THERE AT ONCE!

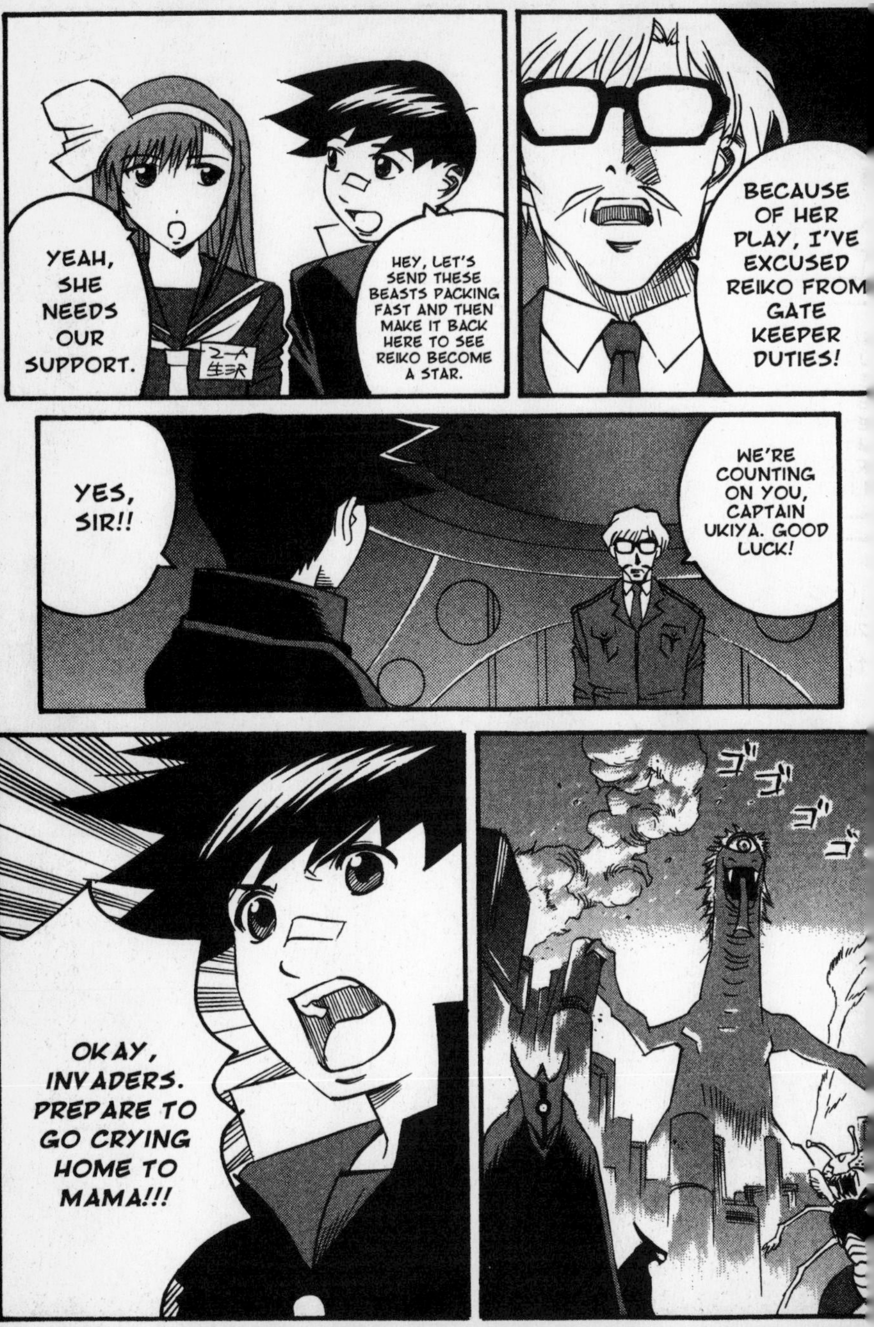
BECAUSE OF HER PLAY, I'VE EXCUSED REIKO FROM GATE KEEPER DUTIES!
HEY, LET'S SEND THESE BEASTS PACKING FAST AND THEN MAKE IT BACK HERE TO SEE REIKO BECOME A STAR.
YEAH, SHE NEEDS OUR SUPPORT.
WE'RE COUNTING ON YOU, CAPTAIN UKIYA. GOOD LUCK!
YES, SIR!!
ゴゴゴゴ
OKAY, INVADERS. PREPARE TO GO CRYING HOME TO MAMA!!!

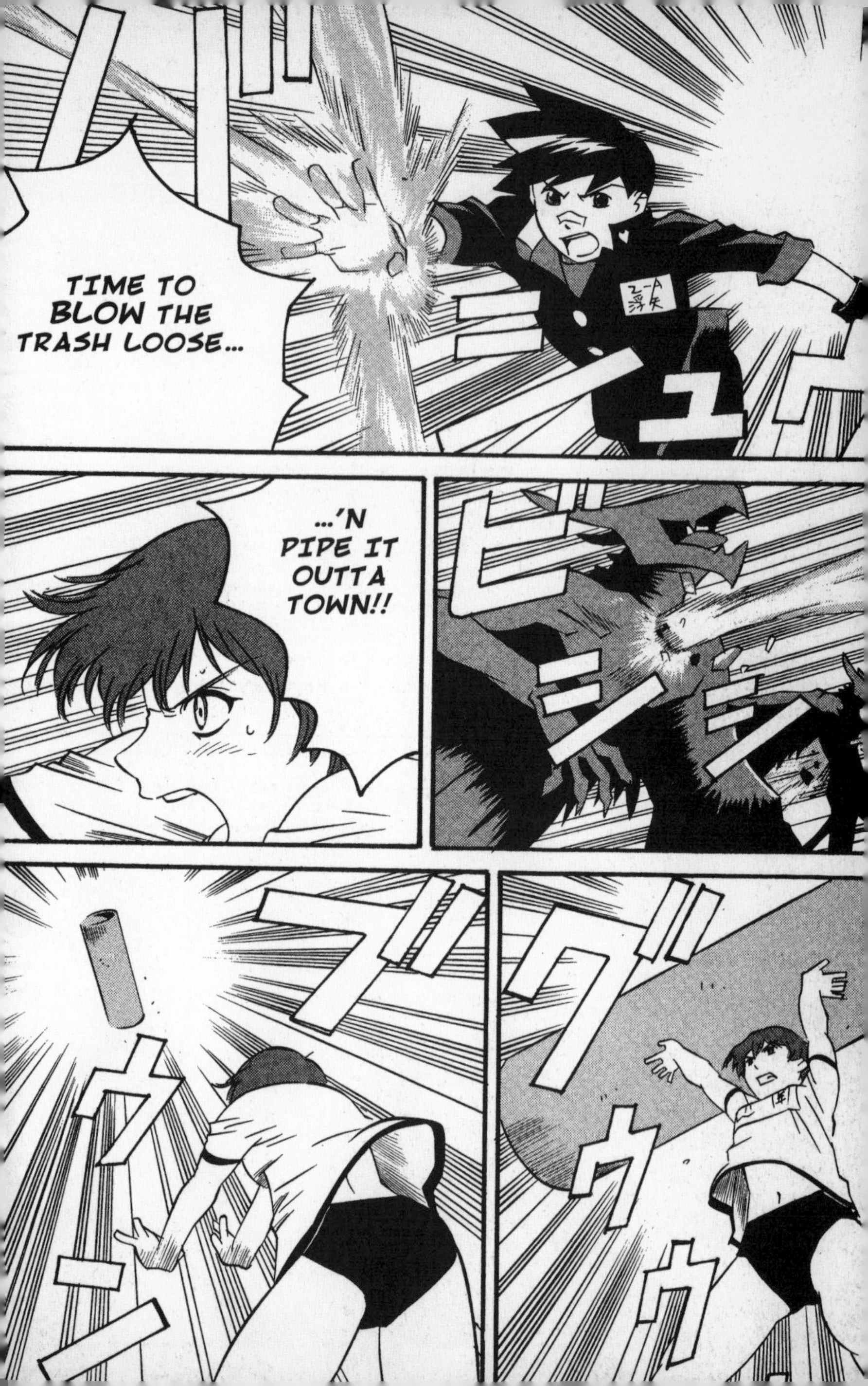
TIME TO BLOW THE TRASH LOOSE...
...'N PIPE IT OUTTA TOWN!!

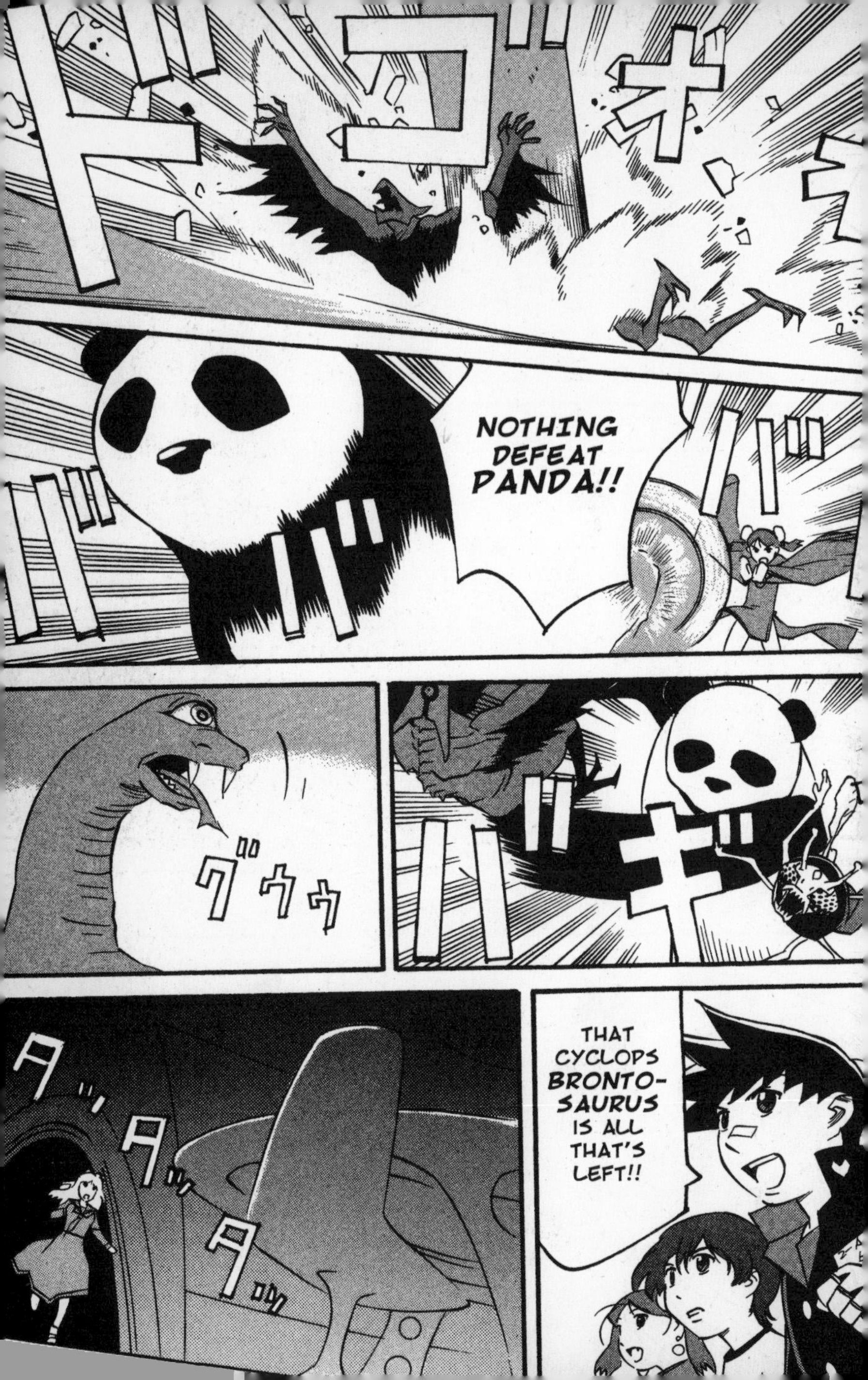
NOTHING DEFEAT PANDA!!
THAT CYCLOPS BRONTO-SAURUS IS ALL THAT'S LEFT!!

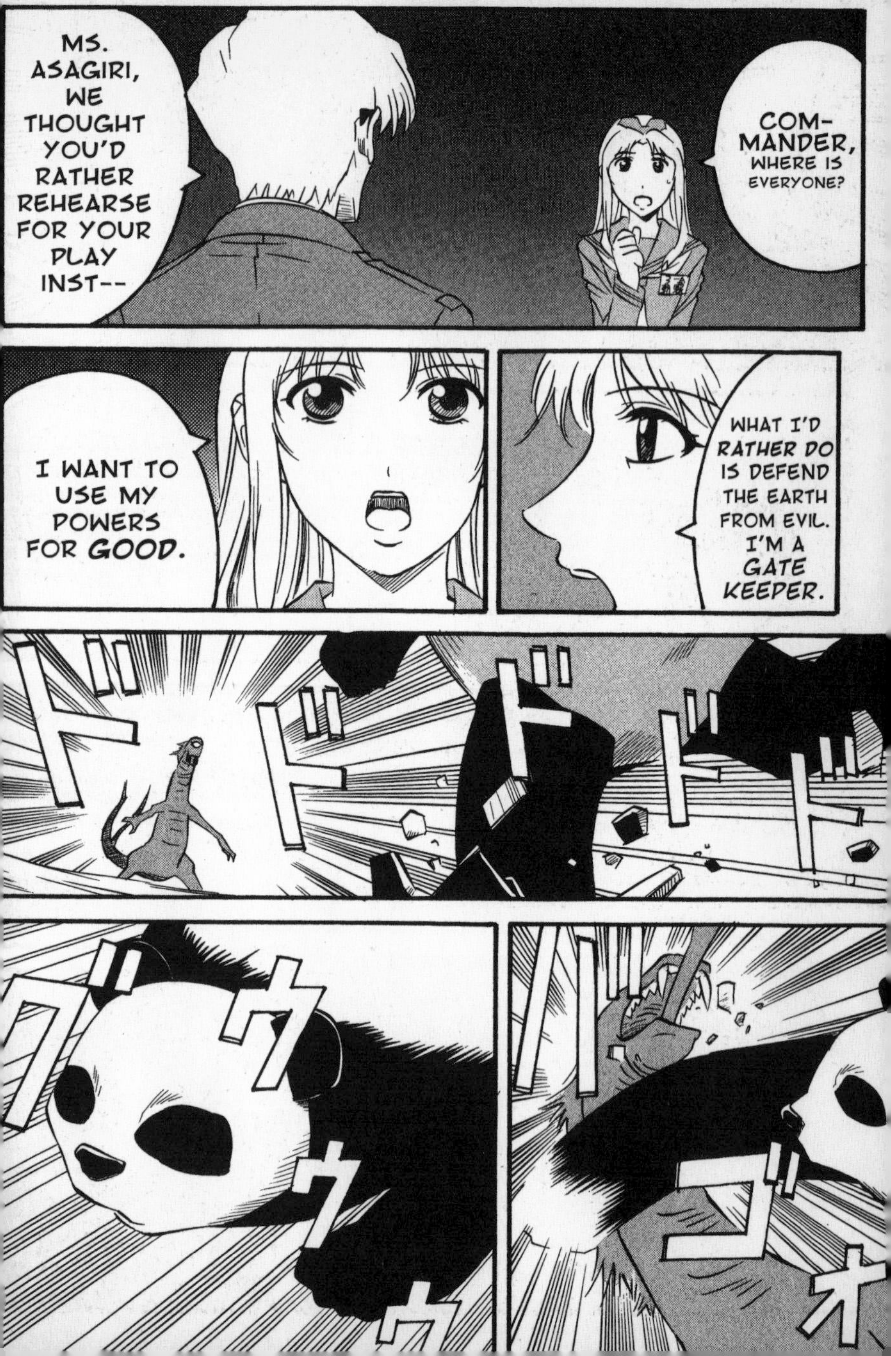
COM-MANDER, WHERE IS EVERYONE?
MS. ASAGIRI, WE THOUGHT YOU'D RATHER REHEARSE FOR YOUR PLAY INST--
WHAT I'D RATHER DO IS DEFEND THE EARTH FROM EVIL. I'M A GATE KEEPER.
I WANT TO USE MY POWERS FOR **GOOD**.
ドドドドド
ゴオ
ヴウウウ

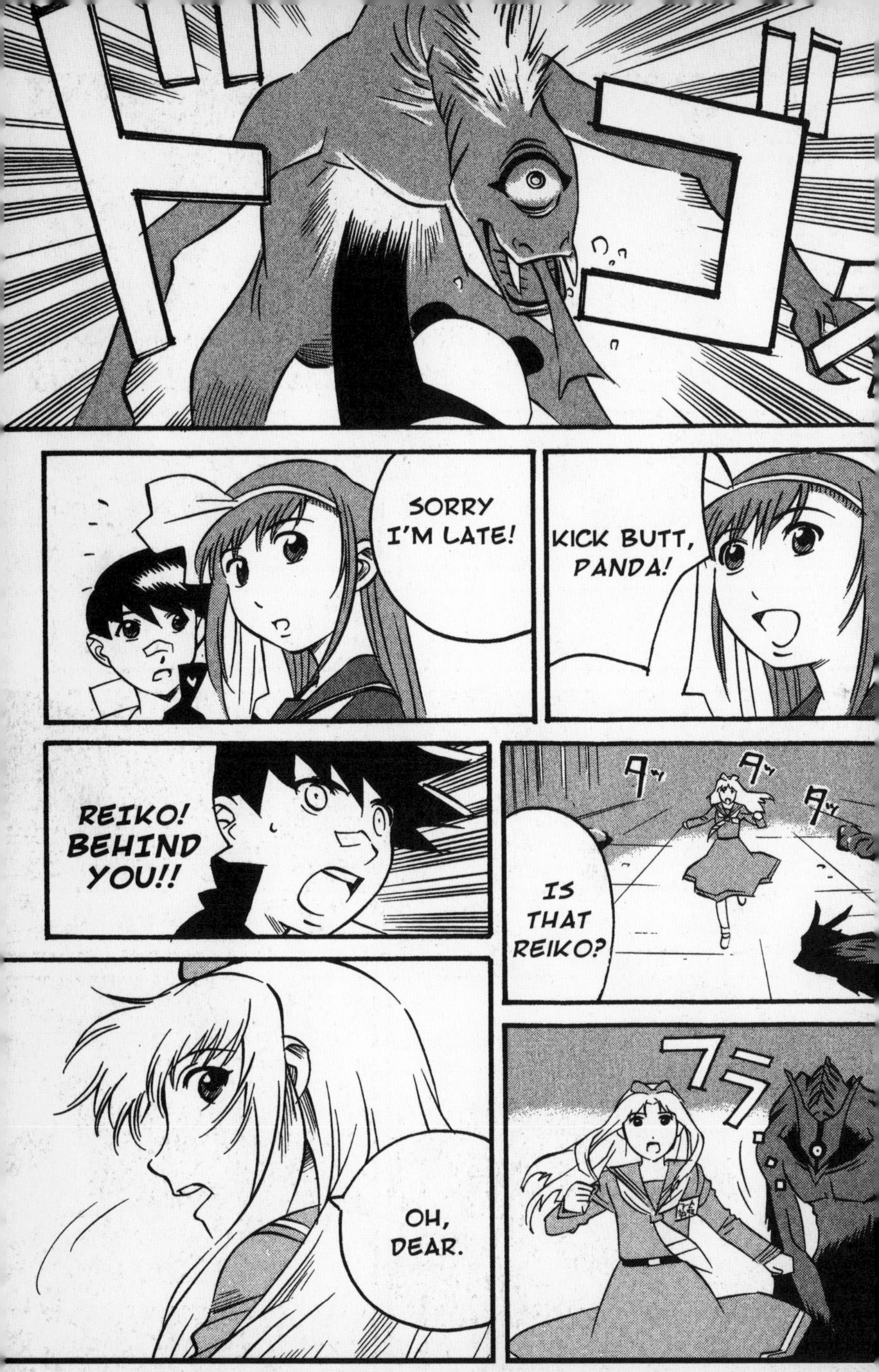
KICK BUTT, PANDA!
SORRY I'M LATE!
タッ タッ タッ
IS THAT REIKO?
REIKO! BEHIND YOU!!
フラ
OH, DEAR.

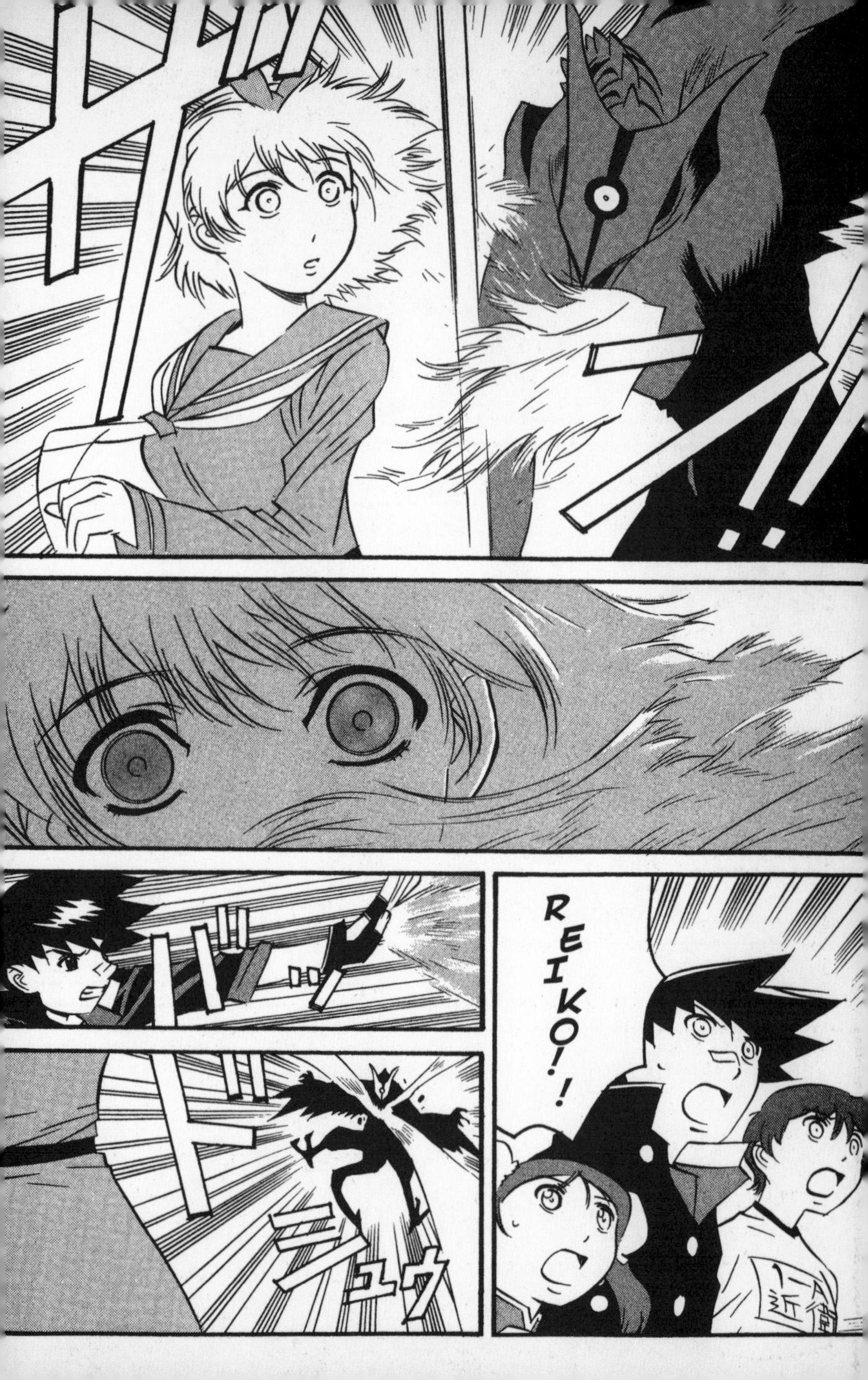
REIKO!!

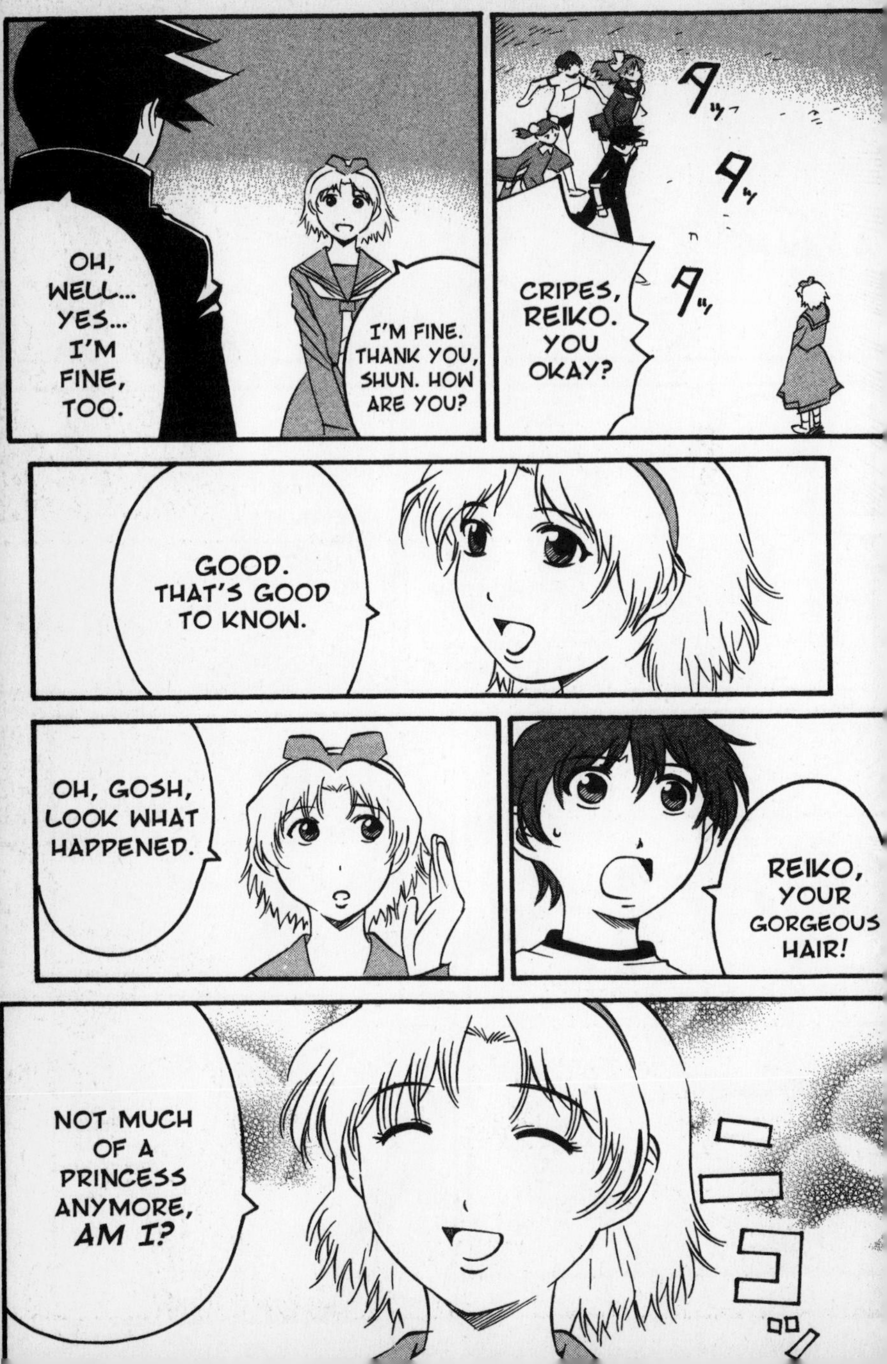
タッ
タッ
タッ
CRIPES, REIKO. YOU OKAY?
I'M FINE. THANK YOU, SHUN. HOW ARE YOU?
OH, WELL... YES... I'M FINE, TOO.
GOOD. THAT'S GOOD TO KNOW.
REIKO, YOUR GORGEOUS HAIR!
OH, GOSH, LOOK WHAT HAPPENED.
NOT MUCH OF A PRINCESS ANYMORE, AM I?
ニコッ

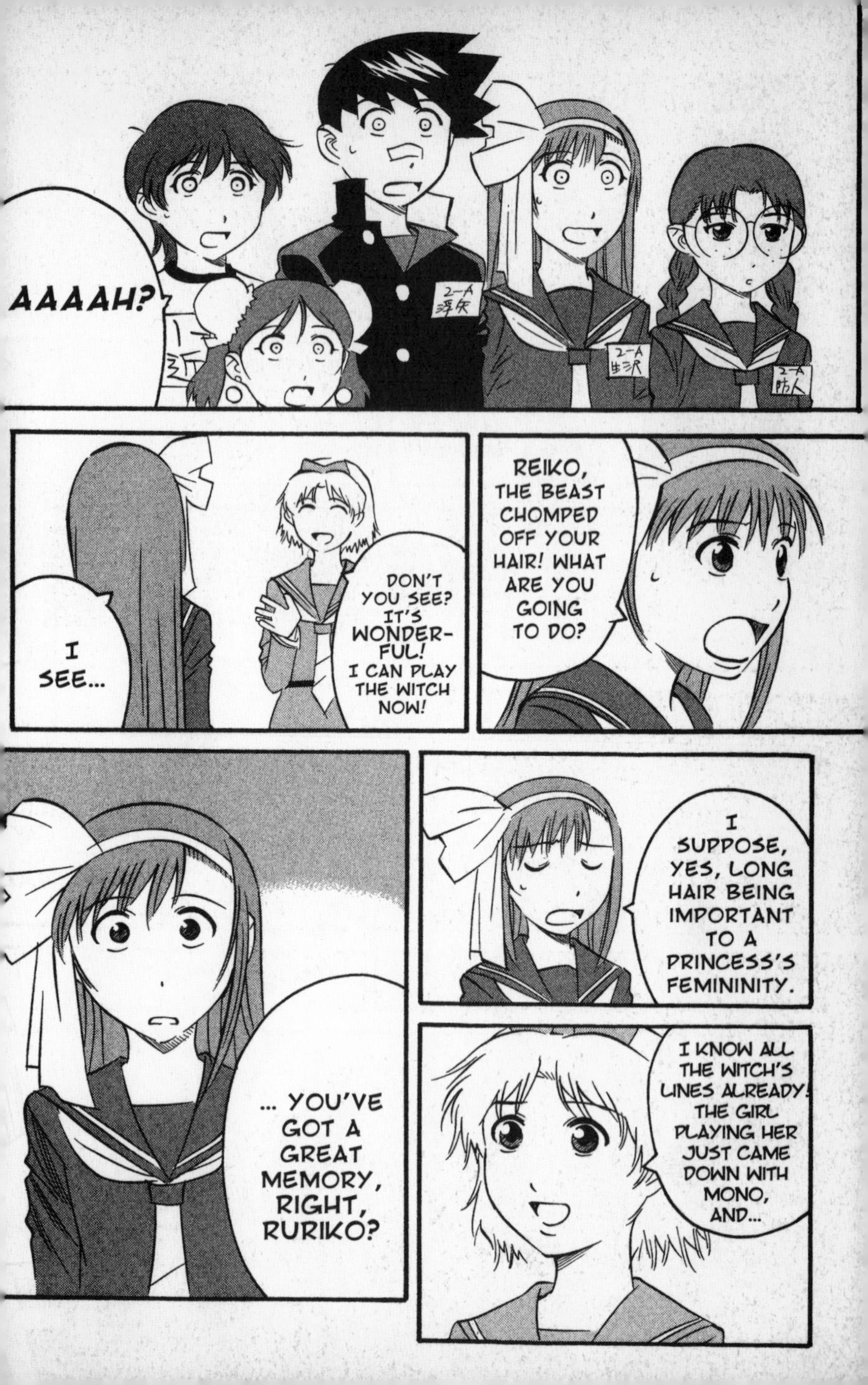
AAAAH?
REIKO, THE BEAST CHOMPED OFF YOUR HAIR! WHAT ARE YOU GOING TO DO?
DON'T YOU SEE? IT'S WONDERFUL! I CAN PLAY THE WITCH NOW!
I SEE...
I SUPPOSE, YES, LONG HAIR BEING IMPORTANT TO A PRINCESS'S FEMININITY.
I KNOW ALL THE WITCH'S LINES ALREADY! THE GIRL PLAYING HER JUST CAME DOWN WITH MONO, AND...
... YOU'VE GOT A GREAT MEMORY, RIGHT, RURIKO?

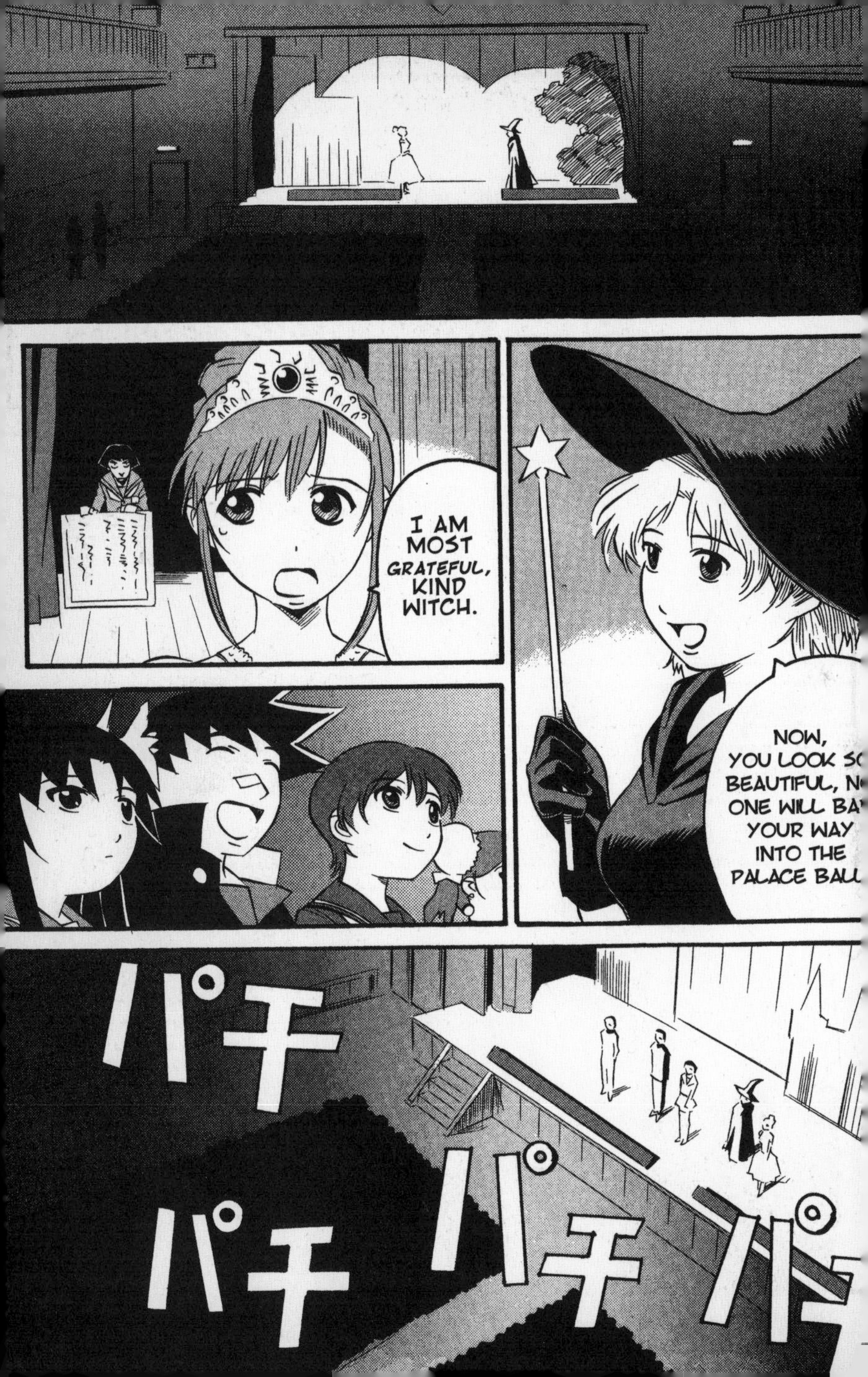
NOW, YOU LOOK S BEAUTIFUL, N ONE WILL BA YOUR WAY INTO THE PALACE BAL
I AM MOST GRATEFUL, KIND WITCH.
パチ
パチ
パチ
パチ

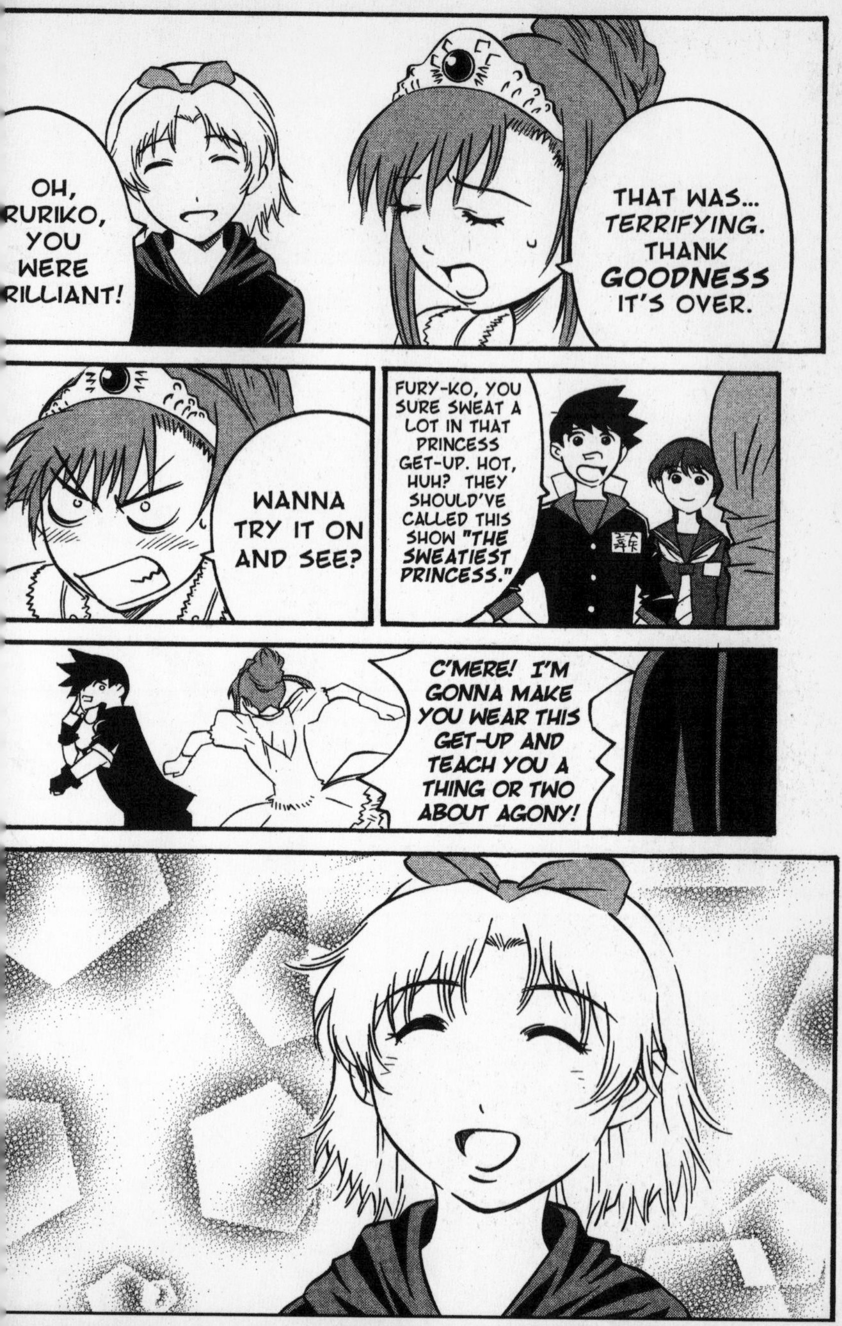
THAT WAS... TERRIFYING. THANK GOODNESS IT'S OVER.
OH, RURIKO, YOU WERE RILLIANT!
FURY-KO, YOU SURE SWEAT A LOT IN THAT PRINCESS GET-UP. HOT, HUH? THEY SHOULD'VE CALLED THIS SHOW "THE SWEATIEST PRINCESS."
WANNA TRY IT ON AND SEE?
C'MERE! I'M GONNA MAKE YOU WEAR THIS GET-UP AND TEACH YOU A THING OR TWO ABOUT AGONY!

GATE #13

DARKNESS RETURNS

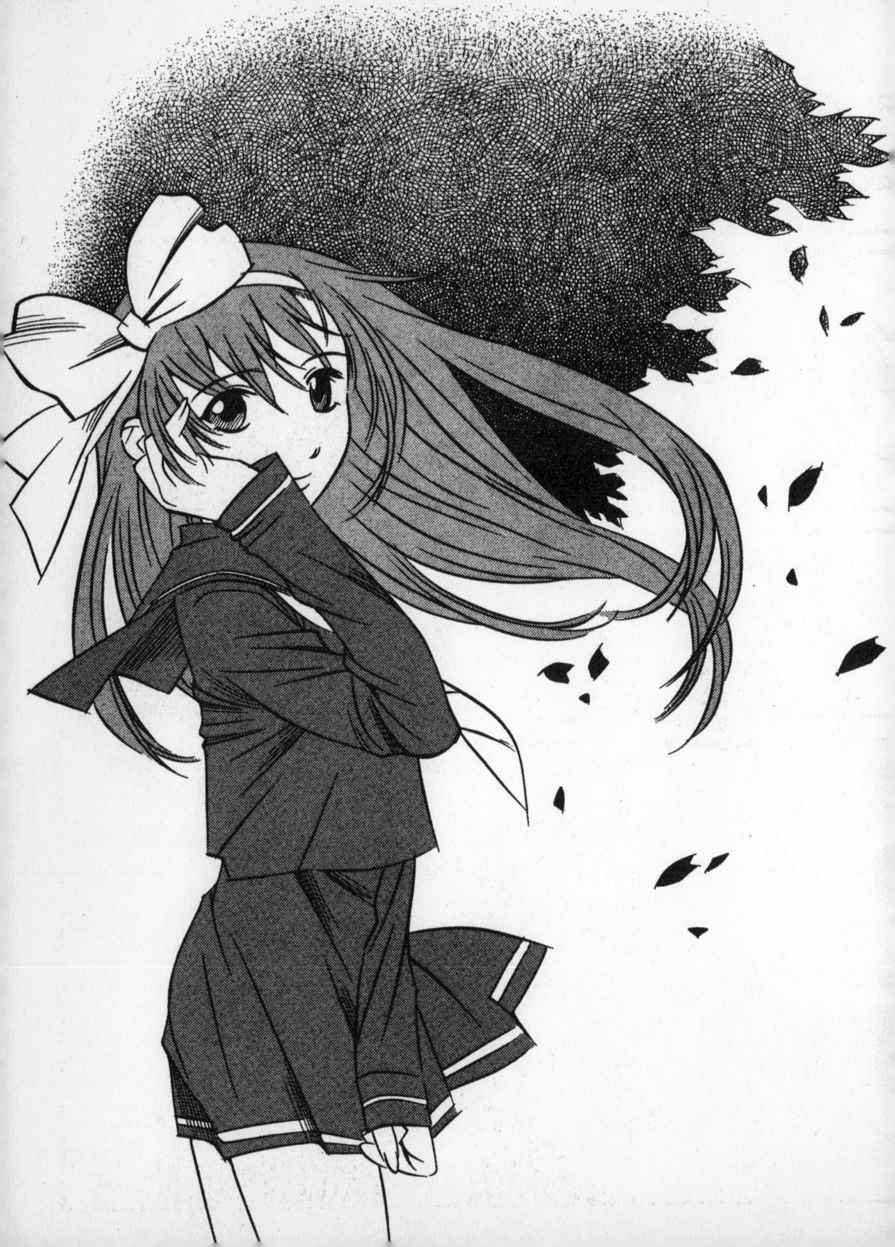

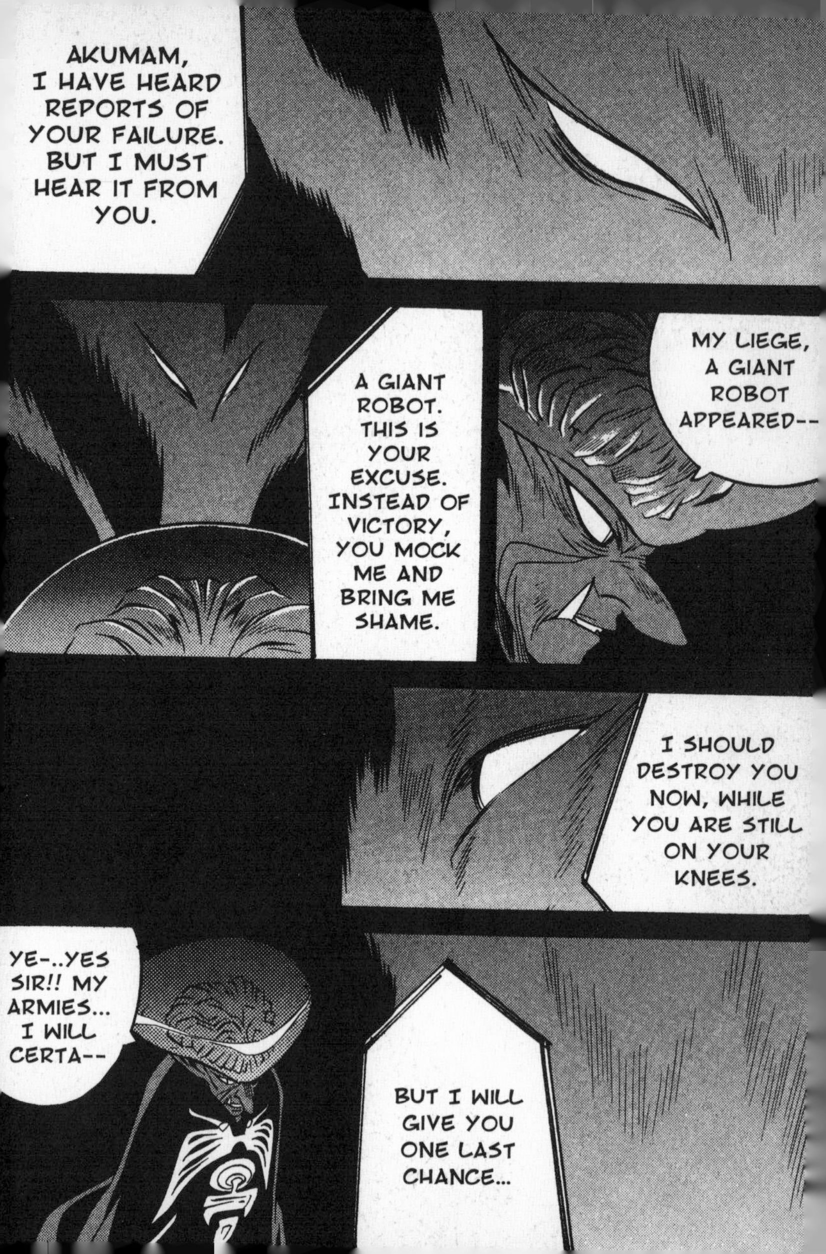
AKUMAM, I HAVE HEARD REPORTS OF YOUR FAILURE. BUT I MUST HEAR IT FROM YOU.
MY LIEGE, A GIANT ROBOT APPEARED--
A GIANT ROBOT. THIS IS YOUR EXCUSE. INSTEAD OF VICTORY, YOU MOCK ME AND BRING ME SHAME.
I SHOULD DESTROY YOU NOW, WHILE YOU ARE STILL ON YOUR KNEES.
BUT I WILL GIVE YOU ONE LAST CHANCE...
YE-..YES SIR!! MY ARMIES... I WILL CERTA--

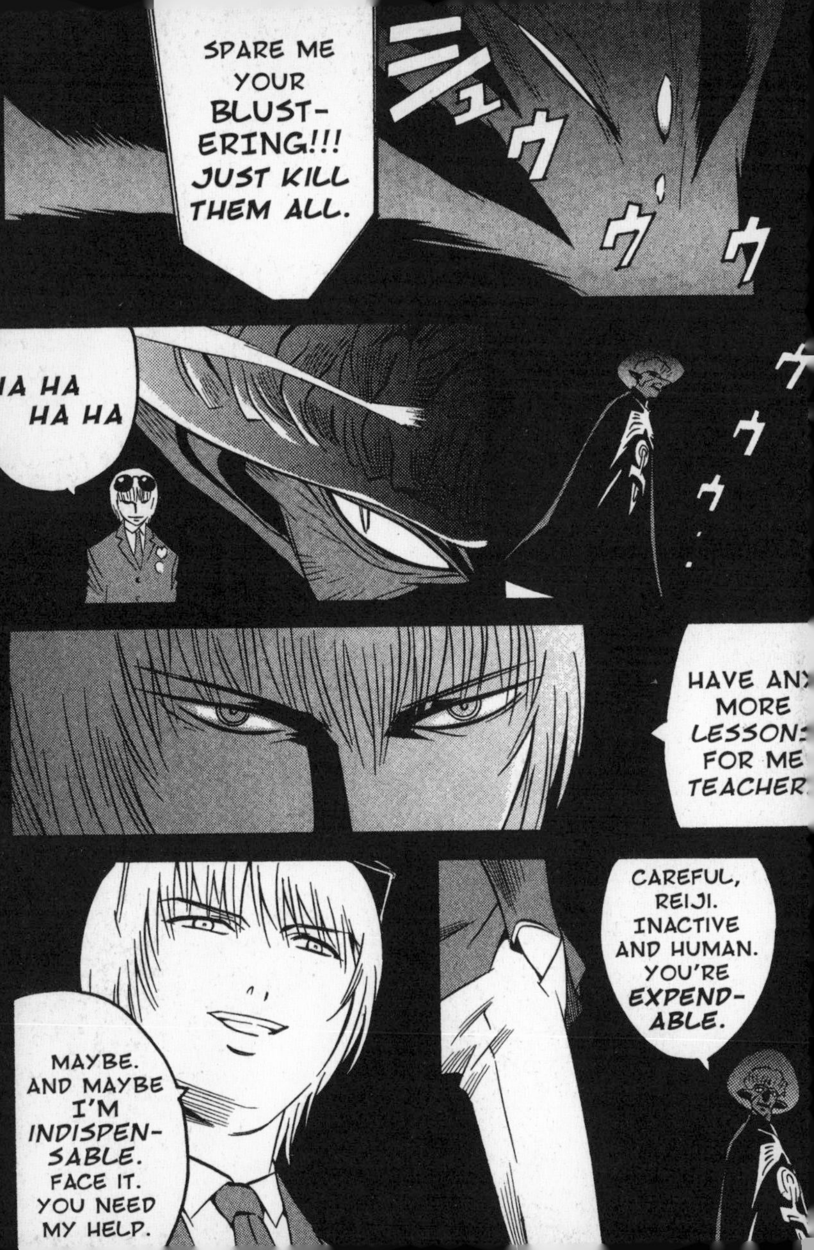

シュウヴウ
SPARE ME YOUR BLUST-ERING!!! JUST KILL THEM ALL.
ウウウウ...
HA HA HA HA
HAVE AN MORE LESSON FOR ME TEACHER
CAREFUL, REIJI. INACTIVE AND HUMAN. YOU'RE EXPENDABLE.
MAYBE. AND MAYBE I'M INDISPENSABLE. FACE IT. YOU NEED MY HELP.

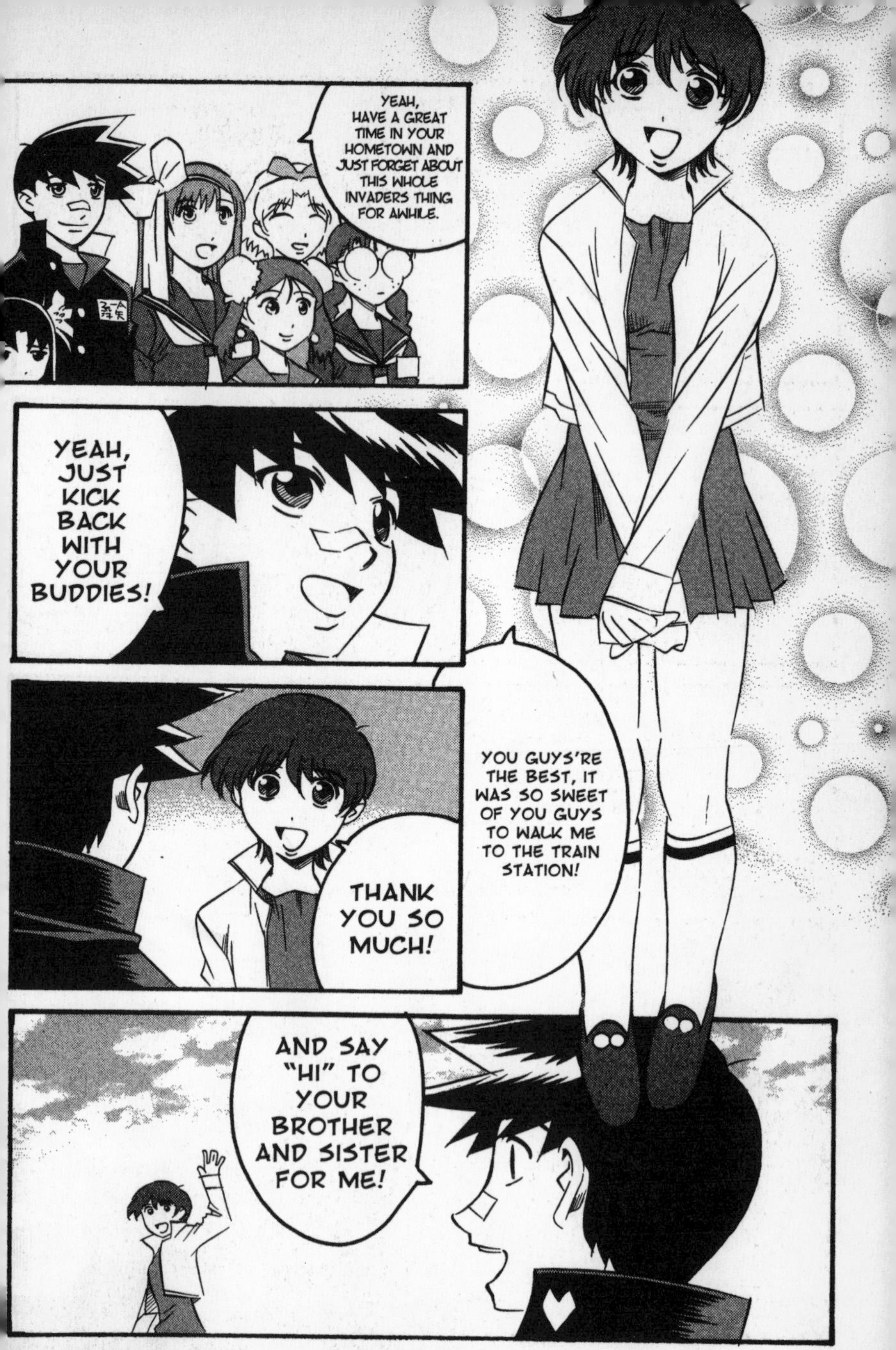
YOU GUYS'RE THE BEST, IT WAS SO SWEET OF YOU GUYS TO WALK ME TO THE TRAIN STATION!
YEAH, HAVE A GREAT TIME IN YOUR HOMETOWN AND JUST FORGET ABOUT THIS WHOLE INVADERS THING FOR AWHILE.
YEAH, JUST KICK BACK WITH YOUR BUDDIES!
THANK YOU SO MUCH!
AND SAY "HI" TO YOUR BROTHER AND SISTER FOR ME!

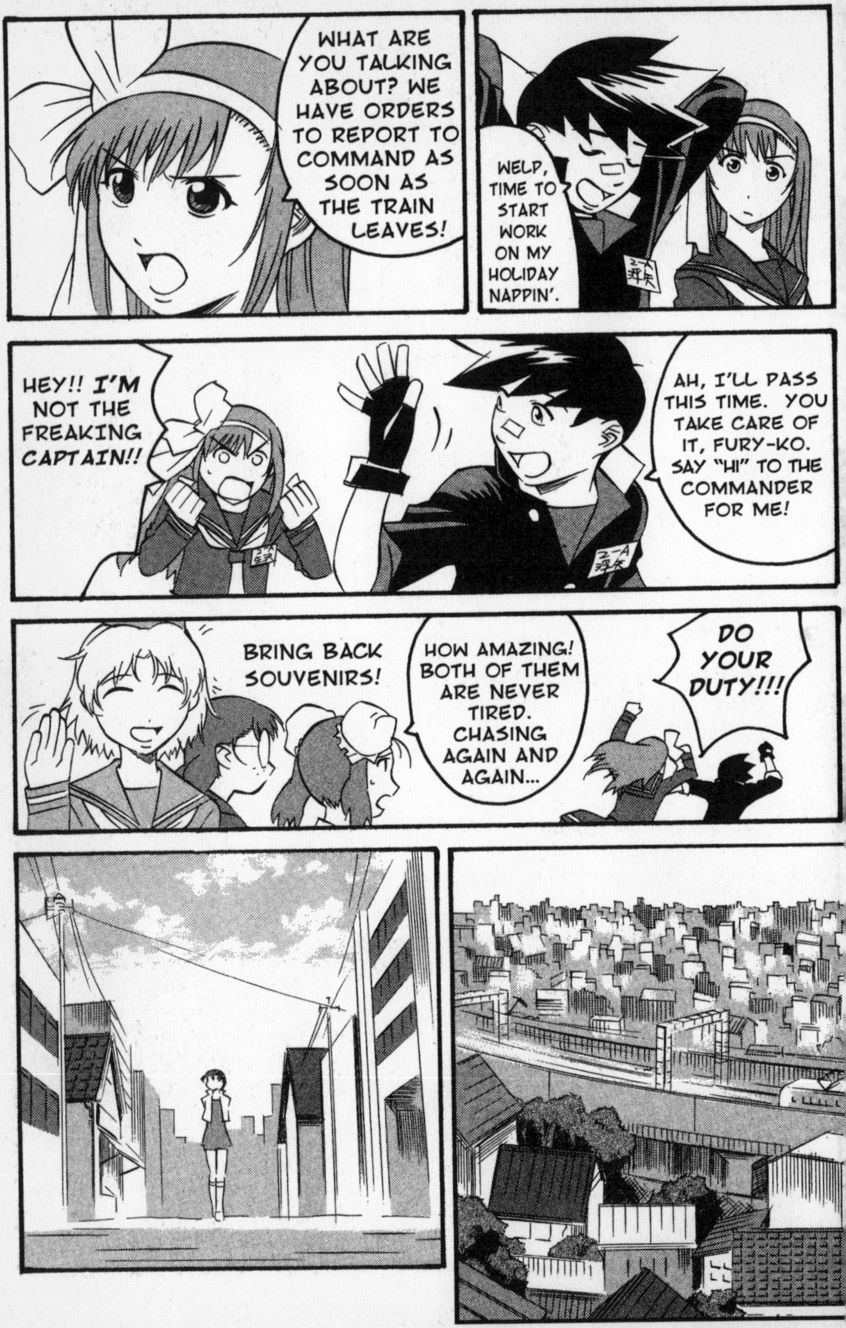
WELP, TIME TO START WORK ON MY HOLIDAY NAPPIN'.
WHAT ARE YOU TALKING ABOUT? WE HAVE ORDERS TO REPORT TO COMMAND AS SOON AS THE TRAIN LEAVES!
AH, I'LL PASS THIS TIME. YOU TAKE CARE OF IT, FURY-KO. SAY "HI" TO THE COMMANDER FOR ME!
HEY!! **I'M** NOT THE FREAKING **CAPTAIN!!**
DO YOUR DUTY!!!
HOW AMAZING! BOTH OF THEM ARE NEVER TIRED. CHASING AGAIN AND AGAIN...
BRING BACK SOUVENIRS!

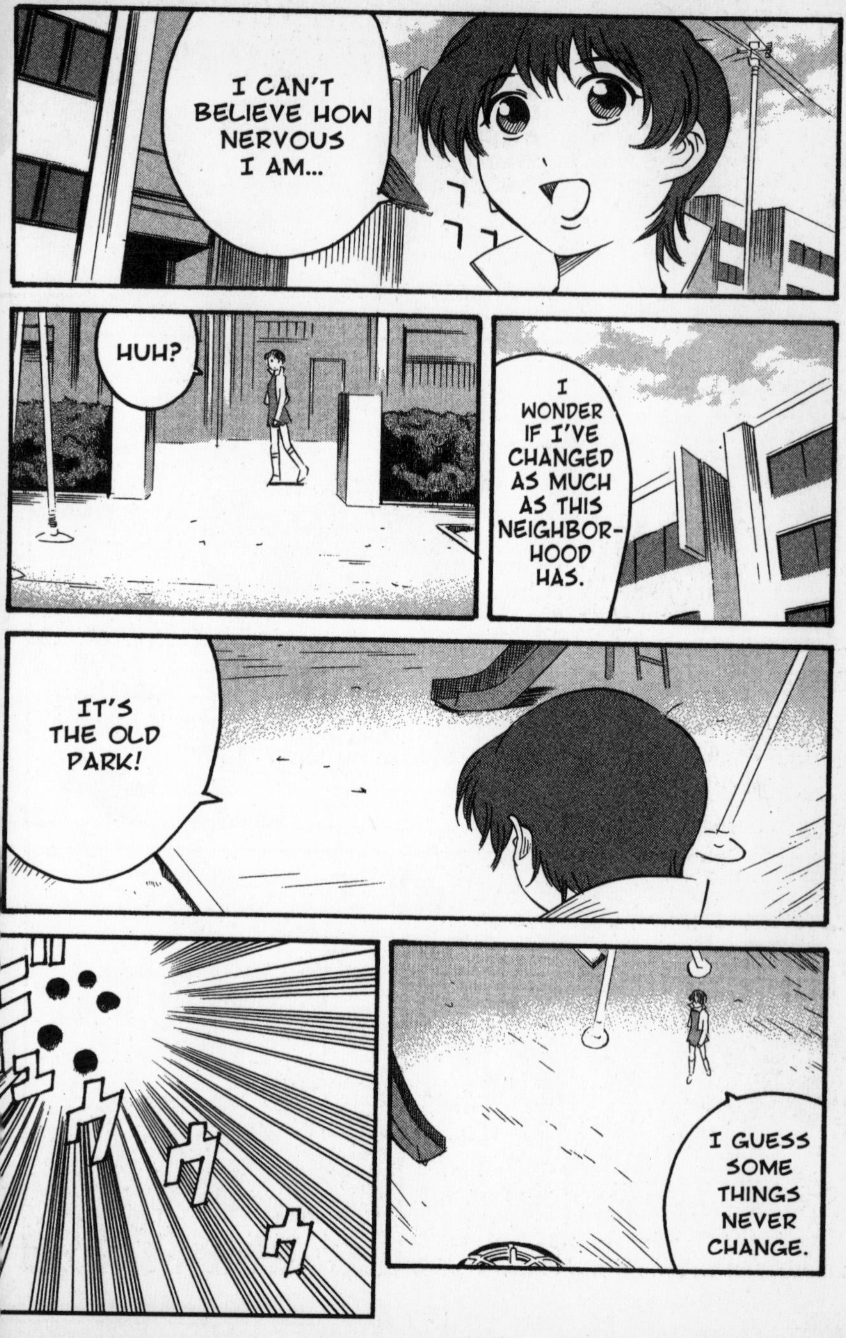
I CAN'T BELIEVE HOW NERVOUS I AM...
I WONDER IF I'VE CHANGED AS MUCH AS THIS NEIGHBOR-HOOD HAS.
HUH?
IT'S THE OLD PARK!
I GUESS SOME THINGS NEVER CHANGE.

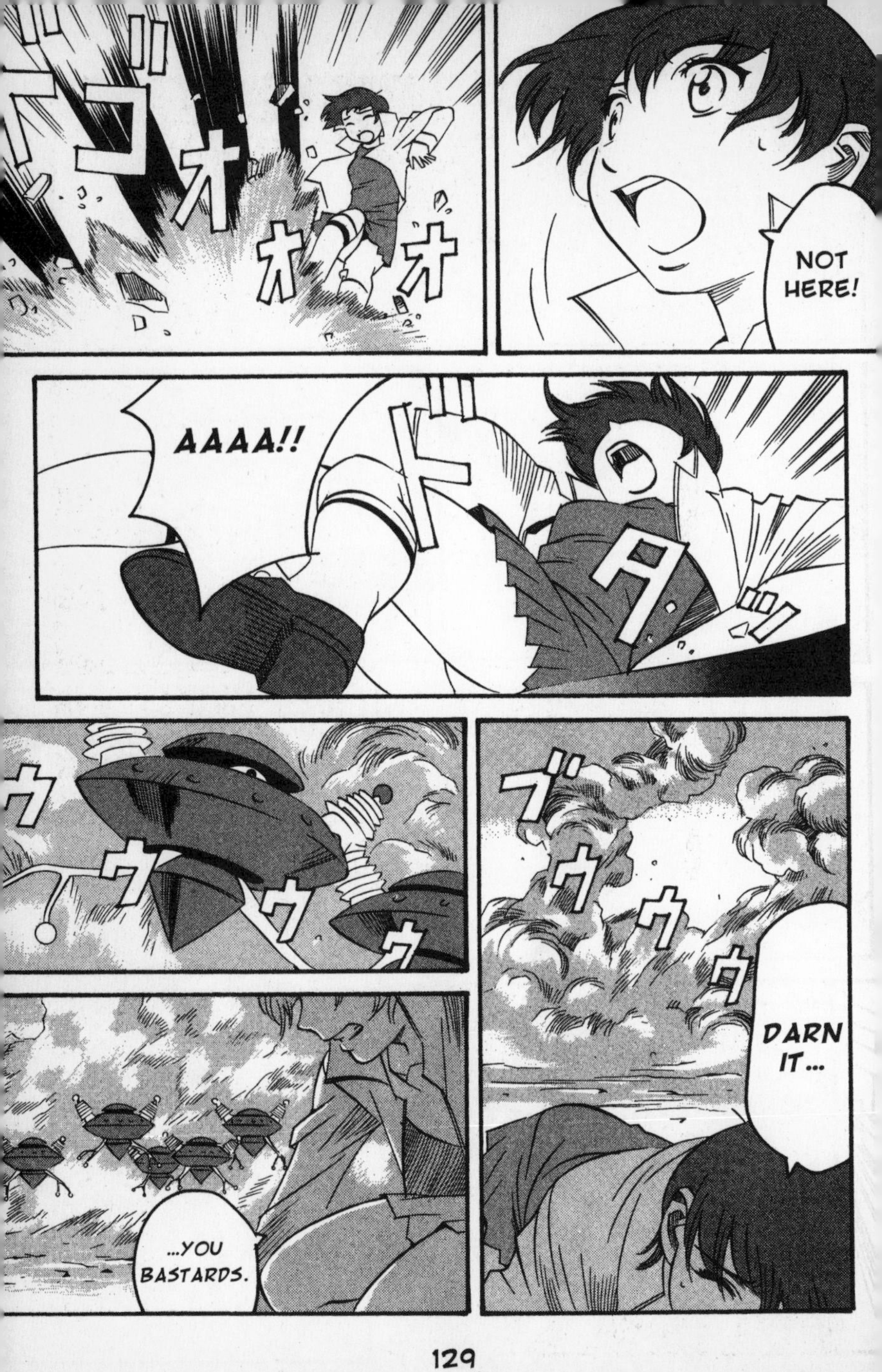
NOT HERE!
AAAA!!
ブウウウウ
DARN IT...
ウウウウ
...YOU BASTARDS.

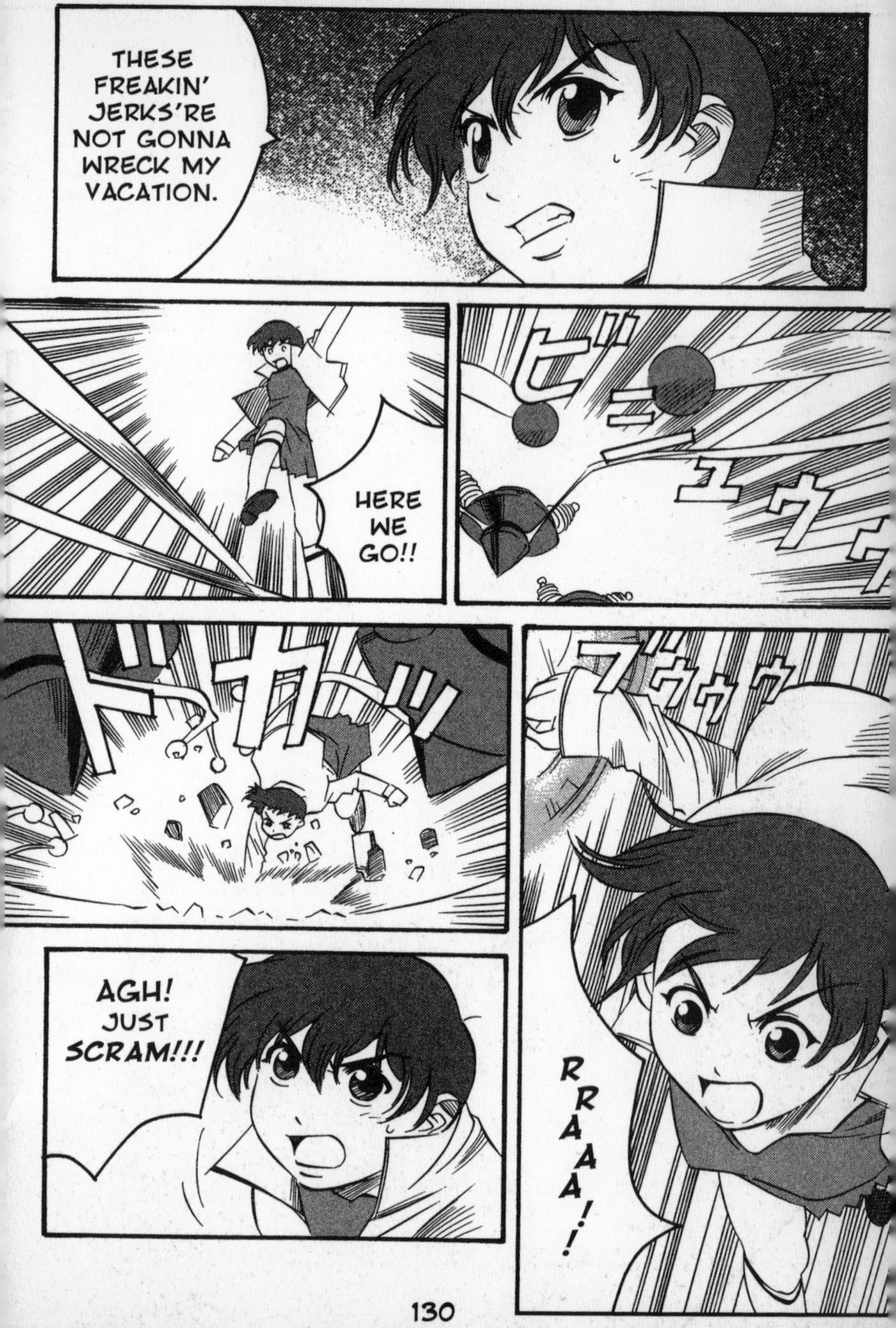
THESE FREAKIN' JERKS'RE NOT GONNA WRECK MY VACATION.
HERE WE GO!!
RRAAA!!
AGH! JUST SCRAM!!!

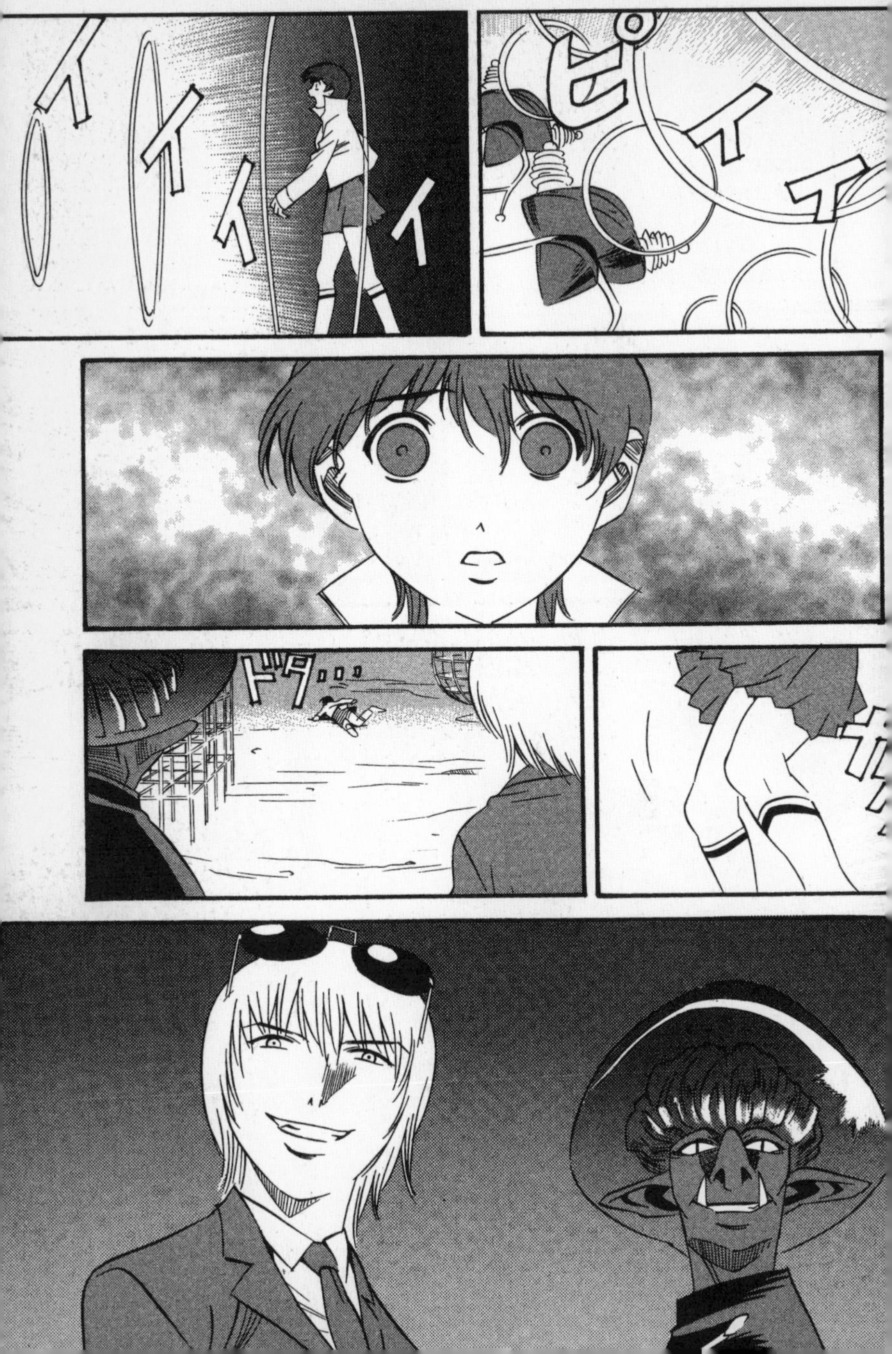
ピィィ
イイイイ
ドタ…

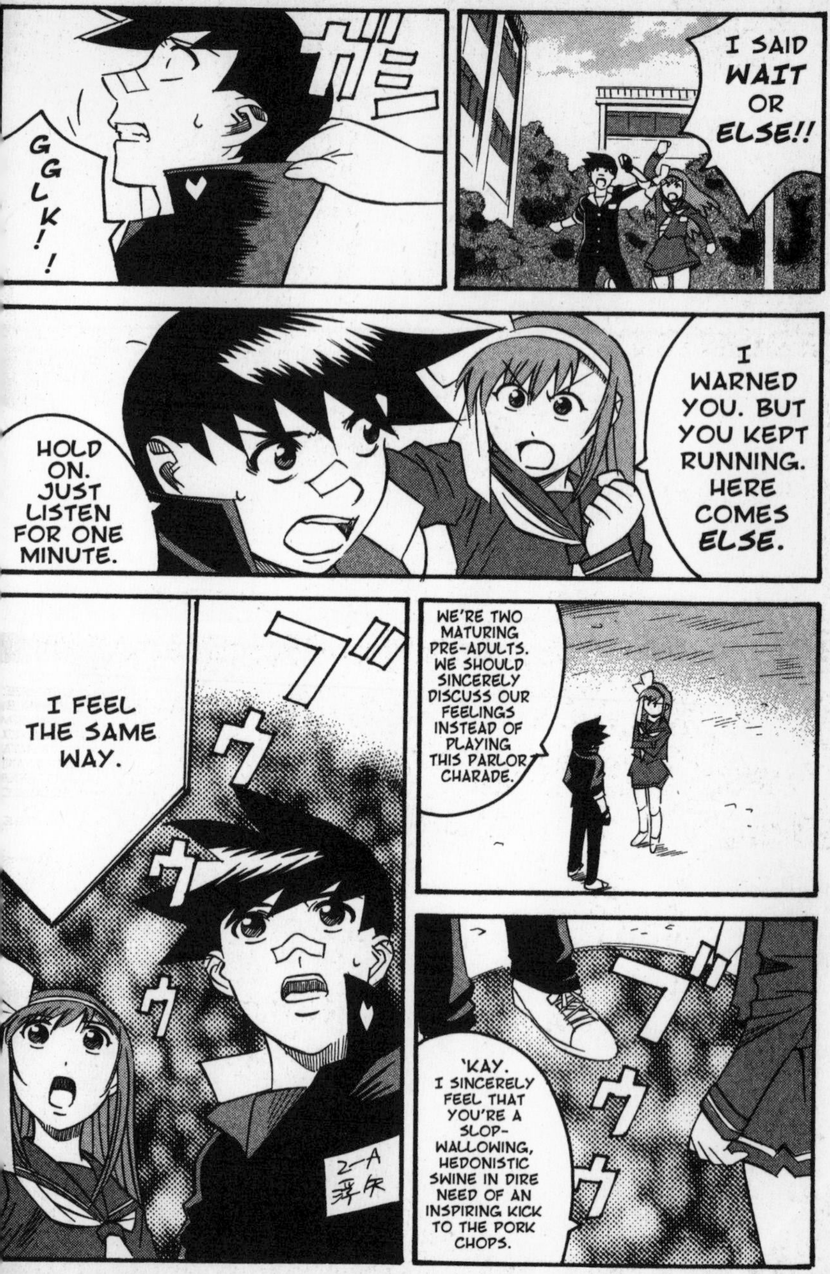
I SAID WAIT OR ELSE!!
GGLK!!
I WARNED YOU. BUT YOU KEPT RUNNING. HERE COMES ELSE.
HOLD ON. JUST LISTEN FOR ONE MINUTE.
WE'RE TWO MATURING PRE-ADULTS. WE SHOULD SINCERELY DISCUSS OUR FEELINGS INSTEAD OF PLAYING THIS PARLOR CHARADE.
'KAY. I SINCERELY FEEL THAT YOU'RE A SLOP-WALLOWING, HEDONISTIC SWINE IN DIRE NEED OF AN INSPIRING KICK TO THE PORK CHOPS.
I FEEL THE SAME WAY.

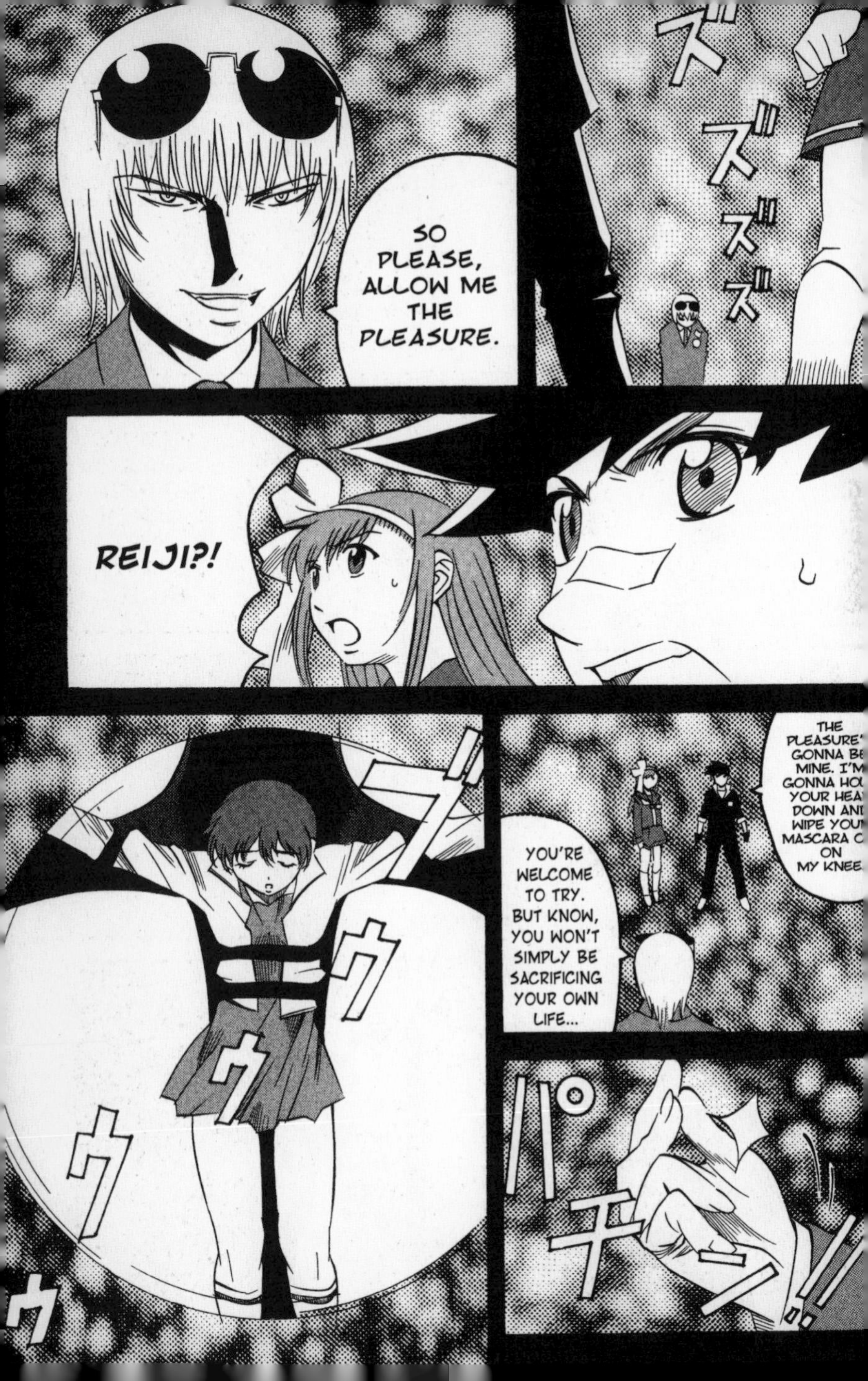

ズズズズ
SO PLEASE, ALLOW ME THE PLEASURE.
REIJI?!
THE PLEASURE' GONNA BE MINE. I'M GONNA HOL YOUR HEA DOWN AND WIPE YOUR MASCARA O ON MY KNEE
YOU'RE WELCOME TO TRY. BUT KNOW, YOU WON'T SIMPLY BE SACRIFICING YOUR OWN LIFE...
パチーン!!
ウウウウウ

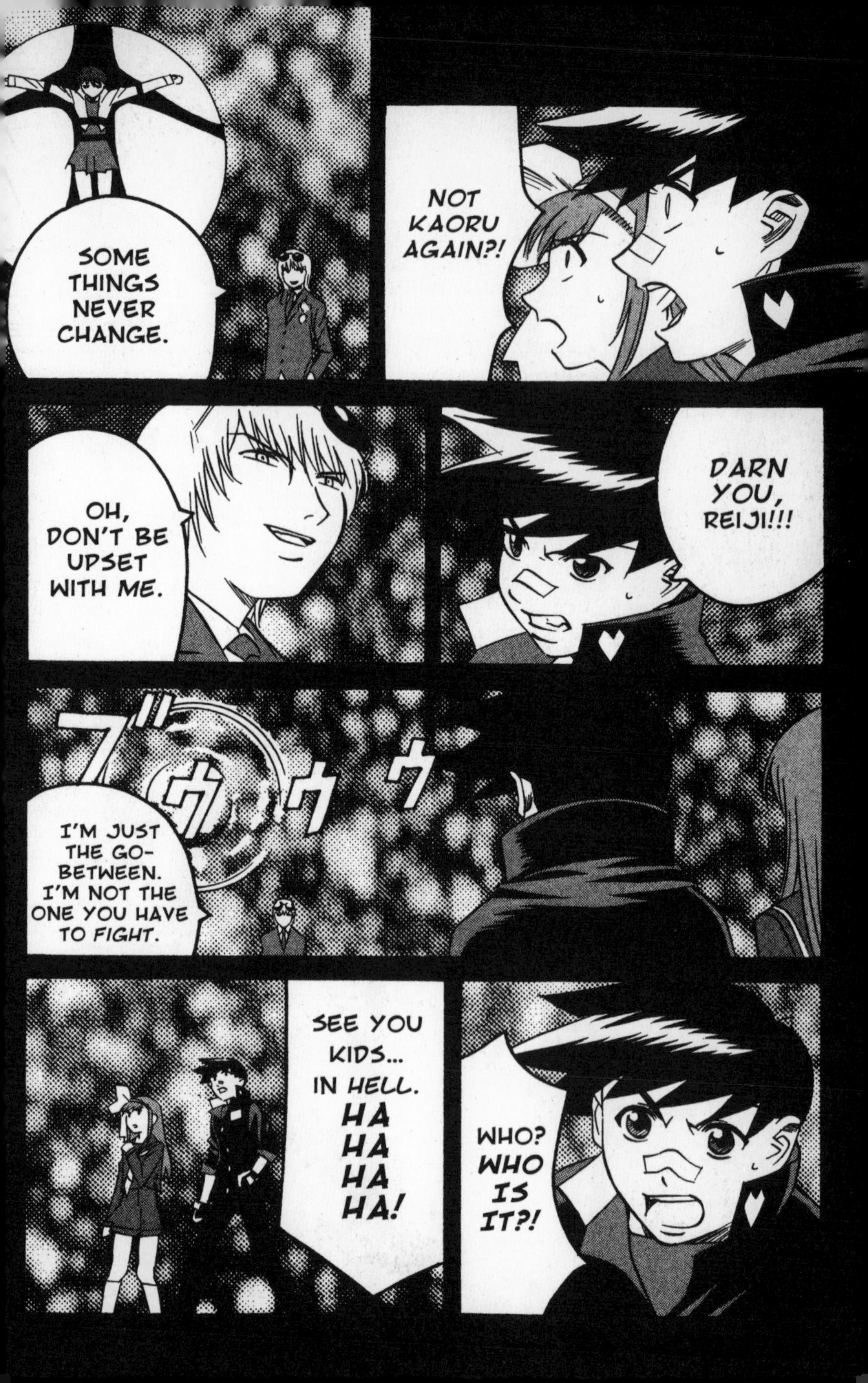
NOT KAORU AGAIN?!
SOME THINGS NEVER CHANGE.
DARN YOU, REIJI!!!
OH, DON'T BE UPSET WITH ME.
I'M JUST THE GO-BETWEEN. I'M NOT THE ONE YOU HAVE TO *FIGHT*.
WHO? WHO IS IT?!
SEE YOU KIDS... IN *HELL*. **HA HA HA HA!**

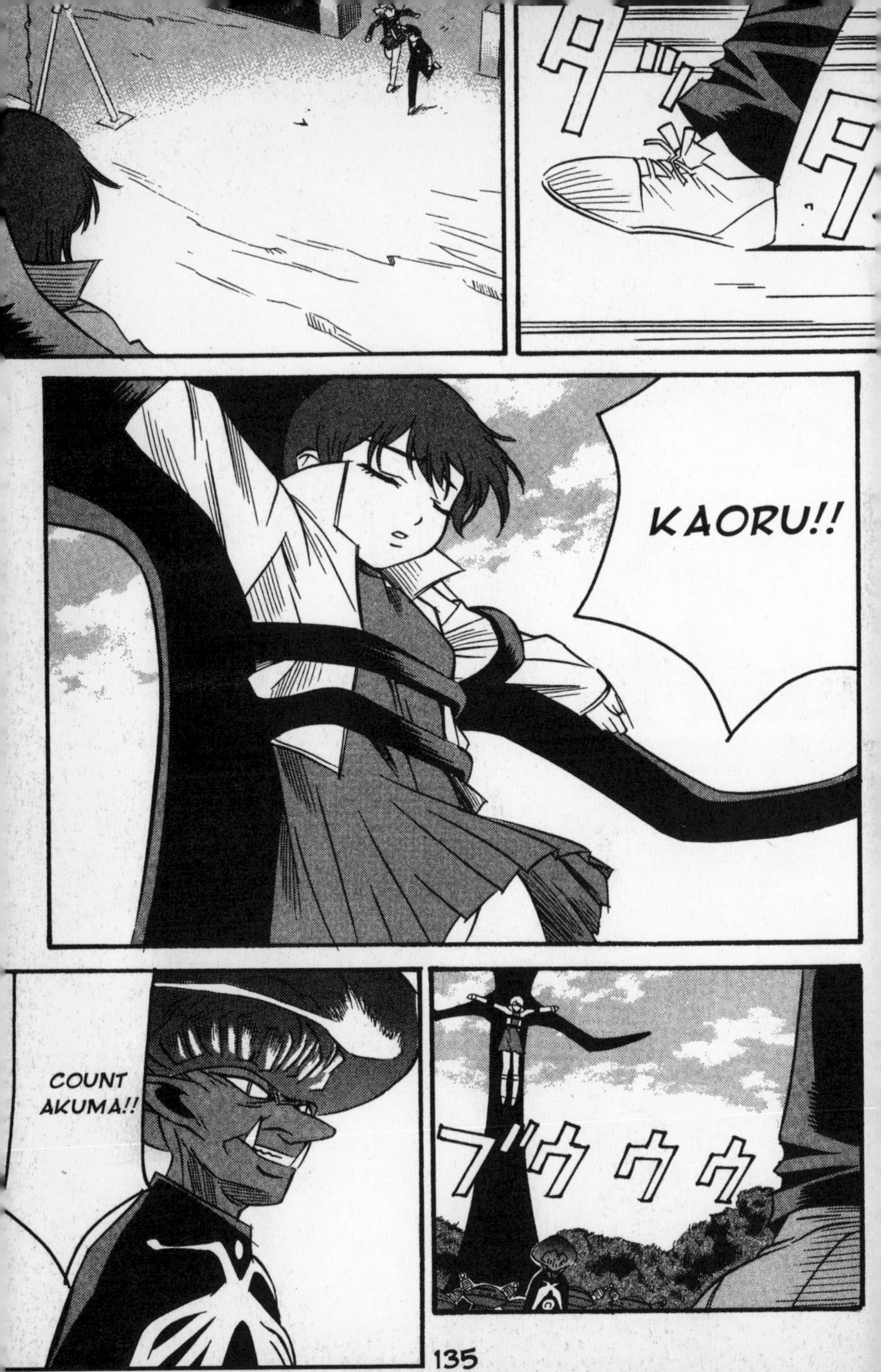
ダッダ
KAORU!!
ブウウウ
COUNT AKUMA!!

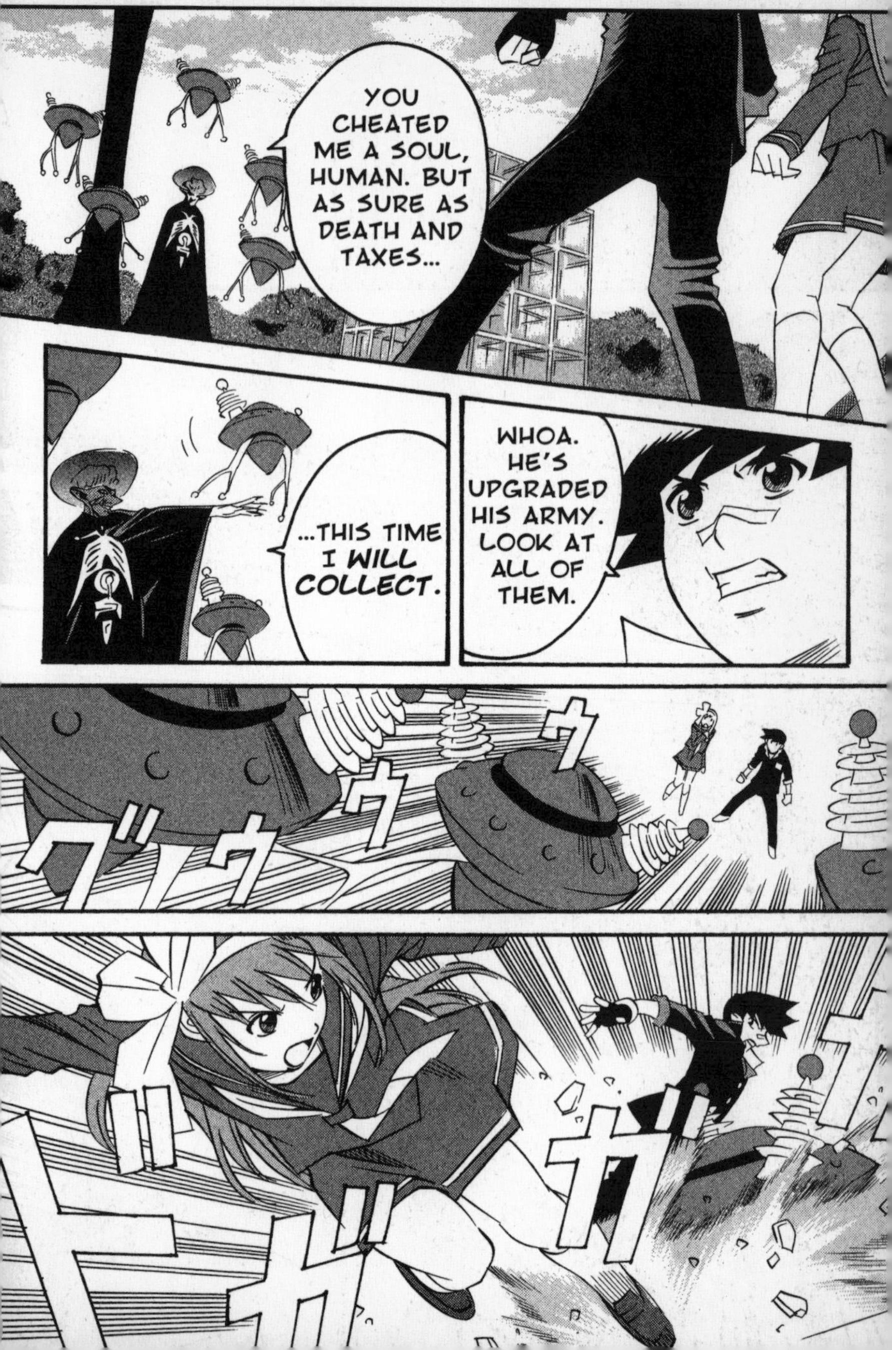
YOU CHEATED ME A SOUL, HUMAN. BUT AS SURE AS DEATH AND TAXES...
...THIS TIME I WILL COLLECT.
WHOA. HE'S UPGRADED HIS ARMY. LOOK AT ALL OF THEM.

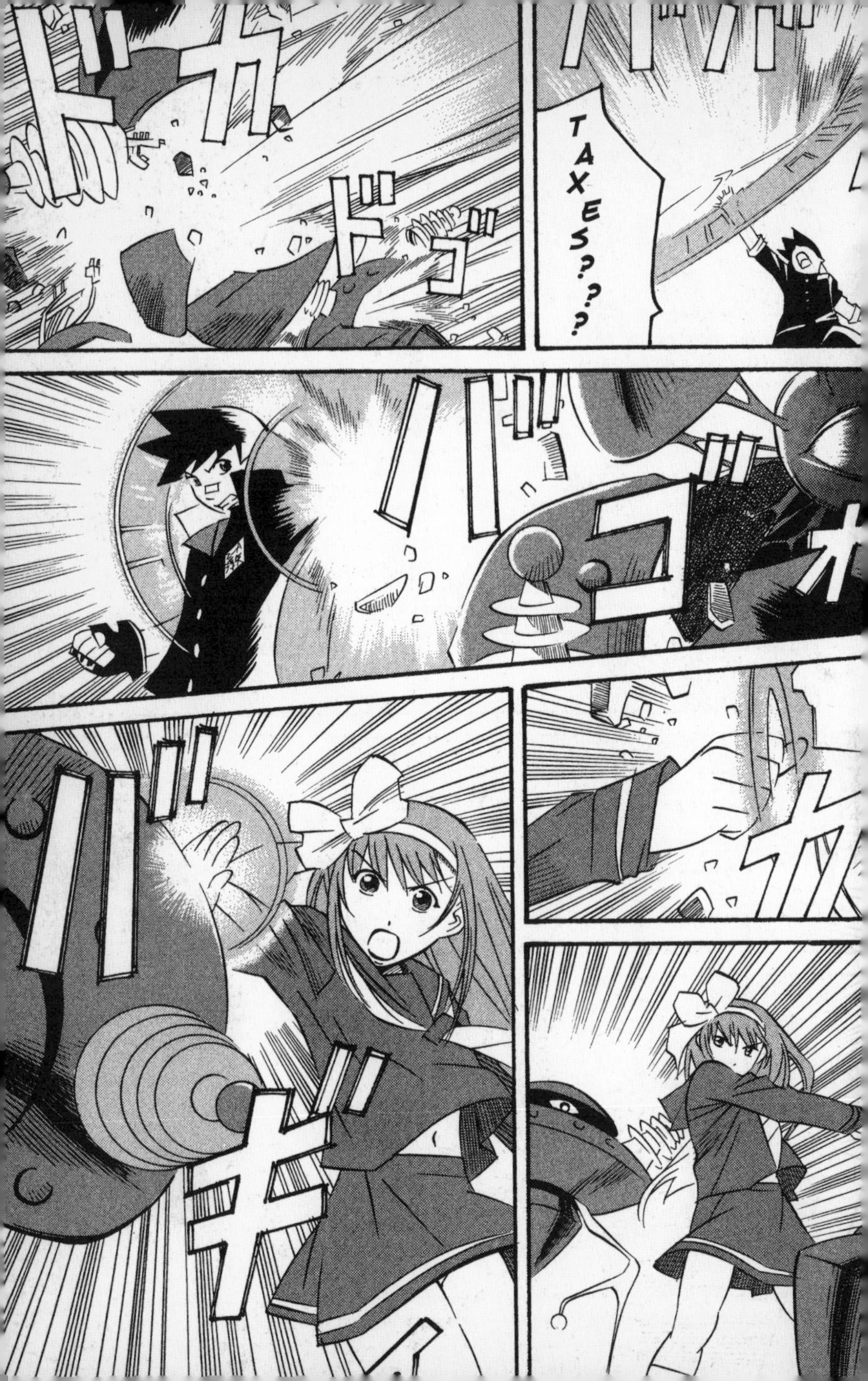
TAXES???

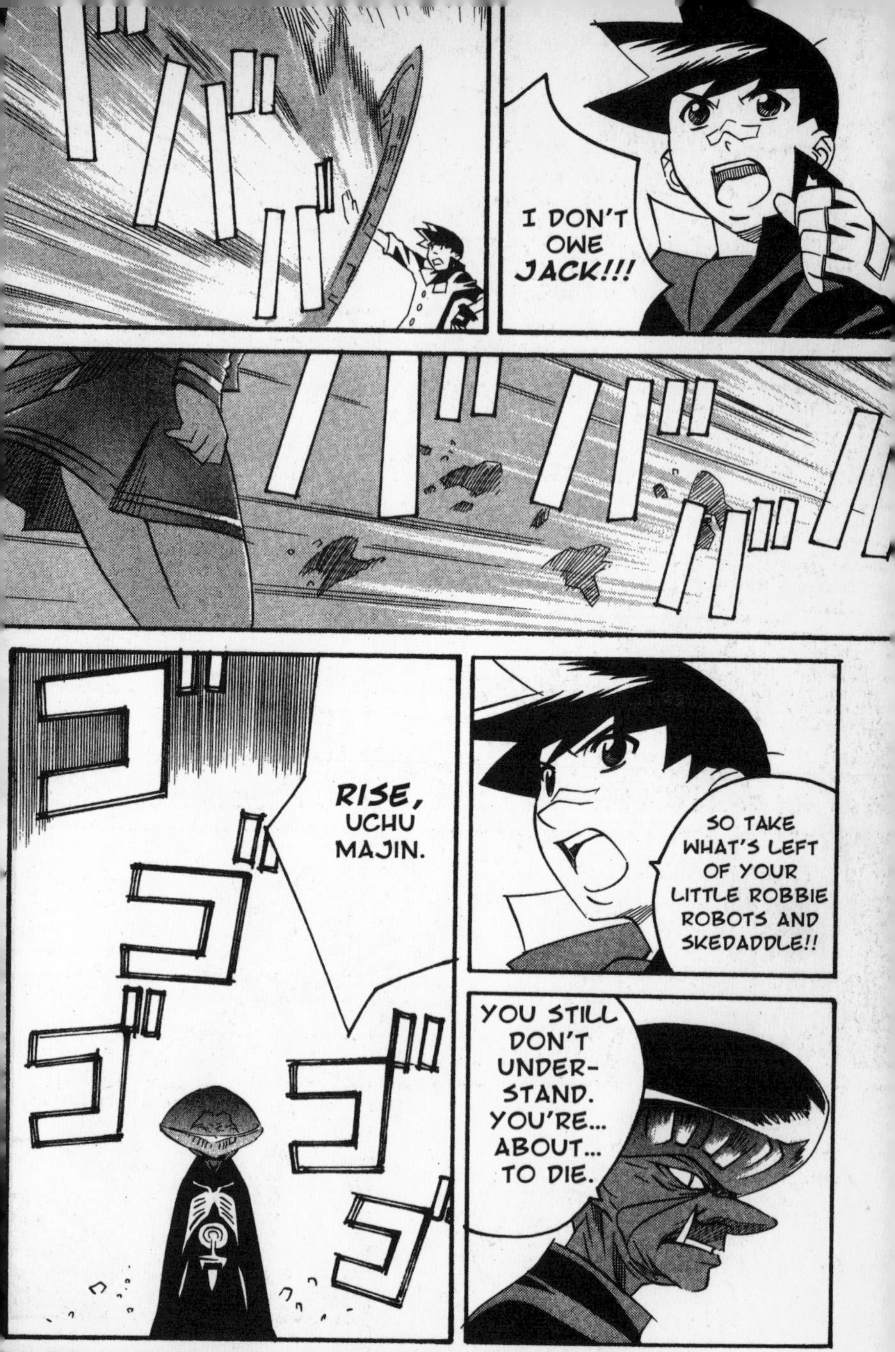
I DON'T OWE JACK!!!
SO TAKE WHAT'S LEFT OF YOUR LITTLE ROBBIE ROBOTS AND SKEDADDLE!!
YOU STILL DON'T UNDER-STAND. YOU'RE... ABOUT... TO DIE.
RISE, UCHU MAJIN.

Uchu Majin: From the Japanese Uchu (universe or cosmos) and Majin (evil spirit or devil).

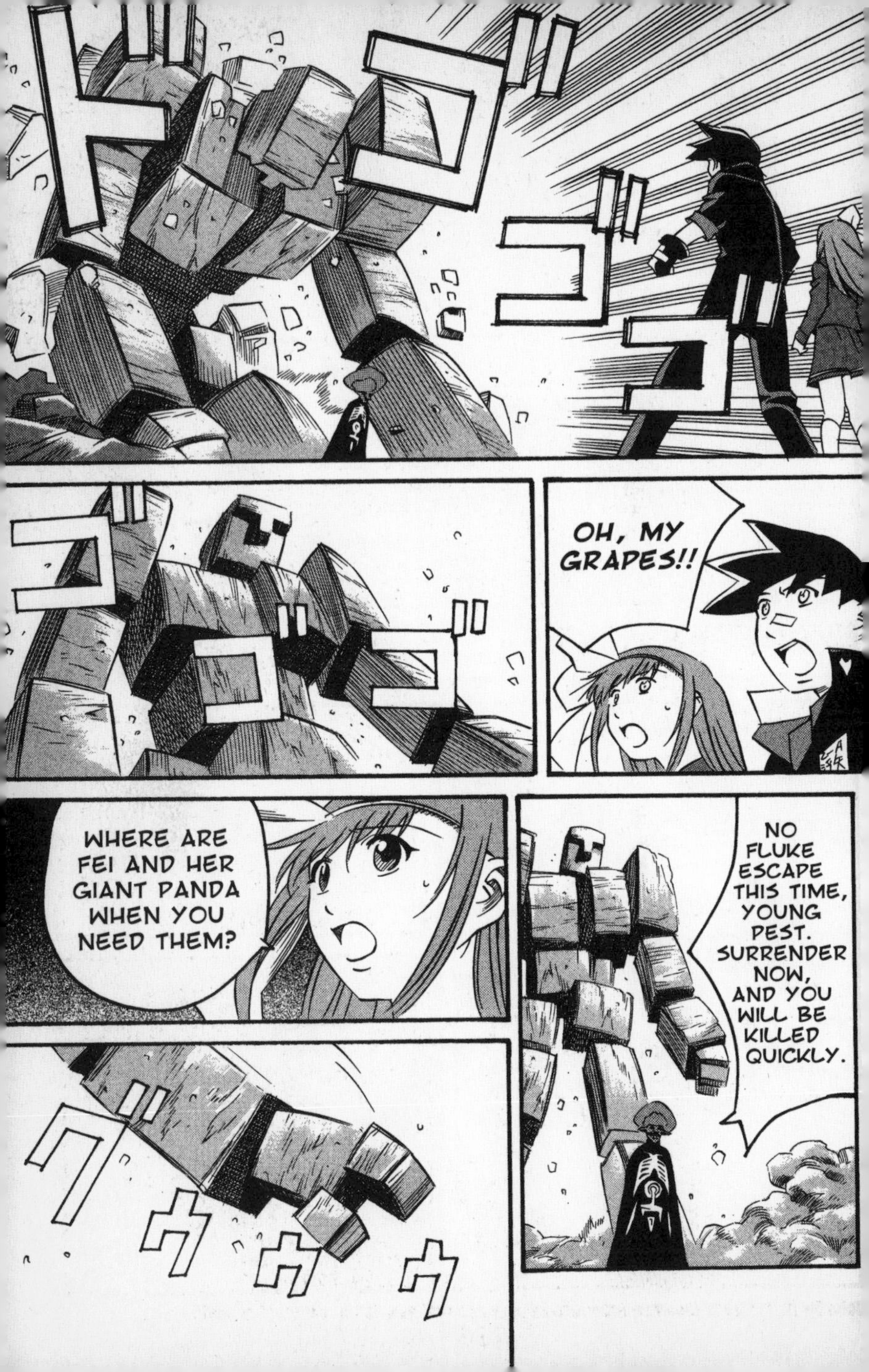
OH, MY GRAPES!!
NO FLUKE ESCAPE THIS TIME, YOUNG PEST. SURRENDER NOW, AND YOU WILL BE KILLED QUICKLY.
WHERE ARE FEI AND HER GIANT PANDA WHEN YOU NEED THEM?

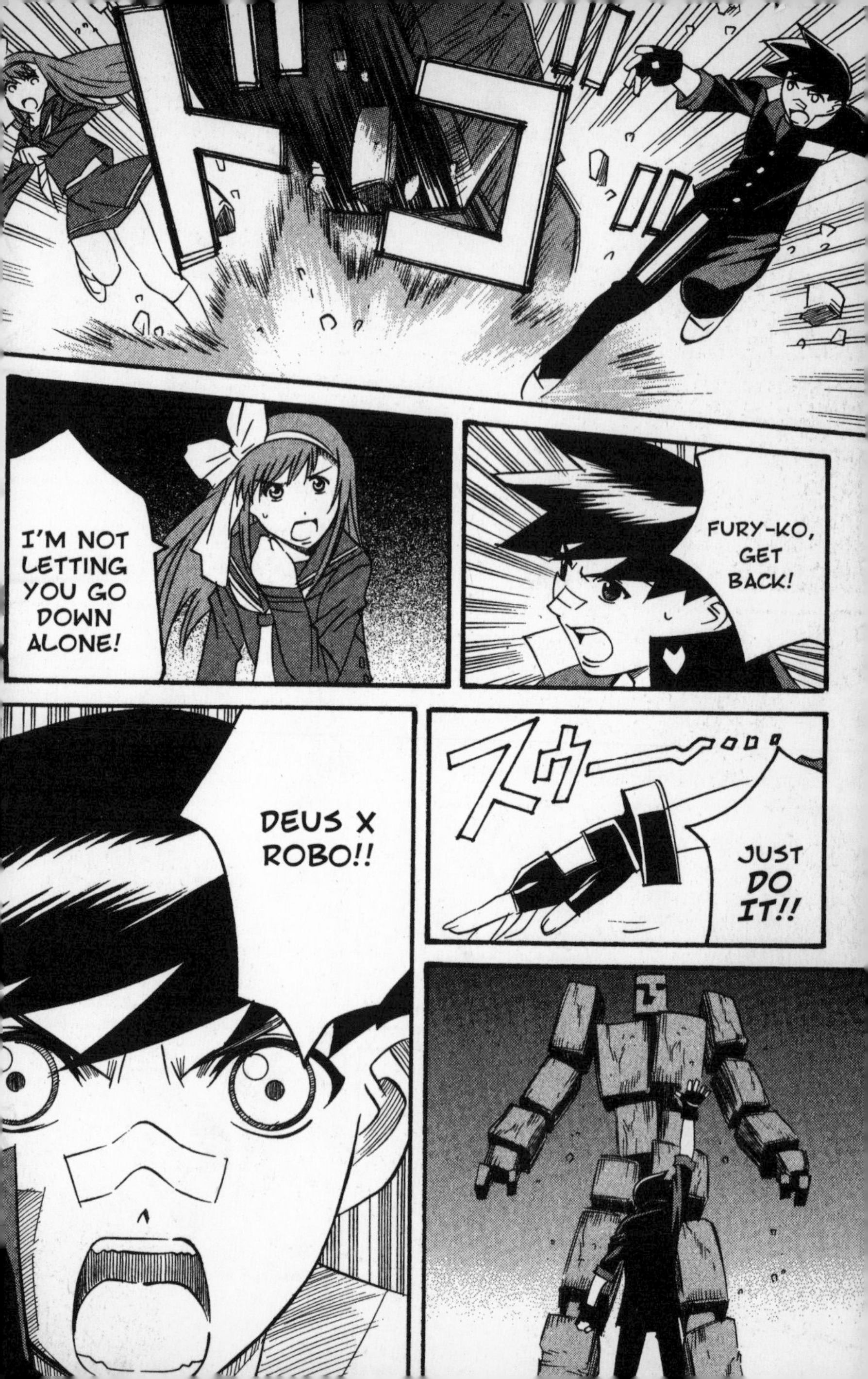
ドゴッ
FURY-KO, GET BACK!
I'M NOT LETTING YOU GO DOWN ALONE!
スウー…
JUST DO IT!!
DEUS X ROBO!!

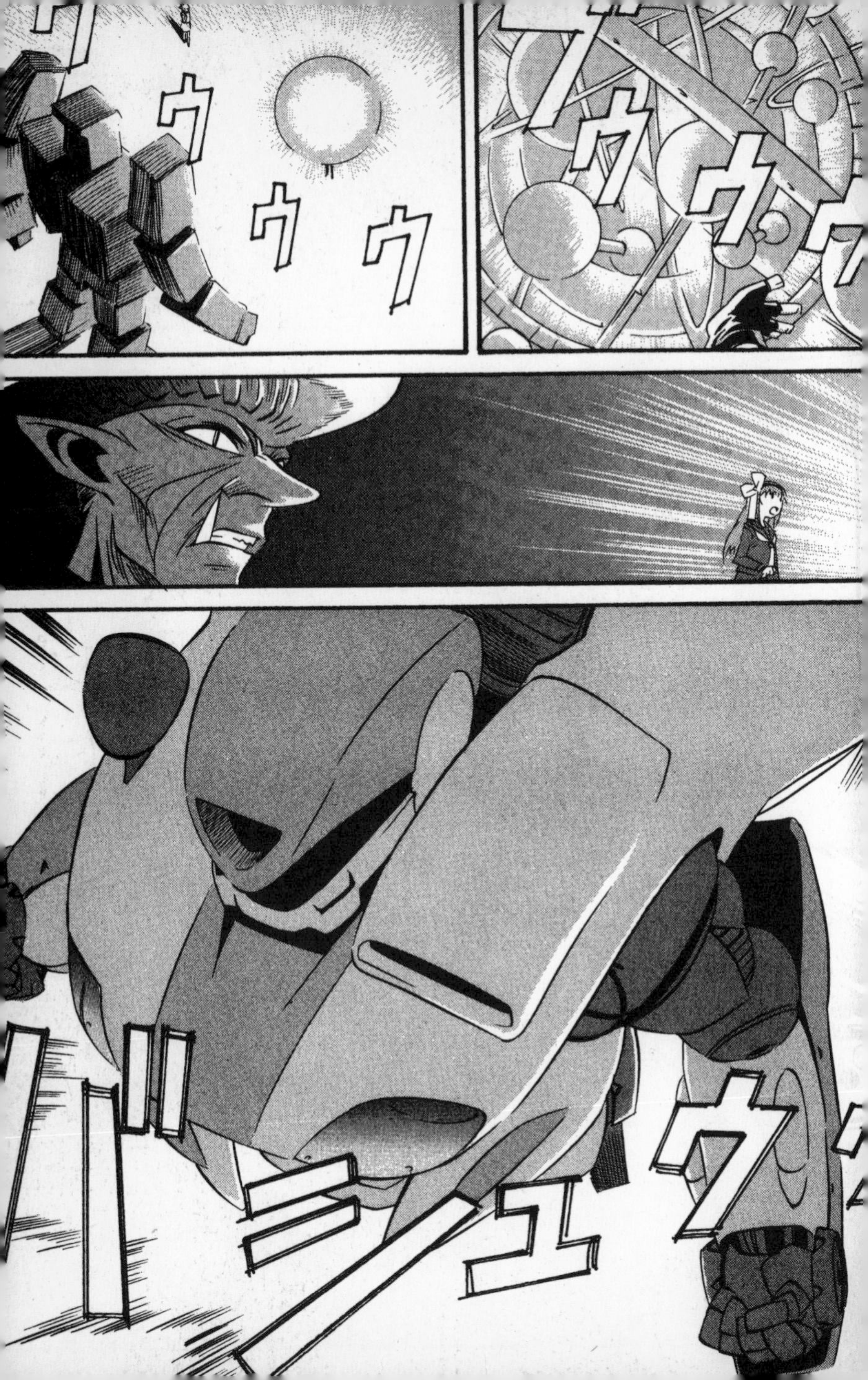
ヴウウウ
ウウウ

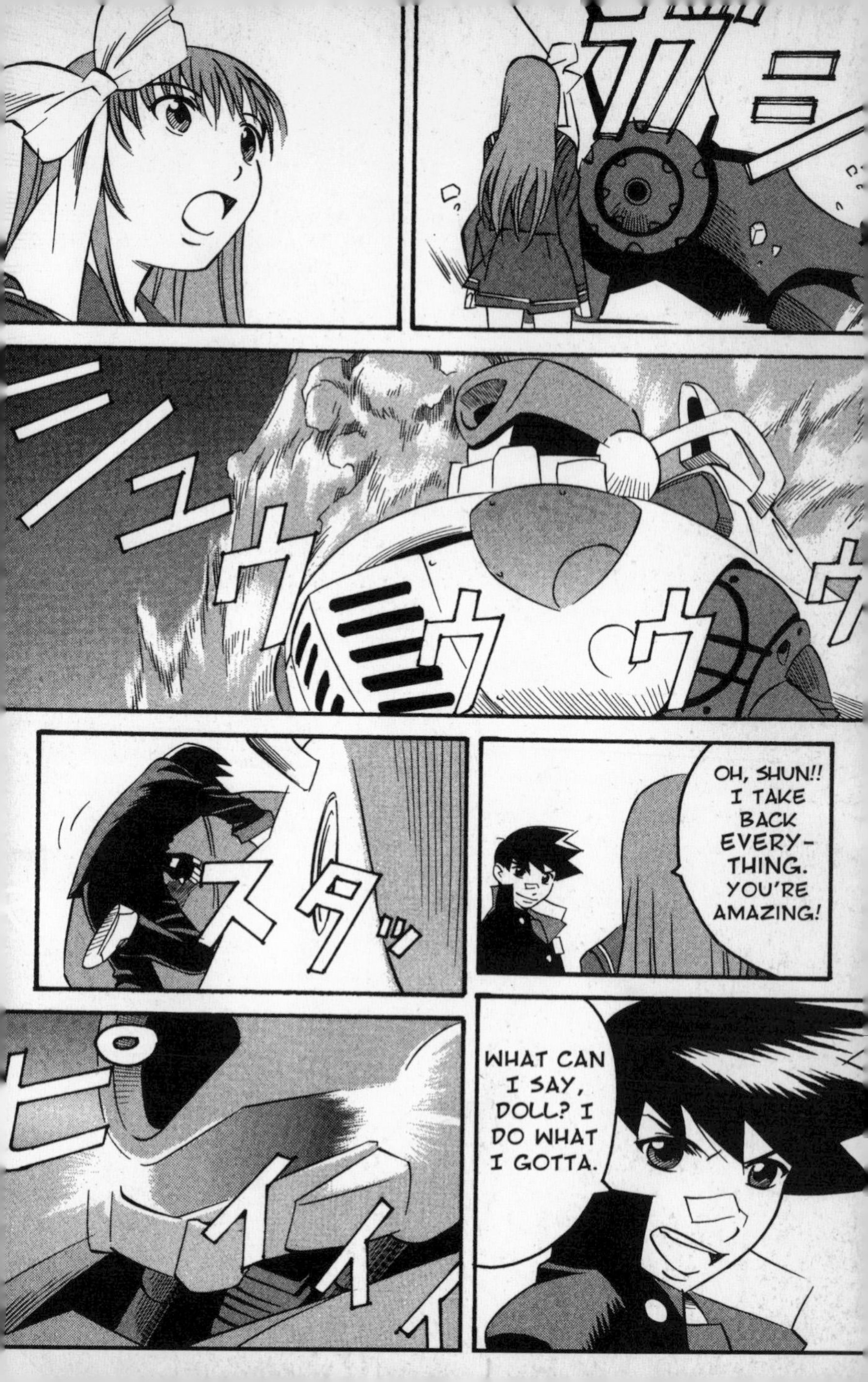
OH, SHUN!! I TAKE BACK EVERY-THING. YOU'RE AMAZING!
WHAT CAN I SAY, DOLL? I DO WHAT I GOTTA.

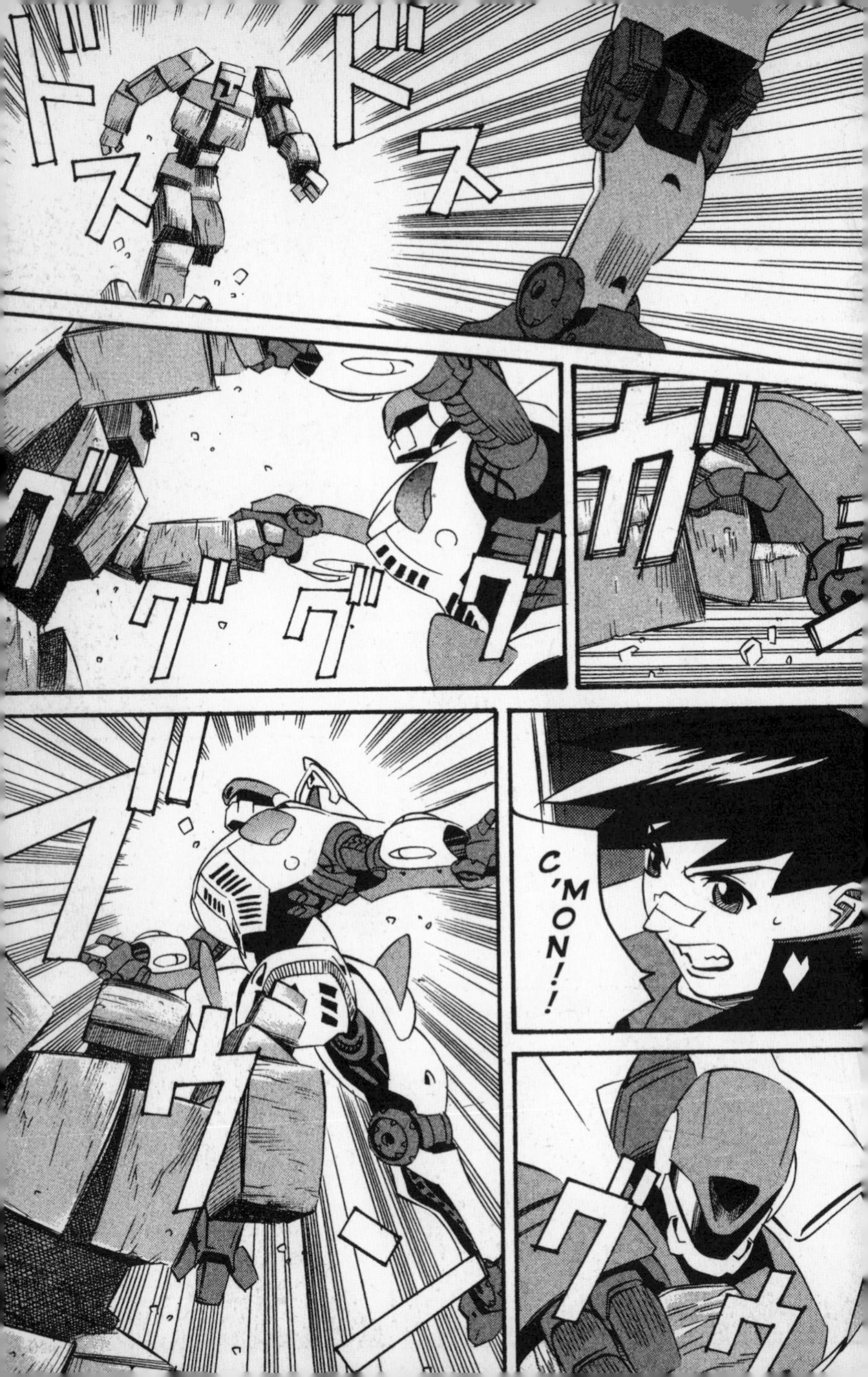
ドス
ドス
C'MON!!

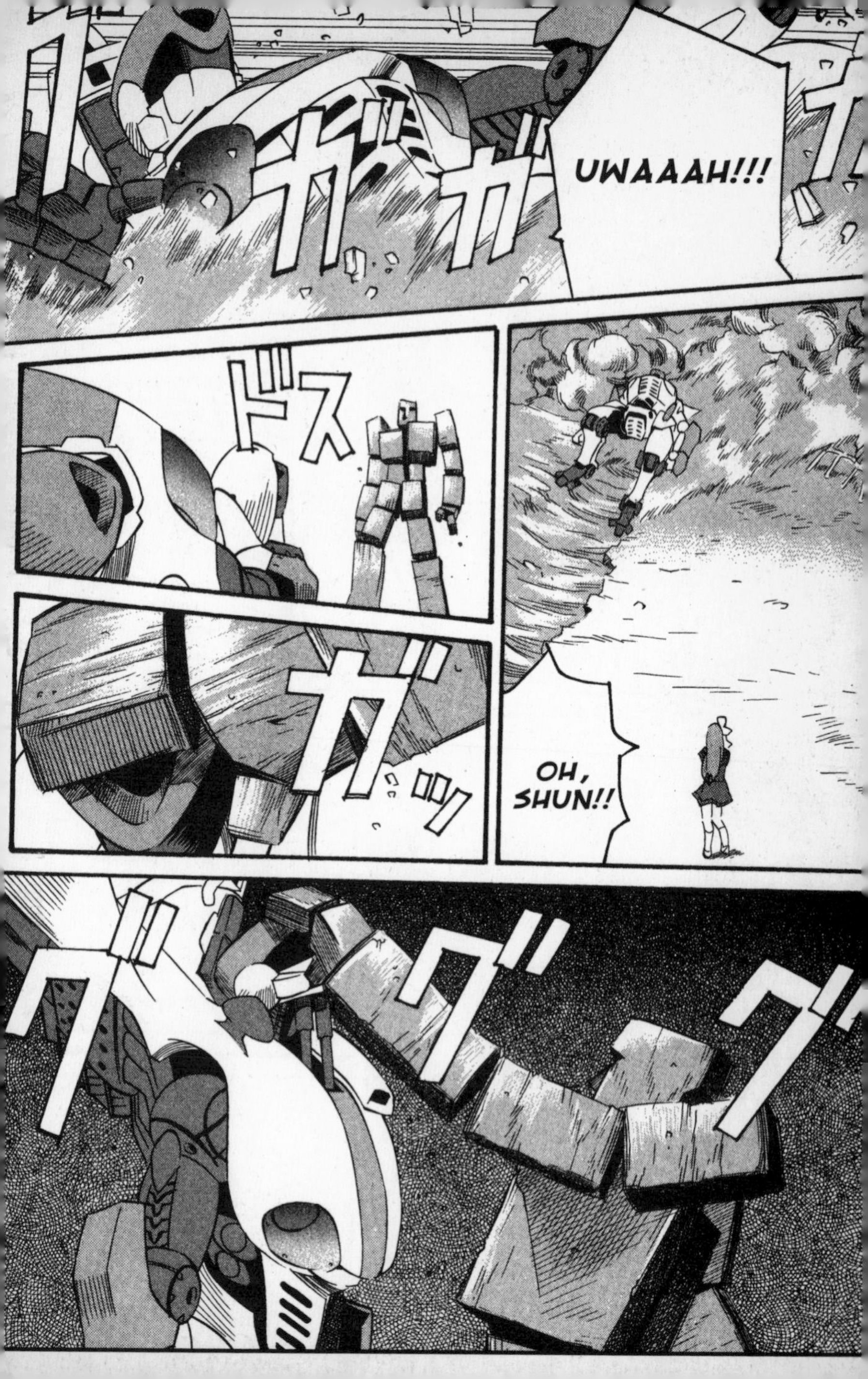
UWAAAH!!!
OH, SHUN!!

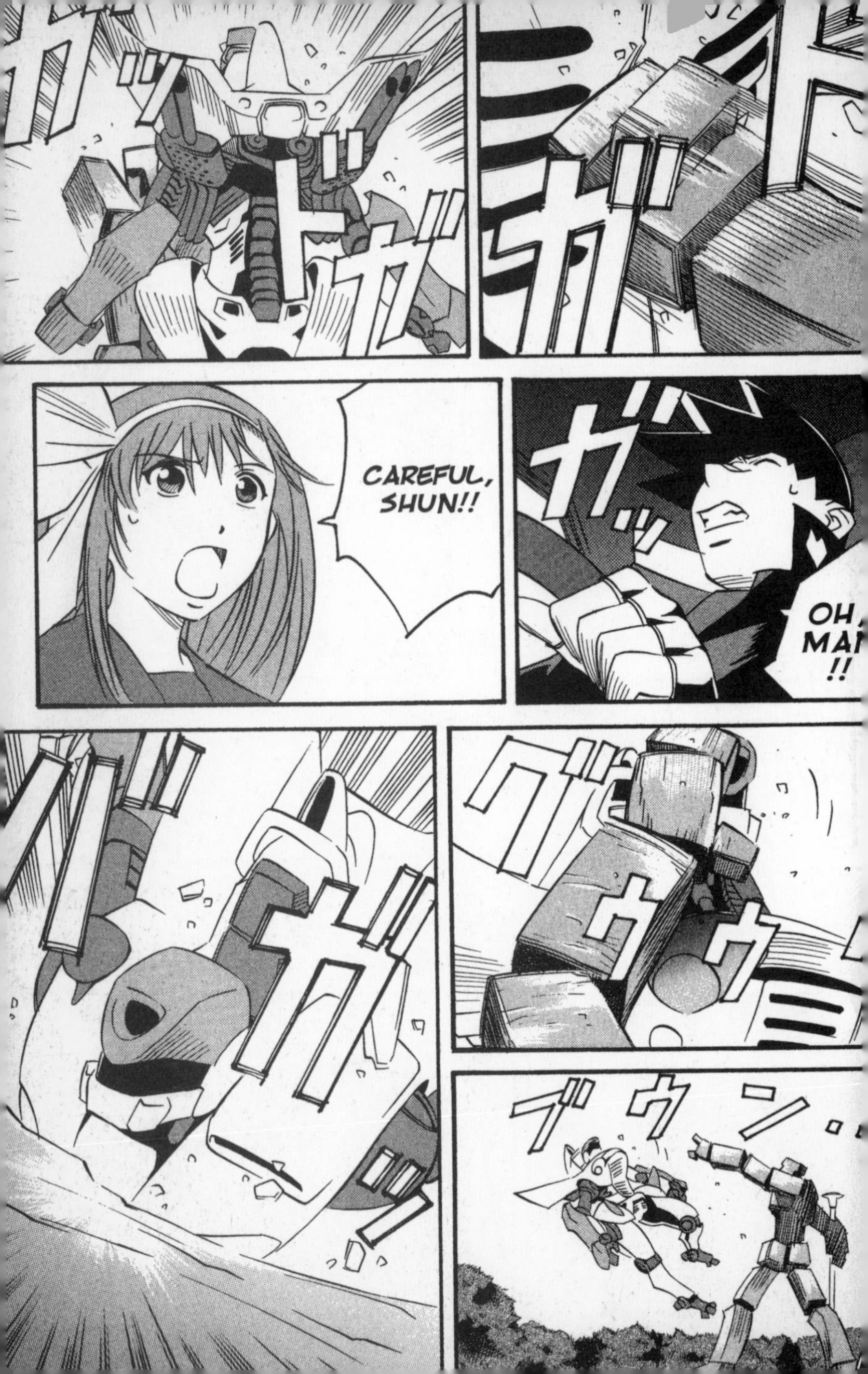
OH, MAN!!
CAREFUL, SHUN!!

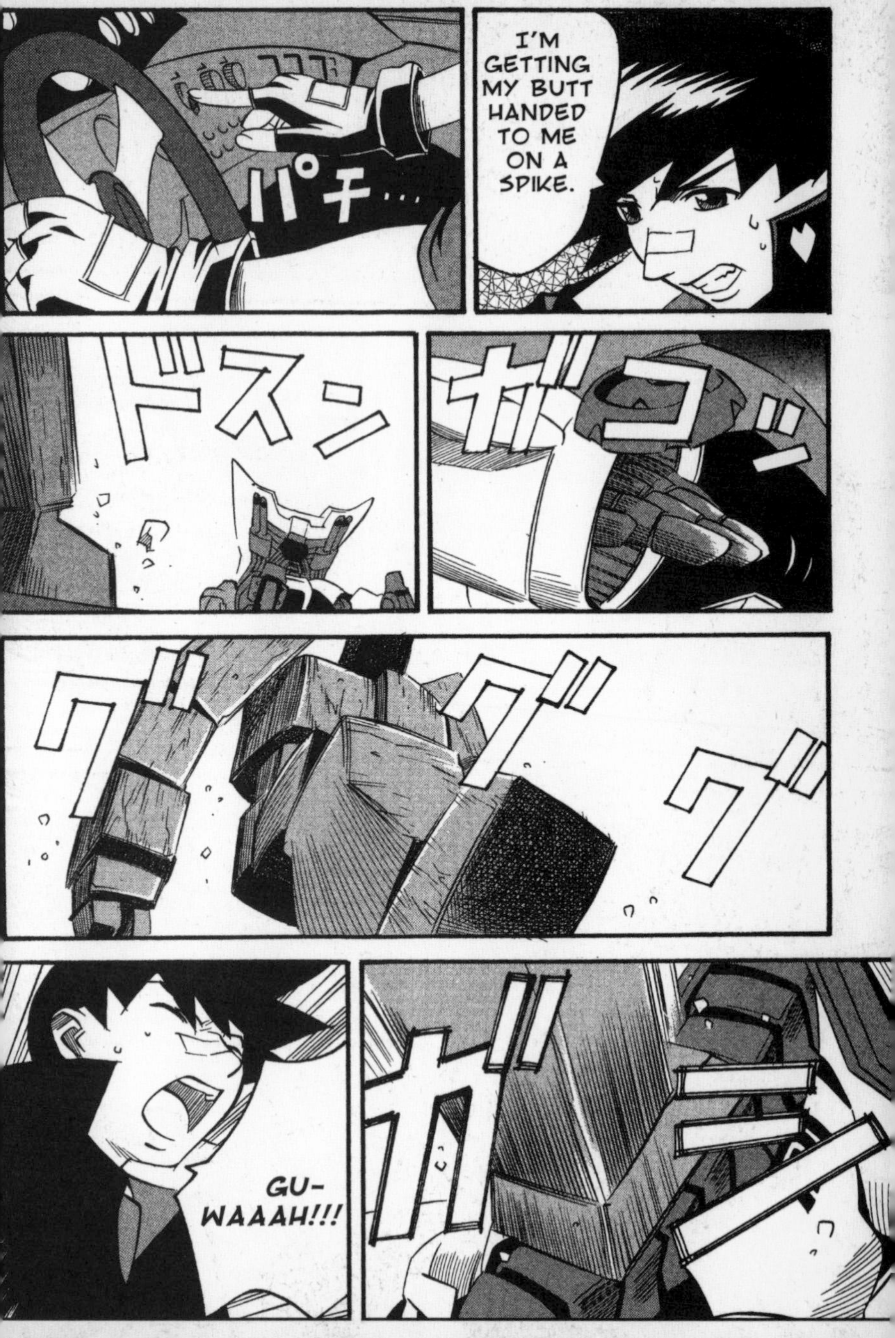
I'M GETTING MY BUTT HANDED TO ME ON A SPIKE.
パチ…
ガゴン
ドスン
グググ
GU-WAAAH!!!

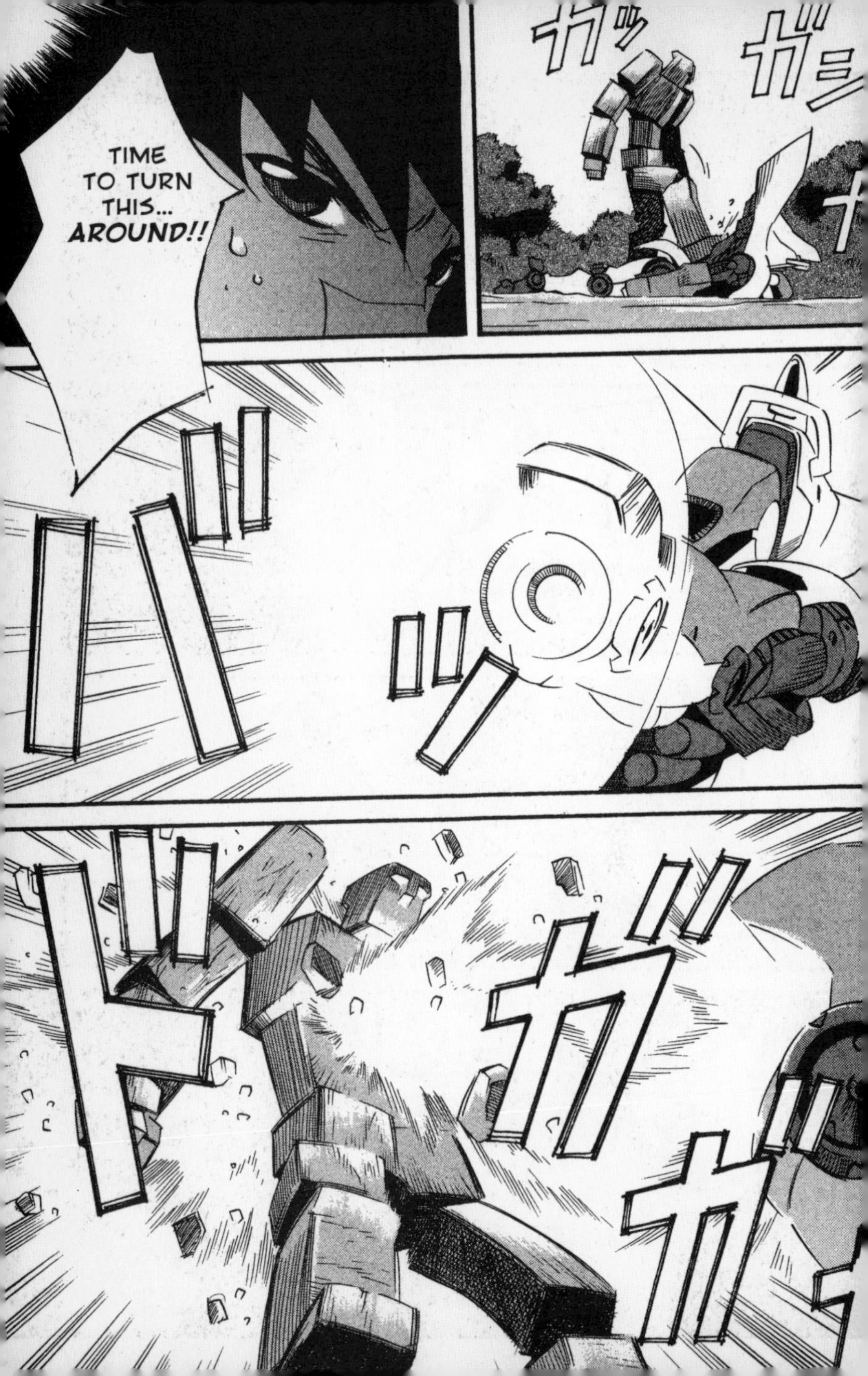
TIME TO TURN THIS... AROUND!!

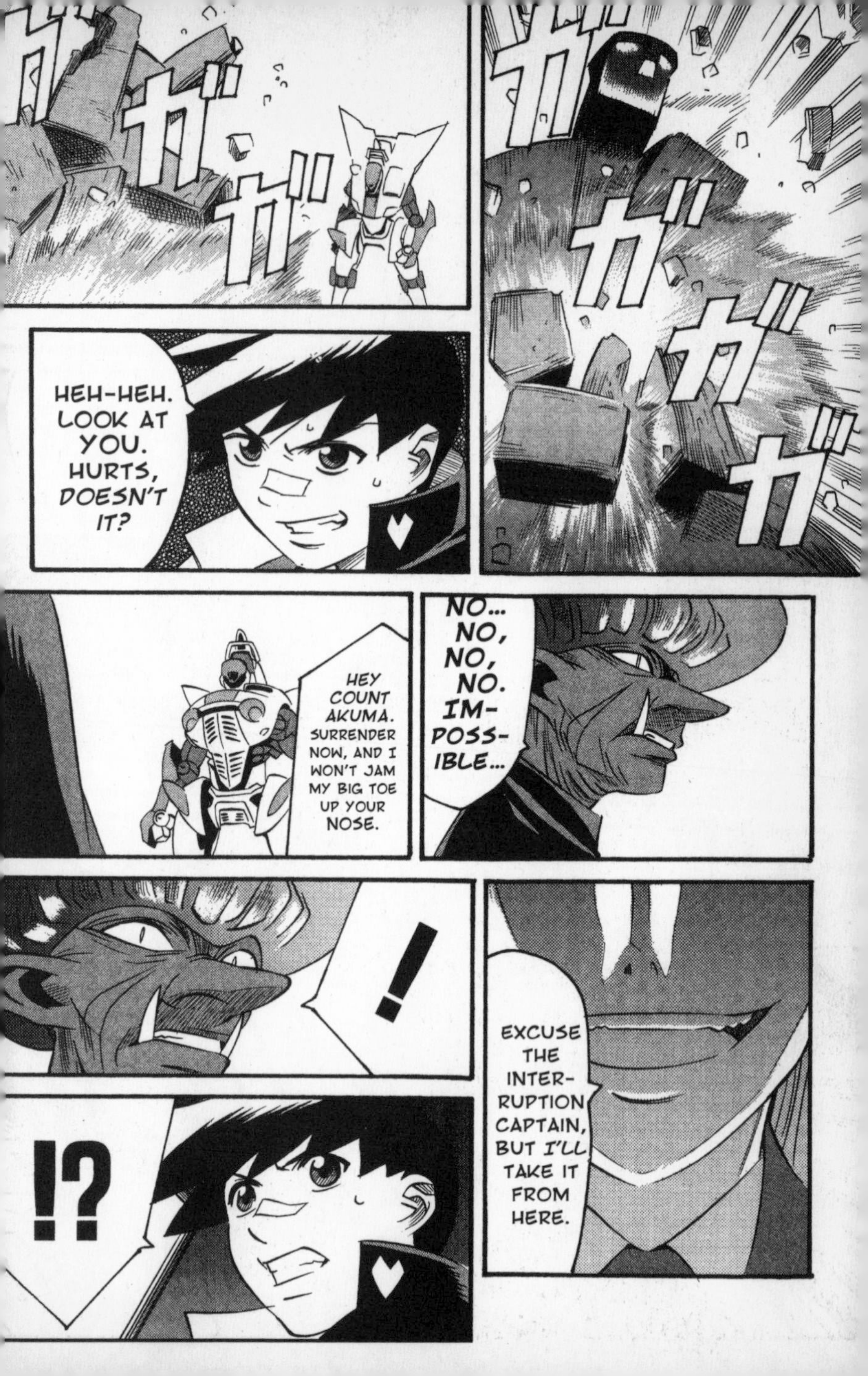
ガガガガ
ガガガ
HEH-HEH. LOOK AT YOU. HURTS, DOESN'T IT?
NO... NO, NO, NO. IM-POSS-IBLE...
HEY COUNT AKUMA. SURRENDER NOW, AND I WON'T JAM MY BIG TOE UP YOUR NOSE.
EXCUSE THE INTER-RUPTION CAPTAIN, BUT I'LL TAKE IT FROM HERE.
!
!?

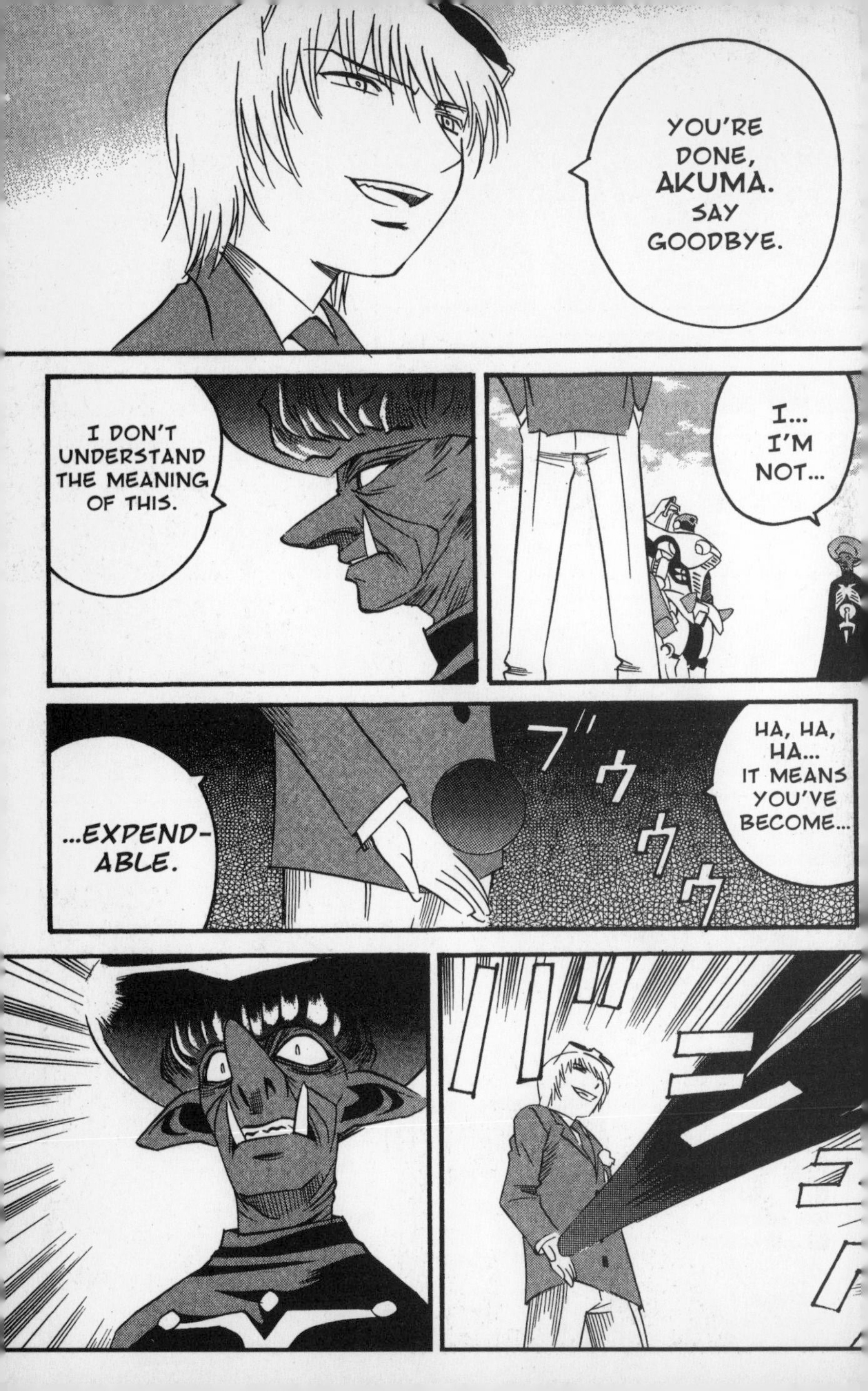
YOU'RE DONE, AKUMA. SAY GOODBYE.
I... I'M NOT...
I DON'T UNDERSTAND THE MEANING OF THIS.
HA, HA, HA... IT MEANS YOU'VE BECOME...
ブウウウ
...EXPEND-ABLE.

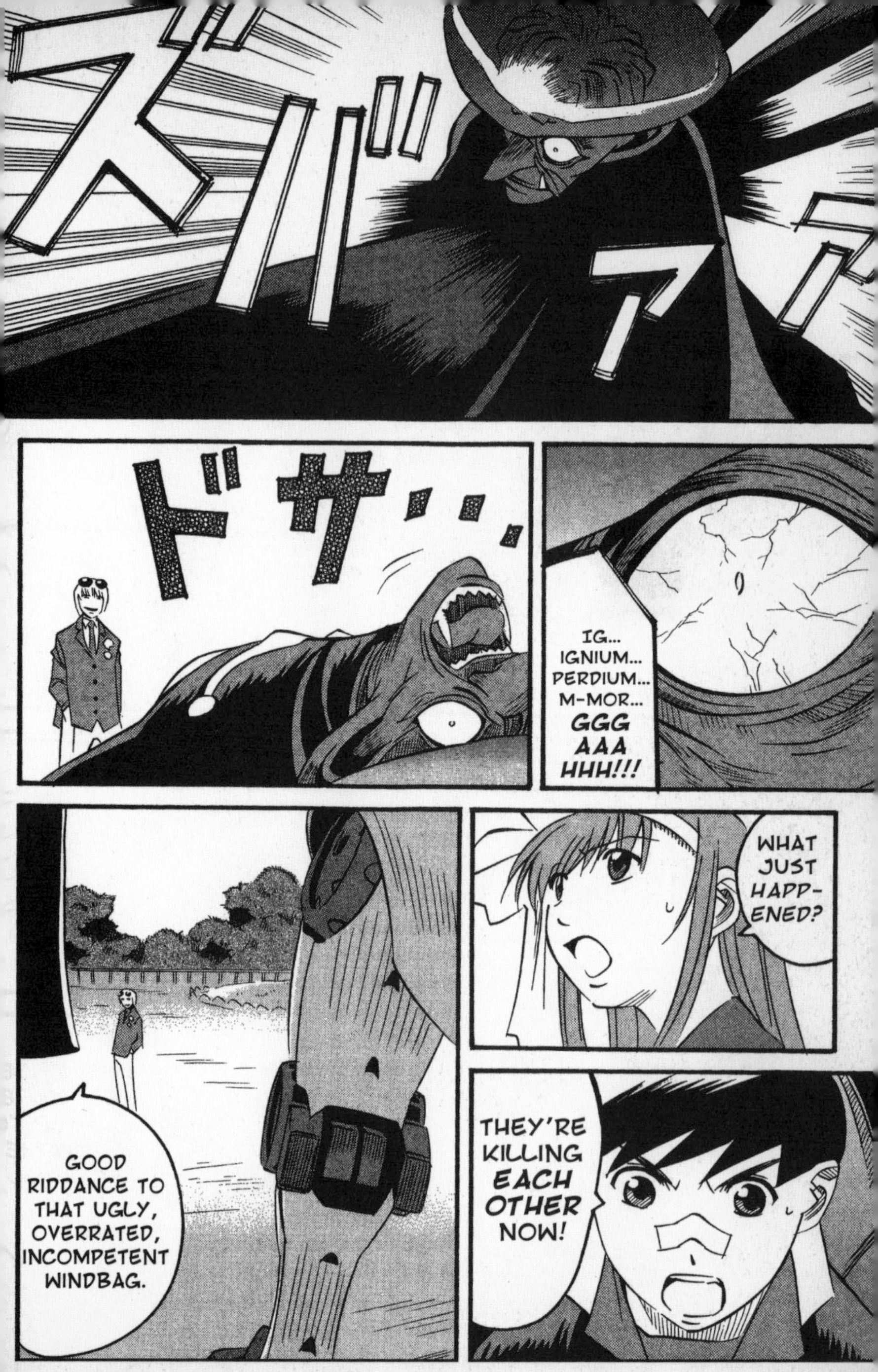
ズバァァ
ドサ…
IG... IGNIUM... PERDIUM... M-MOR... GGG AAA HHH!!!
WHAT JUST HAPP-ENED?
GOOD RIDDANCE TO THAT UGLY, OVERRATED, INCOMPETENT WINDBAG.
THEY'RE KILLING EACH OTHER NOW!

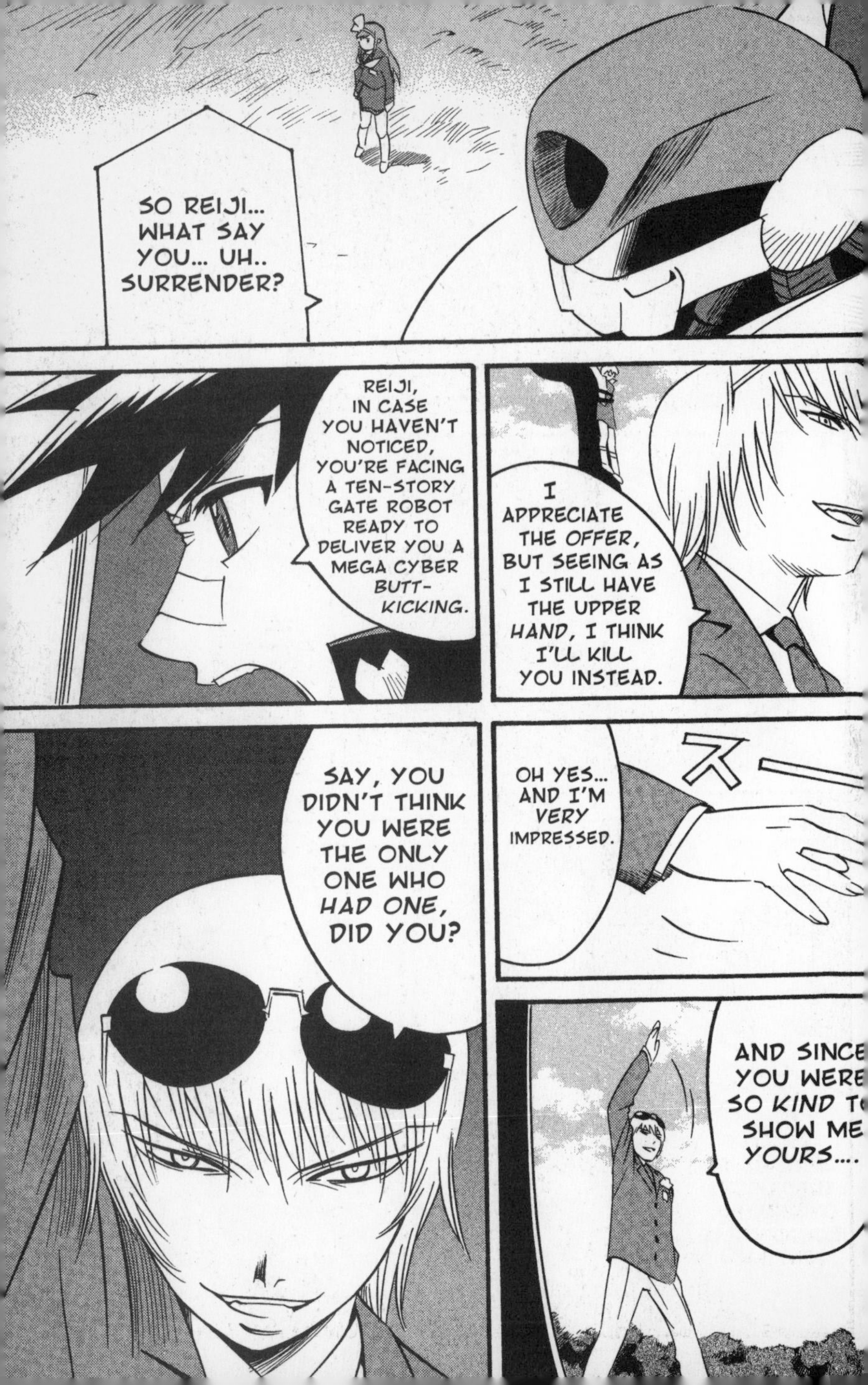
SO REIJI... WHAT SAY YOU... UH.. SURRENDER?
I APPRECIATE THE OFFER, BUT SEEING AS I STILL HAVE THE UPPER HAND, I THINK I'LL KILL YOU INSTEAD.
REIJI, IN CASE YOU HAVEN'T NOTICED, YOU'RE FACING A TEN-STORY GATE ROBOT READY TO DELIVER YOU A MEGA CYBER BUTT-KICKING.
スー
OH YES... AND I'M VERY IMPRESSED.
AND SINCE YOU WERE SO KIND T SHOW ME YOURS....
SAY, YOU DIDN'T THINK YOU WERE THE ONLY ONE WHO HAD ONE, DID YOU?

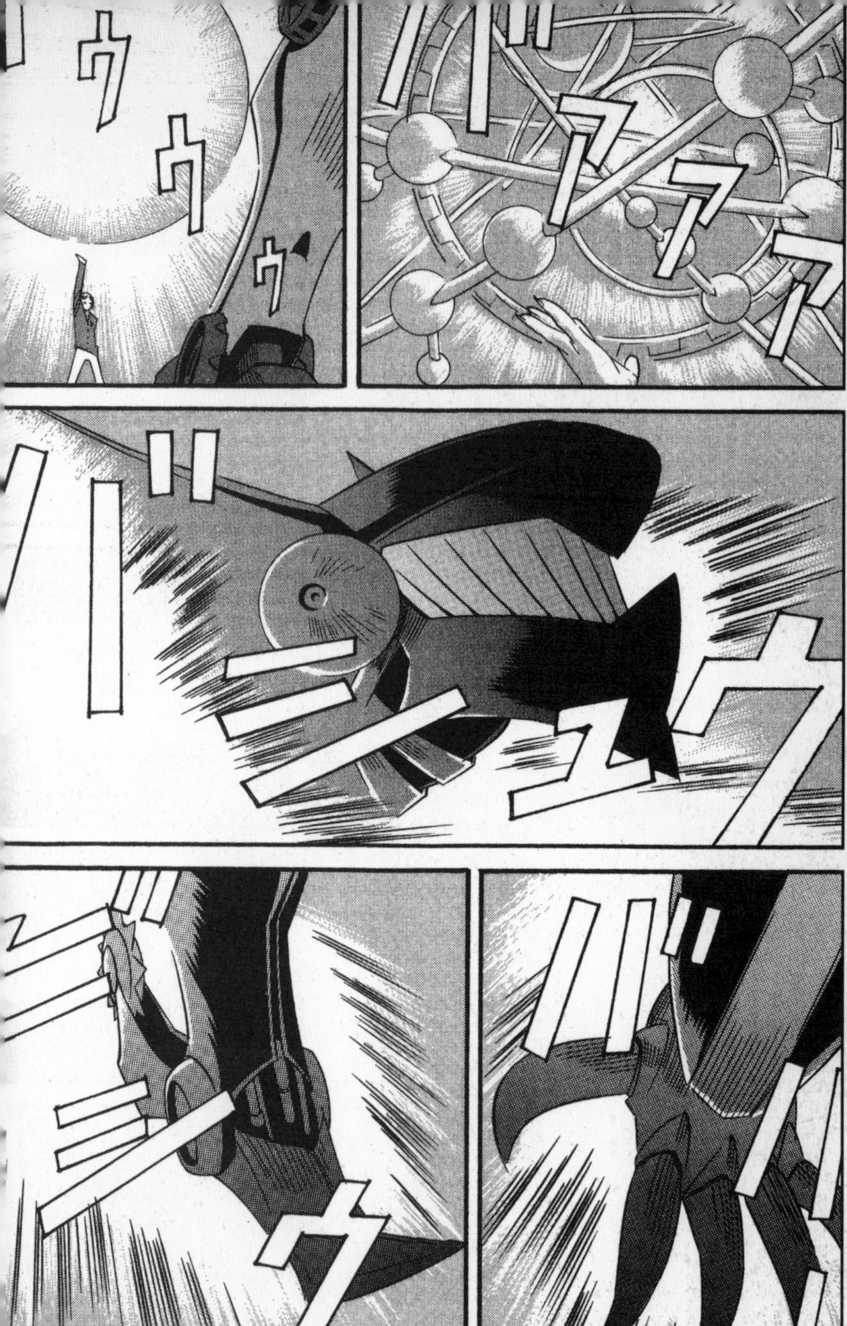
バアアアア
ウウウ

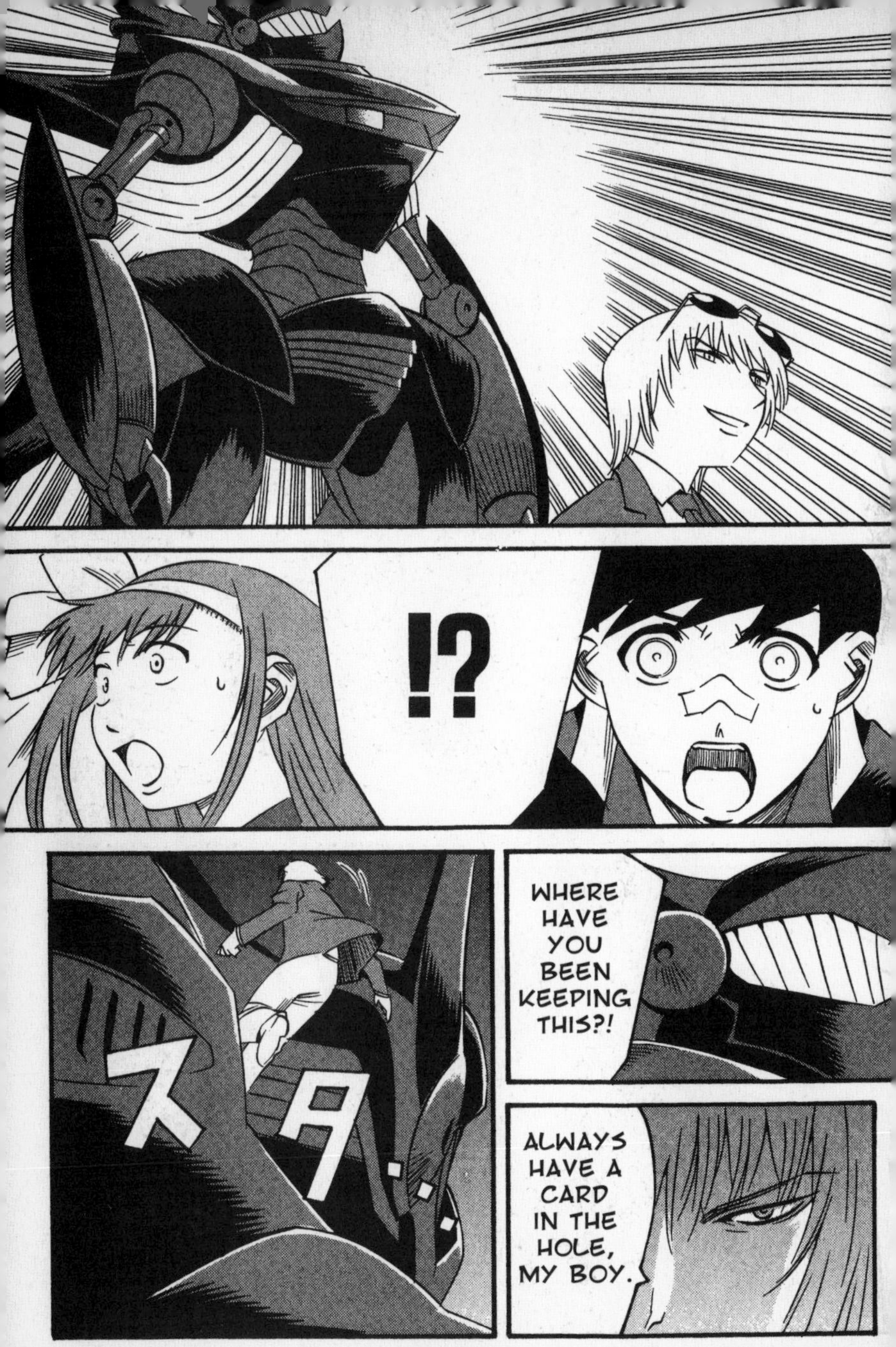
!?
WHERE HAVE YOU BEEN KEEPING THIS?!
ALWAYS HAVE A CARD IN THE HOLE, MY BOY.
スタ...

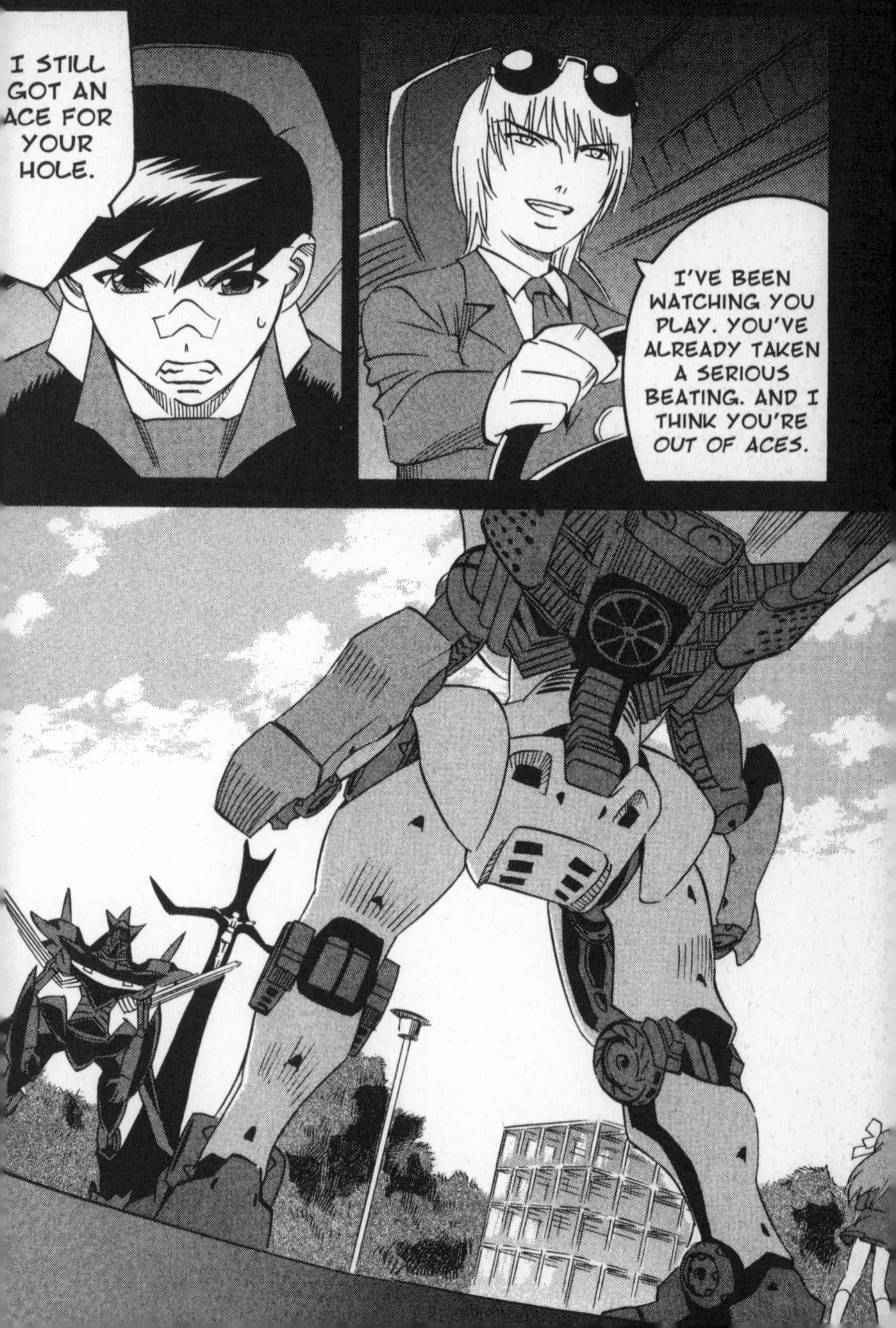
I'VE BEEN WATCHING YOU PLAY. YOU'VE ALREADY TAKEN A SERIOUS BEATING. AND I THINK YOU'RE OUT OF ACES.
I STILL GOT AN ACE FOR YOUR HOLE.

GATE #14 THE THIRD GIANT

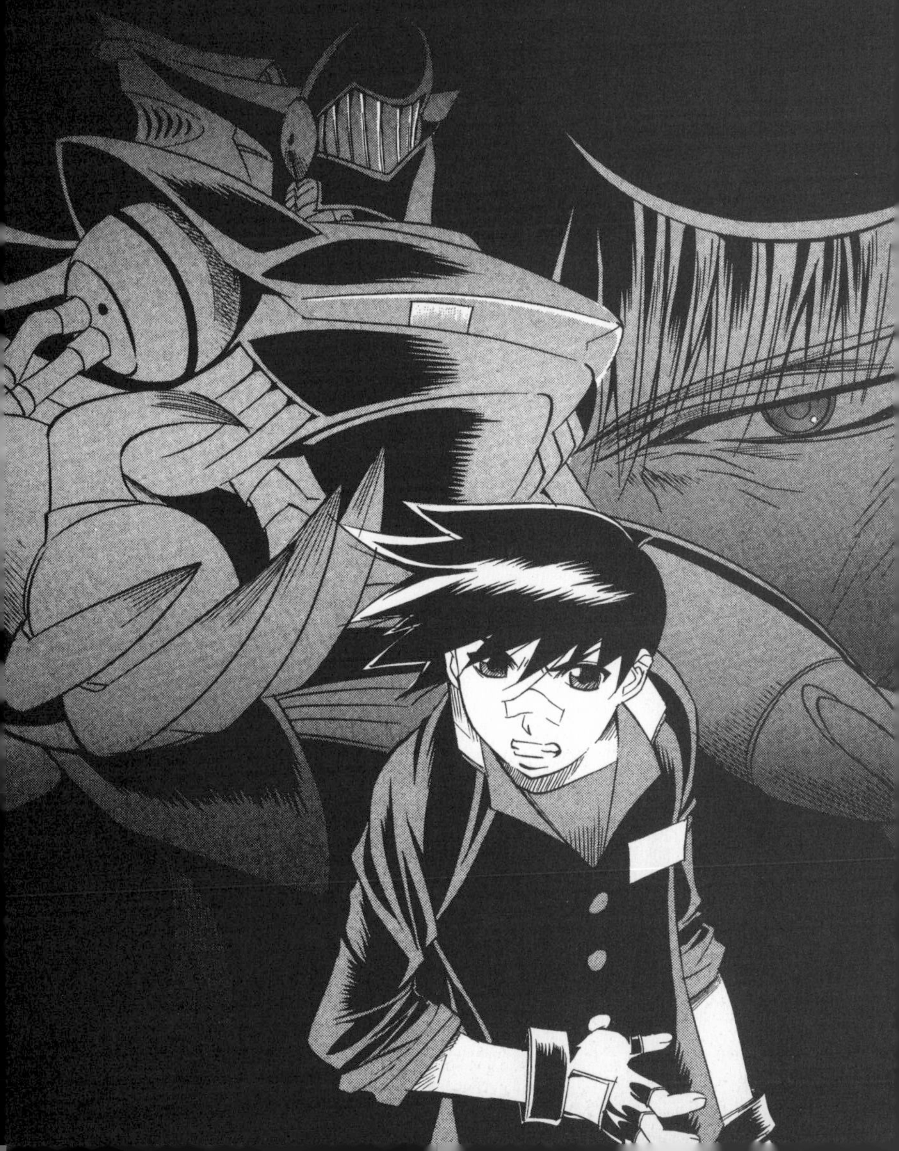

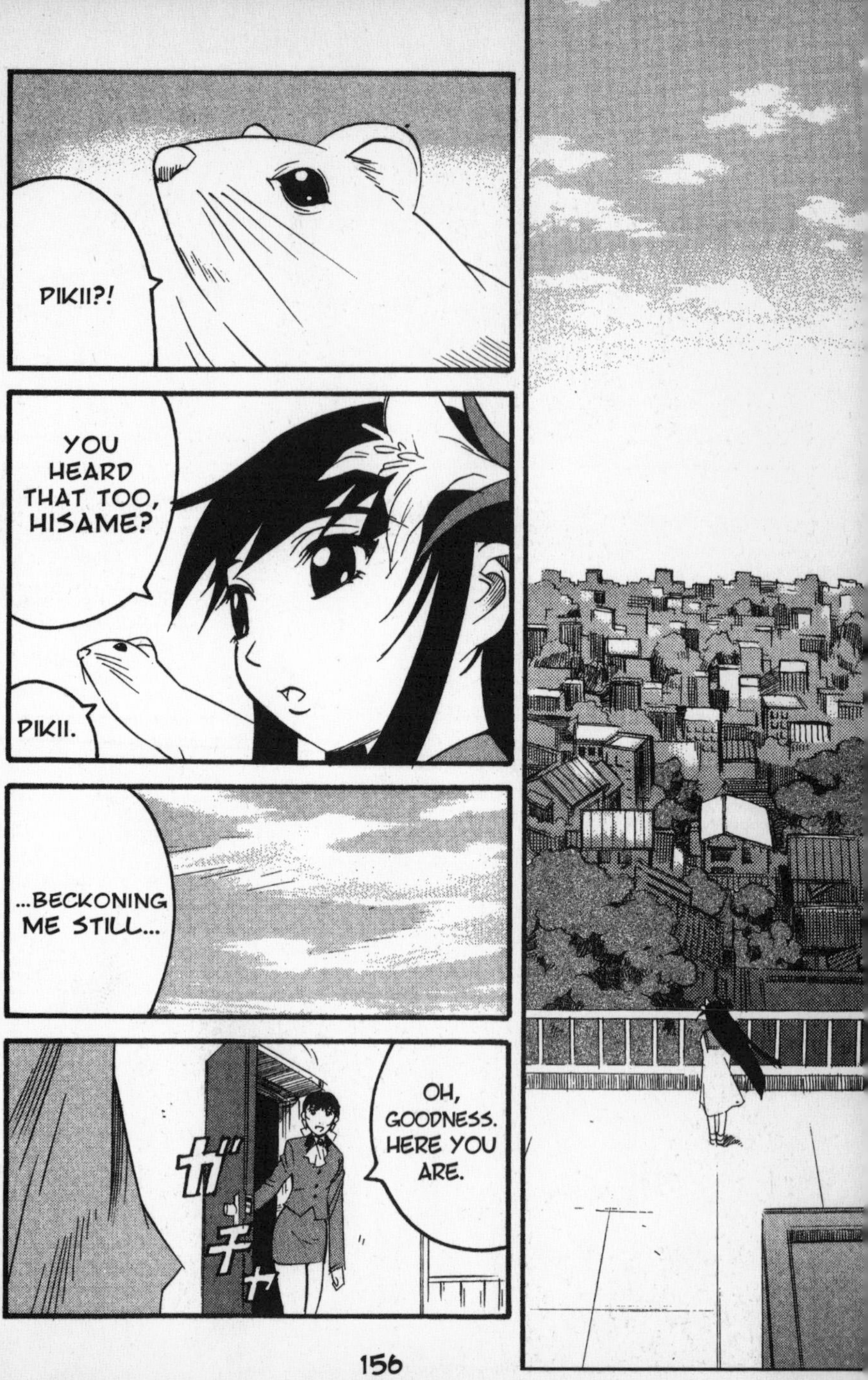
PIKII?!
YOU HEARD THAT TOO, HISAME?
PIKII.
...BECKONING ME STILL...
OH, GOODNESS. HERE YOU ARE.
ガッチャ

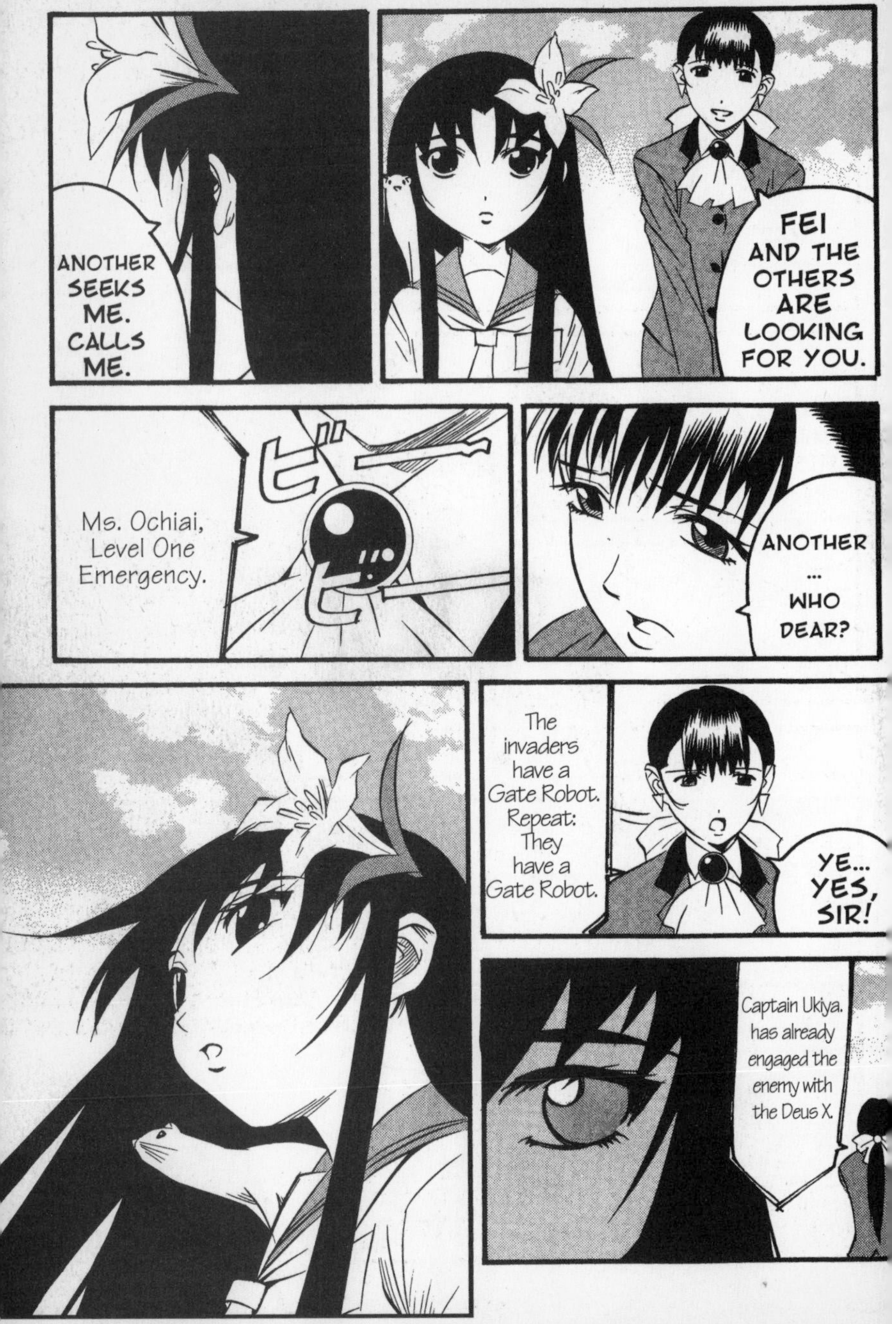
FEI AND THE OTHERS ARE LOOKING FOR YOU.
ANOTHER SEEKS ME. CALLS ME.
ANOTHER ... WHO DEAR?
Ms. Ochiai, Level One Emergency.
YE... YES, SIR!
The invaders have a Gate Robot. Repeat: They have a Gate Robot.
Captain Ukiya. has already engaged the enemy with the Deus X.

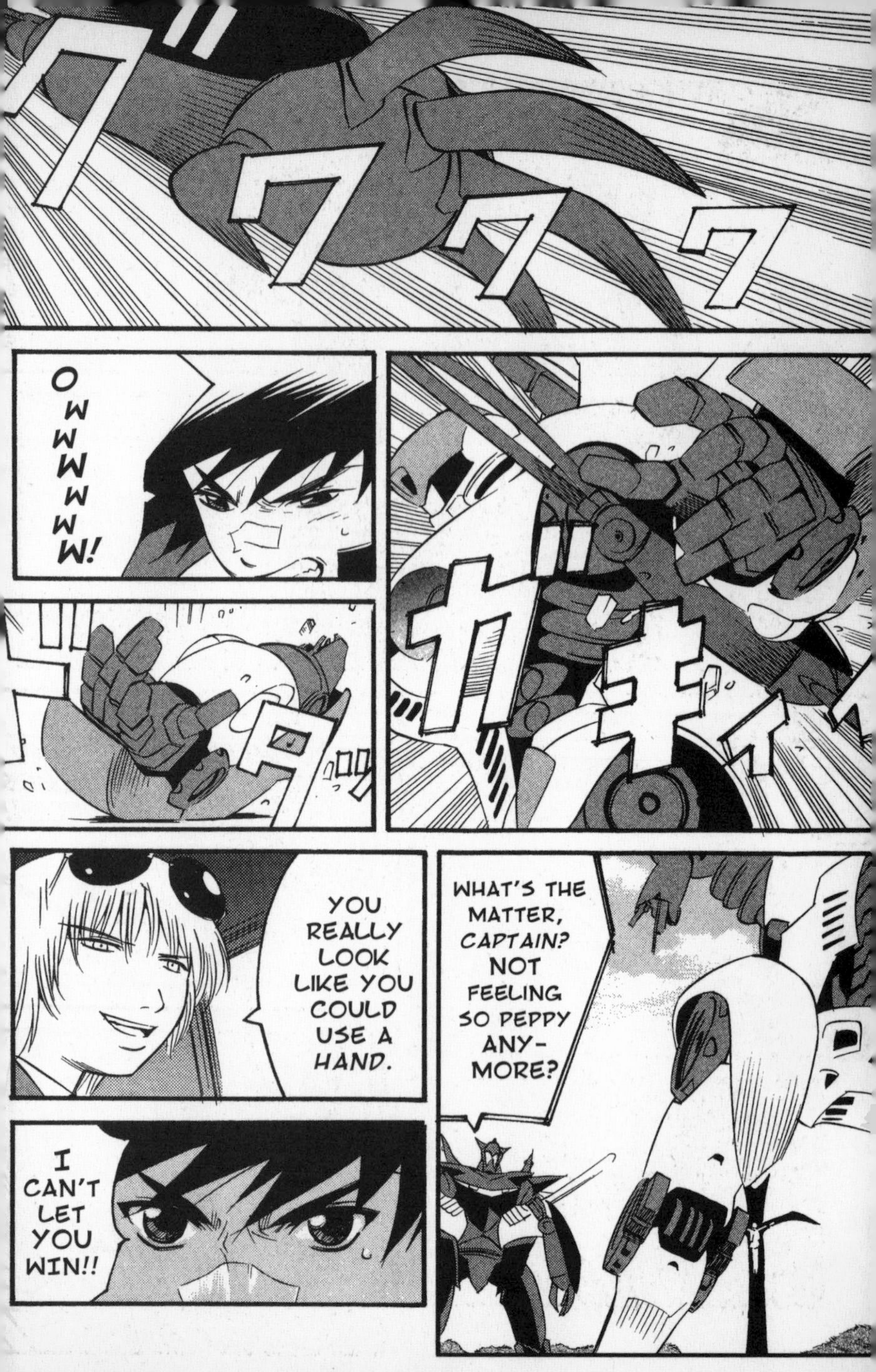
OWWWWWW!
WHAT'S THE MATTER, CAPTAIN? NOT FEELING SO PEPPY ANY-MORE?
YOU REALLY LOOK LIKE YOU COULD USE A HAND.
I CAN'T LET YOU WIN!!

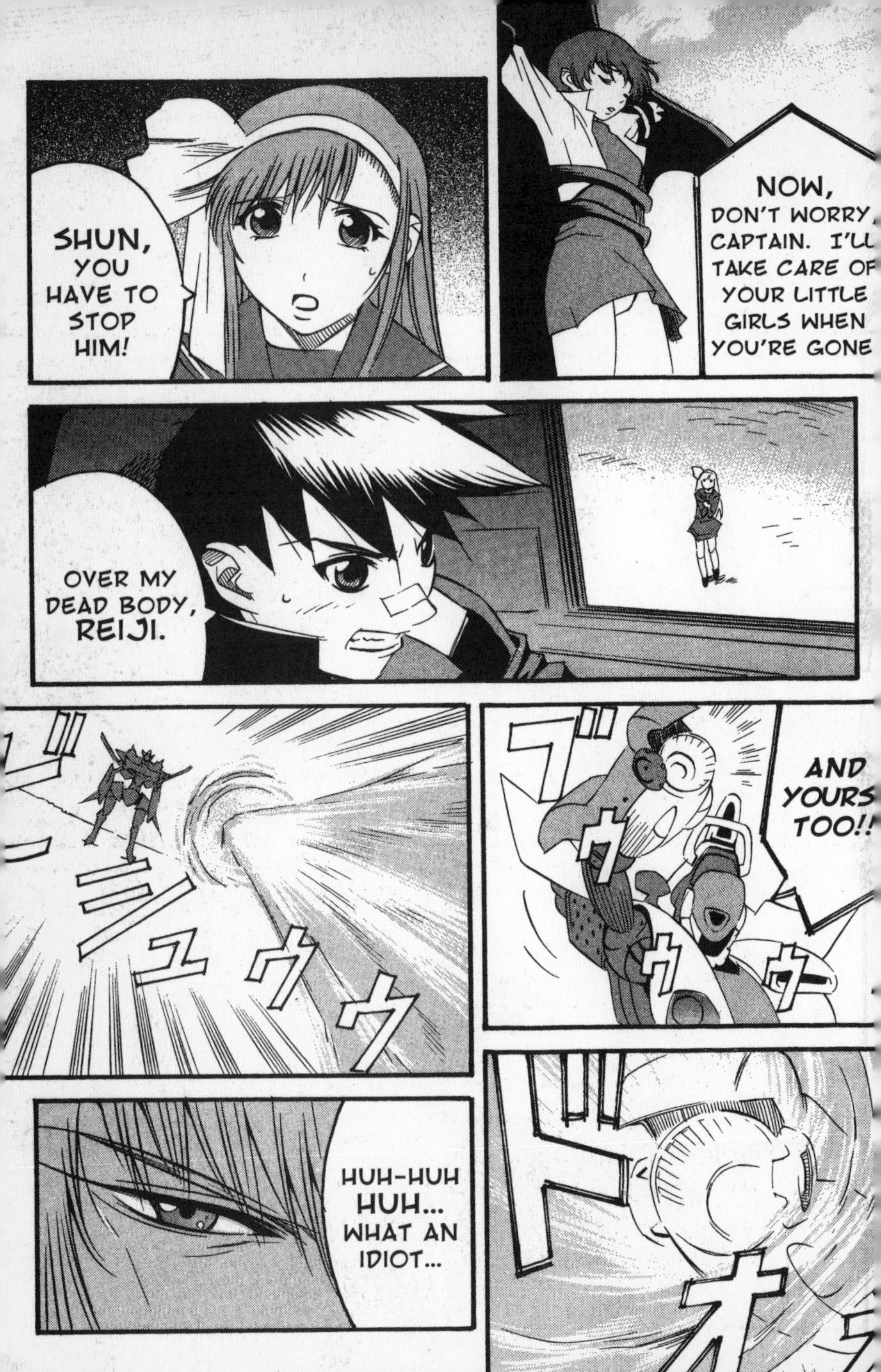
NOW, DON'T WORRY, CAPTAIN. I'LL TAKE CARE OF YOUR LITTLE GIRLS WHEN YOU'RE GONE
SHUN, YOU HAVE TO STOP HIM!
OVER MY DEAD BODY, REIJI.
AND YOURS TOO!!
HUH-HUH HUH... WHAT AN IDIOT...

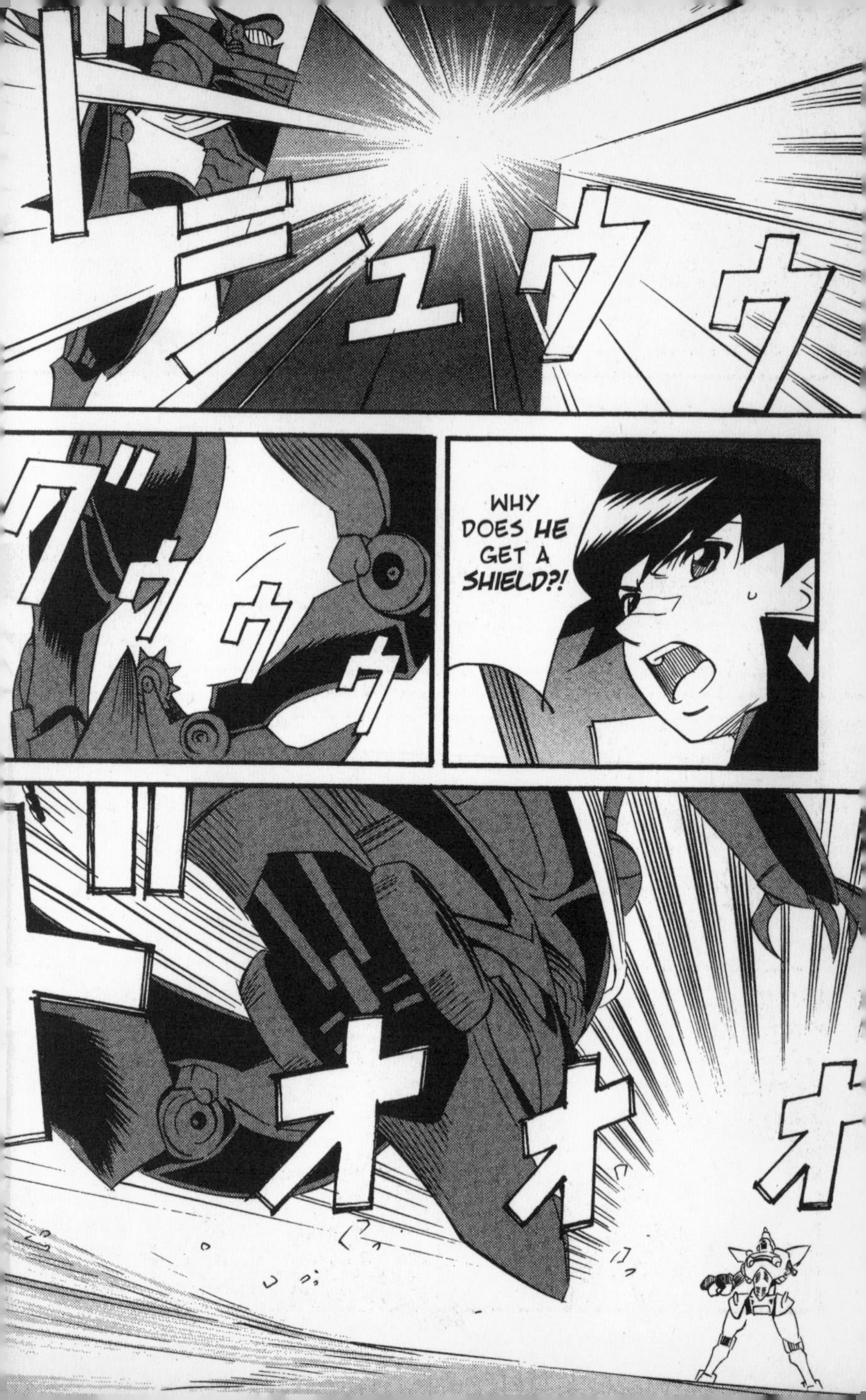
WHY DOES HE GET A SHIELD?!

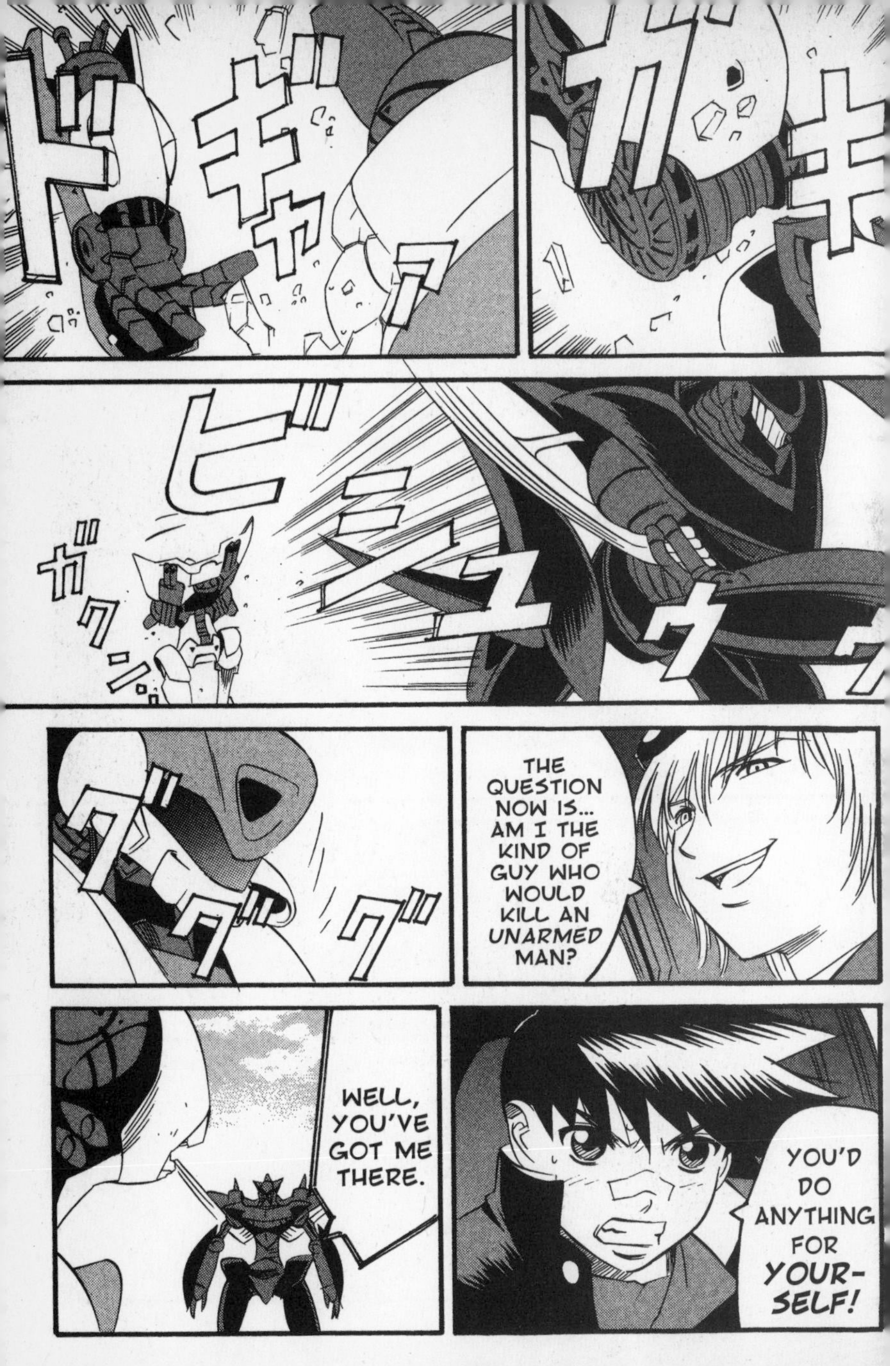
THE QUESTION NOW IS... AM I THE KIND OF GUY WHO WOULD KILL AN UNARMED MAN?
YOU'D DO ANYTHING FOR YOURSELF!
WELL, YOU'VE GOT ME THERE.

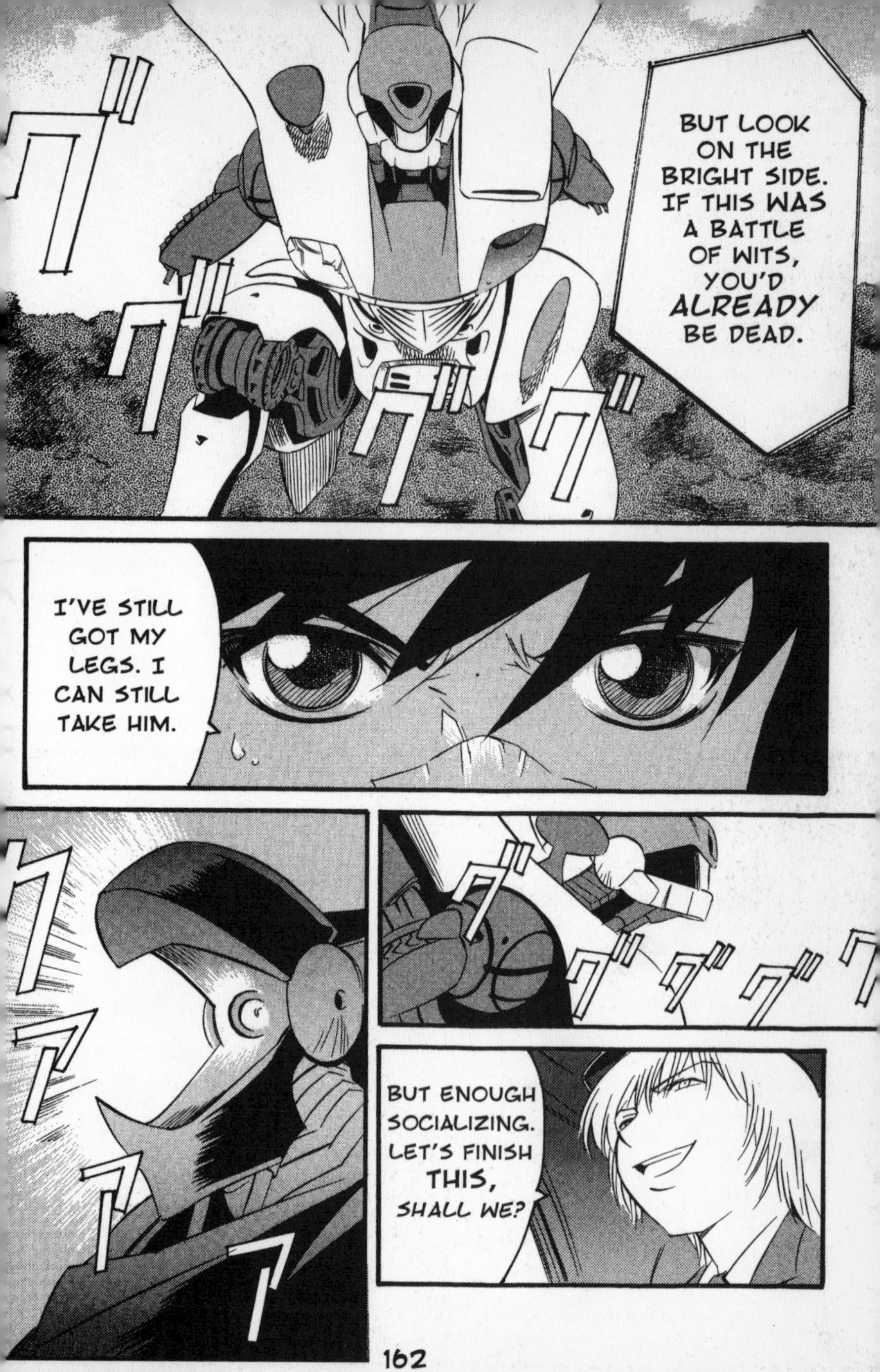
BUT LOOK ON THE BRIGHT SIDE. IF THIS WAS A BATTLE OF WITS, YOU'D ALREADY BE DEAD.
I'VE STILL GOT MY LEGS. I CAN STILL TAKE HIM.
BUT ENOUGH SOCIALIZING. LET'S FINISH THIS, SHALL WE?

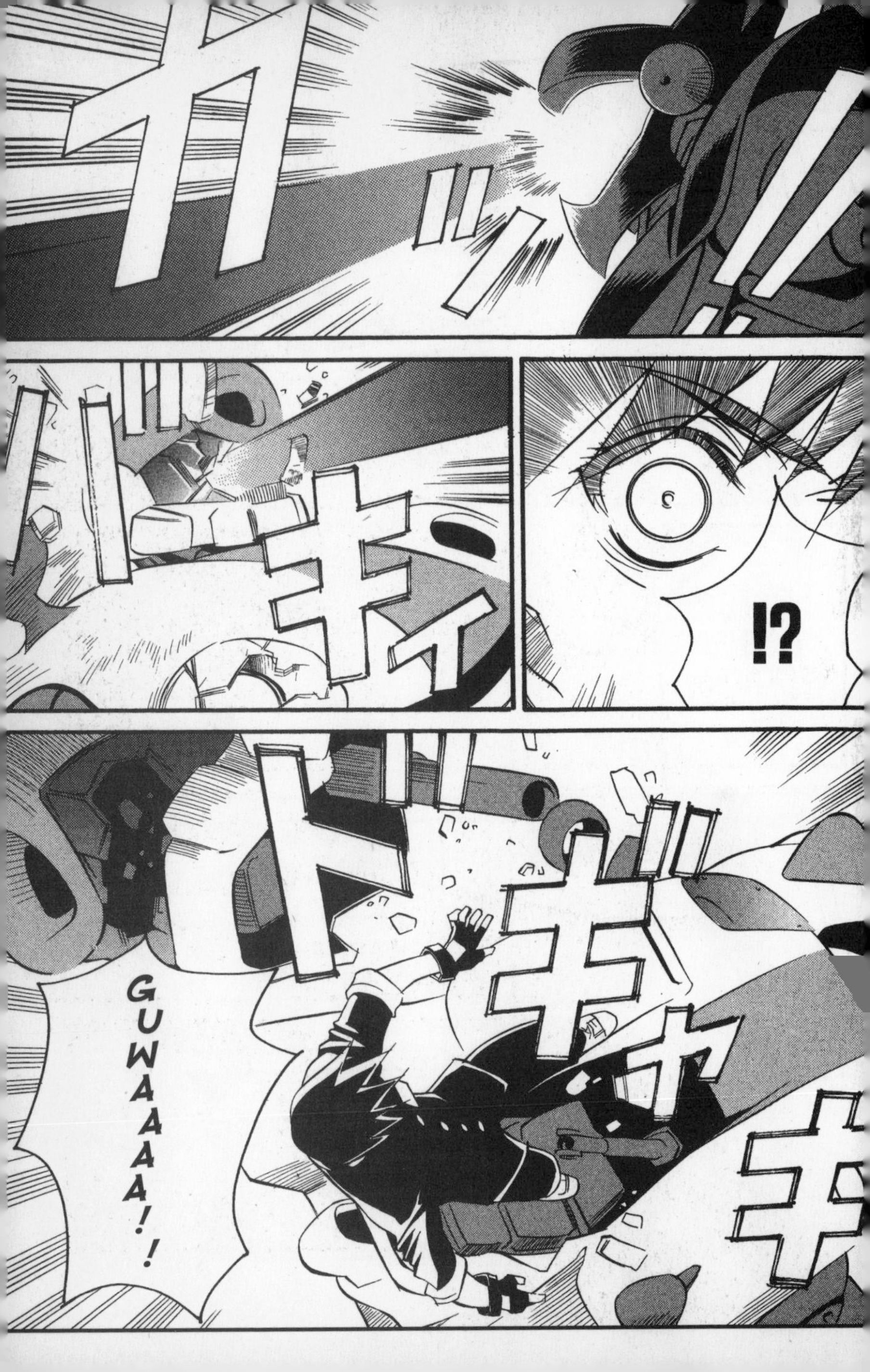
!?
GUWAAAAA!!

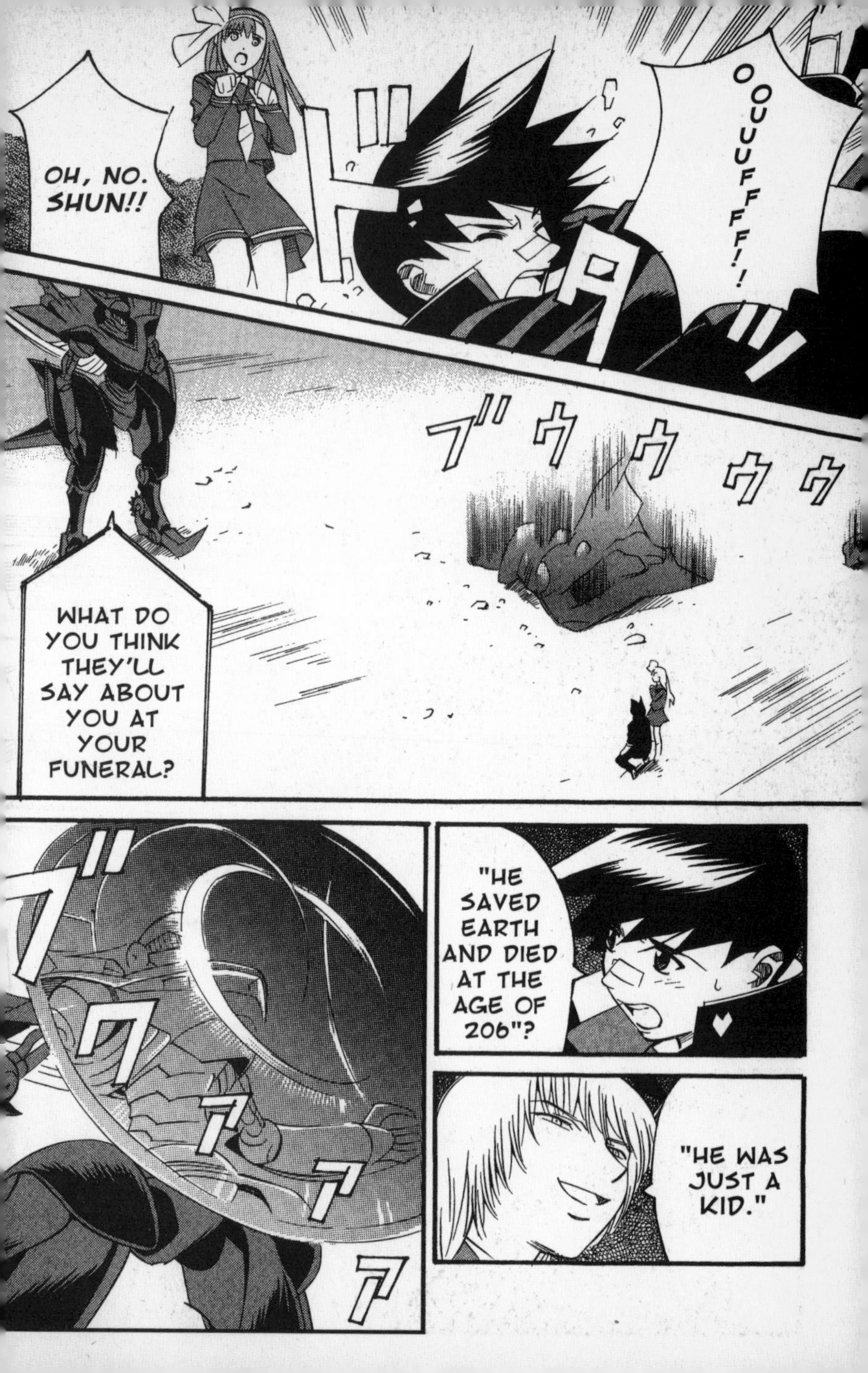
OOUUUFFFF!!
OH, NO. SHUN!!
ブウウウウウ
WHAT DO YOU THINK THEY'LL SAY ABOUT YOU AT YOUR FUNERAL?
"HE SAVED EARTH AND DIED AT THE AGE OF 206"?
"HE WAS JUST A KID."
ブワアアアア

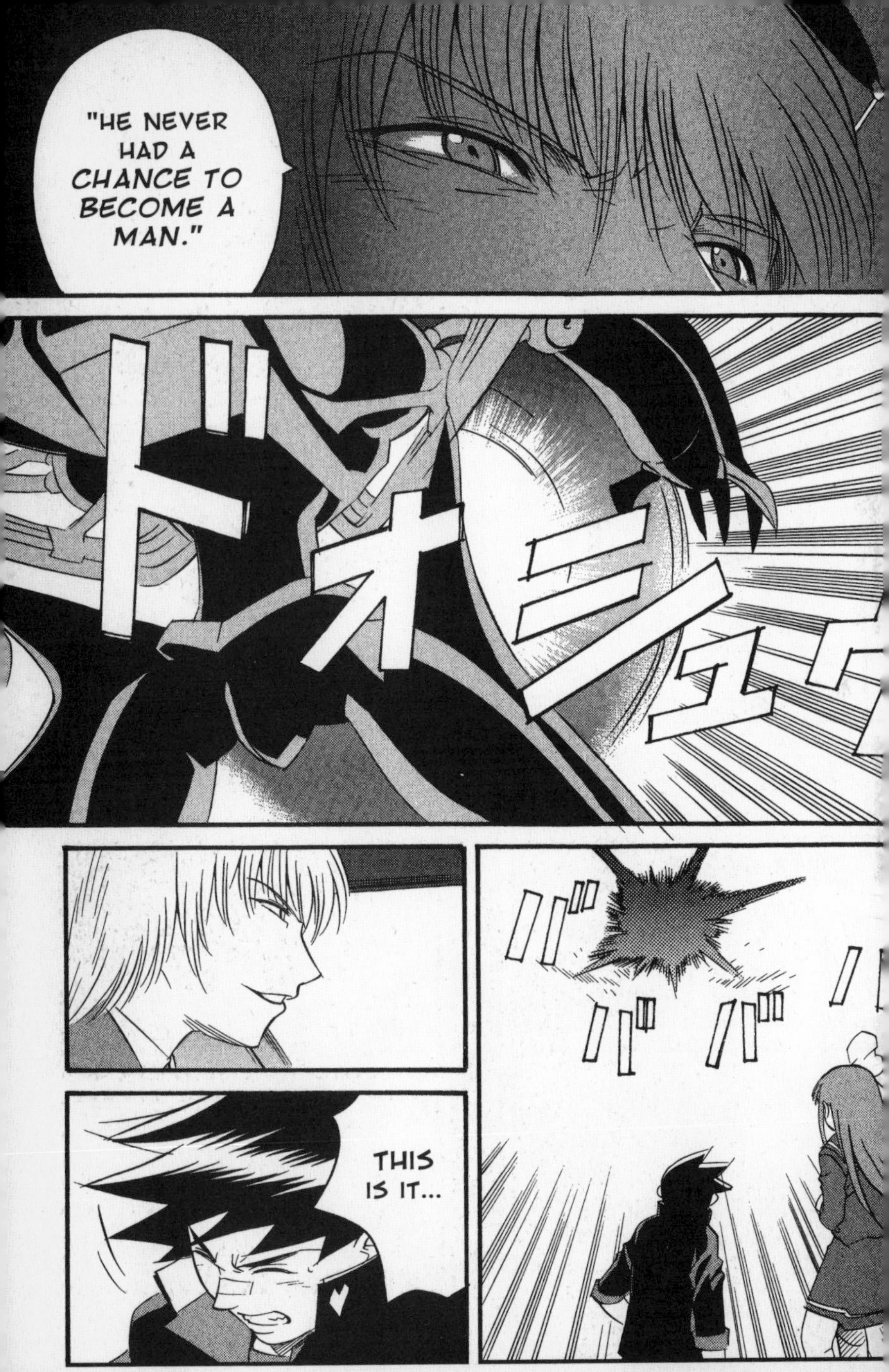
"HE NEVER HAD A CHANCE TO BECOME A MAN."
THIS IS IT...

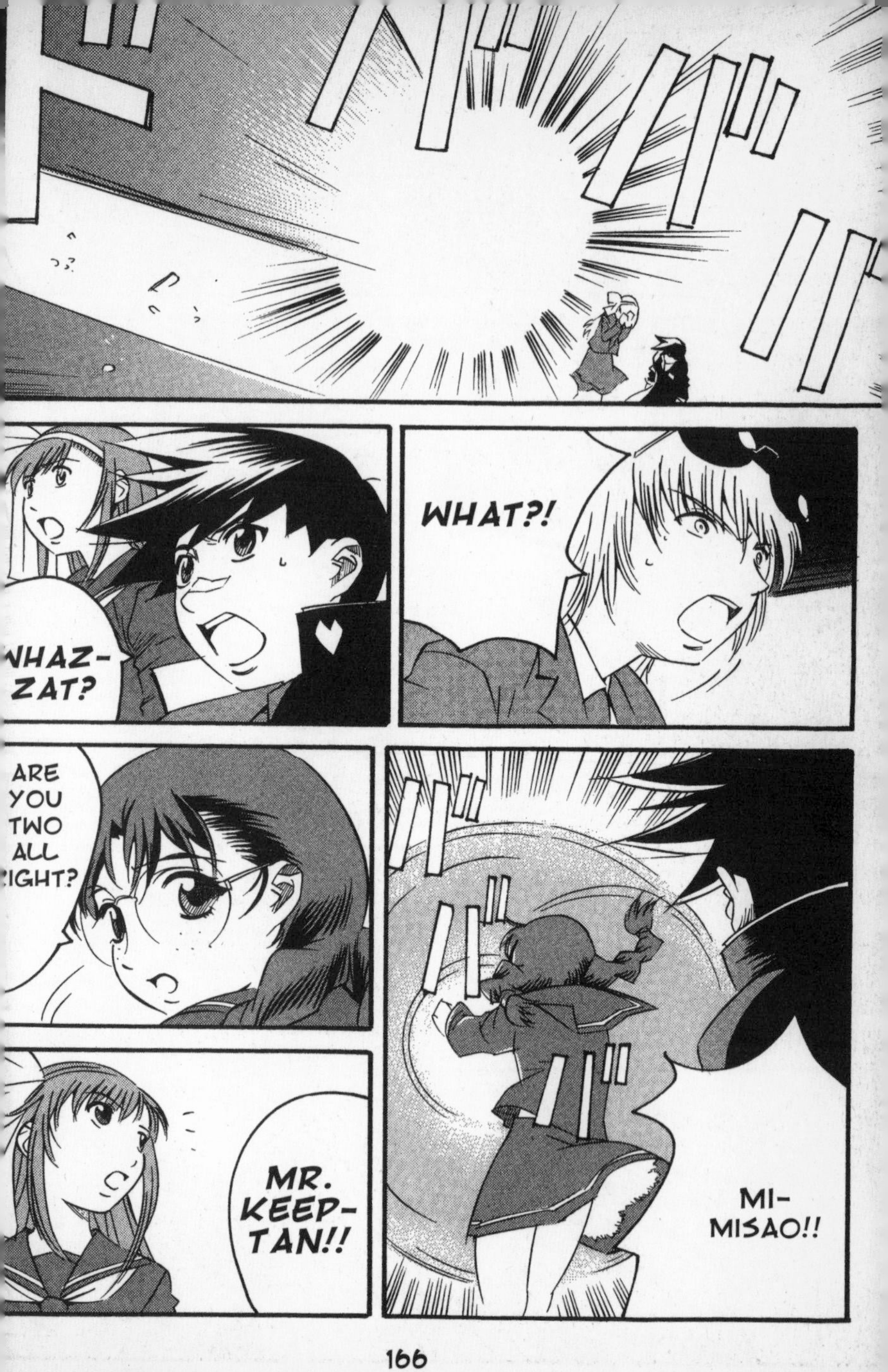
WHAT?!
WHAZ-ZAT?
MI-MISAO!!
ARE YOU TWO ALL RIGHT?
MR. KEEP-TAN!!

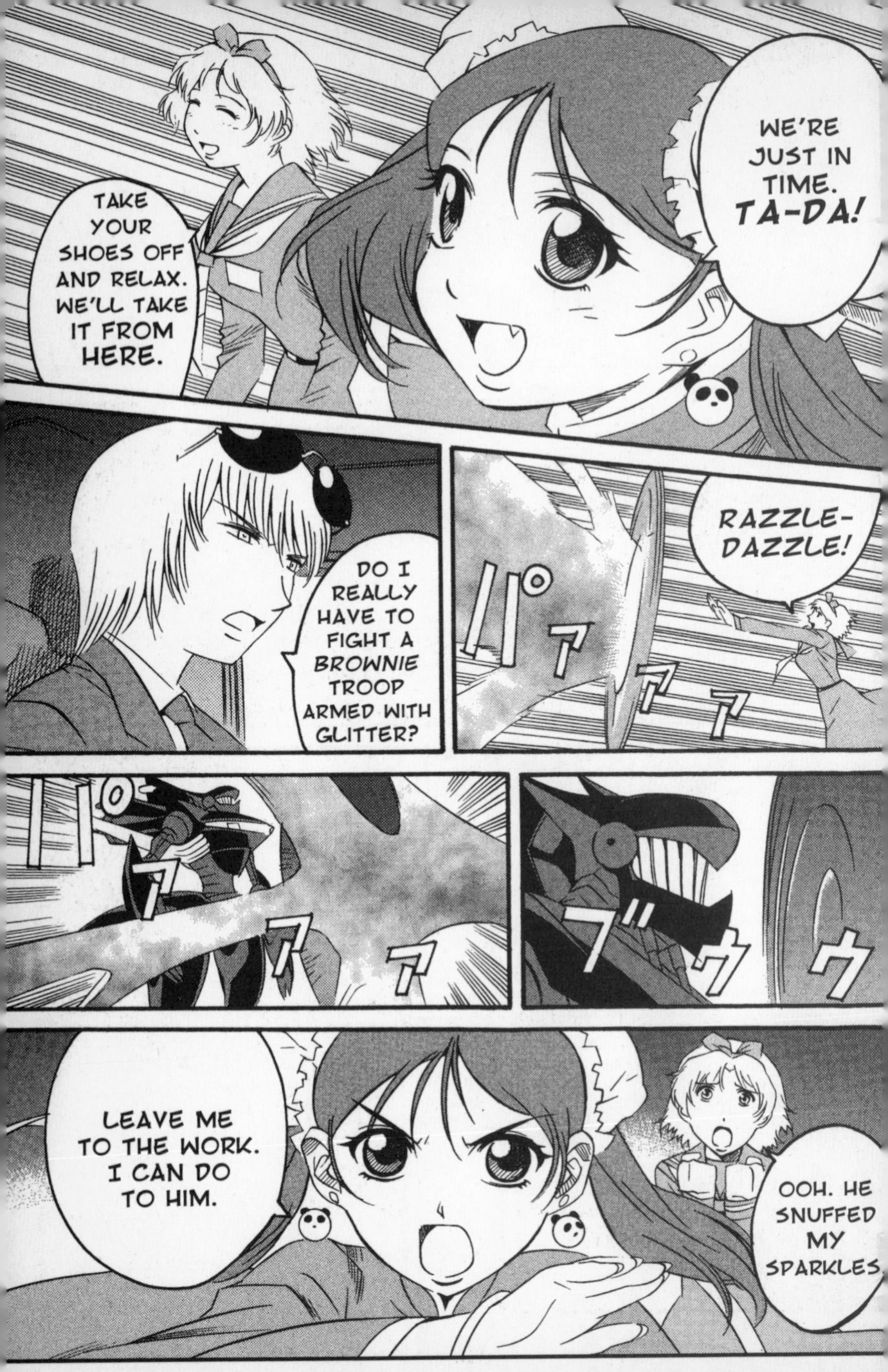
WE'RE JUST IN TIME. TA-DA!
TAKE YOUR SHOES OFF AND RELAX. WE'LL TAKE IT FROM HERE.
RAZZLE-DAZZLE!
パアアア
DO I REALLY HAVE TO FIGHT A BROWNIE TROOP ARMED WITH GLITTER?
ブウウ
パアアア
OOH. HE SNUFFED MY SPARKLES.
LEAVE ME TO THE WORK. I CAN DO TO HIM.

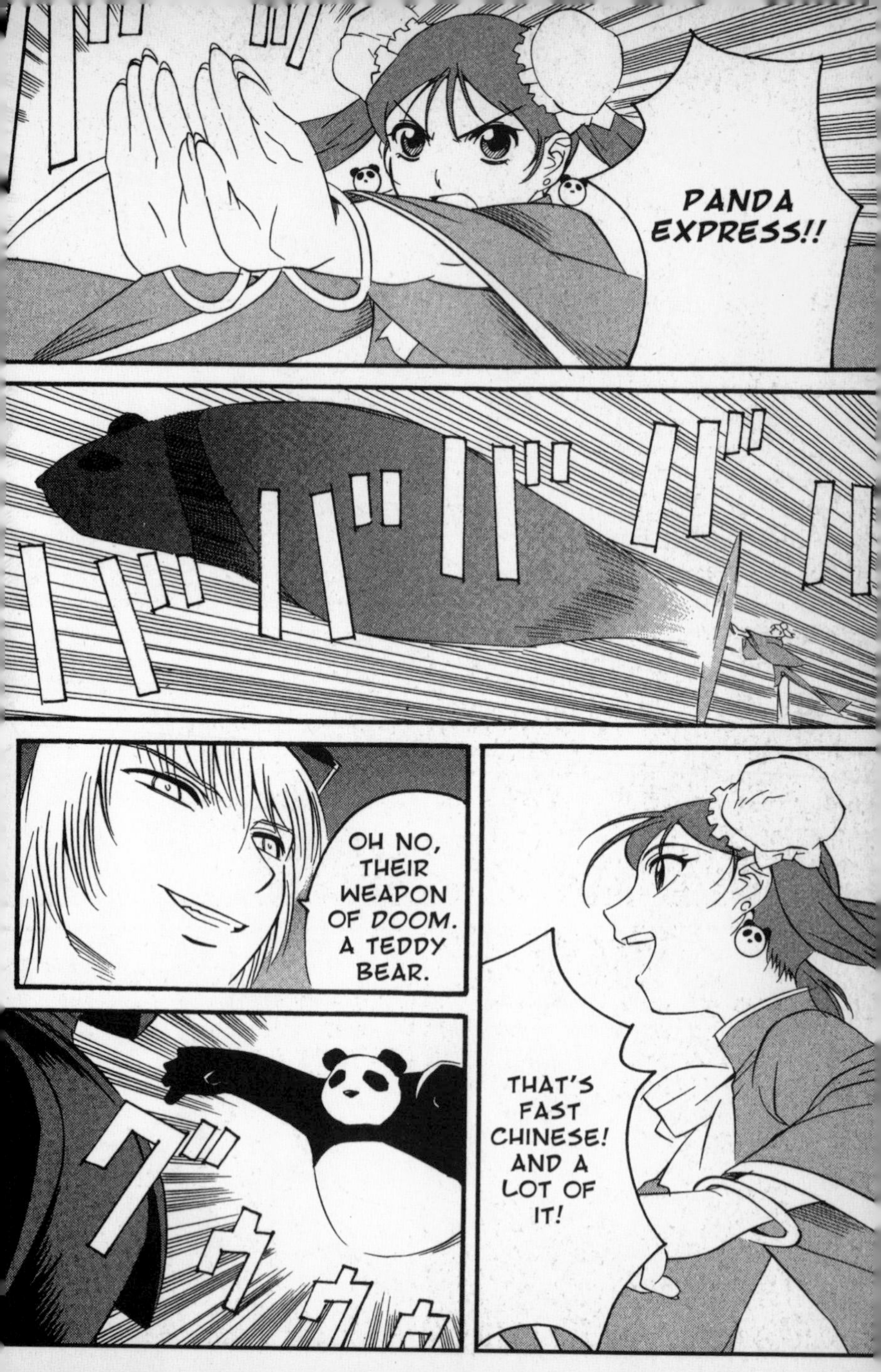
PANDA EXPRESS!!
THAT'S FAST CHINESE! AND A LOT OF IT!
OH NO, THEIR WEAPON OF DOOM. A TEDDY BEAR.

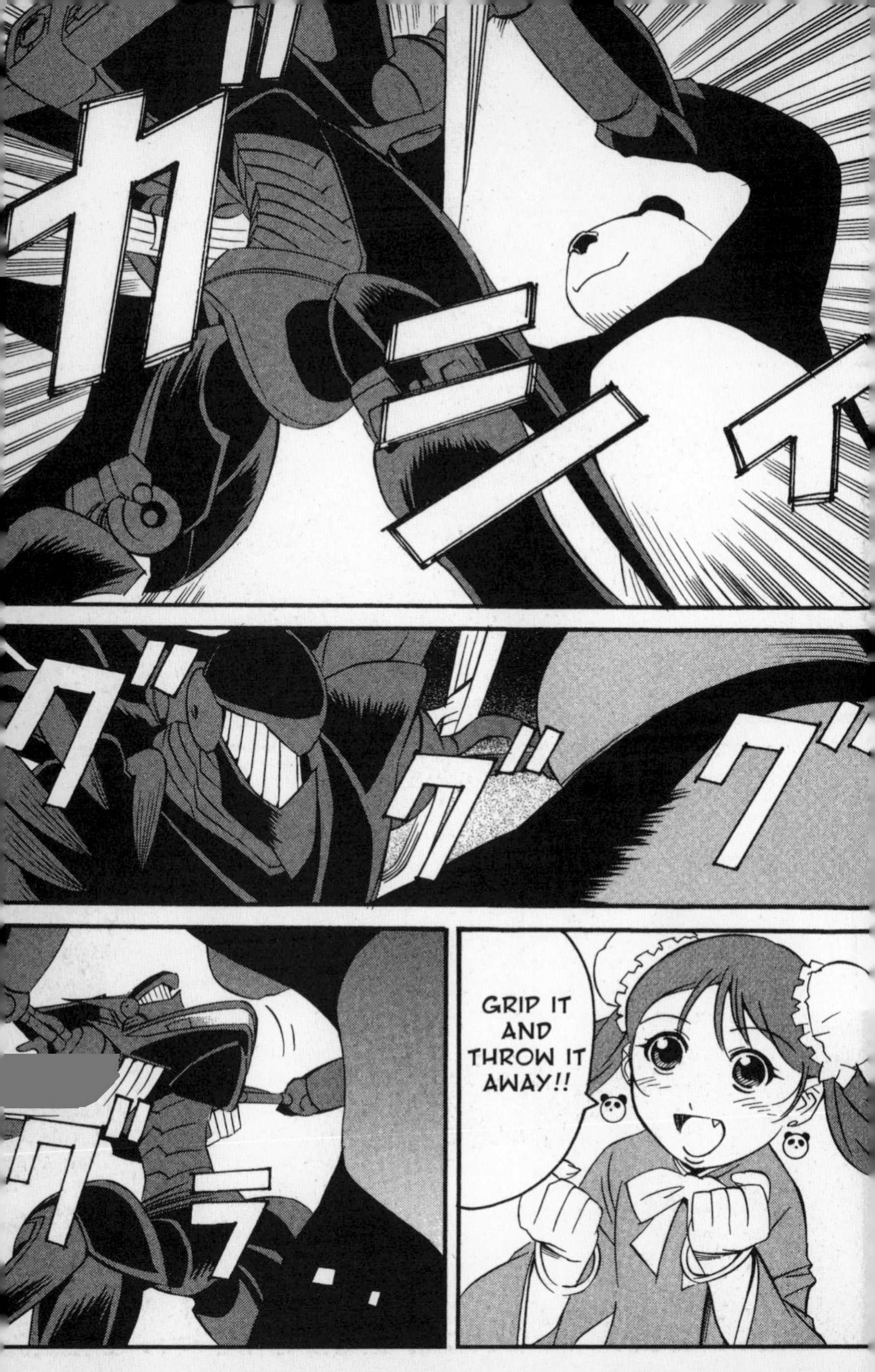
GRIP IT AND THROW IT AWAY!!

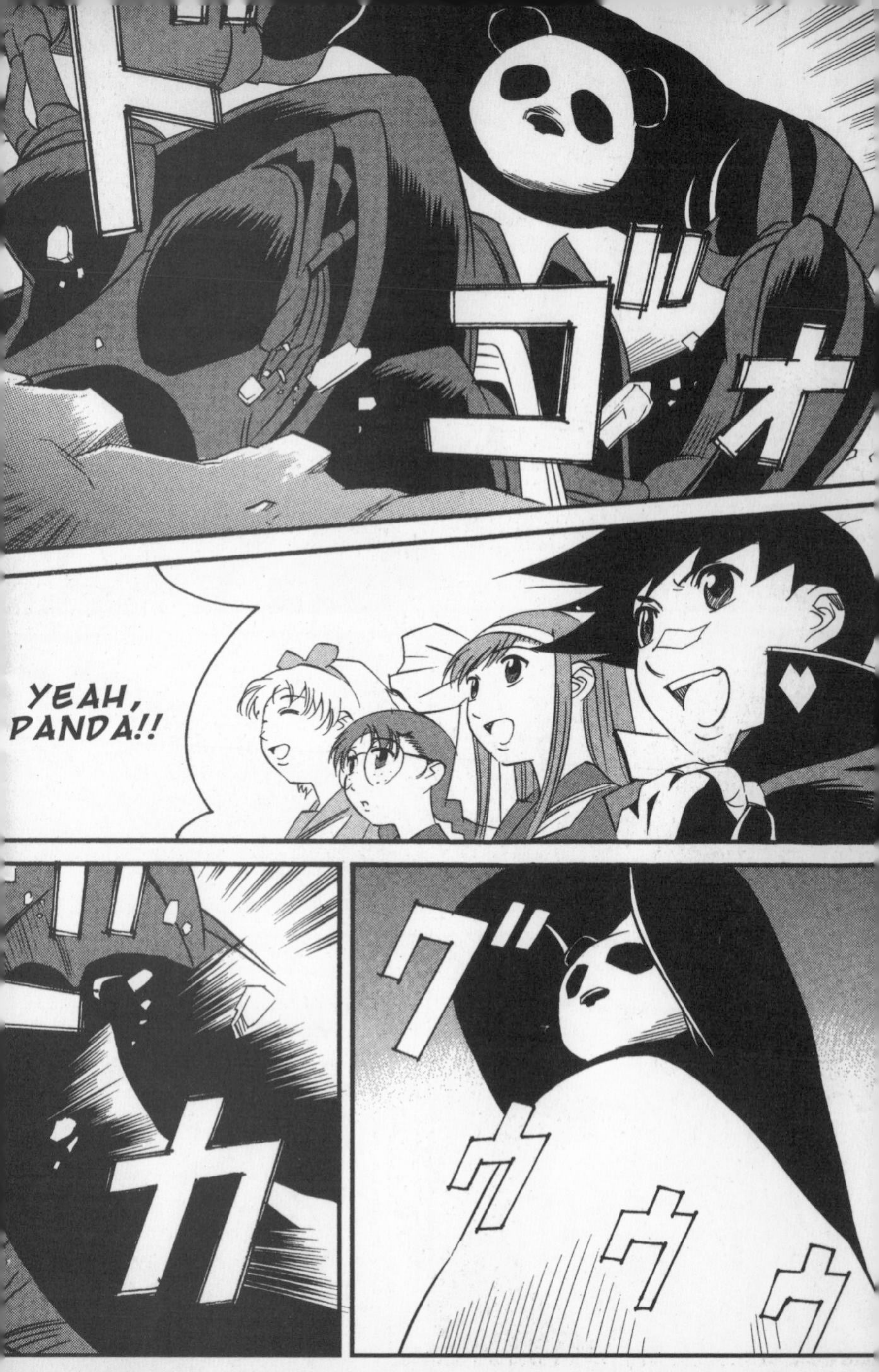
ドゴオ
YEAH, PANDA!!
グウウウ
ガ

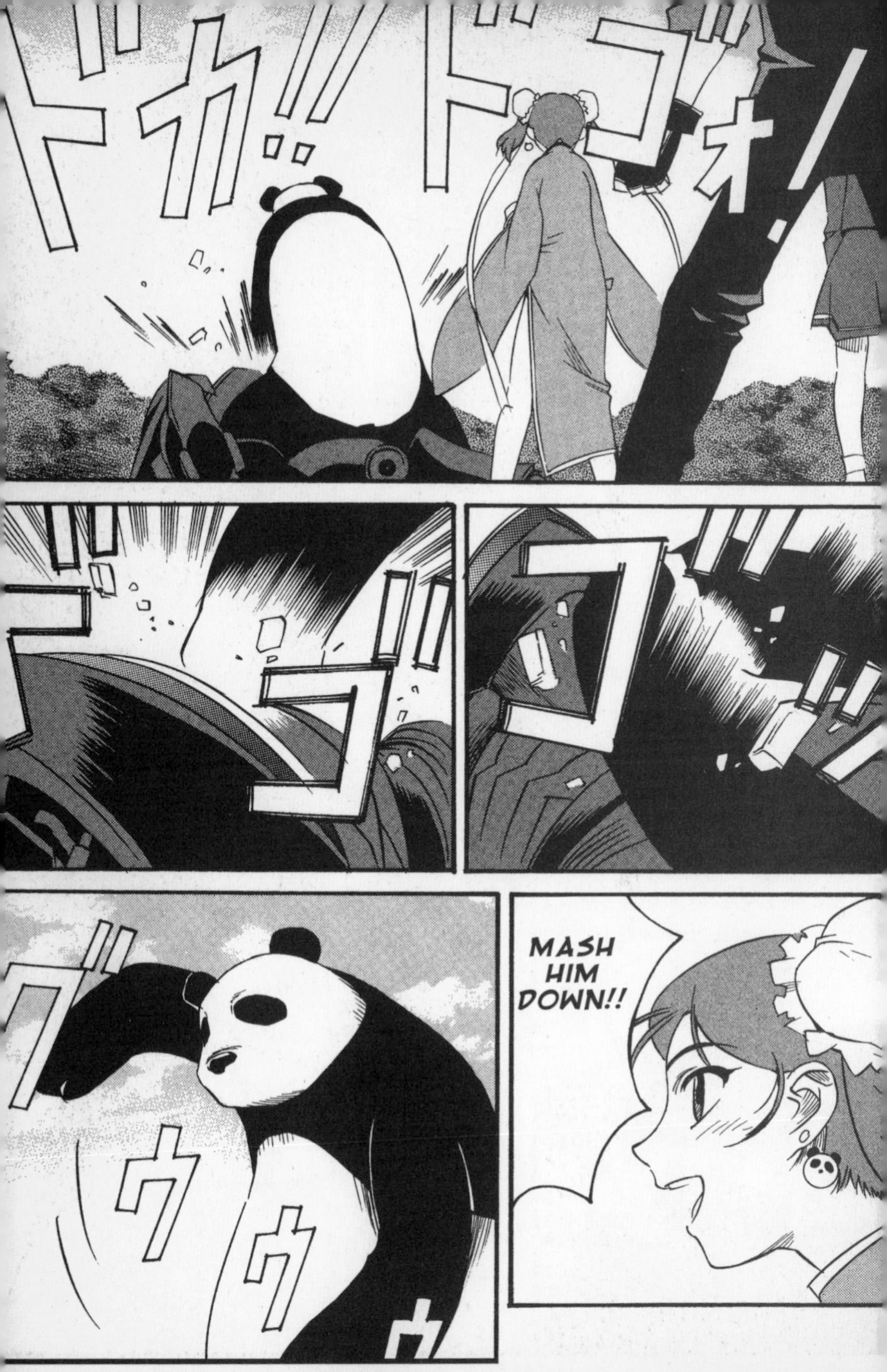
MASH HIM DOWN!!

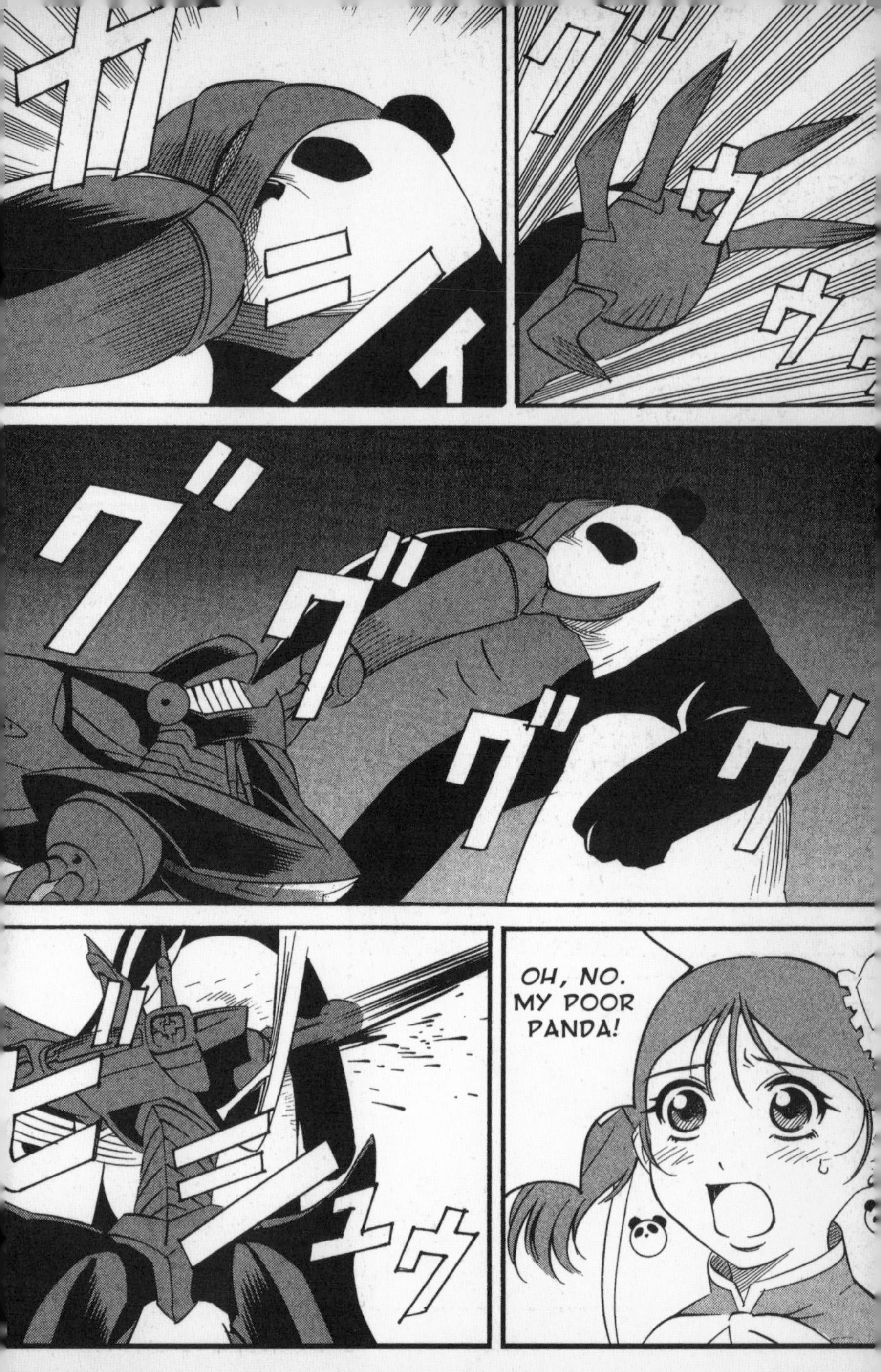
OH, NO. MY POOR PANDA!

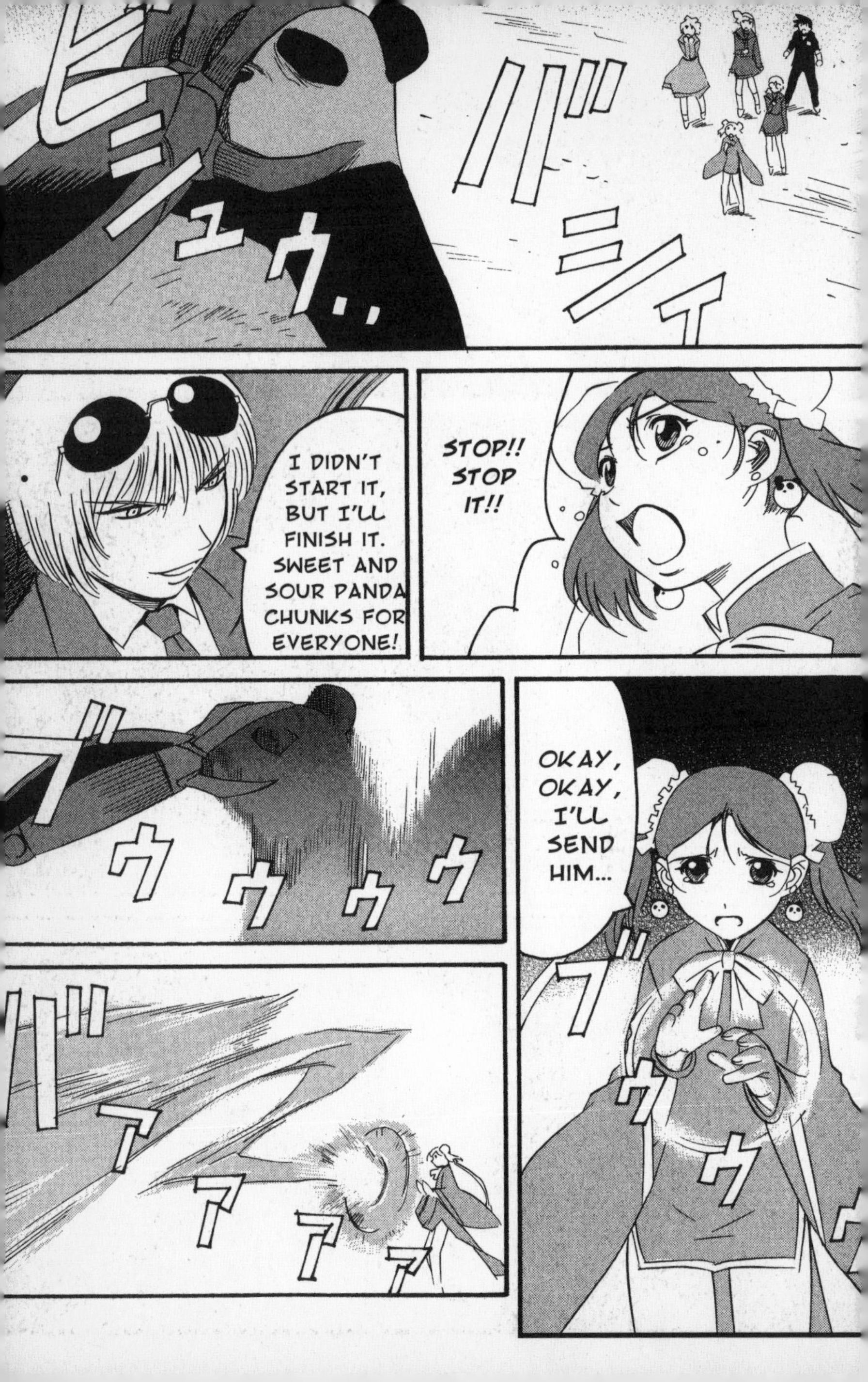

バシィ
ビシュウ..
STOP!! STOP IT!!
I DIDN'T START IT, BUT I'LL FINISH IT. SWEET AND SOUR PANDA CHUNKS FOR EVERYONE!
OKAY, OKAY, I'LL SEND HIM...
ブウウ
ブウウウウウ
バアアアア

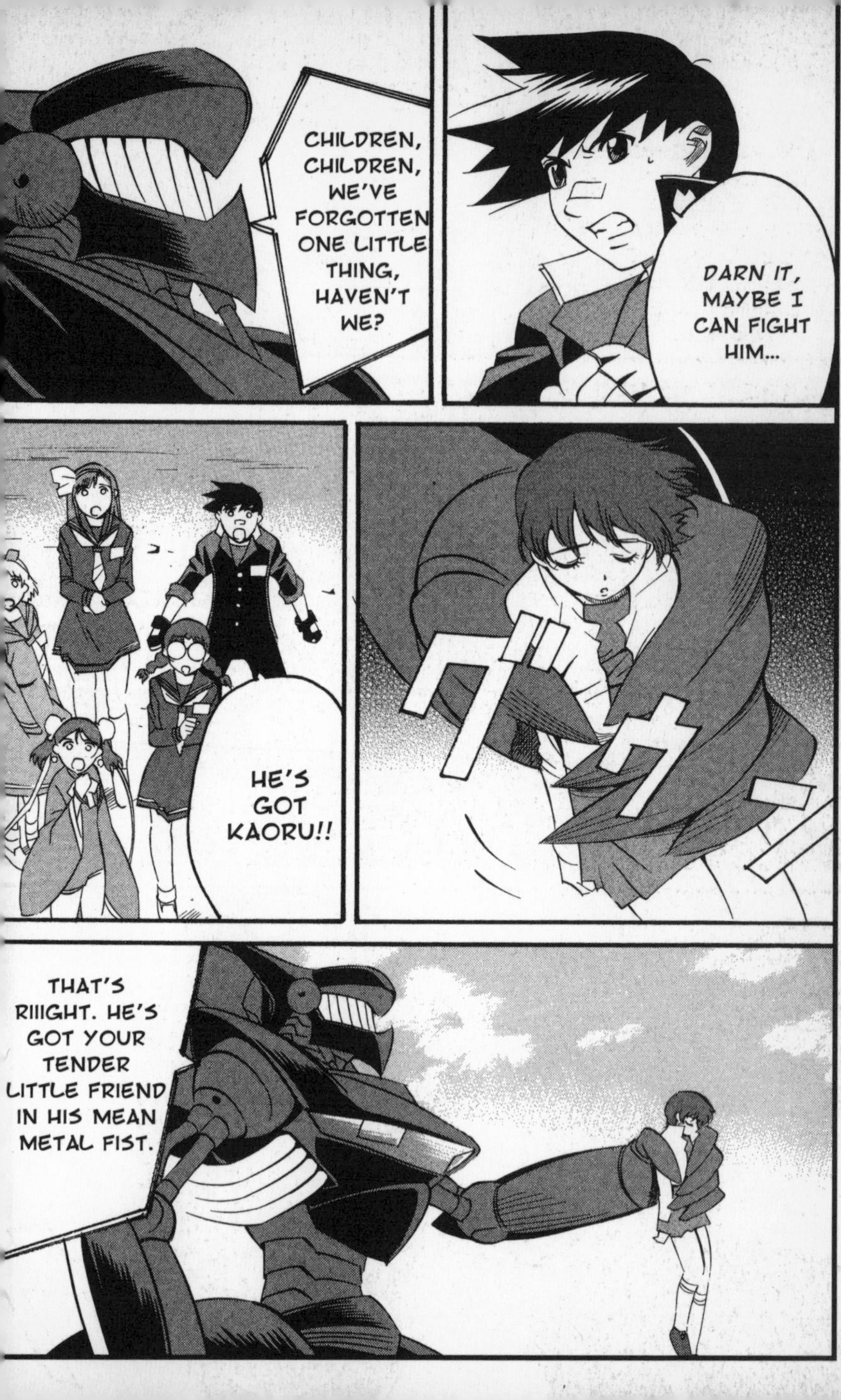
DARN IT, MAYBE I CAN FIGHT HIM...
CHILDREN, CHILDREN, WE'VE FORGOTTEN ONE LITTLE THING, HAVEN'T WE?
グウー
HE'S GOT KAORU!!
THAT'S RIIIGHT. HE'S GOT YOUR TENDER LITTLE FRIEND IN HIS MEAN METAL FIST.

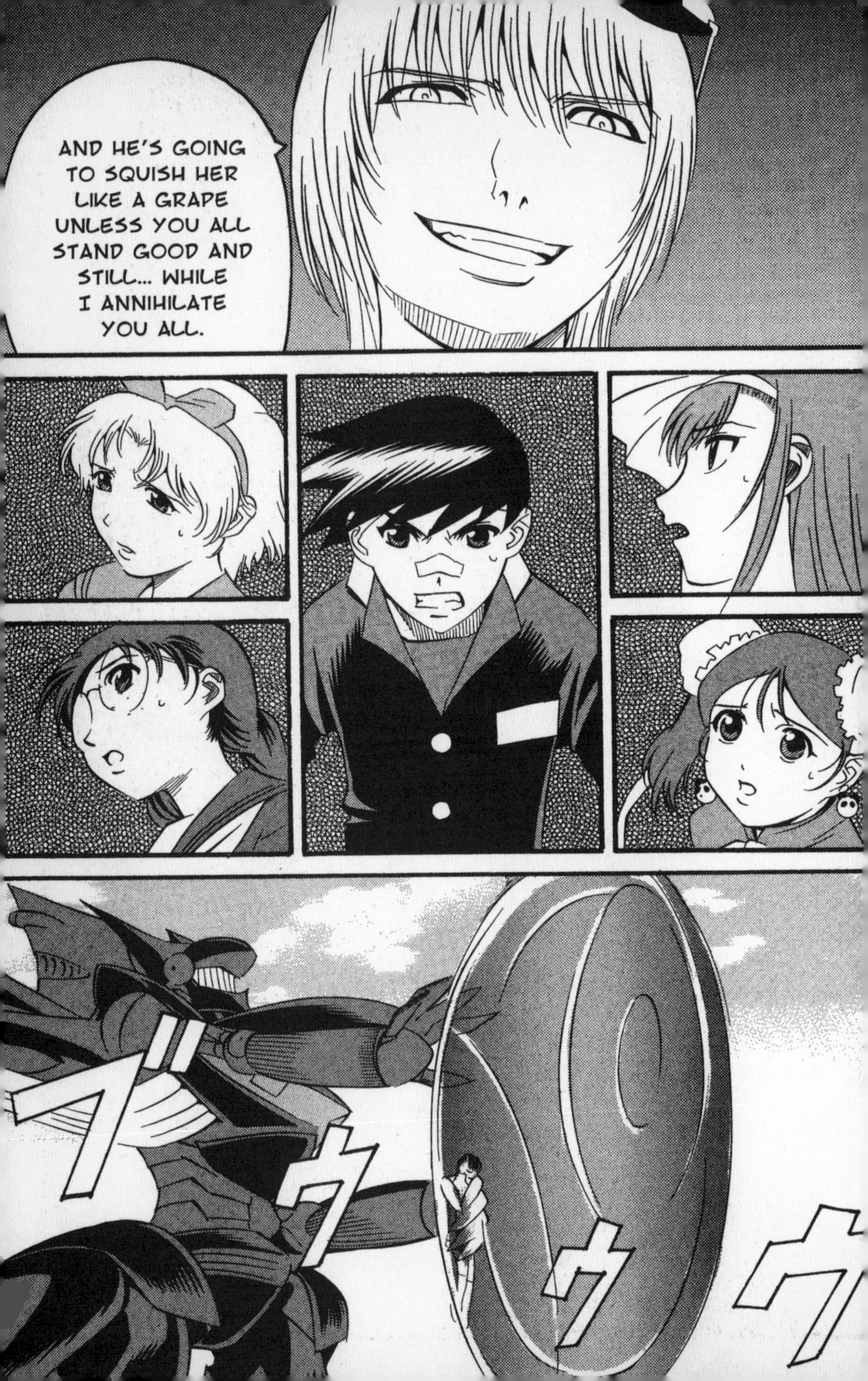
AND HE'S GOING TO SQUISH HER LIKE A GRAPE UNLESS YOU ALL STAND GOOD AND STILL... WHILE I ANNIHILATE YOU ALL.

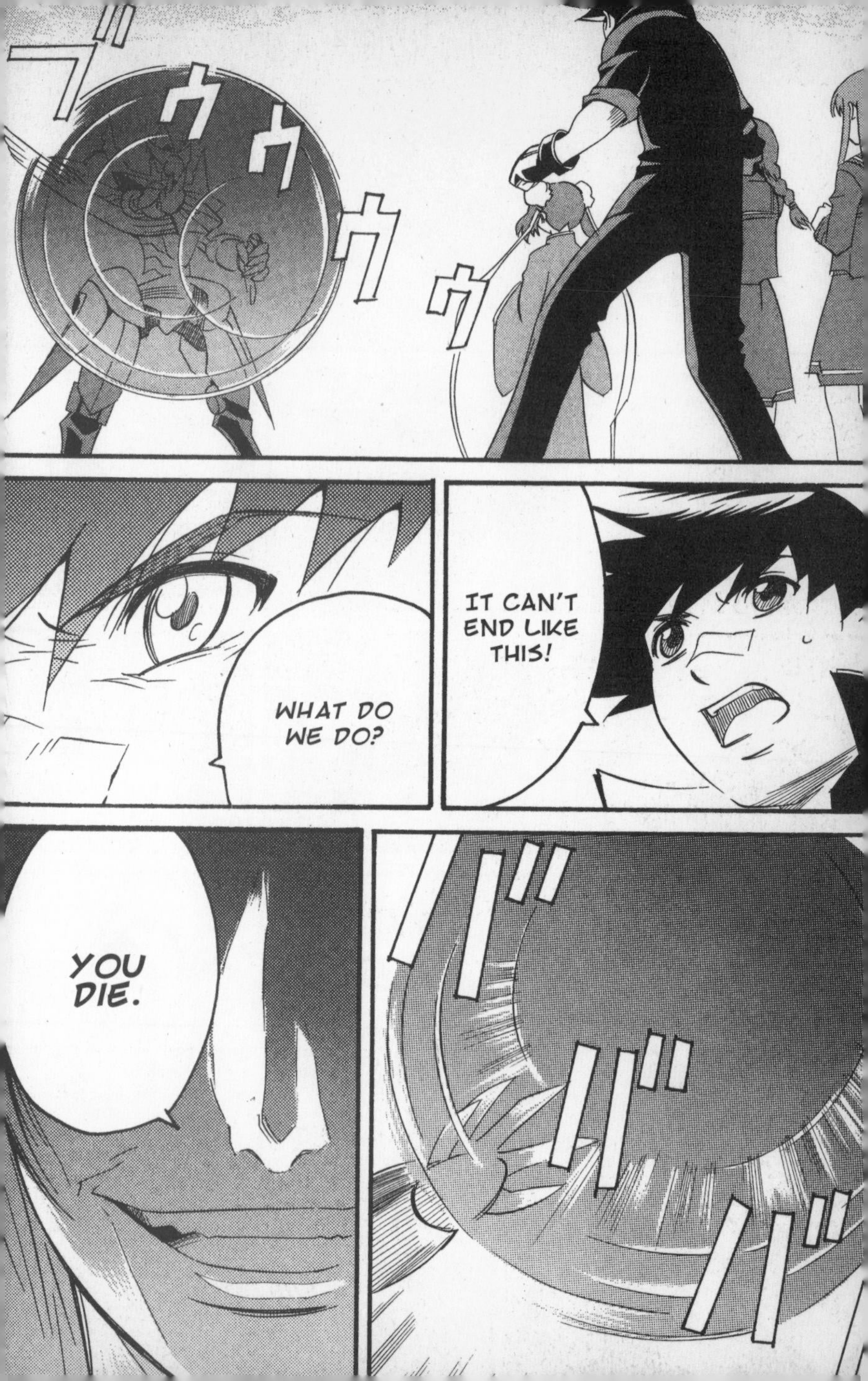
IT CAN'T END LIKE THIS!
WHAT DO WE DO?
YOU DIE.

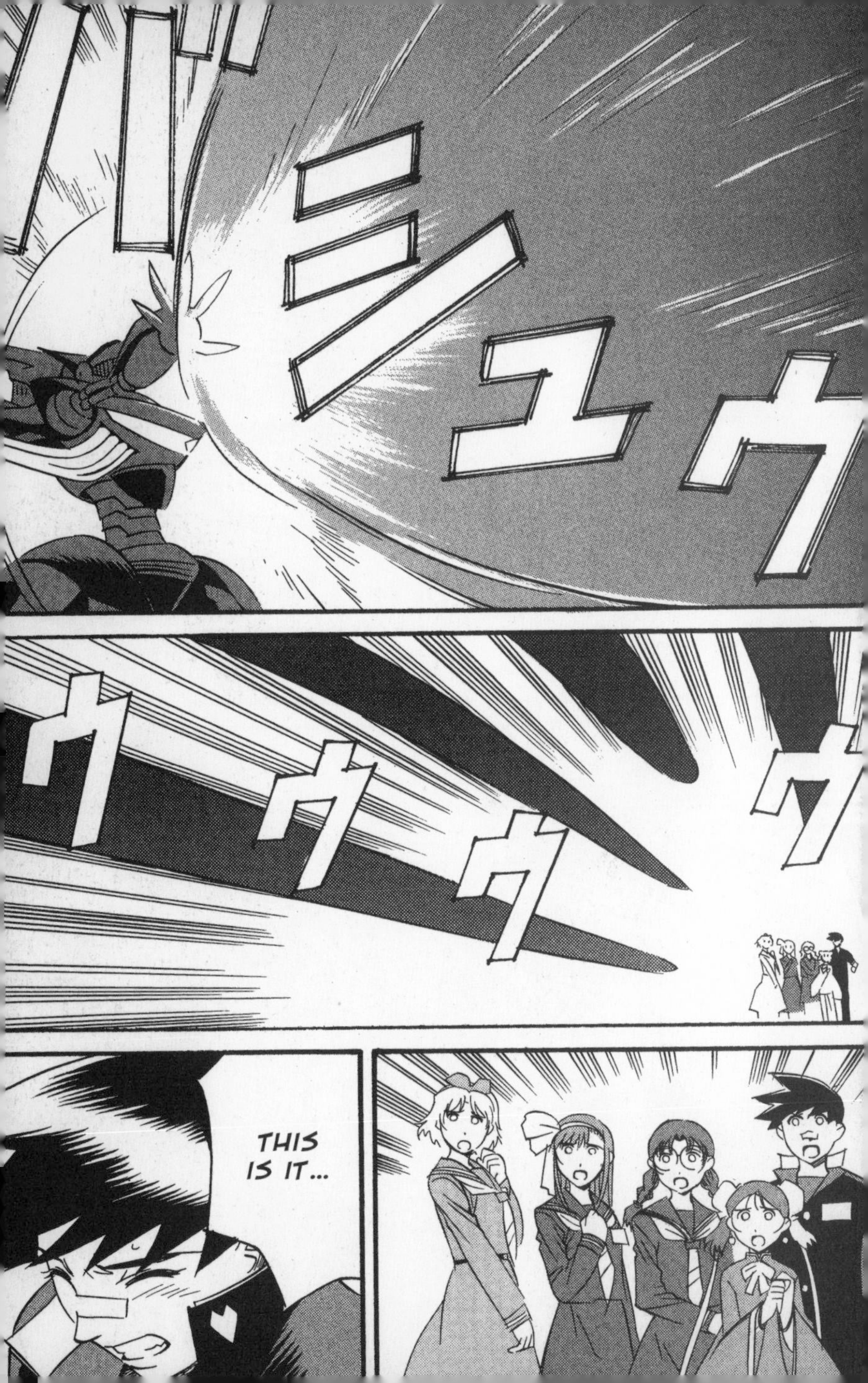
シュウ
ウウウウ
THIS IS IT...

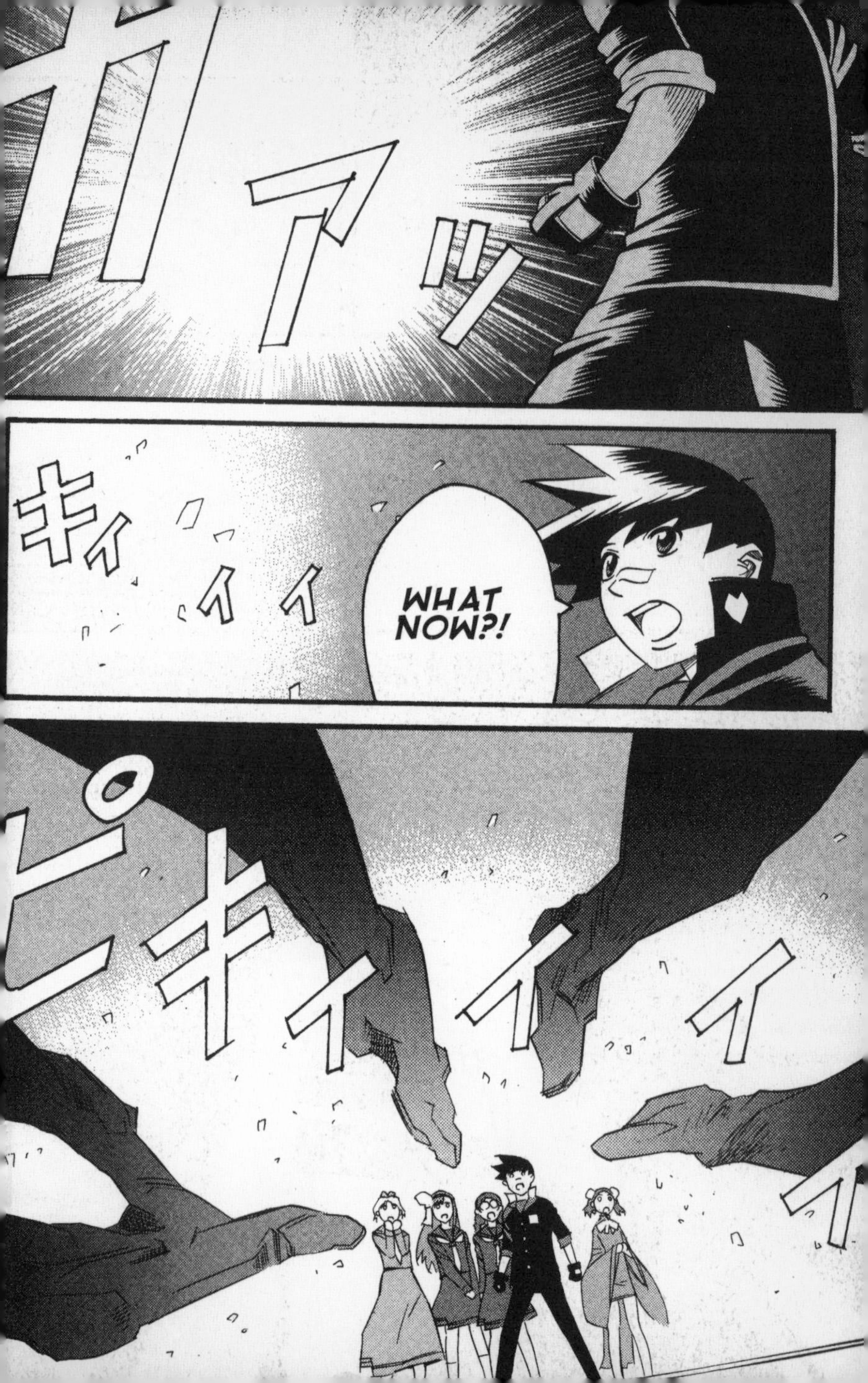
ガアッ
WHAT NOW?!
キイイイ
ピキイイイイ

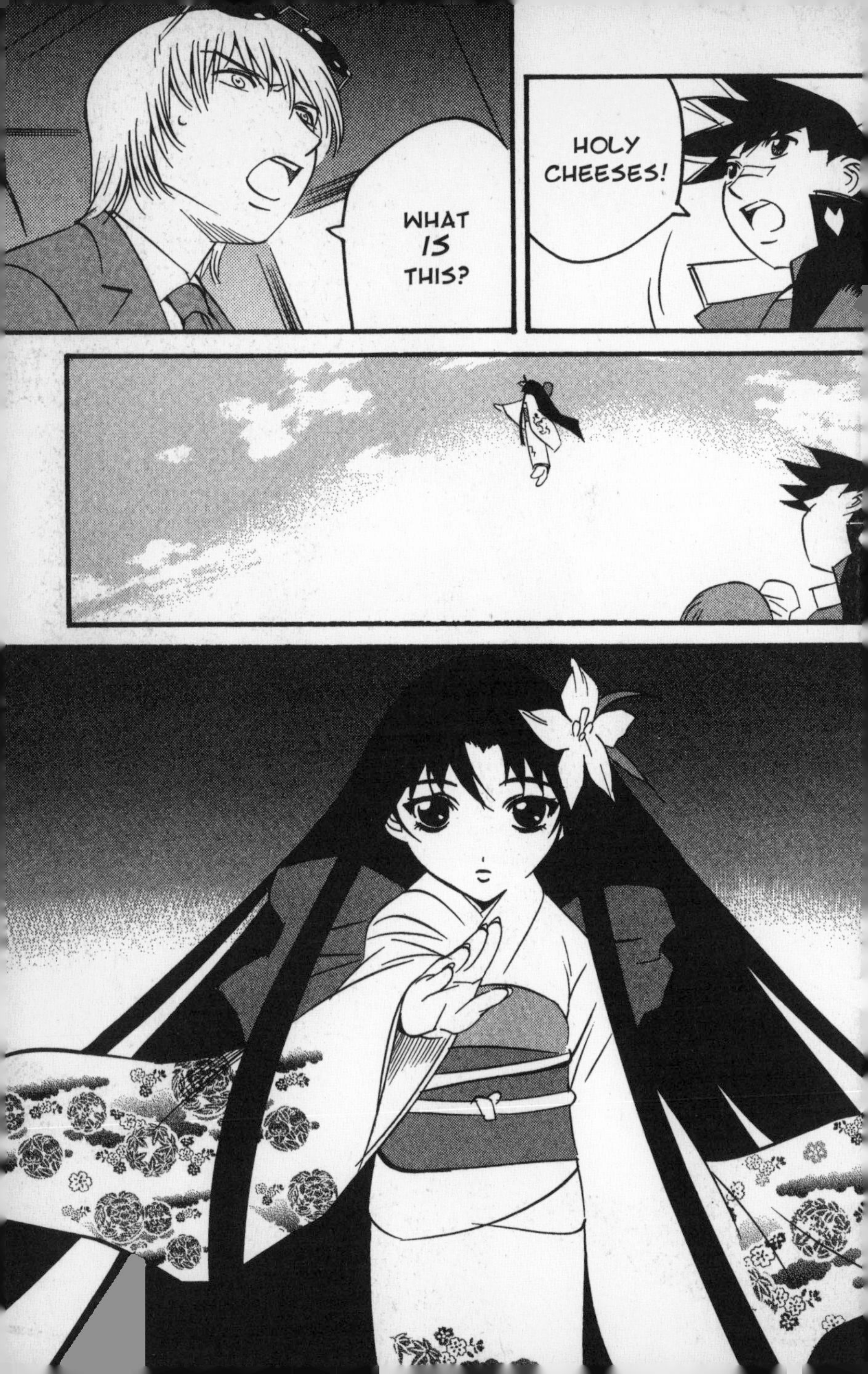
HOLY CHEESES!
WHAT IS THIS?

WHACHA DOIN' UP THERE?!

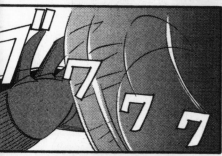

I'VE HAD ABOUT ENOUGH OF THIS.

SNOW. ICE. BLIZZARD. BLOW!

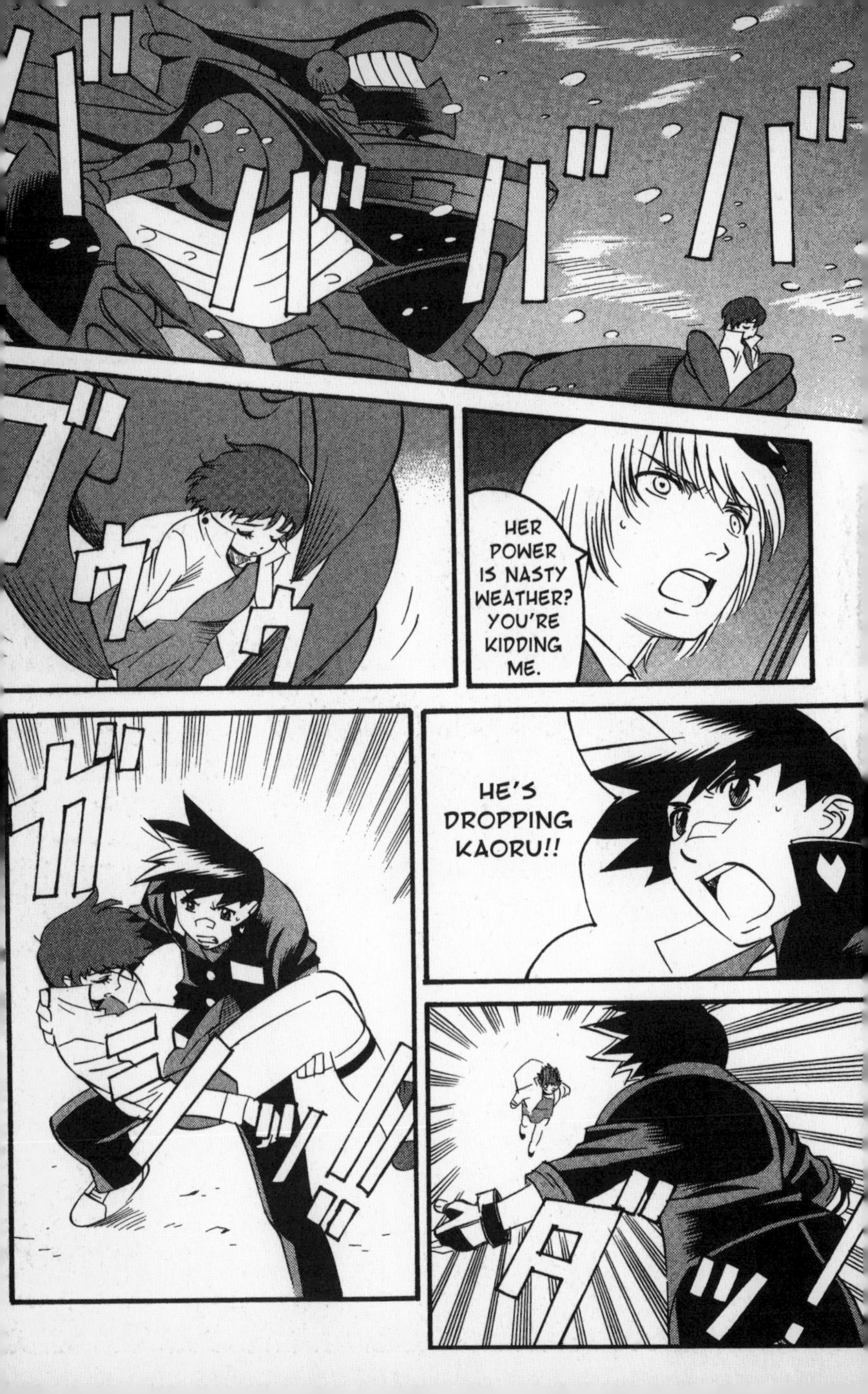
HER POWER IS NASTY WEATHER? YOU'RE KIDDING ME.
HE'S DROPPING KAORU!!

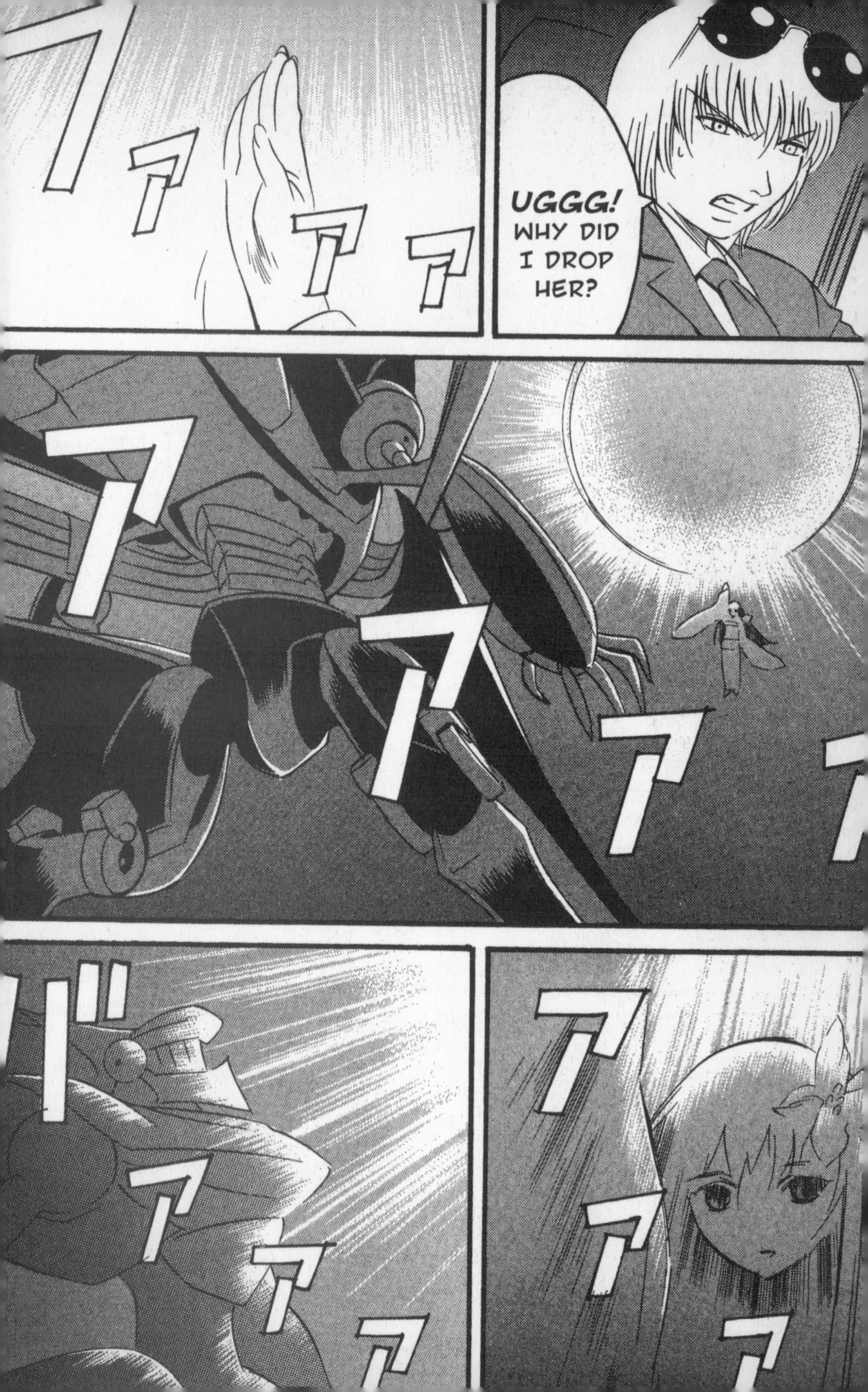
UGGG! WHY DID I DROP HER?

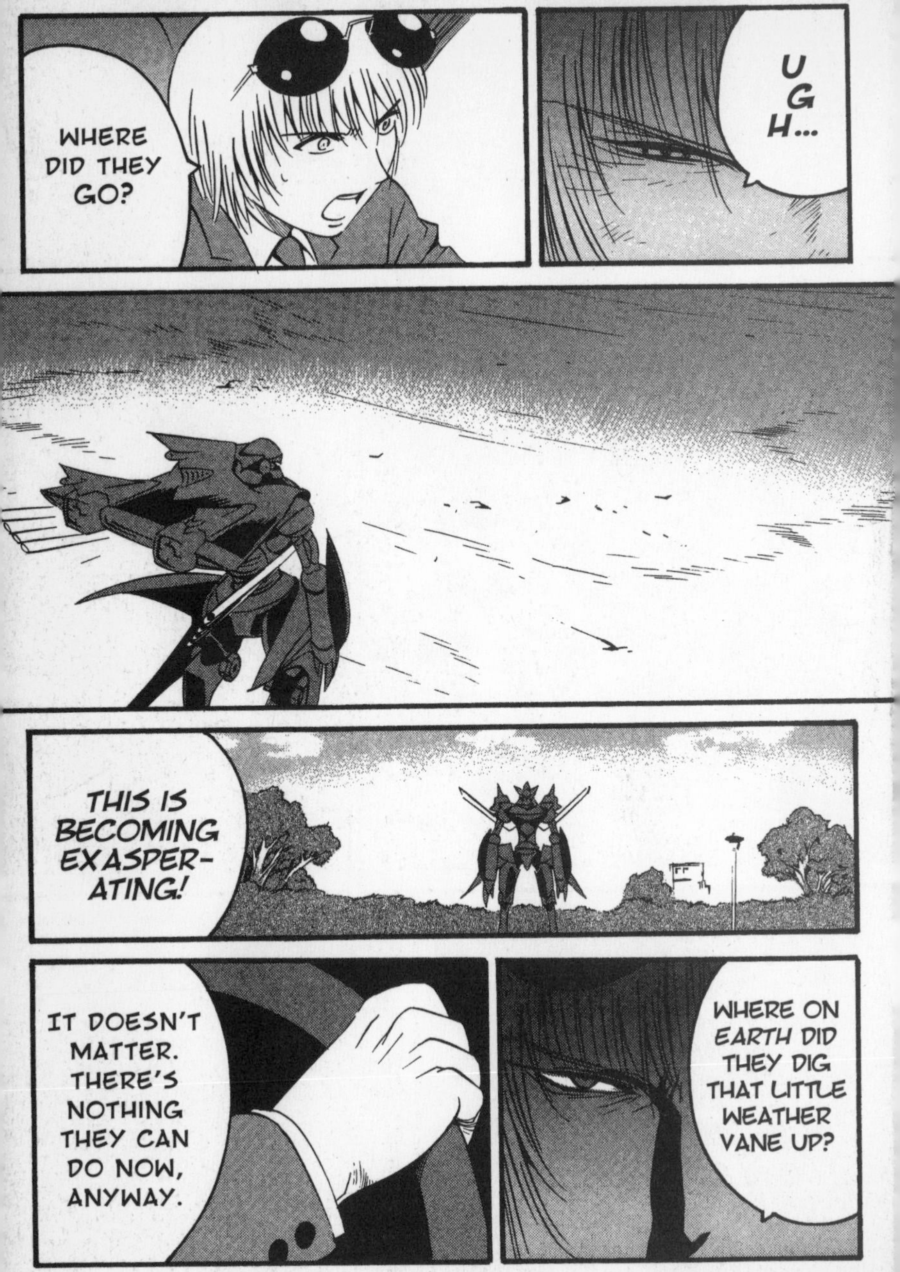
UGH...
WHERE DID THEY GO?
THIS IS BECOMING EXASPER-ATING!
WHERE ON EARTH DID THEY DIG THAT LITTLE WEATHER VANE UP?
IT DOESN'T MATTER. THERE'S NOTHING THEY CAN DO NOW, ANYWAY.

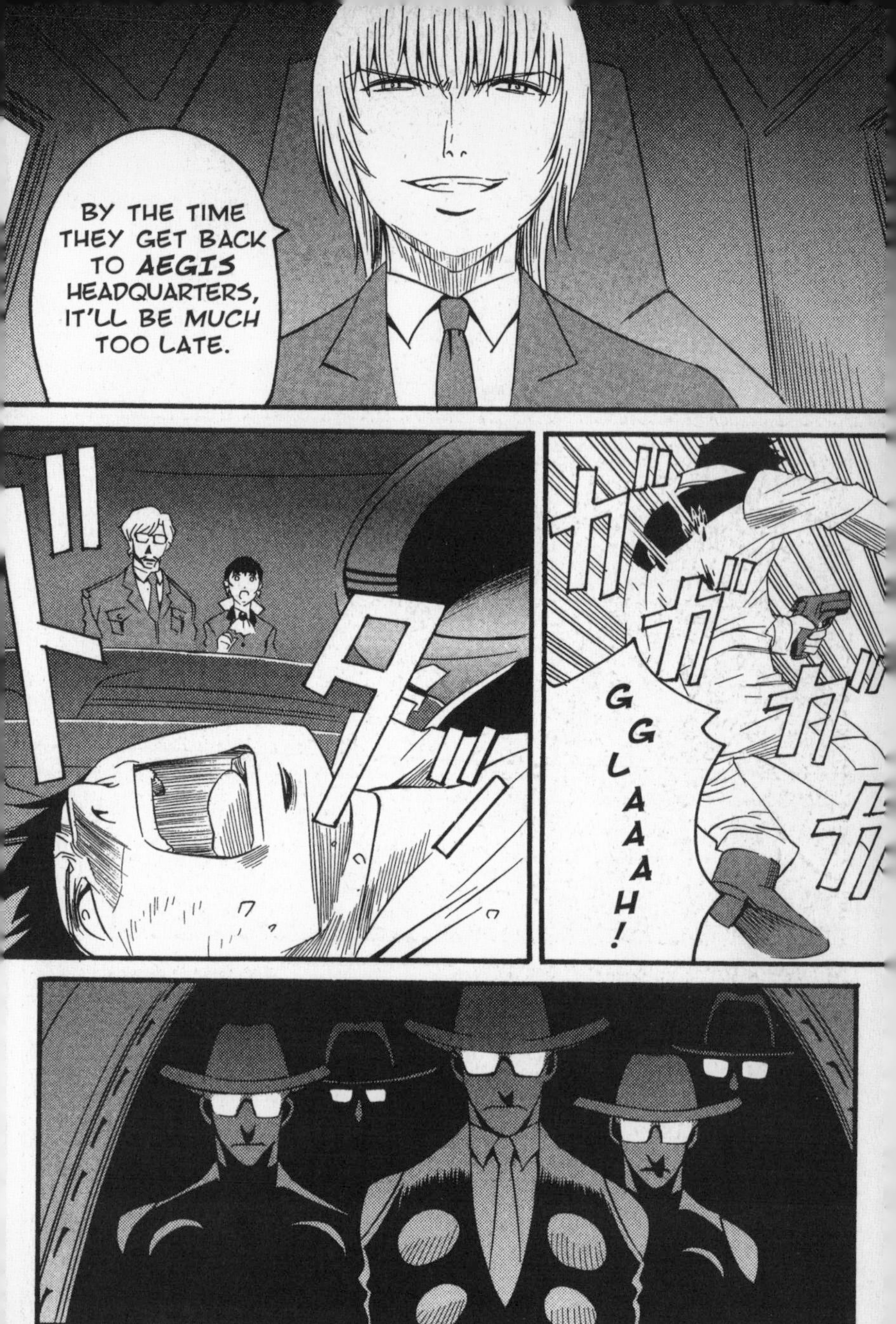
BY THE TIME THEY GET BACK TO AEGIS HEADQUARTERS, IT'LL BE MUCH TOO LATE.
ガガガガ
GGLAAAH!

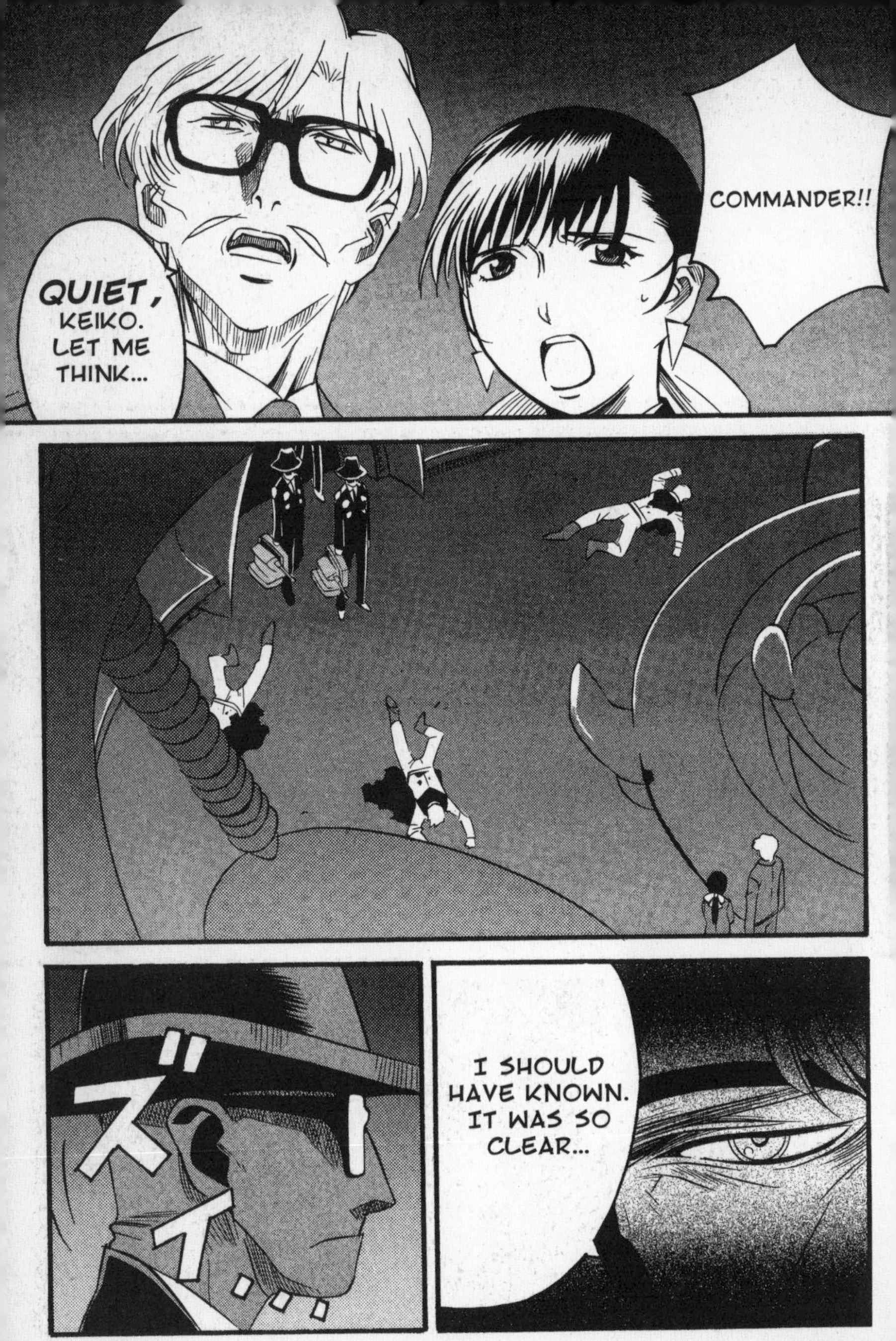
COMMANDER!!
QUIET, KEIKO. LET ME THINK...
I SHOULD HAVE KNOWN. IT WAS SO CLEAR...
ズイ

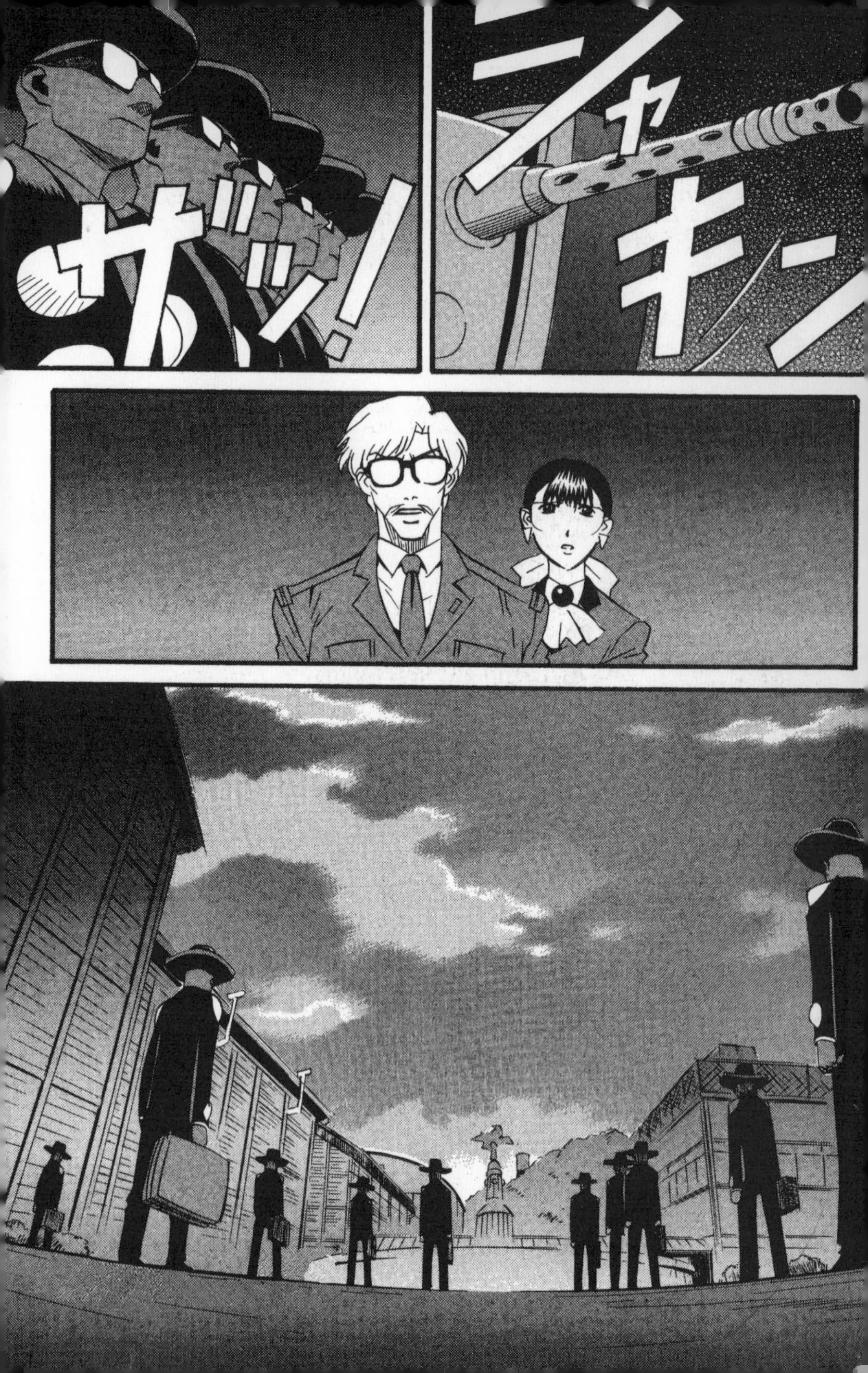
シャキン
ザッ!

THE END OF...

GATE·KEEPERS
ゲットキーパーズ

VOLUME 2

WHAT'S GOIN' ON WITH VOLUME 3:

THE INVASION IS IN FULL SWING, AND WITH ALL THE GATE KEEPERS AWAY, AEGIS MUST STAND ALONE TO DEFEND THE PLANET AGAINST THE DREADED BLACK SUITS. HAS MANKIND FINALLY MET ITS MATCH? ALL WILL BE REVEALED IN THE ACTION-PACKED THIRD VOLUME OF GATE KEEPERS— COMING SOON.

Mess with me...
Mess with my friend!
TOKYOPOP
BRIGADOON
Everyone should have a
Gun-Swordsman Protector of their own.
DVD Available
May 2003!
© SUNRISE · WOWOW. TOKYOPOP is a registered trademark of Mixx Entertainment, Inc.

★★ KODOCHA

SANA'S STAGE

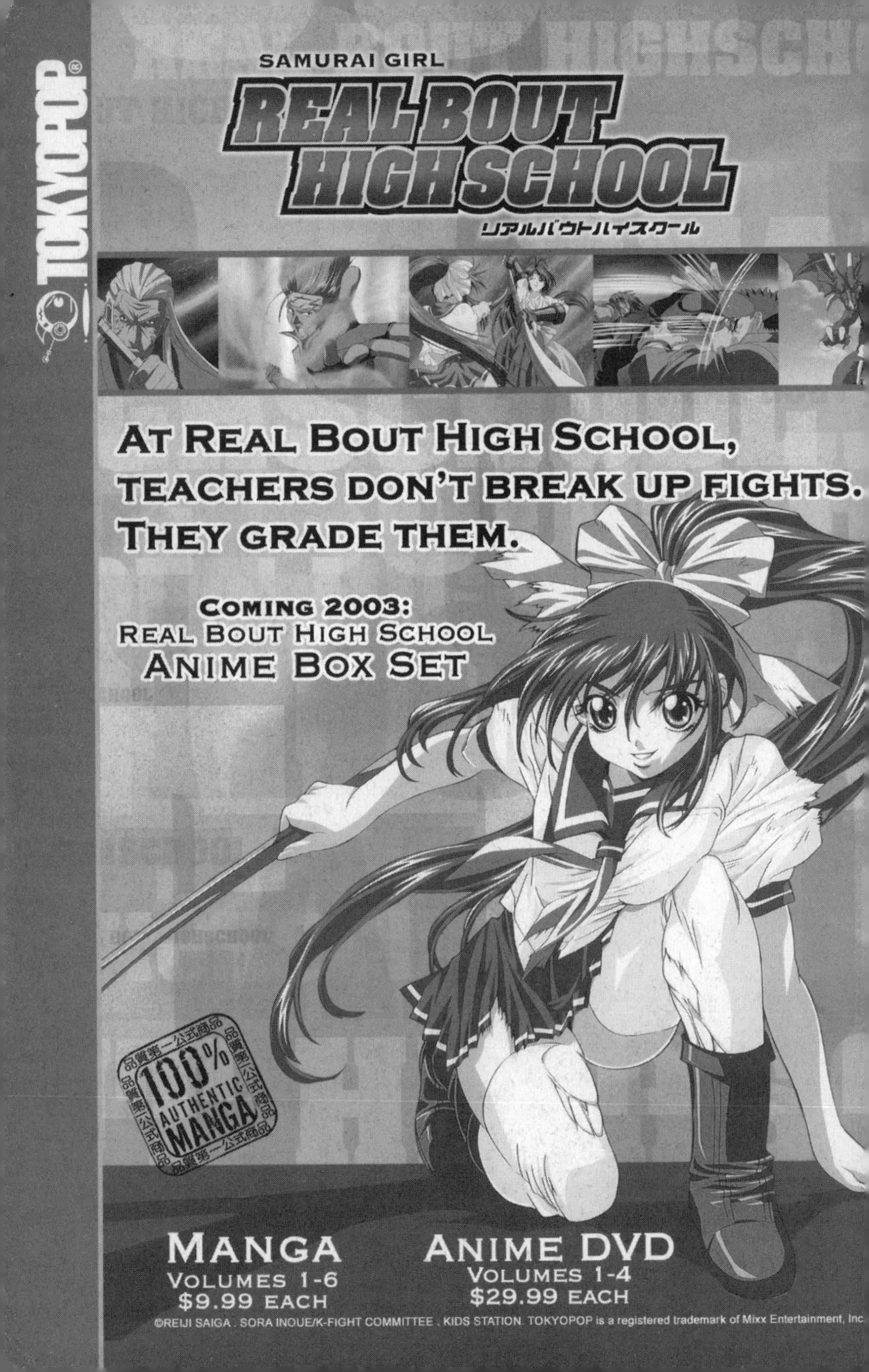
TOKYOPOP®
SAMURAI GIRL
REAL BOUT HIGH SCHOOL
リアルバウトハイスクール
AT REAL BOUT HIGH SCHOOL, TEACHERS DON'T BREAK UP FIGHTS. THEY GRADE THEM.
COMING 2003:
REAL BOUT HIGH SCHOOL
ANIME BOX SET
100% AUTHENTIC MANGA
品質第一公式商品
MANGA
VOLUMES 1-6
$9.99 EACH
ANIME DVD
VOLUMES 1-4
$29.99 EACH
©REIJI SAIGA . SORA INOUE/K-FIGHT COMMITTEE . KIDS STATION. TOKYOPOP is a registered trademark of Mixx Entertainment, Inc.

STOP!

This is the back of the book.
You wouldn't want to spoil a great ending!

This book is printed "manga-style," in the authentic Japanese right-to-left format. Since none of the artwork has been flipped or altered, readers get to experience the story just as the creator intended. You've been asking for it, so TOKYOPOP® delivered: authentic, hot-off-the-press, and far more fun!

DIRECTIONS

If this is your first time reading manga-style, here's a quick guide to help you understand how it works.

It's easy... just start in the top right panel and follow the numbers. Have fun, and look for more 100% authentic manga from TOKYOPOP®!